Charles A. Beard

An Intellectual Biography

Ellen Nore

Southern Illinois University Press

Carbondale and Edwardsville

Edited by H. L. Kirk
Designed by Dan Gunter
Production supervised by John DeBacher

86 85 84 83   4 3 2 1

Library of Congress Cataloging in Publication Data
Nore, Ellen, 1942–
 Charles A. Beard, an intellectual biography.

 Bibliography: p.
 Includes index.
 1. Beard, Charles Austin, 1874–1948. 2. Historians
—United States—Biography. I. Title.
E175.5.B38N67 1983 973'.072024 [B] 82-19452
ISBN 0-8093-1078-3

To Barton J. Bernstein
for kindness and questions

Contents

Preface

The sources for a biography of Charles A. Beard are, as he remarked of his own researches, "frankly fragmentary." Mary Beard noted that her husband had "destroyed some letters, indeed all his letters, a short time before he died . . . We had only kept confidential letters and he felt obligated not to release them. I shared that feeling." Later she added, "It should be a precious liberty to bypass the press and public life by communing in personal letters on matters of the heart and mind."[1]

The Beards surely intended, then, that people who wrote about them would do so on the basis of their published works. And for the curious biographer there is really not a great deal more. Lacking a core of personal diaries and intimate, self-revealing letters, I have not really succeeded in calling Beard back in an immediate way. From my manuscript an identifiable individual does not emerge, and I must admit that this is perhaps more than a failure of sources. There remained a distance between author and subject. Yet to be written is a fuller biography which will achieve that bonding which distinguishes the finest efforts to re-create the lives of individuals.

Beard himself did not really approve of biography. The lives of individuals, he thought, left out too much. His personal code of honor forbade him to deal in personalities, and he seldom did so. "Biography," he once commented when discussing Franklin Roosevelt, whose policies were the subject of many of his scholarly efforts, "is not a science or an art inexorably bodying forth 'the truth.' It is more nearly a form of village gossip, sublimated, elevated, and transfigured. Like gossip, it is amusing, diverting, moving, tragic, comic, or grandiose, according to the social setting, talents, and animus of the biographer." Beard's historical reputation illustrates well his conclusion that "as prevailing interests, conflicts, and ideas change, the images of distinguished historic characters, whether ancient or recent, will be altered, retouched, or perhaps broken for a time."[2]

Possessing a disarming simplicity, humor, and directness that won him friends wherever he went, Beard also had an uncanny sense of and taste for the major issues of his time. Although he is usually discussed with Vernon L. Parrington and Frederick J. Turner in accounts of American historiography, I urge that he had very little in common with these academic intellectuals. Beard was a noninstitutional, if not an anti-institutional figure, less a theorist than an activist. Nothing in his intellectual life was ever "final." The books he wrote were challenges, questions, segments of what he saw as an ongoing dialogue among concerned citizens. He learned about society by actively participating as a reformer of social institutions. However, he was also an omnivorous reader. Reading combined with practical experience gave him a confidence in the power of critical individual effort for social change. This confidence produced his greatest works of history and political science, yet it also kept him from participating in a larger political movement for social change. Bound by no sect or party, he wanted to do "emancipated thinking."[3]

As I and many others read him, he belongs on the left of the spectrum of American social thought of the twentieth century. His radicalism was eclectic and not particularly original. It had its roots firmly in late-nineteenth-century European and American efforts to grapple with the social and political problems resulting from industrialization. Although he tried to phrase ideas in language that Americans would understand, Beard learned from Juan Jaurès, Eduard Bernstein, Peter Kropotkin, John Hobson, Max Weber, Karl Manheim, Benedetto Croce, and many other distinguished European students of modern society. He admired and respected Karl Marx. American teachers such as Thorstein Veblen were important, too, but my contention is that Beard's was not a narrowly native American form of radicalism, that it cannot be understood outside the international context of his reading, friendships, and travels.

The fact that he came from a relatively wealthy family of landowning midwestern gentry and the fact that his family had a tradition of independent reflection on the verities of various American times and places cannot be ignored either. In Indiana he was nourished on the social conscience of nineteenth-century England. The idol of his favorite college professor was William Gladstone. Beard lived in England during a period of intense ferment in British social thought, a time when the differences between socialism and the liberal tradition were being explored, and, in some cases, diminished. He seems to have adopted as the maxim of his life the message of the nineteenth century that the world was a place of constant change and development and that intellectuals must adopt principles that would survive in such a world, principles that would be firm and would serve through tumultuous futures. Beard's guiding suppositions—that the common people could be trusted to know what was best both for themselves and for the country and that the rational aspect of human nature is more powerful than the irrational—were such principles.

Beard's American religious heritage was the most radical possible. To use Herman Melville's words, he was "another phase of the Quaker, modified by individual circumstances."[4] This fiercely nonsectarian and independent "inner light" prevented him from becoming stale and conservative when confronting the gordian problems of life in the twentieth century. From his family's Quaker tradition he early learned that authorities outside the individual conscience were always to be carefully scrutinized. To the end of a magnificent career of scholarship, friendship, and social activism, Beard retained the ability to ask significant questions, to remind Americans that the achievement of economic and social, as well as political, democracy would depend on the quality and quantity of individual critical citizenships.

Of course, I am thoroughly indebted to the many and wonderful historians who have previously ventured opinions on the life and thinking of Charles A. Beard, particularly to Richard Hofstadter, whose chapters on Beard in *The Progressive Historians,* though I have criticized them, remain a powerful example of creative and provocative endeavor. Numerous writers are acknowledged in the footnotes to follow. I have mined a rich vein.

For her wise and often amusing suggestions and for sharing so generously materials from the papers of Charles and Mary Beard in her possession, I thank Miriam Beard Vagts. Librarians everywhere were splendidly cooperative, particularly Judith Schiff of the Yale Archives, who notified me of the many Beard letters in the Edwin Borchard Collection while it was being processed; David Horn, the Archivist of DePauw University; and Joyce Giardana, of the Interlibrary Loan Desk at Southern Illinois University, Edwardsville. Elizabeth Duvall, former Archivist at Smith College, gave bed, board, and cheer to a migrating researcher. Doris Neumann graciously sent me the letters between her husband, William Neumann, and Charles and Mary Beard.

Barton Bernstein is the sort of mentor that every would-be scholar should have. He thoroughly and explicitly criticized every chapter of this manuscript and was never too busy to put aside his own work and give counsel and encouragement. Professors Hal Kahn and Alasdair Macphail read an earlier version of this work and made many useful and imaginative suggestions. I thank Professor Dorothy Ross for a critical reading in the final stages. Because I did not always follow their advice, they are absolved from responsibility for problems remaining, but they certainly prevented a number of errors.

For support during five long, exciting years, I am especially grateful to Norman Nordhauser and to my dear sisters, Betsy Nore and Ann Nore. Kate and Eric Nordhauser provided joyful diversion. Dolores K. Kohler typed expertly. Betty Kennedy provided invaluable assistance in photographing the photographs in the Beard Archives. H.L. Kirk edited the manuscript with skill and patience. For permission to reproduce much of Chapter 12 as it appeared in *The Journal of American History* (66 [March 1980], 850–866), I thank the editor.

Life in Indiana, 1874–1898

C harles Beard once commented that optimism or pessimism in the individual thinker was "a matter of temperament, not of philosophy."[1]
Beard's own optimism, his sense of competence, his permanent, unwavering
faith in the possibilities of individual achievement, his humane rationalism,
his belief in the power of the printed word (based on experience) to bring a
more just world was the legacy of his family's circumstances and tradition,
an inheritance reinforced by the formal educational experience of his first
twenty-four years.

Beard's memories of those early years in the rich, varied county of east-
central Indiana, that green and gold land of large oaks and hills and healthy
fields, were written down when he was more than sixty years old.[2] Through
"the mists of time" he recalled working hard on his father's land: a sixty-
acre parcel near Knightstown, on which Beard had been born in 1874, and
a smaller thirty-five-acre tract in Spiceland township, to which the Beards
had moved in 1880 in order to enable their two sons to attend Spiceland
Academy, a Quaker school of excellent local reputation. His recollections
of life on these farms have a mythic quality: "By the time I was fifteen I had
had enough exercise to last me a lifetime. My muscles and body were hard
as steel. I could ride wild horses bare back, and split an oak log with a maul
and wedge."[3] Years later Beard replied to European critics of the brutality
and materialism of modern, machine-oriented urban society by saying, from
his own experience, that he found it hard to believe that "the machine system

is more dehumanizing than agriculture and handicrafts, beautiful as the latter may seem to dreamers who have never wielded a manure-fork or swung an axe."[4]

Beard remembered himself "out of doors, at hard work in field and forest," but the other great theme in his recollections was the cooperative spirit of the surrounding community. "Co-operation," he wrote, "was the chief characteristic of the neighborhood. In season and out, the neighbors were always helping one another in the harvest fields, at threshing, in times of sickness and tragedy." Individuals and families did not stand alone. "The spirit of the frontier as I knew the pioneers was not," he wrote in 1938, "the spirit of individualism that characterizes the war for trade, jobs and profit in the cities. . . . Their profit was the spirit of neighborly helpfulness—in work, in times of adversity, in hours of celebration." The urban writers of American history, Beard thought, living "among the asphalt flowers," were able to think of rural life only "in terms of their own economy, not in terms of the reality itself."[5]

We cannot know the reality of this Indiana countryside, of course. Beard grew up and observed that life from a privileged position in the community. In the world of agriculture, however, there are certain unities that transcend class—the weather as an omnipresent subject of discussion, the smell of land in different seasons, the condition of crops and animals. Beard wanted to believe—did believe—that his milieu fostered a positive attitude toward cooperation. There were no ethnic and religious divisions among the farm folk of his memory; class lines were neither visible to an intelligent, excitable red-headed boy nor admitted by the white-haired remembrancer of sixty.

Throughout his life Beard relished group efforts, the company of others in some common task. Debating in high school and college, improving the DePauw University newspaper, founding a labor college, renovating Columbia's approach to political science, researching for the city and state of New York, planning a modern capital in Japan, thinking about the role of social studies in elementary and secondary American education, presenting the issues of relativism to the mass of history professors in American universities—all of these endeavors were done in or by committees, and Beard was always a superbly energetic and responsible team member. He was not precisely a leader, *the* leader, but he was always a strong contributor. His personality enabled him to take his cooperative vision of his childhood community as his own ethic.

Beard's sense of competence, his ability to perform many and varied tasks well, to analyze situations and to act appropriately, came from close contact with strong family models, particularly his father and his maternal grandmother, Sarah Payne. William Henry Beard (1840–1913), Charles Beard's father, came from a long line of farmers, artisans, and petty merchants—English Quakers who had settled in Virginia and North Carolina in the seventeenth and eighteenth centuries. Raised on a farm near the village of

Beardtown in Guilford County, North Carolina, by parents who were on principle non-slaveowners and who were, according to family lore, involved in aiding fugitives from slavery, William Henry Beard had come to Indiana from North Carolina in 1861, at twenty-one, because he preferred, in the words of a local historian, "to live in a land that still honored the institutions of the Revolutionary heroes, and the cluster of undimmed stars that decorated the sacred old banner." In other words, he had refused to fight for the Confederacy. He worked in Indiana as a teacher, carpenter, clerk in a warehouse and drygoods store, and farm laborer. In 1863, after saving $1000, he married Mary Payne, the daughter of well-known pioneers of Henry County. According to a *History of Henry County, Indiana* written in 1884, Charles Beard's father became comfortably wealthy by speculating cautiously in real estate a short time before the Panic of 1873. In politics he was and always remained, as his son said on many occasions, "a rock-ribbed Federalist-Whig-Republican."

During the years after Charles Beard was born his father farmed and did some building on contract, including the design of several local churches and bridges. He "loved wood," Mary Beard recalled, "and was an expert craftsman with it." However, the county historian, writing when Charles Beard was a boy of ten, felt that the most interesting aspect of William Beard was his status in the countryside as a traveler and author of accounts for local newspapers.

In 1863 William Beard had returned to North Carolina, impelled by curiosity about the war and the fate of family members, and had written about battlefields, demoralized cities, and the "most interesting regions connected with the Rebellion" in letters to local newspapers. In 1883 he had gone with a group of friends, "to the Pacific Coast, visiting Colorado, Arizona, New Mexico, Oregon, Washington, Wyoming, Idaho, Montana, and Utah Territories." He had interviewed "exotic" Mormon officials in Salt Lake and had visited the mining regions of California and the Rocky Mountains. For local Indiana editors, he had penned "vivid and entertaining descriptions of climate, agricultural resources, and mining interests, as well as grand, varied and charmingly beautiful scenery which he witnessed. . . ."[6] Stories to thrill a boy of nine or ten. Did the man Charles Beard think of his father as he wandered over America, rode in a push-car railroad to visit camphor extraction works in the jungles of Formosa, or flew over the Great Wall of China in a converted World War I bomber?

William Beard was apparently a generous, capable person, the sort to whom members of the community often turned in difficult times. He gave space to black people who wanted to have camp meetings when no one else in town would cooperate; he loaned money on reasonable terms to needy neighbors; his advice was frequently sought.[7] The younger of William's two sons, Charles was recalled by surviving neighbors of the Beard family in Spiceland as "a curly-red-haired, freckled, homely, little boy, with long dangling arms, a great deal of mischievousness, curiosity, and high-temper, and a precocious mastery of 'big words.'"[8]

This precosity was supplemented by another family institution, the library. William Henry Beard had brought from North Carolina and continued to maintain a large family library, described by Charles as "more than a thousand books in history, science and various branches of knowledge." His father, Beard remembered, had taught him to read "hard books" early and also to memorize passages of significance. A fire in 1906 destroyed this family treasure, but among the surviving volumes bearing the names of both William Beard and of his father Nathan are Howitt's *History of Priestcraft*, Thomas Paine's *The Age of Reason*, and John William Draper's *History of the Conflict between Religion and Science*. "My eyes have been good," Charles Beard noted sixty years later, "and I have read day and night."[9]

Not only was this large library unusual for its time and place but so also, as the extant titles indicate, were the Beard family's religious views. Charles Beard's grandfather, Nathan Beard, had been a Quaker until he was "read out of meeting" for marrying a Methodist, Caroline Martin, "out of unity" in 1830. Thereafter Beard's grandfather, who died in 1883, had interested himself in many religions, studied the Koran, and read about Buddhism. He often described himself, Charles fondly recalled, as "a one-man church." According to an undated newspaper clipping written while she still lived, Caroline Martin Beard shared her husband's outlook. She "never attached herself to any church, or subscribed to any creed" after her marriage. Their son William Henry did send his sons to a Quaker school and did require that they attend the meetings of that sect held at the school, but he himself belonged to no church and contributed funds to many. "Well I remember," Charles Beard later wrote, "sitting on the hard benches, my feet far from the floor, while the elders sat in high places. No music. No song. Just the silence of meditation; unless, forsooth, the spirit moved some aged saint to deliver a discourse. . . ." At the age of twenty-three, in an editorial arguing against the holding of revival meetings on the campus at DePauw, Beard perhaps summed up the family's religious outlook. For much of his life Beard questioned the authority of established institutions, and his family's unorthodox religious outlook was surely an important source of this attitude. "Religion," he wrote, "is a matter of growth, of education —that is, rational religion. Religion that is deep and abiding . . . comes as the product of long and deliberate thought. It cannot come from emotional excitement."[10]

In his own family Beard must have seen that people could be effective, perhaps more than usually effective, community members without being religious in a formal way and without belonging to institutions dedicated to a particular ideology. In an urban and academic setting the mature Beard would maintain this independent, rational approach, vowing to "be the member of no party, church, club (except the Faculty beanery), association (except the AHA & c.) or other organization. I realize," he added, as his paternal grandparents and father might have when speaking of churches, "the necessity of parties, but I think there is room for one or two people who refuse to have anything to do with them." "I have been many things," he wrote with satisfaction in the last year of his life, "but never a pacifist or any other kind of absolutist."[11]

Of Beard's mother little is known. In his scattered autobiographical statements, he does not refer to her. From her, however, he inherited the progressive deafness that was to bother him from the 1920s until his death. It was his maternal grandmother, not his mother, who earned, along with his father, a notable place in Beard's memories.[12]

Sarah Wilson Payne died when Beard was eight. Yet sixty years later he described a woman whose hands and "body skilled in the nursing of fourteen children had a magic gentleness," a tenderness that had given him "a sense of peace and security" when she had gathered him into her arms and "softly sang old tunes." She knew "just what to bring, to do, and to say in enhancing her mystic powers on my imagination." The gentle old woman young Beard knew had a history that included, along with bearing fourteen children, homesteading in the early days of Henry County, disposing of wildcats and wolves at the door, and nursing neighbors through an epidemic of smallpox. When Beard knew her she was a "magnificent matriarch" living in a large house on a thousand-acre farm. Beard remembered her as a wonderful manager—"strong, active, commanding, a mistress of many arts. . . ." His grandfather, he wrote, depended upon her as much as upon himself, "for dressing and preparation of food, for medical care, for spinning, weaving, making the woolen clothes and generally keeping the household going."

Not only did this maternal grandmother furnish still another family model of competence and strength, but in retrospect she seemed also to symbolize for Beard the vast changes in technology and society that so impressed him during his own life. Her kitchen in the "big brick house, high on a hill, amid hundreds of acres of fields and forests" was "as big as a New York flat." The attic, with "the big spinning wheel for wool, the little wheel for flax, the reel which checked off skeins of yarn," with loom, candle molds, and herbs hanging from the rafters, became in memory a museum of "strange utensils of the handicrafts."[13]

Thus Charles Beard grew up in the fresh country in a small, financially secure family with strong, humane, rational traditions that were aspects of the privileged independence of prosperous gentry. Beard's memories tell us that books were important; questions were asked; travel and practical experience were regarded as necessary; men and women of the family were powerful, confident people who did many things well, who served the community and, in the family tradition, left the world a better place.

In Beard's case, the values of school and home complemented each other. Spiceland Academy, which Beard attended for all but the last year of high school, was a small, excellent private elementary and secondary institution run by local Quakers. "There was," Beard noted, "strictness without harshness, gravity without heaviness, in the atmosphere of the place." It had a library of more than two thousand books, lively debating societies, speakers from near and far such as David Starr Jordan and local politicians, plays and musical evenings given by the students and by wandering troupes. Beard remembered with pleasure his study of Latin, his introduction to the English classics, "Wordsworth, Ruskin, Carlyle, and the great men of old," and his teacher who taught both American history and physics "with equal proficiency."

On Friday nights, members of the debating societies would meet in the school's library "to solve the burning problems of the hour. Shall the tariff be reduced? Is fame to be preferred to great riches? Shall the Federal government regulate railway rates? Local option or prohibition? With much eloquence and gusto the fledglings displayed their wisdom and learning." For more than forty years, dinner parties at the home of Charles and Mary Beard recalled these evenings. With his friends in Spiceland, young Beard played baseball and football, skated and sledded, and each autumn enjoyed a great "battle of the walnuts" in a nearby grove.[14]

For this part of his life, there are only Beard's fond and happy memories. However, his term at Spiceland Academy came to an abrupt close. He was expelled one year before his graduation and had to finish high school at the public institution in nearby Knightstown. His brother, Clarence, five years older, was simultaneously expelled from the University of Indiana at Bloomington. Beard never wrote about this incident, but it must have been traumatic and humiliating.

William Beard had given his sons, for their own amusement, a printing press. On this press the young men printed, when Beard was sixteen and his brother twenty-one, a pamphlet, now lost, criticizing the faculty and administration of Indiana University, which Clarence was then attending. This incident survived in local memories for more than sixty years, as surviving contemporaries of Charles Beard in the 1950s obviously relished recalling this bit of gossip about a leading family. One neighbor described an enraged William Henry Beard breaking up the press and scattering the pieces on his farm near Spiceland. Someone else remembered that Charles had ridden into town early "to salvage his belongings before the Academy heard from I[ndiana] U[niversity]. (Charles had been doing the printing.)" Charles may have run away from home for a brief time. His daughter Miriam remembered him telling her as a child, "If you ever do anything crazy, child, I think you can tell me about it and I shall try to understand. I was crazy too when I was young. I ran away from home when I was sixteen." Beard did not share with his daughter the details of his adventure, except to indicate that he had been fleeing his father's anger. "But William Henry Beard," she added, "embraced his son and wept, like the biblical patriarch."

In 1898, after his graduation from college and before he embarked for Oxford and graduate study, Beard returned to Spiceland to give students of the Academy a temperance lecture, a talent for which he was famous locally. A friend recalled that the leader of the meeting "reached under his chair, picked up a diploma and presented it to Charles with, 'We think thee have rediscovered thyself in the sight of the meeting, and here is thy diploma.'" With tears Beard accepted the honor and was henceforth listed with the Spiceland graduates of 1898. It was a curious case of adolescent rebellion, which may have strengthened his sense of independence. After the initial and terrible humiliation of being the subject of town gossip for being expelled from the Academy, he still was able to finish high school, go on to college, and see that his father's ire was not sustained and that he would be welcomed back to the safety of the family fold. It had been a limited rebellion, not costly in the long run, and Beard had learned that one could survive the bruises of controversy.[15]

After Charles graduated from Knightstown High School in 1891, William Beard purchased and gave to his sons one of the two local newspapers in Knightstown, the *Sun*. According to Mary Beard, the father took no part in managing the paper after making the gift. It was to be a business experience for the younger Beards. In this paper, partially subsidized by the Methodist Ladies Home Missionary Society, the Beard brothers loyally supported prohibition and the Republican party until the venture ended in 1894, when Clarence went to New Castle, bought out the populist *People's Press*, and established the *Henry County Republican*, to which Charles occasionally contributed during summers while he was at DePauw.[16] Beard must have enjoyed this venture as a small-town editor. In college he repeated the experience by becoming editor of the *DePauw Palladium* and, for the rest of his life, he adored the company of reporters and journalists.

Floyd J. Newby, a fellow Knightstowner and Beard's roommate at DePauw in 1896, remembered (as did another contemporary) that Beard had been persuaded to attend DePauw, a rather conservative Methodist institution with a good academic reputation, by the Reverend Mr. Preston, a local Methodist minister and friend who had seen Beard as a brilliant young man "throwing away his life" in Knightstown.[17] In any case, Beard's father supported his decision and financed him entirely while he attended DePauw for three years and two summers.[18] After Indiana University, to which another Beard perhaps would not have been welcomed, DePauw University was a sound educational choice.

At DePauw, a cluster of seven buildings on a green within the small city of Greencastle, "college life was" in the absence of automobiles, Beard recalled, "lived rather intensively on the campus or near it."[19] Beard belonged to a fraternity, held various offices in his class of sixty-one, and frequently displayed for the community his skill in oratory. Before he became the editor of the college paper, it was a genteel literary sheet carrying on its front page articles such as "The Art of Keats." Under Beard's leadership as editor during his senior year, the front page was transformed by news of the football team, the debate squad, local speakers, faculty publications, and other features representative of the "hurly-burly" of student life. The old *DePauw Weekly* became the *DePauw Palladium*, although still a weekly. The editor announced in his first issue a policy of not trying to please everybody, of "hewing to the line and letting the chips fall where they will." Letters from readers were invited. A General News column that discussed national events from a distinctly Republican point of view was added to the editorial page. At the end of his term Beard left the paper, unlike several previous editors, financially solvent.[20]

Under Beard the newspaper became a forum for discussion of changes in the university: history should be required of all students, the university should advertise itself in this "age of advertising" by creating a board "whose duty it shall be to keep the university before the public"; students should write about DePauw for their home newspapers; women should be admitted to Phi Beta Kappa; the university should "teach young men and women to know the social and political institutions" rather than "bury them beneath the dust and rot and rubbish of hair-splitting subtleties and antique vagaries"; the science, language, and English departments should have special libraries similar to those for history and political science classes; religious revivals should be held elsewhere.[21] In the pages of *The Mirage*, DePauw's yearbook of 1899, Beard is depicted in jest as the author of a book titled *How to Run a University*, which "treats of the best methods to be employed in handling a conservative faculty, of instigating revolts and of crystallizing and directing public sentiment."[22]

The outstanding nonlocal issue for people at DePauw during Beard's senior year, 1897–1898, was certainly the coming of the war with Spain. Many men at DePauw belonged to "the cadets," a military drilling group that volunteered its services en masse at the declaration of war. Beard was not a cadet, and although the editorial page was strongly committed to "Free Cuba" and "Remember the *Maine!*," Beard advised students not to be swept away by the war spirit. "War may be a quick road to the heights of fame for the brave and capable man, but it is one where he must mount over the bodies of his comrades–it is a gory path to glory." He congratulated his fellow students on "the absence of the cheap patriotism and jingoism which have been so prevalent at many other institutions." He praised those who did not choose "to drop their college work and rush away. . . . The duties of peace," he reminded them and perhaps himself, a rejected volunteer, "are as sacred as the duties of war. The courage of the citizen must be no less than that of the soldier."[23]

Asked in 1939 to reminisce about his years in college, Beard's first response was to acknowledge "the fact that the faculty at old DePauw did more for me than I could ever tell." Certainly the faculty member and close friend who most affected Beard's views was his professor of history, Andrew Stephenson, a proponent of the theory that democratic institutions had originated in primeval Teutonic forests, been transplanted to England by invading tribes, and carried centuries later to North America on the ships of white Englishmen. Stephenson had received his doctorate from Johns Hopkins in 1891 and was described by former students as a man of forceful presence, "a roaring lion often," and as a "large, rather gruff, well-liked man," who, like Beard, enjoyed arguments. And, the former classmate recalled, "the two of them had many." Years later, Beard included Stephenson with York Powell of Oxford and Moses Coit Tyler of Cornell as one of the "master lecturers" who had moved him to "rush to the library and find out more for myself."[24]

Stephenson's leading interest was English history, specifically the growth of Parliament, the limitation of the monarchy, and the rise of popular government. He was a Democrat who admired Gladstone's humane liberalism rather than William Jennings Bryan's populism. At DePauw Beard concentrated in history and, with Stephenson, studied general European history, English constitutional and political history, and the political and constitutional history of the United States. History, wrote Beard the student editor, "is the basis of political science, oratory and literature." Students, he argued, should be required to take history before entering those departments. Beard believed for the rest of his life that history is the only true foundation for other social studies. In his last great speech, delivered to the American Political Science Association in December 1947, he deplored the divorce of other social studies from history. Cut loose from history, he said, political science, economics, law, and sociology "would become theoretical, superficial, and speculative, or what might be worse, merely 'practical,' that is, subservient to vested interests and politicians temporarily in power."[25]

During Beard's senior year at DePauw, the "historical seminary" under Stephenson studied the origin and adoption of the Constitution and surveyed the interpretation of that document to 1830. Beard was excited about this investigation. "The class in United States Constitutional History," he wrote on the *Palladium's* editorial page in a youthful burst, "is now investigating the original sources on American nation making. There have been several dangerous explosions of ancient theories, but no lives are recorded as lost. . . ." In another editorial Beard wrote that, while politicians worship the Constitution "as though it were sacred," history "tells us that this crowned Constitution with its halo has been the bulwark of every great national sin— from slavery to monopoly."[26]

Beard was definitely convinced in this period that the institutions of democracy had spread first to England, and then to America, from a point of origin in Germanic forests. If he had learned of the attacks on the "Teutonic Myth" by Charles Maclean Andrews in 1889 and 1891, his senior oration, delivered to the College of Liberal Arts on Washington's Birthday 1898 and titled "The Story of a Race," did not reveal this knowledge. For his audience Beard recreated a panorama beginning a thousand years ago, when Anglo-Saxons from German forests crowded to the shores of Britain bringing "the beginning of a liberty whose expansion shall never cease." He ended this exercise in racist organicism with a plea for the protection of American national life from the "ennervating touch of peace, extravagance and intemperance." Yet Teutonism could be combined with a critical attitude toward social instituions. Continued progress depended on constant effort. "The cry of the hour," young Beard declared, "is reform. . . . Class barriers are rising higher. . . . Side by side are grasping capitalists and idle workmen, luxury and starvation, tax burdened citizens, and pampered officials." The exit from this situation? Americans should not forget "that the Teuton who crossed the Alps into the soft effeminating influences of Italy became the cringing, miserly dago." Reform "must become a resistless moral appeal, striking the minds of men with the truth of God." The "anglo Saxon race," the "race of progress," the source of the Great Charter, the Declaration of Independence, and the Emancipation Proclamation would yet, Beard concluded, "write the new constitution of the 20th century—guaranteeing a broader freedom, based not on equality of wealth or of power" but rather on a liberty "founded on the equality of rational individualism."[27]

In later years Beard shed this racist interpretative structure but not the yearning for a collective nationalism and the urge to make a "resistless moral appeal." The youthful suspicion, based on those Germanic teachings, of nonassimilable ethnic minorities became in mature writings a general unwillingness to discuss ethnic and cultural differences among the peoples of the United States, an effort to create a history of the American people without recognizing individual cultural communities.

Beard's greatest strength, Andrew Stephenson wrote in a letter of recommendation, "is in the line of history and forensics, in which he has excelled all students of my department. . . . It is because of his marked ability in historical research that I have insisted from the first that he give his life to this line of work." It was probably Stephenson who suggested that Beard go to Oxford to study English institutions with York Powell. Stephenson did visit Beard at Oxford in 1900, and Beard may have been influenced by Stephenson's admiration of John Burgess, another Teutonist, to choose Columbia for his doctoral studies. Beard's doctoral dissertation on the origin and development of the office of justice of the peace in England; his volume of excerpts from the English historians, printed in 1906; his interest in researching the origins of the Constitution of the United States; and his later need to think through and follow others such as C.M. Andrews in demolishing the Teutonic theory of American institutions are at least in part testimonials to the power and influence of his friend Professor Stephenson.[28]

The other professor to whom Beard paid written tribute while at DePauw was Arthur Ragan Priest of the Department of Oratory. Priest's classes in debate and oratorical themes were "invaluable aids in working out thesis and papers" and "without equals in enabling students to do clear, logical thinking on any question." He delighted in these "helpful and practical courses," winning as a freshman the right to represent Indiana in the National Prohibition Oratorical Contest in Pittsburgh, where he took the second prize of fifty dollars. During his last two years of college Beard belonged to DePauw's squad of celebrated debaters, arguing such questions as whether or not employers should recognize unions and whether or not the income tax was feasible. Beard, of course, had been debating since high school. In a society that relished verbal contests, debating was a campus sport equal to football in the public eye, commanding front-page photos and captions in the school paper.[29] For the rest of his life Beard took a debater's stance as he had learned it, carefully constructing his arguments, applying social and economic data from reading and experience to issues of the day.

Along with his major concentration in historical studies, Beard took courses at DePauw from James Riley Weaver, a staunch protectionist Republican and veteran of the Civil War who had been an American consul in various European cities between 1869 and 1895, and who was the department of political science at DePauw. Weaver repudiated textbooks. "Students," Weaver wrote, "are collaborators with the instructor in the investigation of specific subjects." His syllabus emphasized contemporary writers as well as the classical authors, whose names and ideas shone for years after in the writings of his students. In political theory, the students read Aristotle, Plato, Machiavelli, Locke, Rousseau, Hegel, Bagehot, and *The Federalist*. The study of social theory was augmented by the Old Testament, Hegel, Greene, Darwin, Spencer, Buckle, Guizot, and Westermarck. For Weaver's class in "principles and application of economics," Beard read Adam Smith, Jevons, Senior, Mill, Marshall, and Marx. Richard Ely, Henry George, Simon Patton, and Edward Bellamy were all part of a course on "socialism—history and philosophy." Weaver was concerned with the role of bias in social thought and he attempted, successfully, to furnish students a number of views that challenged his own. "Who can doubt," Merle Curti has concluded, "that Beard owed some part of his concern with the role of bias and underlying assumptions and presuppositions to his old teacher." Like Stephenson, Weaver emphasized the importance of history for other studies. "All social theory and philosophy must be tested," Weaver insisted, "by historical data properly interpreted. The Historical-Philosophical method is the only safeguard against Ideology on the one hand and Empiricism on the other."[30]

History would become for Beard too the link between all branches of social thought. "Politics, economics, and sociology—while emphasizing the present and practical," he wrote thirty five years later, "have a certain time depth and the degree of their validity depends upon the firmness with which they have grasped the time-dynamics of their subjects. . . . The whole frame of interests and ideas in which modern intelligence works is a heritage from history."[31]

Some writers have placed great emphasis on a field trip Beard supposedly made to Chicago in 1896. Eric Goldman, who made Beard's acquaintance at Johns Hopkins in 1940, has written: "As field trips for a course at DePauw University, he made his first visits up to Chicago and was shocked by the spectacle of raw industrialism." Soon, according to Goldman, "Beard was an avid participant in the discussions at Hull House, listening to Populists arguing with socialists and Clarence Darrow arguing with both, trying this or that heresy for himself, daily moving further from the certitudes of Spiceland."[32]

Beard probably did go to Chicago at least twice during his college years, but there is no contemporary record indicating that his views were dramatically affected at that time by what he might have seen or heard. In James Weaver's classes, the Social Gospel and the experiment of Toynbee Hall in England were discussed, but the nature and impact of any "field trip" is problematic. The Greencastle *Banner Times* noted enigmatically on 13 August 1896 that Charles Beard had returned from a trip to Chicago and had reported that nearly all the workingmen of the city favored protection and McKinley. Records kept by Beard's fraternity indicate that in October 1896 he went to Chicago as a delegate to the Phi Gamma Delta state convention.[33]

Though there is no evidence that he was ever swept away by populist or socialist ideas in this period, Beard's newspaper editorials do reveal some inclination toward the Social Gospel and show that he was stimulated by his teachers and by the ideas in books he was reading. Like many intelligent, sensitive college students of any age, he must have felt that he was looking out of new windows. By the time he was a senior he clearly saw himself as an independent, argumentative scholar with a duty to use his knowledge in the service of general humanity. "The true scholar does not," he wrote then, "seek truth for truth's sake, but that he may pour it out into life's great current to uplift and inspire a burden-stricken humanity." The scholar "catches mighty visions , . . and reads the spirit of the age. The single mind may be wiser than the multitude."[34]

Challenged in his studies, Beard, at twenty-four, rejoiced that "the critical and scientific schools," were "bringing in a new regime of thought." Old idols and superstitions, he thought, were being cleared away by "blasts of iconoclasm." The "true method of study and research" accepted nothing as final, believed nothing "without investigation and verification."[35] Concluding his term as editor of the *Palladium*, Beard penned a final crescendo echoing the rationalism, confidence, and independent spirit of his family tradition, now reinforced by great ideas:

If the truth tears down every church and government under the sun—let the truth be known. And this truth will only be known . . . when men begin to seek the truth in the records of history, politics and religion and science. Let the new school triumph![36]

2

Sojourn In England, 1898–1902

Between 1898 and 1902 Beard spent nearly four years in England, returning to American shores only briefly for a term of study at Cornell and his wedding to Mary Ritter. At Oxford he continued, with the congenial Tory Frederick York Powell, the study of English history and politics he had so enjoyed at DePauw; he met the fascinating Walter Vrooman; and he assisted Vrooman in organizing a new venture in workers' education, Ruskin Hall. Though he might have visited the slums of Chicago in college days, it was in England in his mid-twenties that he got a closer look at life in smoke-filled industrial settings. There he encountered such leaders of trade unions as Ben Tillet and James Sexton of the dockworkers and Kier Hardie, the Scottish miner who a few years before had founded the Independent Labour Party. In a new situation there were opportunities for a direct young man who did not have enough education or sense of class to be awed by Oxonian tweeds and indifference. Young Beard's radiant vitality, ambition, and responsible habits led him to seek experience with both town and gown in the medieval city.

Financed by his father's generosity, Beard arrived in the "city of Oxford with her aged blackened buildings," in the land of his colonial ancestors, the country of Thomas Carlyle and John Morley, of John Ruskin and Walter Bagehot, of John Richard Green and F. W. Maitland, late in the summer of 1898 to pursue graduate study in English constitutional and political history at the university. "My ignorance," he recalled, "was, as American movie magnates might say, 'colossal,' but my enthusiasm was high." Frederick York Powell, the medievalist and Regius Professor of Modern History, welcomed the young man he later described as "the nicest American I ever met," helped him plan a program of studies, and saw that Beard was promptly elected a member of the Stubbs History Club.[1]

On the day he entered Oxford Beard also encountered, quite by coincidence, another tall, red-headed, intense American, Walter Vrooman of Kansas and his wife, Amne Grafflin, a very wealthy woman from Baltimore. Vrooman had come to Oxford, he informed Beard, to study philosophy and to found a new institution for the education of working people. Beard at least knew of the Vrooman name through the Social Gospel activities of Walter's more famous brother, Carl. How Walter Vrooman presented himself to Beard is unknown, but his life had been a dramatic contrast to the relatively sheltered affluence of Charles Beard.

Vrooman at twenty-nine was five years older than Beard. In 1882, while young Beard had been a student at sedate Spiceland Academy, thirteen-year-old Vrooman had been traveling across the Midwest in a wagon selling "lightning cleaning compound" with an older brother. He had had little formal schooling but he knew much of the world. Early in life he had mastered phrenology. In 1884 and 1885 he had looked at the bumps on people's heads throughout the South and Midwest as a paid employee of a lecture bureau. A few years later he had become a "labor agitator," joined the Knights of Labor, and spent time in a Pittsburgh jail for disturbing the peace. Subsequently he had experienced a religious conversion, and as a Christian Socialist had campaigned for parks and playgrounds in Philadelphia and for God and Populism in Baltimore, where he met and married Amne Grafflin and her money. His most recent campaign, before arriving in England, had been against Bossism in St. Louis. There his wife had financed the publication of two populist tracts while he ran for mayor as an independent Christian Socialist and was again jailed for creating a public nuisance in the eyes of city authorities. The Vroomans were recovering from this defeat when they met Charles Beard in Oxford.[2]

Vrooman described himself or rather his ideal self to a journalist from *The Fortnightly Review*. He was, he said, the person who had "originated the movement which [had] succeeded in inducing the largest American cities to open public parks in their most crowded quarters" and was also "one of the most vigorous organizers against" municipal corruption in the United States. C. W. Bowerman and James Sexton, British union officials, persuaded to accompany Vrooman on a trip to the United States financed by Amne Vrooman a few years later, were indeed surprised to learn that they were better known to their American brothers than was Walter Vrooman.[3]

Contemporaries agreed that Vrooman was a compelling personality and a hyponotic speaker. Beard later remembered that, over tea in the Vrooman's living quarters, they had held many conversations on political and social questions of the day, Vrooman being convinced of an impending "uprising on the part of labor throughout the Western world" and of the "duty of 'educated' persons [to] prepare for it." It was Vrooman's idea, Beard said, "to found, with the sympathetic support and financial assistance of his wife, a labor center in Oxford," not a college but a "moral and philosophical movement within the ranks of advancing labor."

Beard was apparently able to separate a good idea from its context, the eccentric Vrooman, and he agreed to outline an educational program and to seek the support of the Oxford Trade Union Council. After much discussion, the fledgling institution was named Ruskin Hall, because Beard wrote later "we were both students of that great moralist and, while we dissented from many of his opinions, we came to the conclusion that Ruskin had laid the best foundation for a humane labor program." Amne Vrooman, who seems to have had a greater grasp of practical issues than her husband and whose interest in Ruskin Hall was to be lifelong, agreed to to put up $60,000 for the venture. Following weeks of planning, Beard approached Professor York Powell after one of his lectures, and he agreed to preside at the inauguration of the Hall in February 1899.[4]

By January 1899, just four months after his arrival in Oxford, Beard had secured endorsements from unions representing 300,000 workers and from Kier Hardie's Independent Labour Party. He had outlined a program of study for the proposed institution, a program that in essence recreated his college courses, such as English Political History, Political Economy, Industrial History, and English Literature. History, Beard told a journalist, was to be "the main subject of study" and the reading lists for proposed courses contained many of the classic and contemporary authors Beard had read at DePauw— Adam Smith, Marx, the elder Toynbee, Alfred Marshall, J. S. Mill, Richard Ely, Richard Jevons, and Herbert Spencer as well as Beatrice and Sidney Webb's *History of Trade Unionism* and other Fabian works that Beard had probably first encountered in England.

Beard had also completed a plan for day-to-day management of the Hall, formulated a project for a correspondence school, enrolled a number of students, and engaged a corps of teachers and lecturers—including, he remembered, such "choice spirits" as Edward Caird, Master of Balliol and a radical in politics and religion, who had earlier in his life supported Toynbee Hall, the well-known social settlement in London, and H. B. Lees Smith, later Postmaster General in the first Labour government. J. Kier Hardie praised Beard's energy and organizational talent, noting early in 1899 that "when in the course of conversation [Beard] closes his eyes, knits his brows, sets his teeth, and pounds his left palm with his right fist one feels that, as this young man progresses through life, something is bound to go down before him."

At the Hall, tuition, board, room, and laundry expenses came to £31 a year. During one year of residence students were to read, hear lectures, and practice their writing skills with the object of returning at the end of the year to their previous jobs, perhaps to continue their education through correspondence courses. Cooking, cleaning, and maintenance duties were shared by the residents in rotation after an early revolt against the first rules, which had provided that those on scholarships should perform the service tasks while those who "paid their way" should not be required to be janitors.

Women could not reside at the Hall, although in theory they could, according to one of Beard's flyers, "enter classes on the same terms as resident members." However, the original group of students were all males, and both Beard and Vrooman appear to have thought of "workers" in masculine terms. As Vrooman put it, "So Ruskin Hall recognizes in the worker not only a producer of commodities, but an individual soul . . . a citizen, husband, and an ancestor."[5]

What was the larger social purpose of Ruskin Hall in the view of the founders? "We do not intend," Beard announced, "to encourage toilers to leave their class, and become barristers, clergymen, physicians, military officers, or financiers." The curriculum therefore did not include ancient languages, mathematics, theology, metaphysics, medicine or law. "We will satisfy our modest ambitions," Charles added emphatically, "by helping to make *men*, expecting students to return when they finish their residence here to their respective shops, factories, farms and mines, to *raise* rather than *rise out of* the mass of their fellow workers." As its first goal, Ruskin Hall would seek to supply "capable political and educational leaders from among the people."

Cartoons in the house journal, *Young Oxford*, contrasting weak, gloomy, gowned scholars with virile, smiling workmen reflected a second purpose of the young Ruskinians: reconciliation between classes. Mary Beard later described Charles' interest "in having the gentlemen of Oxford, who seemed to know nothing of workers in the industrial section, and the workers, who knew nothing of Oxford, know each other in the Oxford center of learning."

A third intention, "the chief purpose of the new education" according to Walter Vrooman, was to "bridge the chasm between scholarship and the real world; between the ideals of the realm of books and the facts of the realm of existence." In 1899 Beard told a journalist that the idea of such education was "not to manufacture a superior class or let loose a horde of half-baked agitators on the world, but to give those who have an aptitude for education that [which] will help them raise their fellow-men, not rise above them." Ruskin Hall, Walter Vrooman promised, would be "the graveyard of agitators. We shall take men who have been merely condemning our institutions and will teach them how, instead, to transform them." Beard rejoiced in the union of "higher learning" and practical life. "We all need to be stimulated in the pursuit of knowledge," he told the students in 1901, "to be encouraged in assumption of broader responsibilities which inevitably accompany increased powers; and above all to have continuously before ourselves visions of our own possibilities . . ."[6]

Looking back in 1936 on these activities at Oxford, Beard described his younger self and his friends as being "wild-eyed cranks lacking in respect for 'academic tradition,'" as "starting a movement in the home of lost causes" by "speaking on streetcorners" and going "to holes-in-corners where trade unions met," and as setting "many of the great and wise at sixes and sevens." In retrospect, Beard's activities appear to have reminded him of the activities of those bustling bourgeois disparaged by Marx and Engels in *The Communist Manifesto:* "economists, philanthropists, humanitarians, improvers of the condition of the working class, organizers of charity . . . hole-in-corner reformers of every possible kind," who were "desirous of redressing social grievances, in order to secure the continued existence of bourgeois society."

Beard and the Vroomans in 1898 and 1899 certainly did not think of themselves as defending the existence of decadent bourgeois privileges. The young Ruskinian activists saw education, enlightenment, knowledge as a transforming weapon in the hands of the working class. Yet the purpose for which the weapon might be used, beyond a sort of vague citizenly uplift, remained mostly unexamined. In 1899 Charles Beard had not yet begun to analyze in a meaningful way the problems of ending exploitation in industrial society. Walter Vrooman never would .[7]

For one year, 1898–1899, Beard pursued both his studies with York Powell at Oxford and his teaching at Ruskin Hall. He began at this time the research in county histories and records that would become in 1904 his doctoral thesis and his first scholarly publication, *The Office of Justice of the Peace in England: In Its Origin and Development.* How did a young man from the American hinterlands, bearing the degree of an unknown university, become the friend of York Powell, the Regius Professor who sported his prejudices against Americans, Germans, Jews, and learned ladies "like a flower in his coat"? The answer is that York Powell made exceptions to each of his prejudices, and Beard was one. Their friendship must have been a meshing of compatible personalities, for in fact their enthusiasms were very different.

York Powell's main interest was not history at all but ancient Icelandic folklore, of which he did many distinguished translations; Spanish literature; the avant-garde art of his time, especially the French impressionists; and his collection of many hundreds of pictures by Japanese artists. Though he wrote practically no large work of history(except a textbook for the middle schools, *History of England to 1503,* which hardly qualifies as a major work), he was known throughout Oxford as a man of great learning and congeniality. In 1894, when a man had been needed to take the place of J. A. Froude as Regius Professor and when the most distinguished and obvious candidate S. R. Gardiner had declined, York Powell had accepted Lord Roseberry's invitation to the post.

An exuberant man, the Regius Professor was full of sunshine and humor though not an overwhelming conversationalist. He always spoke in brief phrases punctuated by laughter that was, his biographer reported, "the first thing noticed by strangers and gave a kind of choric effect to his talk." John Butler Yeats, a close friend, wrote that York Powell "never looked about for people to respect; he looked for people who would give him plenty of delight, excite his sympathy, and make themselves beloved." Someone once said to Powell, "I do believe, Powell, you would not object to a murderer," to which Powell replied, "No, not if he was a really good fellow." Charles Beard was witty, passionate, intelligent, and not enamored of Oxonian tweeds and stuffiness. He had no pretensions. There was about him what his daughter described as "a kind of Quaker innocence and directness" that must have attracted and charmed the unorthodox Regius Professor. Perhaps they also discovered their common delight in the sport of boxing, which Beard had done in college and which York Powell regularly judged at Radley College. Whatever its bases, their friendship was as much personal and political as intellectual.[8]

Lord Acton had spoken for the great majority of British historians of York Powell's era when he wrote in 1887 that "there is no escape from the dogma that history is the conscience of mankind." York Powell's view of history was the opposite, and he delighted in expounding it. "The formation and expression of ethical judgments, the approval or condemnation of Caius Julius Caesar or Cesare Borgia is not a thing within the historian's province." The historian's business was to collect facts, collate them, and "lastly to consider and attempt to see what scientific use can be made of these facts he has ascertained." On another occasion, York Powell had been even more definite. He would regard "History as an absolute science, as much as, for example, Botany." Practical politics, had "no more relationship to History, and no less than, say the art of gardening to Botany. . . . It is not the function of the historian to pass judgments at all."[9]

York Powell did not read European writers on politics and theory. He did not, according to Oliver Elton, refine his simple proposition that ethics and history could be separated except to say that the growth of moral ideas was a subject within the historian's province, a field for descriptive analysis. As Regius Professor he was required on occasion to pontificate on the meaning of history, and he did so, but Elton suggests that he used Darwinian ideas that were "in the air" as a source of his viewpoint. Perhaps because his own intersts were mainly in the field of literature, Powell was particularly concerned to make a rigid distinction between history and literature.

"The proper view" of history, he wrote once when drawing this line, was "as an accumulation or assemblage of facts respecting humanity *en masse,* and not respecting single individuals." Literature, on the other hand, was "concerned with the expression of human emotions in an artistic manner." History could, he admitted, "be a model of exposition," but that was not its true *raison d'être.''* York Powell attacked Froude and Macaulay as perpetrators of a confusion between history and literature. They could be read for style but not for content.[10]

Although York Powell frequently stated his belief that Charles Darwin had been the "greatest of modern historians," that the evolution of political institutions could be explained scientifically, and that the duty of the historian was to "observe, not to preach," there is little reason to believe that as a scholar he presented Beard with any thoughts about history that Beard had not already acquired from his Anglophilic professor at DePauw, Andrew Stephenson. York Powell's concern with the intrusion of personal bias into scholarly products had, moreover, been shared by Beard's other teacher at DePauw, James Riley Weaver. Beard's thesis on the Justice of the Peace was a model of the sort of nonjudgmental, detached, purely institutional history that was attractive to all of these men.[11]

It was probably York Powell's personal social ethics, similar in turn to the aristocratic dismay of Thomas Carlyle and John Ruskin at the human and aesthetic costs of industrialism, that made the deepest imprint on young Beard. In his own way, York Powell provided a model for the scholar-activist. Though he was a Conservative and unenthusiastic about mass democracy, York Powell welcomed Ruskin Hall as an effort to educate the working classes. At Beard's request, on 22 February 1899 he shared the stage of Oxford Town Hall with dignitaries from unions and cooperative societies, and, one observer wrote, "with John Bull, bludgeon-like sententiousness," welcomed the venture. He continued his interest in Ruskin Hall, and in 1901 he wrote a personal and thoroughly "unscientific" prefatory note for Beard's small book of lectures, *The Industrial Revolution.* Democracy, "of all goverments," Powell informed readers of Beard's pieces, is the least able to afford mass ignorance. "No system of government," he continued, "no set of formulas, can save a state unless the people who work the system or formulas are wise, honest, and healthy." The factory system had been a deadly blow to the vitality of the English people. In their ignorance, the people had allowed their taste to become debased. They had come to tolerate such things as "wax flowers" instead of real ones, "wretched drawing room suites" instead of Windsor chairs, "painted vases" and other machine-made "symbols of snobbery." In York Powell's view, the teacher of working-class people should inculcate a taste for "good work, not sham work; good art, not bad nor even mediocre art; good food, not the bad bread . . . and the bad beer; good news, not party lies and foolish flattery and idle or malicious gossip; real information . . . not chopped-up rubbish and dirty garbage."[12]

"It is so hard not to 'preach,' and I dread 'preaching'" York Powell wrote to Beard after putting down these "Thoughts on Democracy." "But this is a time in this country when plain speaking has become a duty one dare not shun at any risk."[13]

Echoes of this sort of paternalistic indignation can be found in Beard's writing thirty years later, although similar sentiments can be found in the writing of a few generations of American intellectuals and academicians. "It is the business of social ethics to criticize and expose the perils inherent in animal materialism," Beard wrote in *A Charter for the Social Sciences* (1932), and York Powell would surely have agreed with Beard's conclusion that "social science in the schools has a duty" to encourage literary interests among students, in this way counteracting "the cheap, flashy and degrading trash which floods the market," to set up "standards of judgment" and to raise "the tone of those who write as well as the taste of those who read."[14]

In this period of his life Beard could trace in the manner of York Powell's ideal, detached historian the institutional development of the Justice of the Peace while simultaneously writing on other subjects, with passionate didacticism, as an exponent of "THE NEW MORALITY, which centres around the words brotherhood, social organism, new democracy, and kingdom corporate." Beard here paused and added, as though York Powell were looking over his shoulder, "In taking up this work I do not pose as an historian for it is his duty to leave ethics alone and 'find out what can be known of the characters and situations with which he is engaged.'"[15]

In the summer of 1899 Beard returned to the United States, where he studied for one semester at Cornell, taking courses from Moses Coit Tyler and George Lincoln Burr. In the spring of 1900, he and Mary Ritter were married in Indianapolis and the couple returned to England, where "The Hall," *Young Oxford* reported, "was in full force at the station" to greet them on 23 March 1900. "How we all looked out for the approaching train and with what enthusiasm. What shall we say more! Mr. Beard has returned and is as ever. The same wholehearted, happy optimist of yore. The same as ever did we say? No, because he was accompanied by a lady who has become his life partner."[16]

Mary Ritter Beard was a warm, sympathetic person, a listener, and like her husband possssed great energy. She was less withdrawn and abstract than Charles, and less bookish. According to their daughter, the original union was not between two determined young scholar-reformers but rather between two attractive, popular young people from similar social backgrounds.

The Ritters lived in Indianapolis, and Mary was one of two daughters in a family of seven children. Narcissa Lockwood Ritter, Mary's mother, was the daughter of parents who had been slaveowning Kentucky gentry before the Civil War. She was not, as has sometimes been asserted, a leading suffragist, although she may have belonged to some organizations that supported the vote for women. Eli Ritter, her father, had left the Quaker faith to join the Union Army, from which he had emerged a captain with impaired eyesight. After the war he had returned to Indianapolis and become a prosperous lawyer with the aid of Narcissa, who helped him by reading from legal books until his eyesight had improved. According to his granddaughter, Eli Ritter was a "monomaniacal temperance crusader" and an activist in Grand Army of the Republic veteran's organizations. He was strongly interested in civic affairs and was responsible for Indianapolis' first zoning laws and for persecution of tally-sheet forgers, who had consistently rigged local elections.

Her daughter has suggested that Mary Ritter may have felt stifled in her proper, Victorian family: her mother a Southern lady, her father a crusader whose example she as a female was discouraged from following. She was the valedictorian of her high school class and followed several older brothers to DePauw, where she again excelled in her studies, concentrating on classical history and law. She was denied admission to Phi Beta Kappa at DePauw because of her sex. Contemporaries who knew her in college described her as a woman of strong and definite opinions, small and round, holding her head high, as women of that time were often trained to do.

Charles and Mary encountered each other at several meetings held for the purpose of learning to dance, soon after dancing was allowed at DePauw in 1897. Mary Beard recalled that Charles had preferred not to dance but would sit for hours talking and reading to her passages from Fustel de Coulanges, "which meant nothing to her." She graduated from DePauw a year before Charles, in 1897, and began teaching in the public high school in Greencastle. She and Charles had become engaged before he went to England. Returning with him to Oxford after their wedding in March 1900, she was shocked by the sights in the industrial North. However, she soon found her own tasks in connection with Ruskin Hall—writing for *Young Oxford* and teaching German to cooperative extension classes.

In Amne Vrooman, a feminist with a great ego and a talent for organization, Mary Beard found not only a lifelong friend but also a fountain of stimulating ideas. Vrooman carried books wherever she went, and it was probably she who introduced Mary Beard to the writings of Charlotte Perkins Gilman and who encouraged her enthusiastic younger friend to follow her inclinations and to write some articles on feminism.[17] Because of Mary's developing feminist consciousness, Charles would become in the future more likely to include women in his images of "workers" and "citizens."

On his return from America, Charles became director of the newly formed Ruskin Hall Extension Department. Soon after his arrival he spoke to a "Sunday meeting" at the Hall, affirming his intention of staying in England. The account of the speech in *Young Oxford* reveals Beard's radiant enthusiasm and idealism. He "had never felt a deeper joy," according to the report, "than when he came back and found them at the station to welcome him." He recalled that

> The first time he came to England on a steamship he met a gentlemen who told him that he would find the cultured society of this country delightful but the working people were scum. Since then he had freely associated with the workers and he had found that they *were* scum. There were two kinds of scum, and the working men of Britain were the scum that comes on milk . . . the only social

position was the strength of a man's character . . . he would not soon cross the Atlantic again. . . . They would labour together until the workers who bore upon their shoulders the burden of the world should realize the identity of their own interest and rise to take possession of the means of life . . . he knew that their love for him was as deep as his love for them.[18]

These years at Oxford were the beginning of a happy partnership. That first summer the young Beards traveled to the Continent and "with knapsacks on their backs," Mary Beard remembered, tramped along the Neckartal in Germany and up to the mountain village of Dilsberg, spending nights in farm homes along the way and practicing their German. On returning to England, they moved to Manchester. There Charles "broke new ground" in the Extension Department of Ruskin Hall, enrolling more than two thousand students during the next two years. As director, Charles Beard toured the "black towns" in the center of industrial England, lecturing to union meetings and cooperative societies and encouraging groups to form correspondence classes. For example, between 1 October and 20 December 1900 he delivered fifty-four lectures in nearly as many towns for one guinea apiece, hospitality, and railroad expenses. This was a rather steep fee for working-class groups, and the number of invitations Beard received was a tribute to his attraction as a speaker.[19]

The themes of these lectures, many of which were reprinted in *Young Oxford* and in his book *The Industrial Revolution*, were various. Beard did not openly advocate socialism or any specific remedies for the conditions he described; rather, he seemed to feel that he was riding and measuring the tide of social evolution. He urged his listeners to consider how they could affect its course. Self-education was possible, he told them. As "the watchmaker takes apart and puts together tiny bits of inticate machinery, the student can examine the phenomena of society. . . ." People had an "invariable instinct for freedom from ignorance." Disease, want, poverty, and misery had not been ordained by God, "but by the ignorance and blindness of man." The healthy mind would attack these problems, for their solution was "the only thing in the world worth the energies of man." Abstention from liquor, he thought, was important for the reason that it was a test of "self-mastery." In the hands of the common people, he told the members of the Macclesfield Equitable Provident Society, lay the destiny of the nation, and therefore it was "essential that the people should study the problems bearing upon their life and labour."[20]

Beard was excited by the books he had read, and one has the sense of him expounding the great self-evident truths of the late nineteenth century. "Environment," he proclaimed, was "the great factor in determining the outcome of men's lives." Man shared in the life of the social organism and was also "capable of modifying by his inter-social activities its structure, function, and lines of development." Reaching beyond the platitudes that had accompanied the opening of Ruskin Hall nearly two years earlier, Beard urged scholars to use their acquired knowledge in an attempt "to analyze present conditions, and to state clearly the industrial problem, regardless of class privileges, vested interests, and political scruples, and to show us 'what ought to be,' and how we can build on 'what is' to attain it."[21] In later life, Beard did not sourly repudiate these ideas. Although the organic metaphor would become less prominent, he retained until his death this passionate optimism and this inspiring vision of the scholar as the servant of society.

In 1900 the Beards spent their Christmas holidays in Oxford at the Hall, and there, standing before the fireplace in the common room, Beard gave a little speech on New Year's Eve, a few minutes before midnight. There was more than an echo of his family's Quakerism as he told the small gathering that "the absolute moral code, which had for so long dominated the civilized world, was, with the Old Century, to pass away forever, to give place to the higher morality in which—more fully and clearly regarding his brother's rights—each man must be 'a law unto himself.'" Then, watch in hand, Beard announced the hour. "The Nineteenth Century," he said, "has been completed; we commence the Twentieth."[22]

One of the great topics of public discussion in this England of the early twentieth century was the connection between foreign affairs, specifically imperial affairs, and domestic policy. The Boer War, which divided politicians and intellectuals so bitterly from 1898 to 1902, coincided with Beard's period of residence. In the spring of 1899 he stood three feet away as Cecil Rhodes, the great capitalist-imperialist, and Lord Kitchener of Khartoum marched by from the Bodleian to the Sheldonian to receive honorary degrees from Oxford University. On this and on many other occasions Beard must have thought about imperialism.[23] In the autumn of 1901, while a debate between Big and Little Englanders raged in the pages of *Young Oxford*, he wrote two articles (which he probably saw as detached and conciliatory) on the subject "A Living Empire." Here, for the first of many times in his career, Beard speculated on the consequences for domestic welfare of an expansionist foreign policy.

Had imperialism hindered "progress"? Not, said Beard, in the case of the North American colonies, since "the Americans, as bad and half-civilized as they are, are better than the howling, scalping Commanches whose places they have taken." On the other hand, Beard was scornful of the Philippine adventure. Sending hundreds of "expensively equipped teachers to the Philippines to instruct naked natives while thousands of white children in American cities" were "under-fed and under-educated," demonstrated, he argued, that American policy-makers were "not brute imperialists but self-destructive lunatics." Before Western nations could become successful imperialists, Beard urged a change of economic conditions in the imperial countries.[24]

But what if the "white" Western nations did succeed in cleaning their own houses? What if these countries assumed control over the economic development of the world? Beard outlined a white-supremacist, vaguely world-socialist utopian future. Under the auspices of an "international bureau," arid plains would be irrigated, swamps would be reclaimed for agriculture, and new canals and railroads would be built to bind the nations. The physical labor would be done by "mongol and negro" workers, "always under white foremen."

No one, Beard wrote, assuming the debater's stance, hated "modern 'Imperialism'" more than he; no one took "a more vital interest in the upward movement of the best life on the globe"; no one had "more feeling of regard and sympathy for other races"; but "reason, love, experience, and humanity" had made him, he said, "know that it is not good for some races to be mixed in the same country, for if they cannot mix in blood the longer they are together the sharper become the distinctions, and the more unpleasant their relations." Beard condemned the practice of segregation in the United States, but he also abhorred, he wrote, "that cursed cant which talks hypocrisy about brotherhood and mixture, and is not willing to prove its sincerity by giving and receiving in marriage." While the "only sane attitude" for statesmen to adopt toward other races was that of "non-mixture," Beard suggested that controlled experiments on islands in different zones of climate be conducted to prove or disprove the common assertions as to the undesirability of "mixed breeds" of people. Cattle breeding was not left to chance; was "man's breeding less important"?

As a method of relieving the United States of unwanted blacks and of alleviating congestion and poverty in temperate zones presently occupied by white races, Beard suggested a scheme of colonization of the tropical regions and the unoccupied temperate regions of the rest of the world. Since he shared the assumption that the white races could never adjust to life in the tropics, the tropics would, in his plan, "serve as a farm, or plantation, as it were, of the temperate zone." With white supervision, the workers on these colonies would be "mongol and negro," as already noted. Meanwhile, "vast settlements from various white countries would be transplanted, not as individuals but as communities" over the temperate zones of the world. The "international bureau" would spare these pioneers from martyrdom and the hardships of settlement by insuring them against crop failure and other calamities. They would be "supplied with the best possible schools for their children, public libraries, gymnasiums and game rooms to help atone for the loss of the incidental advantages of the civilization they had left." Western European countries would settle people in "the rich plains of northern and central Asia and southern South America," while "the United States and England would use the same methods in distributing needed population over the great western plains of America and of South Australia and South Africa."[25]

It is in this curious fantasy of an empire based on racist distinctions and on the needs of poor white people in industrial society that one may see a link between Beard and populism, specifically a book by Mary Ellen Lease, who had been a leading Midwestern organizer of the People's party. Her book, the cover of which featured a huge-breasted figure of "equality" holding a sword labeled "tropical immigration" cutting the chains of "labor" held by the "Shylock of competition," was called *The Problem of Civilization Solved.* It had been published in Chicago in 1895. Perhaps Beard had picked it up in Chicago on one of his trips there as an undergraduate. At any rate, Beard's speculations are a definite echo of Lease's conclusion that the only hope for "the homeless condition of the highly enlightened Caucasian and the debased degradation of the Negro and Oriental" was "the most stupendous migration of races the world has ever known . . . by colonizing the Tropics in America and Africa with fifty million white families as planters on estates of 200 acres each, with three families of negroes or orientals as tillers of the soil." Lease too had thought of colonization as a solution to racial antagonism in the United States. Orientals and blacks had their "natural home" in the tropics and they "should not be brought into a cold region to cheapen the labor of the Caucasian or to suffer from the rigors of an inclement climate." The costs of "the War of the Rebellion" alone might have allowed "the buying" of Latin America. If her plan were adopted, Lease speculated, in fifty years "the white man" would "become the professional man for the remaining two-thirds of mankind" and the world would celebrate a "golden wedding of Justice and Prosperity, by ushering in the era of human brotherhood and equality."[26]

Beard was more specific than Lease in his plans for the creation of an transnational white imperial bureaucracy. He proposed a "World's International University," with centers in each continent that would select the brightest white men and women to advance human knowledge. The single standard for admission to this institution was to be "effectiveness," which Beard defined—perhaps thinking of himself—as "the capacity to see for oneself, independent of whatever has or has not been seen or taught or said or written before."[27]

In constructing his own utopia along lines already suggested by Lease, Beard had carried liberal imperialism and its racist ideology to its illogical conclusion. He never published another such fantastic scheme. Yet these articles represent a lasting aspect of his thought. At Columbia he would learn to question the white supremacist version of history and political economy. However, he would always retain an emphasis on the connection between domestic and foreign policy. The open door at home would always be the most important priority in his thinking.

At the conclusion of the winter session of the Extension Division in March 1902, members of the Co-operative Society in the mill town of Bolton presented Beard "20 volumes of the latest and best works for a social reformer."[28] The Beards were leaving England. Citing Engels' declaration before he died that "the time for small uproars is over, and the people must know what is to be done and how to do it," a few months earlier Charles Beard had written an essay reflecting on his three years of experience with Ruskin Hall and criticizing the "institutional machinery" of the place. The Hall, he charged, was not concentrating social forces in an effort to overcome "the weakness of divided democracy."

What was lacking and what could be done? Finances were needed to support students for two years under an expanded program. Beard had met the "great Kropotkin" in London and had been attracted by the bearded prophet's idea that self-sufficient farming could be combined with an educational routine. Thus "brain work" and "manual work" would not be separated. Ruskin Hall might become self-supporting. Then too, Beard suggested, the Hall should be modernized to include electric lights, hardwood floors, single rooms for the students, and laboratories for sciences such as chemistry and biology. The curriculum, he continued, should be widened to include manual and business training, modern languages, and agricultural science. He called for a return to Ruskin's ideal of a union of honest toil with study, "thus foreshadowing the coming system when workers shall think and thinkers shall work."[29]

Perhaps Beard thought also that he had been doing too much, for he added that men given a more rigorous training, such as he had proposed, would become the leaders in the Ruskin Hall districts "and thus fill the want of competent and sympathetic leaders and lecturers so keenly felt by our classes."[30]

Financial problems may also have influenced the Beards' decision to return to the United States. Their daughter, Miriam, had been born in Manchester in November 1901. Charles had never received a salary from Ruskin Hall, though he may have been occasionally reimbursed for expenses. He had enjoyed a continuing support from his father, and although this was enough for a bachelor, it would not keep a family. Miriam Beard Vagts has written: "I suspect my Grandfather was putting on a little pressure."[31]

Later, Charles Beard said simply that he and Mary had talked things over, as many expatriates had before and since, and had come to the conclusion "that it was 'now or never,' that we 'belonged' at home."[32]

3

At Columbia
Student and Teacher

B eard's last article for *Young Oxford*, "Citizenship in the Twentieth Century," was published in April 1902, the month he and Mary and their infant daughter returned to America. Here Beard summarized the position to which his reading, his temperament, and his experience in England had brought him: One must approach the dilemmas of modern life "with a full comprehension of the profound meaning of the industrial revolution, a thorough grasp of the problems of democracy, a clear knowledge of the serviceableness of applied science, and a complete acceptance of the principles of social evolution. . . ." The world was constantly changing, society was a "vast complex interdependent organism"; systems of thought had little value because evolution had "destroyed the tory, the radical, and the millennium socialist." Men who had "believed in special dispensation for aristocracy," who had staked their lives "on one man one vote," and who had "proclaimed the 'economic breakdown' as the beginning of heaven" had all been betrayed by history. Thoughtful persons, Beard concluded, as he would in all of his subsequent prescriptive writing, "agree at least on the principle of social welfare as the criterion for morals and legislation." This principle, he predicted, would be "the wedge" that would "break through the hindrances to social freedom."

Experiences in England had given substance to Beard's consciousness of the oppression of white industrial workers and had strengthened his vision of the contributions a scholar could make to the achievement of a more humane world. "I cannot progress alone," he wrote. "I cannot be saved alone. My brother's degradation is my own. . . . My brother and I are mutual keepers . . . all talk about free and independent individuals is either ignorance or self-conceit." Yet the social problem was "how to make the most of the individual and the nation." The intelligent citizen seeking to promote the fullest development of both person and community would "promote discussion upon all the great issues which confront us," would try to achieve freedom from "the tyranny of words, dogmas and creeds," would make use of "the light of science," and would avoid "prejudice, bigotry and brutality" as the enemies of "social sympathy."[1]

Thus Beard arrived at Columbia, a confident young man eager to change the world. Intellectually, he was still growing. Unaffected, ready for new ideas, witty, direct, and kind as he was, he learned at Columbia that recent scholarship was disowning the "prejudice, bigotry and brutality" of the Teutonic theory of American institutions. As a student he changed some of his teachers as much as they affected him, and as a teacher, after 1904, he soon enjoyed the esteem of throngs of students eager for his pointed questions and zesty iconoclasm.

Charles and Mary Beard's life-style in New York City appears to have been founded on the unspoken premise that social change would be neither rapid nor destructive of bourgeois luxuries. Supported at first by Father Beard's generosity and later by Charles' salary and investments, the family lived not in any grand style but very comfortably. The Beards' first home was a "large well-built but old, gas-lit apartment" on West 124th Street at the north end of Morningside Park, near the Columbia campus. Mary Beard described it as, from the beginning, "like Grand Central Station." In 1909, partly due to Charles' desire that their children, Miriam and William, aged eight and two, experience life in the country, the Beards acquired their famous summer home on a thickly forested hill overlooking the Housatonic River in New Milford, Connecticut. As befitted his father's son, Beard also became a gentleman dairy farmer. "I think he had the farm because he loved it," wrote one of Beard's grandsons, "because he felt that somebody cut off from the soil was no longer really safe and secure. He loved . . . to talk to the farmer, to get a sense of how the farm was progressing." Beard was comforted by knowing "that it was still there and that the plants came up every spring and that all was right on its course."[2]

At Columbia, where both Charles and Mary enrolled in October 1902 for graduate study in the School of Political Science, Charles Beard's personal magnetism and scholarly talents were soon appreciated. During his first year, in the seminar of John W. Burgess, Dean of the Faculty, he completed a prize-winning master's essay. (As the holder of the George William Curtis Fellowship, named for the notable reformer, Beard had been required to write on "The Present Status of Civil Service Reform.") In 1904, he received a doctorate and published his thesis, *The Office of Justice of the Peace in England,* the result of his earlier researches at Oxford. He had begun, even before completing his doctorate, to contribute reviews to the department's distinguished journal, *The Political Science Quarterly*. During these two years of intensive study he attended lectures and seminars given by many of Columbia's stellar faculty—Herbert Levi Osgood on American Colonial History, John Bates Clark on Economic Theory, John Basset Moore on International Law, John Burgess on American Constitutional History and Governmental Organization of the Territories, Frank Goodnow on Public Law and Municipal Government, E. R. A. Seligman on the History of Political Economy, and, during the first term it was offered, James Harvey Robinson's celebrated History of the Intellectual Class of Europe.[3]

Charles studied conscientiously with Dean Burgess, who aided him in advancing in the Department of Political Science. He had come to Columbia predisposed to agree with the Teutonic theory of the origins of American institutions and with Burgess' racialism—that is, with Burgess' assertions respecting "the three vital nations, America, England, and Germany" as contrasted with "the decadent Latin nations" and the "barbaric populations" of Asia and Africa. Nonetheless, Beard was soon attracted to faculty who represented a different outlook—to the charming and witty James "Hardy" Robinson, who was just developing new courses in social and intellectual history after an early period of concentrating on documents, and to E. R. A. Seligman and Frank J. Goodnow, who were "men of affairs" in civic organizations and who represented the sort of scholarly activism that Beard had already admired and tried.[4] Seligman and Goodnow, in particular, held views of history and politics that were directly opposite to those of Burgess. It was Robinson, Seligman, and Goodnow who led young Beard away from Anglo-Saxon institutionalism toward other approaches to history and politics.

Robinson and Beard became dear friends. They were a natural pair and made popular a fresh approach to the study of history. However, probably Seligman and Goodnow had more to do, intellectually, with the paths of action chosen by Beard at Columbia. It was probably they who turned the young scholar away from dry descriptions of institutional development, abstract and formal legal studies, and Teutonic racism toward the analysis of social and economic forces in history, the collection and classification of data on contemporary institutions, and a concern for practical governmental administration.

The year Beard came to Columbia, 1902, Edwin R. A. Seligman had published a book of essays discussing historically the theory of the economic interpretation of history and replying to critics of a materialist perspective. Seligman had examined Marx's philosophical writings rather than his economic doctrines of surplus value and profits. "It chanced," Seligman wrote, that Marx "also became a socialist; but his socialism and his philosophy of history are . . . really independent." According to Seligman, one could be "an 'economic materialist' and yet remain an extreme individualist. The fact that Marx's economics may be defective has no bearing on the truth or falsity of his philosophy of history." Scientific socialism, he concluded at another point, "teaches that private property is doomed to disappear; the economic interpretation of history calls attention, among other things, to the influence which private capital has exerted on progress." For the wealthy son of a family of bankers, Seligman's reading of Marx was most appropriate.

As he understood the theory of economic interpretation of history, it meant "not that all history is to be explained in economic terms alone, but that the chief considerations in human progress are the social considerations, and that the important factor in social change is the economic factor." Economic interpretation of history meant "not that the economic relations exert an exclusive influence, but they exert a preponderant influence in shaping the progress of society." Replying to idealists who criticized this perspective on history, Seligman agreed that people are certainly moved by ethical considerations, but he emphasized his belief that "the content of the conception of morality is a social product . . . that pure ethical or religious idealism had made itself felt only within the limitations of existing economic conditions." Democracy must, he argued, have a material basis: "Economic equality among individuals creates the democratic virtue."

In this small book Seligman approached most of the questions that were disturbing social scientists of his generation. He rebuked his colleague at Columbia, the sociologist Franklin H. Giddings (a leading proponent of a genetic, racist, racial theory of human development), and indirectly his dean, John Burgess. Genetic qualities may or may not exist, Seligman wrote. They are simply unimportant. Marx, said Seligman, had expressed a profound truth when he had written "'It is not the consciousness of mankind that determines its existence, but on the contrary its social existence that determines its consciousness.'" Finally, Seligman pointed out that economic life could not be separated from ethical and social life: "Deeper than is often recognized is the meaning of Ruskin's statement, 'There is no wealth but life.' . . . The goal of all economic development is to make wealth abundant and men able to use wealth correctly."[5]

Charles Beard already had the moral outlook of the late Victorian critics of industrialism as well as the conviction that democracy must be economic as well as political. What Seligman had done was combine the two views into a "theory" of economic interpretation. In his own numerous later writings Beard never really ventured beyond his teacher's conception. In Madison's *Federalist* Number 10 and, at other times, in the writings of Webster and Calhoun Beard would find his American and philosophical equivalents to Marx. Like Seligman, he would maintain that it was possible to be a historical materialist without committing oneself to socialism; that is, without having any theory of social process. Like his teacher, he would always believe that though economic factors were not the only forces of import in history, they probably explained more than either formal discussions of law and institutions grounded in no particular environment or the collation of abstract philosophical ideas outside their particular social context. "If [the theory of economic interpretation] is true," Beard wrote in 1920, criticizing Harold Laski for writing about Whig and Tory political ideas without mentioning land and commerce, "then what has ethics, metaphysics, Freud, the psychology new or old, or any other emotional or intellectual coloration to offer that compares with it as a hypothesis of illumination?" In Beard's view, the economic interpretation challenged abstract discussion in a way "as sharp and ringing as the challenge of Darwin was to the champions of the Miltonic account of creation."[6]

Beard's other great mentor at Columbia, Frank Johnson Goodnow, was one of the first American students of municipal law and administration. Goodnow was a splendid teacher, and Beard remembered him as striking "from the dull facts of the law sparks which illuminated the heavens for his students." He had "unfeigned simplicity, as natural as the rain and sun, without pride or pique of office or authorship"; he was generous to students and had a keen sense of humor. "Those who cross [Goodnow's] path," Beard said in 1929, found "a new mellow light in their ways."[7]

Goodnow presented an exciting challenge to Burgess' formal, static approach to law and public policy. He constantly told his students that "government could not be understood and lasting improvements could not be made unless the political behavior and the political motivations underlying and eventually controlling constitutional and administrative law were properly mastered." Yet his thinking had positivist overtones, for he proposed that development of policy, "politics," could be separated in practice from the execution of policy, "administration." Along with Seligman, Goodnow combined his critical approach to his field with an active life in the politics of civil service reform and municipal research in the City of New York. Both Seligman and Goodnow were active in the founding in 1907 of the New York Bureau of Municipal Research, and both were in the vanguard of what historian Martin J. Schiesl has called the "progressive 'structural' reformers." Beard was to join them in the campaign for honest, efficient government, which meant "the total reorganization of city administration and eventual creation of a new bureaucratic system."[8]

In the autumn of 1904 Beard was appointed to the post of lecturer in the Department of History, under the supervision of Robinson. Once in his own classroom, Beard immediately followed Robinson in the move away from the institutional approach to history typified by his thesis and by Burgess. That year, in his course of lectures on the expansion of the United States, Beard told students that "the multitude of details" would be "omitted or epitomized" in order to pay attention "to the social and economic forces underlying national growth and the movements now included under the somewhat vague title of 'imperialism.'"[9]

In 1906, as a result of his experience teaching English history to large numbers of undergraduates who complained about not being able to obtain the right books and who took only perfunctory notes on outside readings, Beard published *An Introduction to the English Historians*, 650 pages of extracts from famous writers dealing with great political questions in British history from the Anglo-Saxon Conquest to Labour and socialism in recent years. The selections represented Beard's commitment to recent history: half of them dealt with the last three hundred years and half with the preceding seven hundred. Although such books later became commonplace, in Beard's day this volume was a novel experiment. He was excited and pleased by the idea and made a special trip to England in 1906 to secure copyrights.[10]

Unfortunately, no intimate record of the friendship between Robinson and Beard survives, though Robinson was, Beard later told Albert Beveridge, "one of my few pals—a very wise old owl." The two met each other at the moment Robinson was taking a new direction in his work. Like Beard, he had faith that the world was getting better, and his approach to history had definite political overtones. Except for "the Marxian socialist," Robinson thought, the "radical" had "not yet perceived the overwhelming value to him of a real understanding of the past." The past was "his weapon by right, and he should wrest it from the hand of the conservative." During the 1890s, first at the University of Pennsylvania and then at Columbia, Robinson had occupied himself with what was then the historical rage, editing documents. "We inhaled," he remembered in his delightfully whimsical style, "the delicious odor of first hand accounts, of the 'original document,' of the 'official report.' We had at last got to the bottom of things." However, after 1900 governmental decrees and reports began to seem like a false bottom. In 1902 Robinson published *An Introduction to the History of Western Europe*, which presented students with unique amounts of social and cultural materials. In 1904 he created and taught for a decade a course in Intellectual History, which Arthur Schlesinger, Sr., remembered as "the most provocative" of any he attended as a young graduate student. Peering over his spectacles, Robinson would stand before the throng, speaking "quietly, as though interviewing himself with the class present merely as evesdroppers." Gradually, Schlesinger noted, it would occur to students that Robinson did not want them to think his thoughts, but rather to ask questions of their own, "to think, moreover, not only about the past but about the present state of mankind and what human intelligence, if properly directed, could do to better it."[11]

A book that had a singular impact on Beard and Robinson was the *Histoire Socialiste* by the great humanist leader of the French Socialists, Jean Jaurès, and Gabriel Deville. Here, wrote Beard, was a vivid example of the way in which Marx and his followers had "undoubtably . . . helped to turn the attention of historians from purely political and diplomatic affairs to the more permanent and fundamental forces in the development and conflict of nations. . . ." It was "a monumental contribution to the literature dealing with the [French] Revolution," and Beard rejoiced that one did "not have to accept Socialism" in order to accept many of the authors' conclusions. "Indeed," he added, "Professor Seligman [had] demonstrated that socialism and the economic interpretation of history [were] entirely different propositions." Speaking with similar enthusiasm in 1908 about this "most illuminating history of the French Revolution," Robinson proposed that—while not everything could be explained by a materialist interpretation—it had been "the economist" who had "opened up the most fruitful fields of research" by giving emphasis to "the enduring but often inconspicuous factors which almost entirely escaped historians before the middle of the nineteenth century."[12]

In 1908, Beard and Robinson began a lifetime of collaboration on a series of textbooks in European history. They were frank about their purpose: "to enable the reader to catch up with his own times; to read intelligently the foreign news in the morning paper; to know what was the attitude of Leo XII toward the social democrats even if he has forgotten that of Innocent III toward the Albigenses." Students, the authors urged, should examine their own experience as an example of the dependence of the present on the past. With its chapters on science and invention, social and economic forces, *The Development of Modern Europe* was an effort to endow the present with a vital dimension that records of kings, conquests, and treaties, the staples of orthodox history, did not give. "It is most essential," Robinson exhorted members of the American Historical Association in 1910, "that we should understand our own time; we can only do so through history, and it is the obvious duty of the historian to meet this, his chief obligation."[13]

Robinson adored lecturing. He wished to make history an attractive and popular study, and he was always willing to discuss his enriched view of history with groups of teachers from the primary and high schools. Beard followed him in this interest and gave speeches wherever asked, carrying to elementary and secondary school teachers the message that "the great problems of our time are not the relations of church and state or the fashioning of representative institutions. . . . Our problems are primarily social and economic; they concern the functions of political institutions rather than their form; and they are to be met out of the fullness of concrete experience which history records, not by reference to abstract doctrines set up *in vacuo*." Beard preached "an entirely utilitarian view of history writing and instruction." He did not look down condescendingly on the secondary and primary teachers. Most secondary school students, he knew, would not be going to college. Therefore, in his eyes, teachers of history at this level had a significant role in the making of good citizens. He urged these teachers to take a "topical rather than a chronological" approach. They should explain how monarchies became popular governments, how imperialism developed, "how the whole system of working, living, traveling, and thinking" had been "revolutionized by the great inventions," and "what great problems occupy the attention of statesmen and thinkers today." Teachers who presented history "in a scientific spirit and an interesting fashion" would, Beard told them, "render high service to the democracy in which we live."[14]

In those halcyon days of nonspecialization, Beard soon left the Department of History and joined the Department of Public Law. Columbia was growing rapidly, and in 1907 he was chosen by Burgess to occupy a newly created chair in Politics and Government. This was significant testimony to Beard's charm, for he had not offended Burgess, whose ideas he was daily repudiating. "It was Beard," wrote the historian of Columbia's faculty, "who actually founded the undergraduate courses in government at Columbia."[15]

As a professor, Beard led a full life. Here were numerous opportunities for energy and ambition, and he seized them. He lectured to undergraduates on American Government and Politics, on Party Government in the United States, on American State Government, and on Municipal Functions. He taught a graduate seminar in Constitutional and Administrative Law. From 1905 to 1909 he edited the "Foreign Events" section of the *Political Science Quarterly,* to which he continued to furnish a steady stream of reviews, many of them of works by French and German authors. He coached Columbia's team of debaters, and he founded the Intercollegiate Civic League, an effort "to interest college men in public questions" by staging debates between proponents of differing views on public issues. In 1911 he obtained an endowment from a former president of the board of aldermen and established the "Politics Laboratory," a collection of daily newspapers from all parts of the country, periodicals dealing with public issues, reference works on government, ballots, constitutions, and statutes of all the states for the use of Columbia's students and faculty. A large part of this library was devoted to municipal government in New York City. During these years Beard published articles on the need to shorten and simplify the ballot and on the significance of the downfall of Speaker of the House, Joseph Cannon. In 1911 he published a unique documentary history of the commission type of municipal government in looseleaf form so additions and deletions could easily be made as conditions changed in the country. Here was "living history," emerging on the printed page from "the kaleidoscopic progress of movement" and change in industrial America. The first edition of Beard's massive *American Government and Politics,* which he revised ten times in his lifetime and which survives in print to this day, appeared in 1910. It was an effort, "frankly based" on secondary authorities, to describe "a complex political organism" which was "swiftly changing under our very eyes." The text was to accompany his book of readings in American government and politics, which he had published the preceding year.[16]

Along with his scholarly and organizational achievements, Beard gained the admiration and respect of his students by remaining accessible and interested in their problems. In 1909 he led in a poll of undergraduates who where asked to nominate a successor to J. H. VanAmringe, dean of the college, about to retire. Irwin Edman, a young freshman straight from high school, took Beard's course in American Government and, years later, remembered with pleasure the "lanky figure leaning against the wall drawling wittily with half-closed eyes." Edman could not ascribe to Beard a special technique. He was, the philosopher recalled, suggestive, witty and clear, but "none of these things could quite account for the hold he had on the smug and the rebels alike, on both the pre-lawyers and pre-poets." Edman asserted that Beard had "a certain combination of poetry, philosophy, and honesty" and that he communicated a sense "that politics matter far beyond the realm commonly called political." He conveyed to students his own excitement about reform. One morning, Edman recalled, Beard had walked into the room and said

> Gentlemen, today we are to discuss the budget system in State government. I am sure that must seem to you a dull subject. But if you will tell me, gentlemen, how much per capita a nation spends on its Army, on its Navy, on education, on public works, I shall be able to tell you, I think, as much about that nation as if you gave me the works of its poets and philosophers.

As Edman had learned it from Beard, the ideal of government was "the liberation of the energies of men."

Arthur M. Schlesigner, Sr., who studied with Beard as a graduate student, remembered him as "in no sense a Marxist or single track economic determinist" but rather as a being who "endowed everything he said with a bracing air of realism" and whose "recurrent theme" was "the role of material self-interest in America's political and constitutional development."

Recalling Beard as warm-hearted, accessible, and deferential "to all human beings of whatever age and position," Arthur Macmahon, another of Beard's graduate students, remembered that he had found himself "suddenly thinking one day—unbidden by any personal situation—that if I did not have a father and were free to choose one in all the world, he would be Charles Beard."[17]

Beard joyfully described the prospects then open to the teacher and student of politics and history. "Surely none of the sciences, moral or natural, offers more tempting themes than politics." These themes required "all of the qualities of the scholar—detachment from the clamour of sectarian interests, painstaking observation, keen analysis, sobriety of judgment, and correct generalization." Simultaneously, however, these themes could "serve the practical interests of humanity in its great struggle to secure the highest economies of collective effort in combination with the largest fruitfulness for the individual life." The particularly American combination of research and university teaching, he wrote, "makes the lot of the university instructor in politics a happy one." The teacher who maintained contact with large numbers of undergraduates, Beard wrote, was keeping alive "his powers of exposition, his vital interest in the subject, and . . . his sense of relative values."[18]

At the faculty club Beard usually lunched with a group that included Robinson, John Dewey, the inventor and physicist Michael I. Pupin, and John Erskine, the noted student of English literature. "Such an exchange of ideas,"

Erskine recalled, "I shall never hear again. It seemed then that the world was in a moment of great hope; each one of us personally was conscious of a large opportunity, our university was entering a brilliant epoch, our country had a future, at home and abroad the intellectual horizon was bright, the international mind had almost been awakened."[19]

4

Progressivism and Twentieth-Century Citizenship

Through the years at Columbia the tempo of Beard's already demanding life, within and without the university, increased. In living his vision of the scholar who not only read and talked about social ideals but who also ventured forth to implement them, Beard assaulted the tradition of the gentleman-scholar who experienced the world through the pages of books alone. From 1912 until 1914 he was one of two editors of an important new journal in the field of municipal reform, *The National Municipal Review*. In March 1914 he became director of The Training School for Public Service of the New York Bureau of Municipal Research. In 1918 he became director of the bureau itself. Excluding revisions of earlier textbooks, he wrote five more books between 1912 and 1915, in addition to a civics text for high schools written in collaboration with Mary Beard. He continued to publish articles and reviews in scholarly journals, and he wrote regularly for *The New Republic* after its beginning in 1914. He and Mary were often in demand as speakers, and they worked together and separately in a number of positive civic causes. Charles' books and articles were monuments to his confidence in himself as a "man of affairs" a person with a duty to promote critical thinking among his fellow citizens. Rather than emerging from the competitive context of an academic environment, his writings were a natural extension of his day-to-day practical involvement in the movements for efficient and humane city government, social justice, and woman suffrage.

Where did he get his unflagging energy? Partly he was fueled by passion, by a controlled tension. Miriam remembered her father as filled with a peculiar intensity, an expectation of results that never became rage directed at close associates but that did generate in those who worked with him the constant apprehension of an explosion of emotion. Furthermore, he was bothered from his midtwenties onward by tinnitis. At night, a ringing in his ears kept him from sleeping until he was thoroughly exhausted. During those long, restless evenings, he read books, thought, and composed his arguments.[1]

From 1903 until American participation in the war split its membership into opposite camps, Beard regularly attended the meetings of the X Club, a group of between fifteen and forty literary people, university professors, social reformers, and those Morris Hillquit called "just Socialists" who met every two or three weeks in the private room of a restaurant to discuss topics of current interest relating to politics, science, religion, literature, and art. Among the members were Lincoln Steffens, Norman Hapgood, Hamilton Holt, Edwin Slosson, John Dewey, Owen R. Lovejoy, Walter E. Weyl, W. J. Ghent, William English Walling, and Hillquit. H. G. Wells came to visit, as did George Lansbury, a leader of the British Labour Party.[2] There is one book in particular that may reflect Beard's participation in these wide-ranging talkfests. This is his survey, *American City Government* (1912), which mirrors to a much greater extent than *An Economic Interpretation of the Constitution* (1913) his interests at this time, particularly his sort of progressivism.

American City Government is a great synthesis of the writings of many contemporaries—Lawrence Veiller on housing, Irving Fisher on the economic losses from industrial accidents caused by unsafe working conditions, Franklin Goodnow on the problems of administering New York without home rule, William G. McAdoo on crime, Reta Childe Door on juvenile courts, Frederick Law Olmstead and George B. Ford on city planning, and Frederick C. Howe on the single-tax solution. After more than a half century it has not lost its power and immediacy. Beard read and summarized current reformist thought, but he also transcended it by offering his own criticism of various proposals. Possibly he reproduced the questions and the conclusions of those bracing and earnest sessions of the X Club. According to one reviewer, Beard's survey was "frankly a study of the recent progressive movement using the term in a broad sense, as applied to municipal development."[3]

If Beard knew the city intellectually, through the eyes of activist intellectuals, he also knew it emotionally and physically. In 1906 and 1908 he had campaigned for Hillquit during the latter's unsuccessful congressional campaign as a Socialist on the Lower East Side. Also, Mary and Charles were constantly exploring the neighborhoods and attempting to understand urban problems from the perspective of men and women who had to work long hours, "the people," Charles called them while noting that many of them were foreign-born, a generation removed from another country, or blacks from the rural South. "The people" were those who earned barely subsistence wages, who did not own their own homes, who depended on conditions of employment beyond their control, and who lived in overcrowded, unattractive neighborhoods. In this book Beard showed that he rejected "scientific" racism or racist interpretation of urban problems. He rebuked all who assumed that circumstances would have been different if cities had been inhabited only by "'native' stock" as well as those who thought that "tinkering with political machinery and spectacular 'war on bosses'" would ameliorate these basic conditions.[4] He now saw that reformers must go beyond moralizing to focus on necessary structural changes.

Some "great problems" of government were, of course, common to all cities—"election of officers, efficient management, police, education, housing, transportation, recreation, and city planning." Beard was optimistic that privately funded organizations such as bureaus of municipal research would be a great help in gathering the factual basis for solving these problems. However, he pointed approvingly to the demands of Socialists in cities such as Milwaukee and Schenectady for more radical efforts by the government— public works to relieve unemployment, free employment agencies, free midday meals for school children, municipal markets, and municipal ownership of public service corporations. According to Beard, the Socialists had good ideas for making a decent life possible for urban workers but were wasting their time on municipal elections. The "real seats of power over property" were "in the state and national government."

While acknowledging that the newly popular commission form of city government, because it centralized power and responsibility in a small group constantly in the public eye, might eliminate much waste of public funds, Beard shrewdly pointed out that election at large would prohibit the representation of minorities in the government and that the nonpartisan elections dreamed of by the proponents of this sort of reform were a myth.

Casting his net over the problem of "Raising and Spending the City's Money," he followed Henry George and Frederick C. Howe and supported the plan to tax the "'unearned increment' in ground values," though he doubted that "taxation of land values to the limit" would "of itself provide 'naturally' that improvement in structure, distribution of population, and location of factories and public buildings" which were often part of a "city plan."

Regarding urban crime, Beard rejoiced that America was "beginning to have a criminology that [did] not rest entirely upon the doctrine of original sin." Researchers were beginning "to inquire into the relations between the amount of certain classes of crimes and economic conditions, such as unemployment, low wages, the price of foodstuffs and congestion." If crime had economic causes, he reasoned, then was it not "sheer imbecility" to squander "time and strength on 'exposures' of the police . . . 'raiding' of resorts, and the whole range of coercive measures which divert 'good' people, but do nothing worthwhile to attack fundamental causes."

Beard joined many comtemporaries in urging the improvement of public services through the creation of more efficient bureaucracies and, often, public ownership of utilities and transportation. However, he did not confuse municipal ownership with gains for democratic socialism. Publicly owned utilities, he pointed out, did "not mean necessarily any increase in the power of the working class in government." Private enterprise had failed lamentably in such areas as housing, yet people appeared unwilling to contemplate the alternatives. The American people displayed "an almost pathetic confidence" in education and industrial training "as a guarantee for the stability of republican institutions and a solution of all social problems." City planning was starting, but it often meant "creating civic centers—beautiful showplaces—that is, putting diamond crowns on leprous brows," as Ruskin had phrased the problem.

Replying to Simon Patten, the Socialist economist, and to others who had suggested that vocational education, leading to greater efficiency and higher wages, would help eliminate poverty, Beard objected that this "efficiency theory" for solving the problems of people with low incomes was "hopelessly fallacious." The "whole question of exploitation in every form" was ignored; those "forces which condition the distribution of income among classes" were neglected, the fact that wage increases were absorbed by increased rents was unanalyzed; seasonal and cyclical unemployment, crises, inflation, and contraction in industries received no consideration. Patten called himself a Socialist, yet Beard thought he refused to deal with "the fundamentals of the modern system of production."

Beard might have welcomed the success of socialism as a national party. Having mulled over the leading reform ideas of his generation, he stressed, as did many progressives, that local solutions to the overwhelming imperatives presented by urbanization were best implemented in the context of a national policy. Movements for better government of the city were "to be considered as temporary, not permanent, advances in American politics." It was artificial and ultimately debilitating to tear the "social policy of the city" from "the larger social policy of the nation." Beard represented what Richard Fox has called "a deep simple rationalism." He believed that educating people about modern conditions would produce a demand for a "larger social policy" in the nation.[5]

Working at the New York Bureau of Municipal Research, Beard encountered again the problems of which he wrote. The bureau was a privately funded agency that had been founded in 1907 by three energetic young reformers. Frederick A. Cleveland, a specialist in municipal accounting, and William Allen, a social worker, were both former students of Simon Patten at the University of Pennsylvania, and Henry Bruère was a Socialist lawyer. They were neither muckrakers nor "scientific managers" who assumed that what was good for the corporation was good for society. Their object had been to get the facts about the use of public money in city administration and to introduce administrative techniques, such as budgeting, that would help public officers achieve more efficient and effective results. Frederick W. Taylor's principles of specialization of bureaucratic function, statistical surveys of the need for projected programs, and standardization of work and reports were applied to governmental offices. Yet Taylorism, scientific management, as represented by the bureau, was not simply the application of "business methods" to government. Rather, a major goal was to bring efficient government closer to the people by giving them accurate information about the activities of city departments. As a reform activity municipal research cut across class and occupational lines, was nonpartisan, and attempted to deal positively with specific issues, such as improving the specifications of contracts for sewer construction and eliminating graft and waste in the purchase of city supplies.

By 1911, the bureau had a staff of forty-seven people and would claim that it had been largely responsible for reorganization and improvement in the city's Department of Finance, for system and economy in the Water Department, and for establishment of a Bureau of Child Hygiene. The staff had sponsored well-attended exhibits set up to teach the public about municipal financing. In 1911, a gift of $40,000 from Mrs. E. H. Harriman had enabled the bureau to establish its Training School for Public Service.[6]

The bureau's emphasis on efficient, businesslike government undoubtedly appealed to Beard's instinct for competence. But it must also have attracted him because its philosophy was democratic. Clear-cut procedures would enable the public to understand what went on within the bureaucracy, and thus the government would be brought closer to the people. Also, it seemed to him an opportunity for those outside the usual political circles to contribute to civic improvement. Throughout his life Beard urged private individuals to challenge the public experts. By cutting through mummifying layers of patronage, graft, inefficiency, and mismanagement in the City of New York, the bureau seemed to exemplify a people's challenge to a "hidden government." In the *National Municipal Review,* a forum for the sharing of information and experience in the reform of urban bureaucracies, Beard wrote that "private citizens [were] now doing work which was once regarded as the peculiar function of official persons." These citizens were surveying "questions of law-making and enforcement"; they were "drafting laws, watching administrative officers, employing experts to find out better ways of doing public business, and creating public sentiment on matters of policy." The "line between public authorities and private interest," he reported, had "broken down."[7]

During his years with the bureau, Beard wrote or took a major role in preparing a number of significant reports on problems of the city and state of New York. In 1915, when the state of New York held a constitutional convention, the bureau was asked to recommend structural reforms in the state's government. With Frederick Cleveland, Beard wrote *Government of the State of New York,* which he applauded in a special supplement to *The New Republic* as "the new *Federalist.*" Praising the British model of executive responsibility, Beard argued that the British system exemplified the best method of achieving both maximum efficiency and maximum public scrutiny of governmental activity.

For New York, Beard and Cleveland proposed that, instead of piecemeal appropriations by the legislature, the governor should initiate the budget, which their report called "the very heart of the governing process." The report urged also that 160 boards and commissions be consolidated into seventeen departments, that the ballot be drastically shortened, and that the governor have power of appointment and removal over nearly all executive officers except the attorney general and comptroller, who were to remain elective.[8]

In effect, Beard and Cleveland wanted New York to have something very like a British Parliament. If the legislature refused to pass measures recommended by the administration, the governor could dissolve the legislature and submit the issue to the voters in a new election. At issue was the task of making government efficient *and* accountable. For example, Beard rejected the initiation of legislation by voters as an obstacle to responsible, accountable government. Laws, he speculated, might be drafted by "irresponsible private citizens" and approved in the polling booth only to be sabotaged by an unsympathetic bureaucracy "willing, if not anxious, to discredit them." The initiative was "incompatible with accountability in government," and without accountability there would be no efficiency. "Without efficiency, democracy [could] not carry out effectively any large program of social work."[9]

Adopting a version of the British system was an effort to implement Frank Goodnow's distinction between making policy, the task of politicians responding to the needs of the people, and executing that policy, the task of trained administrators who were nonpartisan. Because he saw a danger to democracy stemming from the emphasis on expertise, Beard emphasized "accountability" and public information. "Power in the hands of public officers," he wrote, "must be commensurate with their obligations." This would result in efficiency. However, "devices for holding them strictly accountable to the electorate" were "as indispensable to good government as the devices of efficiency." Beard urged that a procedure for giving publicity to bureaucratic issues be written into the Constitution, "thus doing away with invisible government." He and Cleveland had sought in their proposals, he wrote—as Goodnow would have written—"to put together those things which should never have been put asunder, organization and system on the one part, and responsible leadership on the other."[10]

The Constitution of 1915 was defeated at the polls. But after the war the bureau was again invited, by Governor Al Smith, an admirer of the 1915 report, to assist in "reconstructing" government in New York. The British paradigm continued to appeal to Beard, and in the 1930s, when he suggested structural and procedural reforms for the Congress, it was to the British example that he turned.[11]

As the director of the Training School for Public Service from 1915 to 1918, Beard frequently spoke and wrote on the problems of reconciling democracy and efficiency. World War I cast a shadow on the German model of efficient administration. The "supreme public question of the hour," Beard wrote in 1916, was "whether democracy and efficiency are inherently irreconcilable." Beard's answer was no. Americans would not have "to choose between bureaucracy and suicide" in the face of urban chaos. He saw the historic reasons for suspecting experts, and he saw the task of administering the Training School as a job crucial to conserving democracy. He would attempt to raise up "the expert who admits his fallibility, retains an open mind and is prepared to serve." If this goal could not be achieved, then there were "many things in this world worse than very dirty streets, a very high death rate and a large percentage of crime." America could learn from Europe, if the bureaucracy was kept close to the people and if public servants recognized "how dangerous" it was "to speak of human life in mathematical terminology."[12]

From the beginning, the bureau's attitude had been that attacking the minions of Tammany, as some reformers did, was wasted effort. Beard adhered to this principle, saying that there was a great gulf between the "mechanistic and impersonal" expert and the "intensely personal" relationship between local politicians and their constituents. Local leaders, election district captains, and assembly district leaders, he affirmed, were "like the country doctor." Knowing everyone in their bailiwick, they gave "food to the hungry, drink to the thirsty, and raiment to the naked." They could carry "to the seats of the mighty in City Hall the tale of woe from the banana-cart peddler" who felt himself persecuted "by some mysterious person with a badge under his coat lapel." This was "the kingdom of democracy," and Beard thought that the administration of the city, to be really effective, must adopt the methods of the ward politicians, must become increasingly decentralized, must have neighborhood offices, and must "reckon with localities and human moods." For example, he told the Ninth Annual Conference of Charities and Corrections in 1918 that social workers should imitate the district leaders. "I would rather," he told the group, "take the word of a district leader as to a minor offender than of a probation officer. They ask no questions and give out no pink and green cards."[13]

In his practical administrative role at the bureau, Beard worked to develop efficient bureaucrats who knew their jobs in budgeting, accounting, municipal politics, and law, and who specialized in specific areas such as managing police and fire departments or engineering and highways. They had to learn to do meaningful research and to write clear reports. They were exhorted to have humane and patriotic ideals and to carry these with them on the job. Yet Beard realized that, if the structure of government did not encourage accountability and if the public was not constantly informed about the newer ways of providing services, the link between the people and their government would be broken and an unresponsive and undemocratic bureaucracy would reign. Efficient bureaucracy was seen by Beard and others as necessary to creative and socially responsive government.

In New York City, the movement for greater efficiency and accountability had produced results in the form of somewhat cleaner streets, more promptly collected garbage, bureaus of employment and child welfare, more parks and playgrounds. Although Beard realized that these reforms were not enough and that enormous breaches remained between hope and reality, he remained optimistic about the urban future. In Beard's day the "public service" had a noble aura that is no longer apparent. Men and women of "character" and integrity were going to provide the services necessary to a good life in the city. The public would know what was happening to their money, and those who managed it would be accessible and accountable. It was, Beard thought, "the function of politics to determine what should be done" and the "function of the trained expert to carry out the public will with all the instruments and methods which modern science—natural and social—can command."[14]

History has betrayed these hopes. Bureaucracy is now seen as a deterrent and obstacle to innovation and reform. James Fallows can now describe "the spirit of a bureaucracy, drained of zeal, obsessed with form, full of people attracted by the side-dressings of the work rather than the work itself."[15] Beard wrestled with these possibilities, suggested ways of ensuring accountability and scrutiny, and urged a decentralization that was never implemented. The hidden government of the bosses became the secret preserve of the experts. "Most of this insulated power of urban bureaucracy," Martin Schiesl has written, "is the unfortunate legacy of the progressive structural reformers."[16] Beard was one of the few reformers who appreciated that this might happen. He was unable, however, to institutionalize the questioning of experts, to suggest a politically viable method of making the people at large feel powerful enough to challenge administrative decisions. And he believed in progress.

As for national politics, Beard rallied to neither Theodore Roosevelt nor Woodrow Wilson. Neither man shared his own vision of what was possible or desirable in America. Beard admitted the appeal of Theodore Roosevelt's language; that is, of his speeches to the middle classes and especially to social reformers. However it was difficult to find "much that is concrete" in the accomplishments of Roosevelt's administration. "Mr. Roosevelt," Beard concluded in 1913, "in all of his recommendations" had taken "the ground that the prevailing system of production and distribution of wealth was essentially sound, that substantial justice was now being worked out between man and man, and that only a few painful excrescences needed to be lopped off."[17]

In his *Autobiography* (1913) Robert La Follette made the same point, saying that Roosevelt was not the constructive leader needed and that he lacked a clear grasp of the economic problems of the day. Beard wrote to La Follette that his "analysis of Roosevelt" was "true to the last degree" and confirmed the opinion he had "always had concerning that shifty gentleman."[18]

Nevertheless Beard did not agree with La Follette's views on the necessity for breaking up the trusts. "I do not think" he wrote, sounding like the Walter Lippmann of *Drift and Mastery* (1914), "that it is possible or desirable to restore real and effective competition." Thus he approved of the "New Nationalism" but saw it as a "counter-reformation" resulting from the growing power and influence of the Social Democratic Party. "Dissenters," populists in state legislatures, the Socialists led by Eugene Debs—these groups, especially the Socialists, were making people in power see the problem as one of a centralized national economy operating within a federal system made for wholly different conditions. Beard had read the works of the German revisionist Eduard Bernstein, and he was impressed with the idea that socialism might be adopted gradually and without a revolution. Hence he labeled the platform of the Progressive party in 1912 a "socialist program."[19]

Beard expressed strong antipathy toward Woodrow Wilson. With a smile he observed that Wilson's view was that the government was "too weak to force the trusts to obey certain rules and regulations, but it was strong enough to take their business away from them and prevent their ever getting together again."[20] Reviewing Wilson's *The New Freedom* for the *Political Science Quarterly*, Beard remarked that Wilson had perceived "the central problem of American democracy: the distribution of wealth and opportunity" but that his dream of laissez faire had never been "quite realized in any social order." Moreover, Beard noted that the President exhibited little sympathy for the "working class" and that it was not clear whether women were included at all in his thoughts about great questions of public policy.[21]

Wilson's Anglo-Saxonism and policy of intervention in Mexico were also distasteful to Beard. In the aftermath of the incident at Tampico, in which Mexican nationals had been forced at gunpoint to salute the flag of the United States, and of the occupation of Veracruz by troops of the United States, Beard agreed with the Mexican socialist L. G. de Lara that "the key to Mexican history" was "to be sought in the contest of the peon against feudalism, lay and ecclesiastical, buttressed by foreign capitalism." He scorned "loose talk in the United States about restoring order by bayonets." Social issues "are not settled by bayonets, for we cannot sit on them or live by them. If a process is inevitable, it is better to let it alone or to aid in its culmination."[22]

Mary Beard was also an active reformer, and her activities influenced Charles' choice of reform causes. She joined the Women's Trade Union League as an ally, the term for members who were not of the working class, helping to arrange meeting places and to raise bail for strikers arrested during the league's major effort to organize the shirtwaist workers in 1909. Together, the Beards spent many a Saturday afternoon ringing doorbells to collect money for workers' causes. [23]

Together, they expressed their humanitarian sympathies in *American Citizenship,* the civics text for high schools that was their first collaborative effort, which they published in 1914 as an alternative to current textbooks that seemed to them "to regard civic life as static or settled rather than dynamic or progressive," which treated government "as a machine rather than a process," and which were "written from a masculine point of view" in a world where the majority of high school students were women. [24]

Perhaps thinking of their happy experiences with their own children Miriam and William, the Beards devoted an entire chapter to the family as an institution. "How deep and important," they exclaimed, "are the ideals of fatherhood, motherhood, child life, affection, loyalty, care for the helpless, and unselfishness which develop wherever there is a wholesome family life!" They were nevertheless careful to point out, perhaps as an antidote to some fellow progressives intent on "uplift," that the middle-class home was not universal. Many men worked on night shifts; there were numerous mothers who labored, and many homes were headed by mothers who were the sole breadwinners; many families depended for survival on the incomes of children. [25]

Though the Beards were not cultural pluralists like Horace Kallen or Randolph Bourne neither were they nativist in their view of the immigrants. "Instead of denying the ballot to persons of foreign birth," it would be better, they suggested, "to educate them, to improve the conditions under which they live and labor, and to give them a fair chance to become valuable American citizens." During this same period Charles spoke of "the melting pot [that was] slowly merging the races that come to the United States into one nationality." His point was not that ethnic cultures were bad in themselves. He had no nativist fears of a threat to "Anglo-Saxon" democracy from competing cultures; rather, his idea was that by "inhibiting" (the term is his) intraethnic hostility between "the warring nationalities of Europe," economic necessity, which had brought everyone to these shores in the first place, might overcome prejudice and produce Socialist internationalism in the United States.

Here, in this book for high schoolers, the Beards dealt seriously with socialism and the single tax; they argued that spending 72 percent of federal revenues on military purposes was folly "when there is so great need [sic] of making this world a better place to live in." Even the illustrations, compelling photographs of "A Policewoman" and of "Those on Whom We Depend for Coal," seemed to ask for a fresh, creative approach to the challenges of citizenship. [26]

Both of the Beards were active suffragists. Mary Beard was an editor of *The Woman Voter,* a journal of the Woman's party of New York, during 1911 and 1912. Women both at home and in the factories, she wrote in an early editorial, "are bound to have a voice in choosing the public authorities who are to be charged with the conscious direction of human affairs." In January 1913, while they were in Washington for Charles Beard's research in the Early National Period, she joined the little group around the talented Quaker Alice Paul, who was beginning her campaign to revive interest in a national woman suffrage amendment. Two months later, all four Beards participated in a large suffrage parade in Washington, planned by Alice Paul for 3 March 1913, the day before Wilson's inauguration. Amid the turmoil of a near-riot, Charles marched with a men's contingent, Miriam and William rode on a horsedrawn float, and Mary Beard walked with a section of black women.[27]

During 1914, Alice Paul's Congressional Union, which demanded an all-out campaign of direct political action to secure immediate passage of an amendment, emerged as an alternative to the National American Women's Suffrage Association (with its emphasis on dignified campaigns to amend each state constitution). In New York City Mary Beard was the "one firm original defender" of Alice Paul and Lucy Burns "during a trial of the C[ongressional] U[nion] by the regular suffragists council. I was," she remembered later, "wholly in favor of its plan for political action to expedite victory for the enfranchisement of women."[28] On behalf of the Congressional Union, in 1914 and 1915 Charles used the pages of *New Republic* to discuss strategy and to debate with members of "the National" who wrote to defend their own state-by-state policy, while Mary joined other Congressional Unionists in testifying before congressional committees and threatening Democratic legislators with defeat at the hands of enfranchised women in the West.[29]

Suffrage for women was perhaps the immediate issue that prompted Charles, on behalf of a Committee on the Federal Constitution composed of such reformers as Florence Kelley, Edward A. Ross, Owen R. Lovejoy, Clinton R. Woodruff, and Samuel McCune Lindsay, to draft a plan for simplifying the amendment of the federal Constitution. Beard's resolution stated that many social movements were being "built on unstable foundations until the Constitution, which determines and limits the efforts at social and political readjustment, is brought under the control of the people."[30]

One of the most eloquent pieces Charles Beard ever wrote, a summation of his mature progressive faith, was a letter to the conservative *New York Times* in response to a letter from Dr. Simon Baruch, who had written that women were biologically unfitted for original and inventive work. "It makes me laugh," Beard replied,

> to hear a comfortable, protected New York citizen speak of "courage" as a masculine virtue, when I recall my own pioneer grandmother, who often drove howling wolves away from the front door with flaming firebrands and on more than one stormy black night rode on horseback ten or twenty miles along blazed forest trails to do errands of mercy for distant neighbors—and incidentally bore fourteen children.

Clearly aligning himself against scientific racism and sexism, Beard warned that the time had come "to beware of generalizations about races or sexes," for example that kings were called by God to rule, that the Jew was inferior to the Gentile, that workingmen and peasants were "of inferior clay," and that "the negro" was "inferior to the white man" and therefore suited only for slavery.

There were, Beard wrote, borrowing the language of Oliver Wendell Holmes, no "biological laws" that could be applied to broad civic and ethical questions: "Our decision rests upon our judgment, our experiences, our sympathies, our associations, our interests, our lives of reading and thought, our notions of justice and a thousand other considerations." The great qualities of human nature, "courage, industry, patience, wisdom, endurance, virtue, honor, originality, and sympathy," were not the monopoly of one sex.[31]

During the winter of 1916 Charles, John Dewey, and thirteen other men, calling themselves a "flying squadron" to line up congressmen for suffrage, heckled Democratic speakers when they appeared at meetings in New York City. In November 1917, after the passage of the New York State suffrage amendment and during the imprisonment and force-feeding of Alice Paul, Lucy Burns, and others who had picketed the White House with slogans reminding Wilson that "Democracy Should Begin at Home," Mary Beard led a Committee of One Thousand Women on a pilgrimage to Washington to embarrass the President further and to gain more publicity for the national amendment. On that historic day in January 1918 when exactly two-thirds of the House voted for the Anthony Amendment, the Beards could feel that they had done their share in the harvest. What Charles Beard had once called "the male state" was set on the long path to extinction.[32]

There have been times in the history of the United States when the problems with which the Beards and many of their contemporaries grappled did not seem very real. Some liberal historians of the forties and fifties, perhaps preoccupied with the Cold War and worried by McCarthyism, perhaps unwilling or unable to recognize basic conflicts between the theory and the reality of American society, and perhaps unready to understand a critic of Franklin Roosevelt, promoted an image of Charles Beard as a muckraker during his years at Columbia, an example of the "Progressive mind" on the prowl for "hidden realities."

Charles Beard's record as a progressive reformer does prompt a question: Was reality hidden from Beard and from his contemporaries? Might it not be more fruitful to abandon discussions of what Gordon Allport has called "the abstract motivation of an impersonal and therefore nonexistent mind-in-general" in favor of "the concrete, viable motives of each and every mind-in-particular"?[33] A consideration of Charles Beard's writings on urban problems, of his very practical and useful activities in the Bureau of Municipal Research, and of his and Mary Beard's humanitarian commitment to social justice and woman suffrage suggests that a more suitable label for Beard would be the one that was his own choice for an epitaph: "The discoverer of the obvious."[34]

5

Wealth and Power
An Economic Approach to Constitutions, Parties, and Politics

To the period between 1912 and 1915 belong Beard's first great works in public law and American history: *The Supreme Court and the Constitution* (1912), *An Economic Interpretation of the Constitution* (1913), *Contemporary American History* (1914), and *Economic Origins of Jeffersonian Democracy* (1915). Written by a man ardently committed to bettering the conditions of life in a great city, these books reflect his belief that the future would "not be hideous and mean, but beautiful and magnificent" and his view of himself as a "co-worker in that great and indivisible natural process which draws down granite hills and upbuilds great nations."[1] These volumes certainly fixed Beard's reputation as an innovator among American historians and political scientists. Yet contemporaries who examined Beard's writing closely saw a disturbing problem: the "economic interpretation" did not exist as a unified theory of explanation. Beard shifted from an idea of people acting out of personal interest to a generalization that people represented the interests of groups. He approached an ideological interpretation of the actions of powerful groups and individuals, but he did not embrace it. Wealth and power were connected, and the public law reflected this connection, but his efforts to describe the process by which the law emerged from a social context were imprecise and contradictory.

In his well-known lecture "Politics," given at Columbia in 1908, Beard asserted that "the great question of any age" was "not shall private property as such be abolished," for the "nature of man" had demonstrated that "it cannot be." The problem was "what forms of property shall be permitted, and to what uses shall they be subjected?" Beard had recently tramped about on the Lower East Side in behalf of Socialist Morris Hillquit's congressional candidacy, and he may have been thinking of this experience when he added that these "complicated social questions" could not be settled "in the closet with the philosophers" but rather "amid the multitudinous experiences of the market place where society daily meets the pressing needs of life."[2]

Power, he argued, was "exceedingly elusive" and academic contemplation of "the juristic state" must give way to a search for "that group of persons able to work together effectively for the accomplishment of their joint aims, and overcome all opposition on the particular point at issue at a particular period of time." Beard's perception of government and politics as part of a historic process was strongly influenced by the path-breaking work of Arthur Bentley, whose *The Process of Government* had appeared in 1908. In his speech at Columbia Beard echoed Bentley's witty and cogent critique of political scientists who had lost "sight of the content of the process in some trick point about the form." In his histories and books on public law, Beard would explore the social dynamics of group activity. He would be following Bentley's suggestion: attempting to replace a study of "barren formalisms" with the more "thoroughly practical" (Bentley's phrase) study of people pursuing com-monsense goals.[3]

Contemplation of the question of power in a democracy—who gets it and why in the United States—led inevitably to a consideration of the great extralegal institutions known as parties. What was needed, Beard postulated, were accounts "of the actual historical processes by which the party has arisen and, as an extra-legal institution, controls the legal forms of government." His own history of the origins of parties in the United States, *Economic Origins of Jeffersonian Democracy*, demonstrated his conclusion of 1908 that "the party in general and particular, as a centre of power and a working institution, offers the richest field of investigation now open to the student of politics."[4]

Amid the dust and clamor of construction designed to accommodate a growing student body and a larger faculty, the halls of Columbia in Beard's time reverberated with a vigorous debate on the basis and application of public law, specifically the Constitution of the United States. One one side stood John W. Burgess, holding forth at the Law School, striving with magisterial confidence (as Beard described him) "to indoctrinate rising lawyers with the creed [of] the Constitution as limitations, limitations as economic *laissez faire*, and judges as sovereign in prescribing limitations in concrete cases."[5]

Burgess had a pessimistic attitude toward the great American public. "I have always found," he said in his autobiography, "many men ignorant, narrow, greedy, prejudiced, malicious, brutal, and vindictive." Burgess was therefore concerned to protect American individuals from the possibilities of socialism, which might be perpetuated by "the organ of universal suffrage." In his view, the Supreme Court was frankly a vital "tool of conservatism." The Constitution stood like a Hegelian spirit above the people. He perfectly expressed the formalist position on the study of public law when he wrote:

> It is the consciousness of the American people that law must rest upon justice and reason, that the constitution is a more ultimate formulation of the fundamental principles of justice and reason than mere legislative acts, and that the judiciary is a better interpreter of those fundamental principles than the legislature,—it is this consciousness which has given such authority to the interpretation of the constitution by the Supreme Court.

This is the sort of reasoning about the sources of law that Arthur Bentley called "soul stuff" and "spooks."[6]

Outside Columbia, the distinguished political scientist Westel Willoughby of Johns Hopkins had dissented from Burgess' denial of the power of the representative branches of government to alter a sovereignty interpreted by the courts.[7] Within the faculty at Columbia, the leader of the opposition to Burgess' interpretation of the public law was Beard's mentor and friend Frank J. Goodnow. His *Social Reform and the Constitution* created a sensation at Columbia in 1911. In it, Goodnow attacked Burgess' entire approach to constitutional law, and as a result, despite the attempts of Beard and others to the contrary, Burgess, when he retired from the coveted Ruggles Professorship in 1912, refused to allow Goodnow, the logical candidate, to succeed him. Instead, Burgess secured the appointment of a former student and Wall Street lawyer, a partner of one of Columbia's conservative trustees, a man who took no part in faculty meetings or work with graduate students and who gave one lecture a week for one semester each year.[8]

In contrast to Burgess' Hegelianism, Goodnow described his own sensibility as informed by pragmatic philosophy and the theory of the economic interpretation of history. He did not believe in a static society with permanent political principles of universal applicability. "Political organizations," he argued, "must be so framed and governmental powers must be so formulated as to be in accord as far as possible with the actual economic and social situation," and he asked the ringing question: "Is the kind of political system which we commonly believe our fathers established one which can with advantage be retained unchanged in the changed conditions which are seen to exist?"[9]

Describing reforms recently advocated, such as federal incorporation, state pensions for old age, accident on the job, and sickness, and state-sponsored housing for working people in cities, Goodnow urged that the prospects for amending the Constitution were dim indeed and that to destroy the federal courts or to alter their jurisdiction was "inconceivable." As a recourse, he advocated "a persistent criticism" of those court decisions tending "to regard the Constitution as a document to be given the same meaning at all times and under all conditions" and failing to "appreciate that the courts in our system of government" had been "accorded a really political function." Courts, said Goodnow, "should not absolutely block change, although they [might] quite properly limit the rate at which it may proceed."[10]

Beard's *The Supreme Court and the Constitution* (1912) was a book in public law.[11] It furnished a historical basis for the sort of criticism of the federal courts that Goodnow had advocated. It was a brief against the arguments of such people as Chief Justice Walter Clark of North Carolina, Dean William Trickett of Dickinson Law School, New York lawyers L. B. Boudin and Gilbert Roe, and Theodore Roosevelt (though Beard did not mention him by name), all of whom had asserted that judicial review by the Supreme Court represented the usurpation of a power not granted or intended by either the framers or the ratifiers of the Constitution.

A majority of active framers had probably assumed "that the judicial power might be held to embrace a very considerable control over legislation." He was not prepared, he said, to do "years of research into the lives and opinions of several hundred members" of state ratifying conventions, but "fragmentary evidence" suggested that members of the state conventions, concerned as they mostly were with state powers, did not give much thought to judicial review of acts of Congress. Beard stressed the absurdity of looking back to eighteenth-century positions to support modern goals. What, he asked, would be "our constitutional position" today if it were recognized that each branch of the federal government, in addition to the clearly expressed powers, "possessed those additional powers only which were understood by the ratifying conventions of the states to have been implicitly conferred!"

It was obvious to anyone familiar with the writings of representative men of the period "that the Constitution was looked upon as a bulwark against populism of every form." This was what Burgess and his followers proclaimed and approved. However, Beard's purpose was different. He went on to ask, as Goodnow had done, "whether this system is outworn, whether it has unduly exalted property rights." Then, turning from Burgess to those Progressives who were arguing the usurpation theory of judicial review, Beard added that "those who hold the affirmative cannot rest their case on the intent of the eighteenth-century statesmen who framed the Constitution."[12]

Here was the prism of history in the hands of an activist. Beard was beginning his controversial re-examination and synthesis of the period of American history after the Revolution. People were to be given a fresh perspective on their fundamental law. Thus would they be equipped to compare critically their own views on the function and possibilities of government action with those of the framers. Perhaps they would see that, indeed, times had changed and so also must the fundamental law.

Beard had been thinking about the origins of the Constitution since his days at DePauw and his seminar on the Constitution with Andrew Stephenson.

One of his final editorials in the *Palladium*, in 1898, had announced that the Constitution had "been the bulwark of every great national sin—from slavery to monopoly."[13] Years later, at Columbia, when Beard was feeling his power as a scholar, this longstanding interest in the Constitution coincided with an appropriate moment in a great debate. He had, he wrote, spent "the leisure of several years" reading the writings of men politically active in the post-Revolutionary period. In autumn 1912 he took a leave of absence from professorial duties and went to Washington for four months. Within that time, while simultaneously working on two other books, he completed the research on both *An Economic Interpretation of the Constitution* and *Economic Origins of Jeffersonian Democracy* and wrote the former.[14]

In 1935 Beard issued the rather narrow disclaimer that while writing these volumes he "had in mind no thought of forwarding the interests of the Progressive party or of its conservative opponents."[15] Beard may be taken at his word. It was a narrow disclaimer of an affiliation he had rejected. He certainly wanted more throughgoing reforms than most Progressives. The link between his scholarly and his political position was made clear in a letter to Robert M. La Follette in 1913. Thanking La Follette for his gift of a copy of his *Autobiography*, Beard sent him in return a copy of *An Economic Interpretation*. Frankly disagreeing with La Follette's ideas about restoring government to the people, Beard wrote that he did not think it was "a question of 'restoring' the government to the people"; it was "a question of getting possession of it for them for the first time." Before the Civil War, the Democratic party had been "the agent of slavocracy," and since that war the Republican party had been "the advance agent of plutocracy." This was, he added, how "I read our history, and I may say that my Republican up-bringing was scarcely less thoroughgoing than yours." The book on the Constitution would show La Follette why he believed that "we did not have 'a government of the people' to start with."[16]

Conceived in the context of a particular debate, *An Economic Interpretation of the Constitution* (1913) and *Economic Origins of Jeffersonian Democracy* (1915) were intended to furnish a new historical foundation for the study and application of the public law and to give a fresh interpretation of the sources of political parties. Beard addressed himself in his introduction to the first volume to a very specific contemporary audience: all fellow students of politics, especially lawyers, judges, and teachers of constitutional law and administration. The "legalists," as he repeatedly referred to them in his text, consciously used history in a political way to justify their position on current issues. In the study of public law, history was and should be the primary means of illumination, the basis of generalization and application. Divine guidance in history as interpreted by George Bancroft; the Teutonic school, with its emphasis on the political genius of certain races; and the nonspecific school, associated with no theory in particular and concerned mainly with editing documents, were being challenged by scholars such as Frederick J. Turner and his students, who applied an economic analysis to the past. Generally, economic factors

had been neglected by historians, but Beard's major point on historical interpretation in his introduction was that "the neglect" had "been all the more
pronounced in the field of private and public law." In both England and the
United States, the public law had not been subjected to "a critical analysis of
legal evolution," with the result that "all sorts of vague abstractions" dominated much of the thought in the field of law.[17]

As he so often did in his writing, Beard compared the work of European
scholars, such as Rudolph von Jhering and Ferdinand La Salle, who viewed
the law as an expression of concrete interests rather than abstract ideas, with
writing and thinking about constitutions in America. With some exceptions,
such as Roscoe Pound, Franklin Goodnow, and Arthur Bentley, Beard noted
that American students of the law had generally labored under the spell of
"the juristic theory of the origin and nature of the Constitution." It was this
theory—that the Constitution proceeded "from the whole people," that "the
people" had been "the original source of all political authority exercised under
it," and that it had been "founded on broad general principles of liberty and
government entertained, for some reason, by the whole people and having no
reference to the interest or advantage of any particular group or class"—that
Beard proposed to question. He had listened carefully to Burgess.[18]

He took Professor Seligman's "nearly axiomatic" statement of the theory
of the economic interpretation of history as his starting point:

> The existence of man depends on his ability to sustain himself; the economic
> life is therefore the fundamental condition of all life. Since human life, however,
> is the life of man in society, individual existence moves within the framework
> of the social structure and is modified by it. What the conditions of maintenance
> are to the individual, the similar relations of production and consumption are
> to the community.[19]

However, Beard cautioned that the theory of the economic interpretation
was older than Seligman and Marx. James Madison had anticipated it in *The
Federalist* Number 10, and Beard proposed to replace the Hegelian political
science of the law as "an abstract thing, a printed page, a volume of statutes,
a statement by a judge" with his version of Madison's neglected formulation:

> A landed interest, a manufacturing interest, a mercantile interest, a moneyed
> interest, with many lesser interests, grow up of necessity in civilized nations and
> divide them into different classes, activated by different sentiments and views.
> The regulation of these various and interfering interests forms the principal task
> of modern legislation, and involves the spirit of party and faction in the necessary
> and ordinary operations of the government.[20]

Beard shared with Raymond Moley, then his student, something of the
spirit in which he wrote his books. "The thing to do is to lay a mine, store it
with nitro, and then let it off in such a fashion that it rips the bowels out of
something important, making it impossible for the fools to travel that way any
more."[21]

In essence, the "juristic theory" of constitutional history was the idea that the Constitution proceeded from "the whole people." Hence Beard began his survey of economic interests in 1787 with four groups whose status had a definite legal expression but who were outside the political process: slaves, indentured servants, men who could not qualify for voting because of property tests, and women.[22] Robert E. Brown, attacking Beard's work some forty years later and determined to uphold the hypothesis that "American society was democratic in 1787," wrote disparagingly that "If slaves and women had to vote before there was democracy in this country, we did not have democracy until 1920."[23] This was precisely Beard's point. As in 1787, so in 1913 the law was not proceeding from "the people," broadly speaking so as to include them all. In his view, women and slaves were people.

Next Beard divided the politically active male population into economic interest groups. First there were real property holders (among them smaller farmers with debts, manorial lords, and slaveholders of the South), then there were personal property interests (creditors, holders of public securities, manufacturers and shippers, and speculators in Western lands). Under the Articles of Confederation, the latter group, "personalty" (holders of personal property), was experiencing difficulties. "It was, in short, the dynamic element in the movement for the new Constitution."[24]

Employing the imaginative and novel technique of collective biography, Beard centered *An Economic Interpretation of the Constitution* on a survey of the economic interests of the members of the Constitutional Convention. A majority of these men were lawyers from towns or coastal regions and the dusty *Records* of the Treasury Department after 1790, a source Beard was the first to use, showed him that forty of the fifty-five members who attended the Convention probably held public securities in 1787. Otherwise, they were "mere speculators" who bought securities after they were assured of the passage of Hamilton's funding and assumption of the debt. "Economic biographies" of the membership of the Convention revealed that fourteen of the fifty-five were speculating in public lands, that twenty-four were involved in loaning money at interest, that "at least" eleven members represented "personalty in mercantile, manufacturing, and shipping lines," and that "at least fifteen members" represented "personalty in slaves."[25]

Superficial students of the Constitution, who had "read only the commentaries of the legalists," might have difficulty, Beard conceded, thinking of it as an economic document. It did not mention property qualifications on voting or officeholding; it did not recognize any of those economic interest groups he had outlined. Yet Beard maintained that the "true inwardness" of the Constitution was manifestly revealed in the "correspondence of the period, contemporary newspapers and pamphlets, the records of the debates in the Convention at Philadelphia and in the several state conventions, and particularly *The Federalist.*" Using von Jhering's phrase *Zweck im Recht,* "concrete interest reflected in the law," Beard described the positive powers conferred on the new government to levy and collect taxes, to raise and support military and naval forces, to control foreign and interstate commerce as reflections of "the strong impulse of economic forces in the towns and young manufacturing centres. In a few simple words," he concluded, "the mercantile and manufacturing interests wrote their *Zweck im Recht*; and they paid for their victory by large concessions to the slaveowning planters of the south."

Two clauses, Beard argued, embodied the main demands of personality against agrarianism: the emission of paper money was prohibited and the states were forbidden to impair the obligation of contract.[26] Politicians of the eighteenth century could frankly recognize "class rights" and they "were not under the necessity," as were "modern partisan writers," of clouding "the essential economic antagonisms featuring in law and constitution making. Their clarity of thought," Beard observed, "was greatly facilitated by the disfranchisement of the propertyless, which made it unnecessary for political writers to address themselves to the proletariat and to explain dominant group interests" in such a way that they appeared "in the garb of 'public policy.'" Beard spoke of the "political doctrines" of the Convention rather than about "political theories." *Doctrine* implies something commonplace and unquestioned, while the word "theory" has overtones of abstract speculation. Beard wanted the framers to be seen standing on the ground.[27]

Burgess himself had suggested that the ratification of the Constitution was the equivalent of a coup d'état. "We must therefore," he had written, "give up the attempt altogether to find a legal basis for the adoption of the new constitution." Students were advised to "have recourse to political science, to the natural and historical conditions of the society and state."[28]

There had been, Beard reminded readers, no direct popular vote taken on the Constitution. Using secondary sources such as O. G. Libby's *Geographical Distribution of the Vote of the Thirteen States on the Federal Constitution* and Charles Ambler's *Sectionalism in Virginia*, scattered records of state ratifying conventions, and Treasury Department records, Beard attempted to generalize his thesis about the Convention into a hypothesis that would describe the alignment of interests in the states. He was not prepared, he said, to do "a study of the natural history" of approximately 160,000 men involved in the formation and adoption of the Constitution. Surveying economic interests represented in state conventions, he concluded that those conventions did not "seem to have been more 'disinterested' than the Philadelphia convention"; in fact, "the leading champions of the new government" appeared to have been mostly "men of the same practical type, with actual economic advantages at stake." "Almost uniformly" the opponents came from farming regions and from areas "in which debtors had been formulating paper money and other depreciatory schemes." Contemporary accounts, Beard thought, supported his hypothesis that during the election of delegates to the ratifying conventions in the states there had been "a deep-seated conflict between a popular party based on paper money and agrarian interests, and a conservative party centered in the towns and resting on financial, mercantile, and personal property interests generally."[29]

Beard aimed his final sentences directly at his select audience of judges, lawyers, and students of public law:

> The Constitution was not created by "the whole people" as the jurists have said; neither was it created by "the states" as Southern nullifiers long contended; but it was the work of a consolidated group whose interests knew no state boundaries and were truly national in their scope.[30]

This book was hardly a "long and arid survey—partaking of the nature of a catalogue," as Beard modestly described it in the preface to his conclusions. Page after page radiate with controlled excitement. Again and again Beard pointed to the need for more research to test his conjectures fully.[31] Although occasionally, by the way he stated his conclusions, he seemed to imply a belief that the framers conceived their ideas of government as a direct, conscious rationalization of their property interests ("It was an economic document drawn with superb skill by men whose property interests were immediately at stake"),[32] his discussions of the origins of men's ideas were not so crass. When he did analyze ideas, which was not often, his explanations were overwhelmingly environmentalist. When trying to describe political action, he apparently adhered to Bentley's view of the role of ideas: "The 'ideas' and 'feelings' serve to give the individual man his orientation in the social activity in which he is involved; they serve, so to speak, to define him as an individual. There is no idea which is not a reflection of social activity.[33]

Personal experience, in Beard's view, was the basis for acceptance or rejection of ideas about society. Hence the members of the Convention represented "distinct groups whose economic interests they understood and felt in concrete, definite form through their own personal experience with identical property rights." Alexander Hamilton, "the colossal genius of the new system," for whom "extensive augmentation of his personal fortune was no consideration," thus appreciated "at first hand the stuff of which government is made."[34]

In his 1915 volume, *Economic Origins of Jeffersonian Democracy*, Beard described Hamilton as knowing that the new government "could not stand if its sole basis was the platonic support of genial well-wishers." Hamilton saw that the Constitution had been created "in response to interested demands and not out of any fine-spun theories of political science." In Beard's eyes, he had displayed a "penetrating wisdom which placed him among the great statesmen of all time."[35]

Treating Jefferson's thought in this second volume, Beard distinguished between the interpretation of people's ideas as momentary rationalizations and as products of a larger environment. Jefferson's attacks on "stock-jobbing" and "paper operations" were not, Beard argued, "the trick of a politician seeking to put his opponents in a bad light." The fact was "that the captalist mode of accumulation" had been "foreign to Jefferson's personal economic experience and that of the planting class to which he belonged—a class based, as Calhoun long afterward had pointed out, upon the simple exploitation of slave labor and not upon the arts of finance and commerce." Doubtless, Beard speculated, Jefferson's antipathy to capitalist methods was increased by the heavy indebtedness of planters to British creditors and by the accumulation of the national debt in urban centers, but Beard clearly rejected the view that Jefferson's political views were a direct result of his personal everyday economic concerns. It was not necessary, "to introduce this element to account for the psychology and economics of the slave-owning planter."[36]

Economic Origins of Jeffersonian Democracy carried the analysis of interest groups in politics into the early national period by attempting to demonstrate, again by the technique of collective biography, that—contrary to Orin G. Libby and John S. Bassett—the economic and hence political divisions over the ratification of the Constitution ("realty" versus "personalty") had extended into Washington's administration. Beard contended that Anti-Federalists, who, he thought, generally represented the farmers and debtors in the struggle over ratification become the followers of Jefferson in the 1790s, while the supporters of the Constitution—the financiers, public creditors, traders, commercial men, and manufacturers in the larger seaboard towns—became the Federalists, supporters of Hamilton's programs of finance and foreign policy, as political parties developed in the wake of the Constitution. Thus, within new institutional boundaries, Beard depicted a continuing struggle between politically active capitalistic and agrarian interests.[37]

Beard's concern was not to establish an antithesis between aristocratic Federalists and democratic Jeffersonians. His main focus, as in the book on the Constitution, continued to be on Bentley's politically active groups whose ideas of what was possible for government sprang from a concrete environment, rather than from abstract speculation. Neither party, Beard observed, wanted to "cherish the people" by lifting the restrictions on voting and officeholding, though Jefferson had talked of universal manhood suffrage in private. (Beard was careful to point out that, even in Jefferson's most far-ranging speculations on universal suffrage, women and people in slavery were to be excluded.) Although he pointed out that poorer farmers as well as "the poorer orders" in cities joined the Republicans, Beard did not propose a division between rich and poor. "The southern planters," he wrote, agreeing with Richard Hildreth's work of decades earlier and adding overtones of Veblen, had "formed the 'natural aristocracy' of the South, readily consolidated because they possessed the leisure and the intelligence requisite for travel, communication, and correspondence which fused them into a social group conscious of identical interests." "A curious freak of fortune," Beard speculated, had given "to a slave-owning aristocracy the leadership in a democracy of small farmers." What was the cause?

"In a conflict with capitalism," he answered, "the agrarians rallied around that agrarian class which had the cultural equipment for dominant direction."[38] The rich ruled. They divided over issues related to the possession of different kinds of wealth, but when the agrarians won the battle of 1800 there had been no significant revolution in policy. Jefferson, according to Beard, had followed his own maxim: "'What is practicable must often control what is pure theory.'" Soon after taking office, Beard noted, Jefferson had begun working to "detach the banking interests from the Federalists and to fasten them to the Republican party." Although he had accused Hamilton of corruption, "Jefferson was conscious of the rectitude of his own intentions."

This version of Jefferson as president was a final powerful argument against the abstract, formalistic interpretation of politics: "Jeffersonian Democracy" had not implied an "abandonment of the property, and particularly the landed qualifications on the suffrage of office-holding." There had been no basic changes in the Constitution "which the Federalists had designed as a foil to the leveling propensities of the masses." The coming to power of Jefferson and his party had "simply meant the possession of the federal government by the agrarian masses led by an aristocracy of slave-owning planters, and the theoretical repudiation of the right to use the Government for the benefit of any capitalist groups . . ."[39]

Economic Origins is less tightly organized than *An Economic Interpretation.* The chapters do not form a unit in support of a particular thesis, except perhaps some vague generalization about the importance of economic issues in the thought and activities of members of the federal government between 1787 and 1800. Like its companion, *Economic Origins* is studded with suggestions for further research, with unanswered questions and guesses. When confronted with evidence that did not fit his generalizations, Beard was not above shifting the grounds of his argument, and this lends an unsystematic quality to the book. For example, his economic analysis of party composition suffered a major breakdown in the chapter entitled "Security Holding and Politics." Here, Beard recorded that, in the voting during the First Congress on Hamilton's fiscal measures, "quite a number of security holders voted *against* assumption of the state's debts and contrary to their personal interest." According to Beard's original hypothesis about the basis of support for Hamilton's funding program, these security holders, as representatives of "personalty," as men aware of the advantages to be gained from such a program through their own personal experience, should have voted *for* funding. Beard ignored the dichotomy between this finding and his earlier argument and concluded that these security-holders still represented economic politics and not abstract, philosophical objections to funding, because "an examination of the vote with reference to the geographical distribution of the public securities would seem to show beyond question that nearly all the members, security holders and non-security holders alike, represented the dominant economic interests of their respective constituencies rather than their personal interests."[40] This was begging and confusing the question of motivation by shifting the interpretive framework from focused on personal interest and experience to a Burkean idea of virtual representation.

In his chapter on John Adams' political economy Beard again abandoned the Madisonian analysis. Adams had "built his entire system upon an economic foundation, upon the material needs of human nature." Yet Adams' concepts of society and balanced government were "static." Adams had not thought of the "possibility of new and extra-ordinary modes of accumulating wealth. In his system, there was no inherent opposition between landed property and personalty." At the close of this chapter Beard commented that Adams' system of political economy, as expounded in the *Defense of American Constitutions* (1786), had had "no direct reference to the course of party politics in the United States." Nor, he might have added, to his own theory of the material origins of political conflict.[41]

There are other examples of Beard looking at the evidence and questioning himself and the readers. In 1800 the vote in Massachusetts had not followed the predicted lines between agrarians and capitalists and was, therefore, "puzzling"; he "guessed" that supporters of the Constitution in 1788 in New York City voted the Federalist ticket in 1800; he included, without comment, Madison's note about the importance of the institution of slavery in the debates at the Convention; he only indicated the rich possibilities of an investigation of the Jeffersonians' political use of banks and of the Republicans' attack on the Federalist courts.[42]

Beard had enormous confidence in the basic correctness of his outlook. He was so certain that future research would bear out his conclusions that he offered his "grand scheme" replete with plenty of evidence to contradict it. Then, too, he did not believe in absolute generalizations, in propositions that would cover all occasions. He was more concerned to draw the general outlines of an interpretation than to fill in the details. He was proud but not arrogant. After all, the goal was to replace, in people's thoughts about their past, an abstract idea of the basis for men's actions with a more materialistic view. He was debating, an art he adored. He was speaking to an audience living and dealing with the problems he had described in *American City Government.* The Fathers, he was telling several generations of judges, lawyers, and students of politics, were people with experiences that had shaped their views on public policy. Their ideas, while not conscious rationalizations of their own interests, were yet products of their lives and, as their economic position affected the course of their ideas, made some measures more attractive than others. Modern folk, he was certainly implying, were living in a different world, and judges, lawyers, and teachers should approach the Constitution recognizing the differences between the "instant needs" of their own society and those of society in the time of the Fathers. Patriots, Beard urged, need not shrink from a materialist analysis of history. What kind of government could have been established anyway, he wondered, "if there had been excluded from voting on the great fiscal measures all 'interested representatives,'" if "such momentous issues" had been "left to those highly etherealized persons who 'cherished the people'—and nothing more"?[43]

Because he crusaded, because he opposed the tide of interpretation, he was careless and not really theoretical. "I shall rough-hew it all the way through," Beard wrote of these books to his former student, Arthur M. Schlesinger, Sr., "leaving it to others to correct my perspective and many errors and do the balanced job." In this letter, written when he was forty-one, Beard added that he was in robust health and could "carry more steam now than I could when I was thirty."[44]

Among American historians the story is well known that, after *An Economic Interpretation* was published in 1913, Columbia's President and John Burgess' leading pupil, Nicholas Murray Butler, asked if he had read Beard's last book, replied "I hope so!" The review of *An Economic Interpretation* in Columbia's *Educational Review*, which Butler edited, was similarly brief. Beard had performed, wrote the anonymous critic—perhaps Butler—"a good deal of labour without, we fear, any very important result. . . . We had thought that the myth of the Economic Man had finally disappeared."[45]

Another member of Beard's intended audience, former President William Howard Taft, took the podium at the Waldorf-Astoria before an audience of more than a thousand prominent lawyers and politicians to denounce the book as an example of progressive muckraking. In Marion, Ohio, home of future President Warren G. Harding, the editors of *The Ohio Star*, who had seen only reviews of *An Economic Interpretation*, wrote the famous headline SCAVANGERS, HYENA-LIKE, DESECRATE THE GRAVES OF THE DEAD PATRIOTS WE REVERE and added that Beard's book, "if correctly represented," was "libelous, vicious and damnable" and all patriotic citizens "should rise to condemn him and the purveyors of his filthy lies and rotten aspersions."[46]

These were the sort of criticisms, good publicity for the book, Beard could enjoy and ignore. Not so the more sober thrusts of such highly respected colleagues as William K. Boyd, John Latané, Edwin S. Corwin, and Orin G. Libby. Latané examined the book in the *American Political Science Review* and pointed out that the security holdings of six leading proponents of the Constitution—James Madison, Alexander Hamilton, James Wilson, George Washington, Gouvernor Morris, and Charles Pinckney—totaled $21,046 according to Beard's figures, while a similar group of opponents including Elbridge Gerry, Luther Martin, Oliver Ellsworth, and William S. Johnson were associated with securities amounting to $87,979.90. Latané used Beard's own estimates to show that security holdings were not a reliable basis for predicting men's outlook on the Constitution. Latané said he was willing to accept interpretations which stressed the economic nature of sectionalism or which allowed that members of the Convention were influenced by the economic interests of their constituents, but he concluded that Beard had not demonstrated satisfactorily the connection between the personal financial interests of members of the Convention and their position on the Constitution. Beard responded to this criticism in *Economic Origins* by trying to incorporate it into his larger canvas. Describing the considerable number of security holders who had voted against Hamilton's funding program, he wrote that they "represented the dominant economic interests of their respective constituencies rather than their personal interests."[47] Again Beard showed that he was more interested in bludgeoning the formalists with "things economic" and less interested in a coherent explanation of the political process.

Both Orin G. Libby, in the first issue of a new journal, *The Mississippi Valley Historical Review*, and E. S. Corwin, in *The History Teacher's Magazine*, suggested that Beard's method of using the Treasury's records after 1790 to interpolate the security holdings of members of the Convention of 1787 was dubious—or, as Corwin put it, "With all due respect, this is the most unmitigated rot. . . . Why should not former members of the Convention have invested their money in public securities in 1790 and the years following, when they saw these rising in value and becoming safe sources of income." Beard's evidence, Corwin noted, showed only that seven members of the Convention, excepting Robert Morris, "had held public securities anterior to the meeting of the Convention," that these securities were worth less than $90,000, and that "fully two-thirds" of this amount belonged to Elbridge Gerry, who "however, was so little influenced by this consideration that he refused to sign the Constitution and opposed its adoption!"[48]

Beard replied to this particular critic with a long footnote in *Economic Origins*. He had assumed as a "minor point" in *An Ecomomic Interpretation*, he now wrote, that members of the Convention on the funding books after 1790 were holders of securities in 1787, "on the theory that very few of them could have been in what Jefferson called the 'corrupt squadron' dealing in the funds of the government whose credit depended so much upon their labors." What, then, had been the main point of the economic biographies in his much-misunderstood ChapterV? "The main point of the chapter in question was that the members of the Convention were of the capitalistic rather than the agrarian interest, and whether they made money out of the adoption of the Constitution was specifically stated to be of no consequence to the main thesis." Here Beard was saying that the specific relationship between security holdings and members' positions on the Constitution was less important than the general view of the Fathers as being "capitalistic" rather than "agrarian."

Certain "superficial critics" had imagined, Beard continued, in the fashion of a veteran debater, "the downfall of the whole thesis because it could not be definitely proved that all the security-holding members held their papers *at the time of the Convention*" (Beard's emphasis). These critics could "have the satisfaction of choosing to believe that the framers who held public funds

were men who had risked their money . . . when the fortunes of the government were at a low ebb before 1787, or that most of them were engaged in
buying securities while they were serving" as officials of the government they
had created "and at a time when their influence was determining the value of
those securities. Respect for the framers," he concluded, "should impel us to
choose the former alternative."[49] Beard took the high ground that, in attacking
his thesis, the dastardly critics were slinging muck at the Fathers they longed
to defend—a spirited reply that avoided confronting the questions being raised
about his methodology.

He did not answer those who had challenged his broad outline of the politics
of the period as essentially a battle between politically active men whose main
economic interest was in fluid capital and politically active men whose wealth
was mostly in land. Thus he ignored Libby's perceptive comment that *An
Economic Interpretation* was "principally at fault in its lack of perspective; the
period of constitution making is too narrowly limited" and that Beard had
neglected the impact of the colonial and revolutionary experiences upon the
Founders. Furthermore, Libby argued, "the fundamental factor" in framing
and adopting the Constitution was that "those sections supporting the new
instrument were the ones best situated for keeping in touch with progress"
and that "those sections opposed were those most isolated from their fellow
citizens."[50]

William K. Boyd agreed with Beard that "undoubtably economic matters
were the basis of the movement which resulted in the constitution" but argued
that their scope was much wider. Beard had made the "financial anarchy" of
the state currencies "secondary in importance to the depreciation of continental securities held by the 'fathers.'" Some states, Boyd pointed out, "were
engaged in commercial warfare with each other"; and this "'economic
interpretation'" had been "entirely overlooked." Along with criticizing Beard
for ignoring many available primary sources and for neglecting some secondary
works, Boyd asked two searching questions: "In the choice of delegates to the
convention the 'personalty' interests were successful; if there was so much
economic conflict between the farmers and the security holders and traders,
how could this result have been secured when the landed class controlled the
legislatures which elected the delegates?" and if the Constitution was so clearly
an economic issue, "why was so much of the opposition conciliated by promises
of amendments in which questions of personal liberty and states rights pre-
dominated?"[51]

The critical fray left *An Economic Interpretation* tattered. The original reviewers of the book were clearly as astute as those historians who made their
fortunes raking Beard over the coals fifty years later. Contemporaries, even
those, like Boyd, predisposed to accept a materialist as opposed to an idealist
orientation toward past events, saw that Beard's picture was out of focus. Yet,
like the debater he was, Beard yielded nothing and reiterated his conclusions
on the making of the Constitution with bravado at the close of *Economic*

Origins of Jeffersonian Democracy. It had been "established upon a statistical basis" that the Constitution had been "the product of a conflict between capitalistic and agrarian interests." Supporters of the new government had come "principally from the cities and regions where the commercial, financial, manufacturing, and speculative interests were concentrated"; opponents had come "from the small farming and debtor classes, particularly those back from the seaboard."[52] Thus Beard slipped under the barbed fence, but his interpretive shirt was noticeably full of holes.

Contemporary American History (1914), a textbook, was Beard's "impressionistic" account of the years 1877 to 1913, which he termed "the most wonderful period in American development." However, he did not use the word *wonderful* in a naively optimistic sense. Beard had shed his Teutonic racism, and his first chapter, "The Restoration of White Dominion in the South," with its account of the intimidation and disfranchisement of black voters, its citation of Benjamin Tillman's speech on the floor of the Senate in 1900 ("We shot them. We are not ashamed of it"), and its description of the series of decisions by the Supreme Court upholding segregation and giving "judicial sanction to a view undoubtedly entertained by the major portion of the whites everywhere," cast a long shadow over the brightness of Beard's contemporary America. The emancipation of people from slavery and their enfranchisement had come, he wrote, "almost without effort on [their] own part, without that development of economic interest and of class consciousness that had marked the rise of other social strata to political power." In contrast to many other writers of his era, Beard thought that the differences of opinion on history and tactics between Booker T. Washington and W. E. B. DuBois were of great historical significance.[53]

On this issue, racism, the Beards ranged themselves with such white humanitarians as Jane Addams; William English Walling, the socialist editor of *Independent* whose writing they admired; Mary White Ovington, the social worker; and O. G. Villard. These people tended to attribute the problems of blacks to the hostile climate created by white racism.[54] And yet, in the enormous mass of the Beards' writings, these few lines do not, as Otis Graham has remarked of the social justice progressives in general, "add up to serious attention to the condition of blacks." The progressives—and, among those on the left, the Beards—"had more pressing business than the welfare of the Negro."[55]

Charles Beard explained privately that he aimed in *Contemporary American History* to "give the economic interpretation without calling it such. . . . Battles to the background. Mere talkee facts in Congress ditto . . . and the ordinary political history in a back place."[56] In this book he presented for the first time many of the bold generalizations which would become famous as part of *The Rise of American Civilization* (1927). For example, describing the aftermath of the Civil War, he wrote that "the scepter of power" had "passed definitively from the masters of slaves to the masters of 'free laborers' . . . the old contest between agrarianism and capitalism now took on new vigor." In postbellum America, the character of political leadership had also changed. "Orator-statesmen" had yielded power and authority to "businessmen-negotiators." The latter had refused to learn the lesson of Bismarck's Germany and to put off discontented workers with social legislation. Aided by the Supreme Court, the "businessmen-negotiators" had implemented their belief in the greatest freedom possible for private property. They had ignored, Beard said, "the great intangible social property created by community life."[57]

A "turning point" had been the campaign of 1896, in which the "real" battle had not been over the monetary issue. It had been in fact "a conflict between great wealth and the lower, middle, and working classes, which had hitherto been recognized only in obscure circles." In Beard's view, 1896 had been the first expression of mass politics in the United States. "Terror" had been, he thought, a major aspect of this election—"terror from above" created by Republicans with their vision of factories closing and "terror from below" developed by the Democrats' stirring of "class feeling." Yet, when answering the question Why did the Republicans win?, Beard reverted to an explanation that might well have come from the lips of his father William Henry Beard: "the silver issue could not stand the test of logic and understanding." Beard had once again evaded the task of producing an explanation. The chapter, for all its bold rhetoric and promise, was weak.[58]

According to Beard, McKinley's election had enabled the conservative interests "to further down their opponents by employing that ancient political device 'a vigorous foreign policy' to divert the public mind from domestic difficulties." Here too was a theme that would appear again and again in Beard's writing on the failure of domestic reform. Why did the public accept this diversion? Beard gave the curious answer that "the American people enjoy wars beyond measure, if the plain facts of history are allowed to speak." The public had not seen certain larger forces at work: "the inexorable necessity of the present economic system" for markets and safe investment opportunities for "surplus products and accumulated capital."[59]

Given his experiences in England and America, Beard might have been expected to devote more thought to the fact that most industrial workers in the twentieth century were immigrants and their children and thus to the circumstances that prevented the emergence of a labor party in the United States—to the importance of ethnicity, the psychology of a nation of newcomers, the problems posed for organizers by large numbers of women and children in the workforce, the violent methods used by employers to discourage and kill efforts at bargaining. Perhaps he thought that these things were obvious. Instead of discussing them, he merely recorded the changing "racial composition" of the immigration, the increasing role of women as workers outside of the home, and his disappointment with the petit bourgeois outlook of the American Federation of Labor.[60]

Beard may have grasped an important truth about the AF of L's alignment with the Democratic party when he speculated that this alliance had resulted from skilled workers thinking of themselves as small businessmen strengthening themselves against encroachments by the greater capitalists. Yet, as Eugene Genovese and the Swedish critic Elias Berg have so persuasively observed, Beard had no "theory of social process," no appropriate psychology to explain what he so astutely recorded. His chapters on the election of 1896 and on labor make this criticism valid in the utmost. Beard's background, his upbringing in the family of a wealthy farmer-banker, his Quaker conscience, and his education prepared him to deal in splendid fashion with the relationship between wealth and power in American, yet he never really got close to the society he described. His individualistic wish to stay clear of "systems," to remain outside any particular school of economic theory, made it impossible for him to ask or to answer the question Do people perceive their interests on the basis of an analysis that corresponds to objective reality or are they misled into a series of strategic estimates that do not conform to objective reality? In treating "social forces," Beard drew attention to the connection between wealth and power as no other prominent historian had done before him, but his explanations of the dynamics of social history tended all too frequently to be vague and indefinite. This was more than ambivalence. It was an active resistance to all comprehensive theories of explanation.[61]

Beard's limitations as a theorist were further revealed in a series of four lectures he delivered at Amherst College in 1916 and published in 1922 as *The Economic Basis of Politics,* having subsequently revised the last talk to comment on the Russian Revolution. Beard chose six philosophers—James Madison, Daniel Webster, and John C. Calhoun received equal space with Aristotle, Machiavelli, and Locke—each of whom, he argued, thought of forms of government as historically resulting from the distribution of various sorts of property. These philosophers, Beard urged, had been right: the history of governments in Europe and America illustrated that property in land and other forms of capital was indeed the basis of the power of groups in the government of various states.

However, beginning in the eighteenth century, the theory and practice of government had diverged. The official theory of many Western governments had come to be Rousseau's doctrine of the equality of all persons. In this theoretical view, the law represented the will of a majority of abstract individuals, regardless of their worldly interests. "All heads," said Beard, "are equal and, from the point of view of politics . . . [t]he rule of numbers is enthroned." Yet, in reality, all students of politics knew that group and class interests had endured and that there was "an inherent antagonism between our generally accepted political doctrines, and the actual facts of political life." It was obvious that "a thousand farmers and laborers, going on about their tasks" did not have as much influence in the making of a protective tariff bill as "a thousand manufacturers represented by spokesmen in the lobbies and committee rooms of the Congress of the United States." It was not the people at large but rather the determined efforts of the American Federation of Labor that had procured the exemption of trade unions from the provisions of the Sherman Anti-Trust Act. "Shall we in the field of political science," he asked, "cling to a delusion that we have to deal only with an abstract man divorced from all economic interests and group sentiments?"

Democratic suffrage in Europe and America had not destroyed "economic classes or economic inequalities." Did Beard believe that political democracy could "afford to mankind a mastery over its social destiny"? In his final lecture, revised to discuss the answers to this paradox furnished by the Russian Revolution, Beard gave no answer. Noting that American devices, such as the initiative, referendum and recall, "direct government—more head counting on the theory of numbers and abstract equality" had not given the people more power than specific interest groups and that various European schemes for reconciling interest groups and democracy such as corporatism and various shades of socialism were only "devices on paper," Beard commented briefly on the Russian experiment. And even in Russia, as Beard viewed it in 1921, efforts to socialize property had met resistance from peasants, produced conflict between government bureaucrats and other workers, and led to the recognition that "skill itself is a form of property" even if property in capital had been abolished.

Beard concluded that property could not be abolished, that the connection between material interests and politics could not be altered. Using the term *interest* in an imprecise way, he paraphrased Madison as he imagined Madison would speak of politics in the twentieth century: "a landed interest, a transport interest, a railway interest, a shipping interest, an engineering interest, a manufacturing interest, a public-official interest . . . grow up of necessity in all great societies and divide them into different classes actuated by different sentiments and views." The job of modern statesmen would be to regulate these "various and interfering interests, whatever may be the formula for the ownership of property." In other words, there was "no final solution of eternal contradictions."[62]

Beard was very sympathetic to socialism. Throughout his adult life he appears a person waiting to be a member of a socialist commonwealth. However, as a scholar, he was disappointingly timid in making clear the direction in which his analysis was supposed to lead his listeners. *The Economic Basis of Politics* was delivered from the rostrum to an audience of wealthy, conservative college students at Amherst. Beard seems to have had the Fabian notion of boring from within and to have been distinctly unwilling to present the audience more than a superficial point. Economics and politics have always been linked. Revolutions occur over the issues connected with the distribution of wealth in various societies. The audience is informed of the obvious. But they, and we in later years, are not told how the obvious works. We are not given any clue to the actual relations of direction and control among the people in American society.[63]

Walter Lippmann was exasperated by this book. He quarreled not with Beard's theme of material interest but with his lack of precision in developing his point. "Once you grant," Lippmann wrote, "as I certainly should, that an intimate connection exists between politics and property, you cannot stop until you have made up your mind what that connection is." Yet, Lippmann complained, he had not seen in Beard's work "a clear conception of how he thinks economics determine politics."

"I think he is in doubt," Lippmann continued. "I think his energy is so much occupied in pounding home a realization that there is a deep connection . . . and in the joy of depicting unsuspected connections, especially where there are sacred cows, that he has not stayed to make it clear what kind of connection this deep connection is." Moreover, in Lippmann's view, Beard was too rational. Prediction of the political behavior of people based on the distribution of property was not always possible because "He does not know how men will conceive their property. He cannot tell by analyzing the objective interests of property how those interests will be subjectively regarded." The connection between property and politics could be, Lippmann speculated, "a connection of error, as well as truth, folly no less than wisdom, superstition or technical competence."[64]

Wounded, Beard responded by denying any belief in "the economic man," an issue Lippmann had not even raised. Furthermore, Beard said he could never answer the question "as to 'how' economics ever influences politics . . . any more than the physicist can explain 'how' a dynamo makes electricity." Accusing Lippmann of splitting hairs, Beard wrote "I do not think that economics determines or even explains politics in the philosophic sense." And, he added, making a debater's retreat, "Neither does anything else that I have yet stumbled across in this vale of tears."[65]

Regardless of the existence of mass voting, the wealthy had remained in command. They had always determined "the positive limits on the kinds of things which men may agree to do." In a general way, Beard wanted to change the *language* in which people spoke of politics, defined by him as "manipulation and negotiation." He wanted less talk of voting statistics and more discussion of power and its sources: property, money, labor, contracts, securities—in short, of those material aspects of the political process over which educated citizens in a democracy might hope to secure rational control, acting in the interest of what he called "the great intangible social property created by community life." Unfortunately, Beard remained unwilling to commit himself to any political system for protecting this community life. He had a busy schedule outside of his books and study. He saw his scholarship as part of a drive to educate public opinion on the social basis of the law. Yet, he presented the fact of the power of wealth without any clues as to how such power might be dethroned.[66]

6

A Confident Response
to World War

B eard had a passionate temperament but he attempted always to make
sure that passion informed without controlling his judgments. At first
he did not view World War as an obstacle to reform. On the contrary, he
joined many others in hoping that its nationalizing tendencies would be a
cleansing wave, smashing and clearing away the outmoded institutions, arrangements, and habits of thought that resisted needed social changes. However, he did not speak the messianic language of the Wilsonians. It was
possible to argue that German "autocracy" had to be stopped without supporting the concept of saving the world for some nobler system. Aware of
the ruthlessness of Allied imperialisms, he hoped that the war would finish
this form of exploitation too. Finally, he sought, by setting a dramatic example, to dissociate patriotic support of the war from the repression of civil
liberties that accompanied it. He did not act out of a naive and unreflective
optimism; his life during this period exemplified a feeling of confidence, a
certainty that the world was not beyond the control of competent citizens.

Although the outbreak of war in August 1914 had come as a "horrible
surprise," Beard's sympathies were always frankly, vigorously, and unambig-
uously with England and France. Having no deep moral aversion to war, he
never supported President Wilson's policy of neutrality toward the conflict.
In the autumn of 1914, the acting president of City College forbade him to
speak there again on the war because Beard had given a rousing speech that,

in his words, had "attacked the Central Empires as responsible for that war." While others had cherished hopes for peace in 1914 and 1915, Beard later said that he had taught "the truth, that war has been one of the most tremendous factors in the origin of the State and the progress of mankind."[1]

"Millions of Americans," he supposed in a speech published in May 1916, "would give their life blood to prevent the establishment of [a Prussian state] on these shores. In this [he added with tongue in cheek] I mean no breach of neutrality. With due scientific calm and without expressing any preference in the matter I think I am stating accurately the opinions of most of my countrymen."[2] In March 1917, after the Germans resumed submarine warfare and sank the first of several American merchant ships in British waters, with tears in his eyes Beard told a class at Columbia that "the history of the world" had been altered. "It will now be impossible," he related, "for the United States to stay out of the war. German autocracy will have to be destroyed."[3]

As he had been skeptical toward Wilson's expressed longing for an economy of smaller units, so Beard was never enthusiastic about the President's particular dramatization and explanation of the questions of foreign policy and peace-making thrust forward by the war. Throughout the war he maintained an independent, often critical attitude toward Wilson's diplomacy. In 1916, when *The New Republic* and its stable of intellectuals, including Walter Lippmann, Herbert Croly, Walter Weyl, Felix Frankfurter, Francis Hackett, Randolph Bourne, Harold Stearns, and John Dewey, were converted to Wilson's position—some by his domestic policies, some by hopes for continued neutrality and peace, and some, according to Charles Forcey, by hopes of eventually going to war—Beard, with Henry Stimson and Willard Straight, had voted for Charles Evans Hughes. Hughes supported "preparedness" and also, in important contrast to Wilson, a national woman suffrage amendment.[4]

Before Wilson's dramatic announcement of support for a League to Enforce Peace in May 1916 Beard had speculated that a League of Nations "composed of lawyers and diplomats," instead of "delegates elected by the people of the nations they represent," would simply repeat the "hopeless and helpless condition" of the Hague Court.[5] When the President made his celebrated appeal for "peace without victory" on 22 January 1917, Beard commented to a reporter from *The New York Times* that the speech was "very general—not much of a basis for negotiation" and that, unless Wilson were acting on the basis of information from one of the belligerents, he was "just preaching a sermon, just a sermon." Wilson's suggestion that an enduring peace could be founded only on world recognition of the principle that governments derive all just powers from the consent of the governed prompted Beard to ask sarcastically "Does it mean an independent Ireland? What about Alsace-Lorraine? What about Bohemia? What about Croatia and the scores of little nations in the Balkans? What about India? What about Haiti and Santo Domingo, where the United States is ruling according to President Wilson's orders?"[6]

When the President proclaimed "armed neutrality" on 26 February 1917, in the face of Germany's renewed use of submarines, Beard remarked that he favored "more drastic action" and that he thought that "this country should definitely align itself with the Allies and help eliminate Prussianism from the earth."[7]

Following the declaration of war on Germany and Austria in April 1917, like hundreds of his fellow academicians Beard rushed to offer his services to the government. At a hearing on production and conservation of food supplies he volunteered to coordinate farmers in Connecticut on behalf of the national effort: "I think there are many men of middle age who are not in the military [age] limit who are anxious to do something and be of service. I know that university men—pardon the personal allusion, but I should be glad myself if I could be of service as a resident in that community, to put myself absolutely at the service of the Government without any cost." He added confidently that he "could raise an army in New England and New York of men who would be willing, without any cost to the Government, to do what they could do in forwarding the scheme."[8]

Beard's zeal to "be of service" found employment in the Civic and Educational Cooperation Division of the Committee on Public Information, a section headed by the historian Guy Stanton Ford. Along with Carl Becker, Sidney B. Fay, J. Franklin Jameson, and others, Beard contributed anonymously to *The War Cyclopaedia,* a "handbook for ready reference on the Great War" edited by the prominent historians Frederick L. Paxon, Edwin S. Corwin, and Samuel B. Harding. Many reform-minded intellectuals considered the CPI a superb opportunity to advance social progress and extend democratic concern for labor, women, and the victims of modern industrial society. Collectivism necessitated by the war, they hoped, would be supported after the war by a spiritually awakened public interest. "American democracy, or Americanism," Stephen Vaughn has concluded, "was to be the common denominator, the ideological cement, a secular religion, to unify an increasingly pluralistic society." Beard shared this enthusiasm.[9]

Though he staunchly upheld the war effort, Beard viewed the necessities of diplomacy dispassionately. He called for "poise, cold-bloodedness, and a Machiavellian disposition to see things as they are and to deal with them as they are—whether we like them or not." Previously he had criticized Wilson's moralistic diplomacy in Mexico; now he again censured the President in a letter to the *New Republic* in June 1917. "A painful consciousness of the rectitude of our intentions and the purity of our purposes" was, he said bluntly, "more likely to be a nuisance than a service." The "pat little phrase 'liberty against autocracy'" was, he commented, "more like to deceive ourselves than the Germans." It would "settle nothing."[10]

Words could not replace deeds in completing what Beard saw as the twin tasks of diplomacy in the spring of 1917: first, to break the union of the "Hohenzollern military caste and the German masses whose radical leaders" he was convinced were "Social Democrats" and, second, to convince the Russian revolutionaries that "the things they held dear" were "really at stake in the eastern trenches." Because of the American record of imperialism in the Orient, "our Philippine policies, and our enterprises in the Caribbean," Beard thought these tasks would be rendered difficult. Moreover, there was the fact of Lord Hugh Cecil's recent announcement that Great Britain planned to keep the German colonies. Thus it was imperative, Beard argued, to make clear to the Germans at the beginning of American participation in the war "that the people of the United States" would "not shed one drop of blood to enlarge the British empire" and that Americans did "not contemplate another peace like that of 1763 or 1815." For the moment, late in the spring of 1917, Beard wanted the United States to endorse the Russian formula, "peace without annexations and indemnities."[11]

As for many others, Beard's fear of a German victory intensified following the draconian treaty of Brest Litovsk in March 1918. "A modified and moderate plea against a peace at Russia's cost" would be the best thing, he wrote to Frank Tannenbaum, a student, "but, my dear Sir, we may have to thank God for any kind before the German gets through with mankind. Personally, I am not worrying so much about Russia as the possible triumph of the German War Lord's outfit."[12]

When the revolutionary government of Russia published the secret treaties, Beard's doubts as to the high purposes of the Allies were confirmed. In July 1918 he still wrote of the "justice of the cause for which America took up arms," but he was saddened and disheartened by reports of the terrors of warfare in the trenches. "All things" were "relative in this vale of tears. If we will adhere only to the perfect good, then we shall always be floating around in realms adjoining the kingdom of madness." Half-heartedly he added that Wilson had perhaps done some good by expressing his opinions and using his authority to weave "revolutionary concepts of national life and government and international relations . . . into the very warp and woof of the world's thinking."[13]

The Beards were part of a group including old Columbia friends, such as Robinson, Dewey, Michael Pupin, and Seligman, who announced on 27 November 1918 that they had formed the League of Free Nations Association. During the summer of 1918 Charles had led a seminar at the Columbia University Club on Wilson's alternatives for peace. The group had hoped to construct a statement of liberal principles for general public discussion. The manifesto of the League of Free Nations Association reflected the work of the seminar and illustrated that a number of people were disillusioned with the Allied cause before the Peace Conference, that they doubted the President's ability to meet the issues, and that their interpretation of the war was already the more sophisticated one of trade and imperial rivalries, as opposed to the interpretation based solely upon German military and political ambition.

Specifically, the group supported four principles which were part of the Fourteen Points: first, that no State accord to one neighbor privileges not accorded to others; second, that "investments and concessions in backward countries should be placed under international control" with no special economic privileges being granted to States exercising authority in non-self-governing territories; third, that goods and persons of all States should be transported on equal terms in waterways, railroads, roads and harbors; and finally that landlocked states must be guaranteed access to the sea on equal terms with maritime states.[14]

Unlike Wilson, the group expressed skepticism about a League of Nations that might be "an immense bureaucratic union of Governments instead of a democratic union of peoples." To forestall this result, the League of Free Nations Association suggested that "the elements of (a) complete publicity and (b) effective popular representation must be insisted upon." Essential to peace in the future was some surrender of national sovereignty. The Association suggested that the wartime framework of cooperation among the Allies in the distribution of military resources, shipping, food, raw materials, and finance should be continued in the postwar period, thus providing "the groundwork for a new world economic order." As Charles De Benedetti has pointed out, the social scientists and social workers of the LFNA were confident that an international effort to manage "the fragile interdependence of modern industrial civilization" could succeed. Democracy and nationalism could be preserved "by substituting social scientific calculability for irresponsible violence."[15]

The New York Times did not hesitate to associate this call for "a new world economic order" with Beard and his view of history. "New ideas rule," an editorial writer announced. "The revelation of the economic interpretation of history supersedes the law and the prophets of the ante-Marxian days." The League of Free Nations Association, in the eyes of *The Times*, was a "League for the resuscitation of German Commerce at the Expense of the Allies." It revolved, suggested *The Times*, "into the hackneyed Socialist theory that all wars are caused by capitalist competition for foreign markets." Those who still cherished "a suspicion that certain factors in the German mentality had more to do with bringing on this War than the inevitable necessities of Anglo-German trade rivalry" were being attacked.[16]

Beard did not comment explicitly on the Treaty of Versailles. Years later, he privately expressed his disappointment that Wilson had not "placed before Lloyd George and Clemenceau the vital questions of an independent mind, which he could have done forcefully." Instead, he had "remained *just a professor* after all." But the failure belonged not only to Wilson but also to "the American professors of his expert loyal guard," the Inquiry, who had not reminded him of his "'*Mission*'" to think independently. At home, as in Paris, too many intellectuals had not been critical. They had been "full of wonder and admiration for W.W.—*'one of our boys made it.'*" Only J.M. Keynes had spoken up for "*'the* university'" by early pointing out that the reparations demanded from Germany were completely impractical.[17]

Among those on the left who supported the war there was fervent expectation that in the aftermath society would be "reconstructed"—the metaphorical reference to the years after the Civil War was intended by a generation who still used it as a point of reference—in a collectivist fashion. Beard saw the war as a crucible into which outmoded political science as a "study of constitutions, statutes, and judicial decisions," stale economics as "a millowner's apology," and social economy as "the ambulance of capitalism gathering up the wrecks of industrial anarchy and finding its hope in charity rather than sound public economy" would be thrown and crushed beyond repair. The war would accelerate the tendency to see "the problems of political science . . . as problems of power, not of mere head-counting or judging in accordance with duly constituted rules of law." Although Beard noticed the prominence in the war effort of people who had not been concerned in prewar days with popular battles, he took heart from the fact that the Council of National Defense had representatives of capital, labor, shipping, transportation, and retailing. Women were emerging as "political people" unwilling to "permit men to do their thinking for them in the manner of the grand old patrons." There were "books too numerous to mention" that emphasized "the place of economic rivalry in international relations." John R. Commons and others were preparing "the first worthy history of labor in the United States." To the war Beard ascribed the triumph of pluralism. It was "here to remain."[18]

During 1918, although he expressed an ever-mounting concern about the widespread depredations of civil liberty, Beard continued to hope that the war would produce the longed-for redistribution of national wealth. "Up to the present time," he wrote in 1918, "the work of democracy" had been "to conquer and control institutions already made by superior classes." Now democracy was at work on economic instititions. The War Industries Board, which was setting priorities for "gigantic railway systems" and "huge industrial concerns" was the beginning of economic democracy. The Rockefellers, Morgans, Vanderbilts, and Harrimans had been, he argued, "creative pioneers," and now democracy was attempting to subject their "magnificent economic structures" to "public purposes."[19]

The war brought an explosion to Columbia, as Beard, in a fury, resigned from the faculty in October 1917. It was a gesture of commitment to those values of honor, decency, trust, and freedom of thought the repressive leadership of the university had sacrificed in its drive for conformity. However, the struggle with what Beard termed "the inner administration" antedated the war. First there had been the tussle over the Ruggles professorship in 1912. The Department of Public Law, led by Beard, had backed Frank Goodnow to replace Burgess when he retired. Despite President Nicholas Murray Butler's frequent talk of faculty control of matters relating to appointment and tenure, Goodnow had been passed over in favor of a colorless corporate lawyer handpicked by Burgess. "This was the way," Beard wrote disgustedly, "in which the first important vacancy in the Faculty of Political Science was filled after my connection with the institution."[20]

Beard had encountered the trustees themselves after his speech at the Astor Hotel on 21 April 1916 to the National Conference on Community Centers. A few weeks before this meeting, a speaker at an evening gathering at a public school in New York City was alleged to have uttered the words "to hell with the flag." Some of the speakers preceding Beard at the Conference on Community Centers had therefore argued for censorship and even for closing the public schools to community forums. Beard replied that "even if a speaker at a . . . meeting in a New York school had said 'To hell with the flag' such an exclamation should not be made the excuse for closing the schools to responsible parties for the discussion of public questions." The *New York World,* a Hearst paper, accused Beard in a headline of endorsing the infamous sentiment "To hell with the flag."[21]

A week later Beard was summoned to appear before the Committe on Education of the University's Board of Trustees and was surprised to find that, after he had explained the flag speech, the committee began to discuss whether or not "the government of the United States had been founded 'in disrespect of existing authority.'" His economic interpretations of the origins of the public law had displeased the trustees, and they had apparently seized this occasion to haul him in. One of the trustees, Frederick R. Coudert, told a shocked Beard that "in his opinion the American Revolution had been in fact a revolt against usurpation of authority by a German king on the English throne." At this point Beard suggested adjournment, but Coudert and William E. Bangs, the committe chairman, began to deliver a general harangue against Beard's subversive teachings on the Constitution, Coudert asking the seething Beard if he knew that it was generally understood that his teachings were "calculated to inculcate disrespect for American institutions, particularly for the Supreme Court of the United States."[22]

E. R. A. Seligman, who was present, tried to lower the tension of the meeting by suggesting that the trustees' main concern was really to defend Columbia against further barrages from the sensation-seeking press. Beard rose to leave; as he did so Bangs warned him to advise his departmental colleagues against teaching "calculated to inculcate any disrespect for American institutions, and particularly the Supreme Court." Beard saw that his support of Goodnow's plea for criticism of the court was, in the minds of these guardians of the university, a major sin.

Back at the department, Beard gave a rousing account of the trustees' warning. This report was heralded by "a shout of derision," one of his colleagues inquiring "whether Tammany Hall and the pork barrel were not American institutions!" At this moment, led by Beard, the faculty was ready to support him by passing a resolution against "doctrinal inquisitions" conducted by persons outside the department, but Dean Frederick Woodbridge assured the group that the trustees had "learned a lesson." Also, he cautioned the faculty to think ahead to the future of President Butler, who was popular. Butler's prewar enthusiasm for pacifism, said Woodbridge, had made the trustees suspicious. Butler himself urged Beard to forget this incident—which, of course, Beard did not do, although he did let the matter drop. To a colleague Beard wrote sarcastically that, while he regarded the recent affair as a "clear breach of the principle of academic freedom," several of his colleagues in the Faculty of Political Science had taken the opposite stance: since he had been "allowed" to retain his position "it was a 'gain for academic freedom.'" Beard stopped pressing the issue at this time because of lack of support from his peers.[23]

When the faculty learned a year later, in March 1917, that the trustees had after all established a committee to review what was being taught, Beard successfully marshaled forces on the Faculty of Political Science. Under his leadership the faculty promptly and unanimously passed a resolution stating that they would not, as individuals or as a group, "lend any countenance to such an inquiry." The trustees then compromised to the extent of promising to cooperate with a Committee of Nine, which ostensibly would represent the faculty in all disputes over what was being taught. In reality, as John Dewey pointed out when he resigned from the committee, it overwhelmingly represented Columbia's administration, composed as it was of six deans appointed by the administration and only three faculty members.[24]

These conformist currents at Columbia were strengthened by the declaration of war against Germany in April 1917. That spring, the administration advised the Department of Political Science to drop Leon Fraser from its rolls. Fraser had been a protégé of President Butler in the Association for International Conciliation, and Beard had resisted his appointment to the Faculty of Political Science in the first place, on the grounds that Fraser was unqualified for the post. Butler, however, had forced the appointment of his young follower. When Fraser came up for reappointment, Beard led the faculty in renominating him for his position, but this time Fraser was dropped from the rolls, on the assumption that during fall 1917 the war would reduce the number of students in the department. Fraser's pacifism was now an embarrassment to Butler, but instead of being satisfied with the department's excuse for cutting Fraser, he issued a warning that Fraser was never to be renominated, even if the number of students in the department should warrant his re-employment.[25]

To Beard, Butler was practicing the worst kind of disloyalty and immorality. Having promoted the career of a younger man, he was now abandoning him when his views, formerly endorsed by Butler himself, were under attack. "In truth," wrote Beard, "if not in theory, Dr. Fraser was expelled from the College without notice or hearing," despite the fact that he had been inspired by Dean Frederick P. Keppel and President Butler to engage in pacifist activities in the first place. Keppel and Butler were men without honor, for "they should at least have demanded and insisted upon having a full and fair hearing of the charges against their youthful adherent, especially as those charges grew out of his 'pacifist' teachings."[26]

In his commencement address of 6 June 1917 President Butler announced a firm policy of restriction on academic freedom for the duration of the war. "What had been tolerated before [was] intolerable now. What had been wrongheadedness was now sedition. What had been folly was now treason," and there would be "no place in Columbia University" for those people who counseled opposition to the laws of the United States or who acted, spoke, or wrote "treason."[27]

In accordance with this warning, the firings began in the autumn of 1917. In October, against the recommendations of the Committee of Nine, the trustees summarily terminated the appointments of James M. Cattell and Henry Wadsworth Longfellow Dana. Cattell was bold and radical, a renowned psychologist who had long been despised by the trustees, by Butler, and by many of his colleagues on the faculty. In 1913 he had written *University Control*, a book in which he advocated a restructuring of universities, a taking away of power from administrators and trustees, and the creation of a "democracy of scholars." He repeatedly referred to professors as "'clerks' of the administration" and, according to one historian, "implied that if they *really* were 'gentlemen'—i.e. principled men—they would rise and demand their rightful place in university government." He was famous and infamous among his fellow faculty members for having circulated an ironic private memorandum suggesting that, since Butler had announced that the Faculty Club was to be taken away for other uses, his house—"erected at a cost of $300,000 from funds given for education"—be donated to the faculty for a new club. The memorandum had also characterized Butler as "our many-talented and much-climbing president"; its release to the press by an enemy of Cattell had caused a new move among the trustees to oust him. Cattell was an unpleasant thorn, and the patriotic excuse for pulling him was a letter he had written to members of the House of Representatives on 23 August 1917, while the conscription bill was pending. The letter had not opposed conscription per se, but rather the sending of conscripts to fight in Europe against their will.

Henry Wadsworth Longfellow Dana, a young professor of English, also came within Butler's definition of treason—one who was "not with whole heart and mind and strength committed to fight with us to make the world safe for democracy." Dana had been active in the Anti-Militarism League in opposition to the conscription law during June 1917, before it was passed by Congress, and afterward had joined the radical-pacifist People's Council for Peace and Democracy and had spent the summer of 1917 working for it.[28]

Early in October Beard got word that the trustees had scheduled "another doctrinal inquisition" in the social sciences. In Beard's words, they were proposing "to take advantage of the state of war to drive out or humiliate or terrorize every man who held progressive, liberal, or unconventional views on political matters in no way connected with the war." Columbia, he thought, "was to be reduced below the level of a department store or factory." On 9 October 1917, Beard lectured as usual to a class of seventy students. Then he announced that he had given his last lecture at Columbia. The students, at first silent, rose and applauded for twenty-five minutes, while Beard wept.[29]

Hailed by *The New York Times* as "Columbia's Deliverance" from radicalism, Beard's resignation expressed his growing dismay over the wartime use of the cloak of patriotism to smother free speech.[30] The efforts of the trustees to control opinions expressed within the university had placed a man of his temper in an impossible situation. One of his former students wrote: "Professor Beard could not endure the imputation that he was an active, enthusiastic supporter of the war because it was good for his health, for his salary and for his advancement in Columbia. Nor can any of the rest of us in whose behalf he uttered his ringing challenge."[31]

At the center of Beard's celebrated letter of resignation was the failure of the university. It should have been the guardian of free inquiry and liberty of opinion. Instead it had proved to be just another church whose members were more concerned with upholding one version of the truth than with tolerating diverse opinion. "We stand," Beard said, "on the threshold of an era which will call for all the emancipated thinking that America can command." Many disagreed with his personal opinions on the war, but their views were not going to be changed "by curses or bludgeons," but rather by "arguments addressed to their reason and understanding." A patriot connected with an institution controlled by trustees who had "no standing in the world of education" and who were "reactionary and visionless in politics, narrow and medieval in religion" would be suspect in the eyes of his countrymen. Support of the war, as well as independent thought in the days of reconstruction to follow, "must come from men whose disinterestedness" was "above all suspicion, whose independence" was "beyond all doubt, and whose devotion to the whole country, as distinguished from a single group," was "above all question."[32]

On behalf of the beleaguered trustees, Annie Nathan Meyer replied to Beard in *The New York Times* on 13 October. Her letter showed that Beard had been right to draw attention to issues of academic freedom which transcended the particular moment of the war. "By all means let us have our radical colleges," wrote Meyer,

> our places of learning where one knows that every social law will be demolished, where every established custom will be picked to pieces in the crude alembic of the crass youth; let us have institutions of learning where marriage is laughed

at, religion ridiculed, feminism fostered, picketing apotheosized, but is it not a little too much to expect that the most conservative men and women of the nation be asked longer to cloak these institutions with their own respectability! If the radicals demand colleges, let them have them, but stop letting them run away with our staid, established ones because trustees and parents are too white-livered to demand a halt, to uncover this bogey of academic freedom. [33]

Although Columbia witnessed a few days of intense turmoil, mass meetings, and petition campaigns among students and faculty who were deeply distressed both by Beard's leaving and by the conditions that had provoked the act, only a few colleagues joined him in exile. Few could afford emotionally or mone-tarily to act on their convictions, if they had any. Few were confident of finding another place. Seligman, who had all along used his standing with the faculty to conduct what Thomas Reed Powell called "a supine 'diplomacy'" continued in October to attempt to mediate the troubles between faculty, administration, and trustees. When Beard resigned, Seligman accused him of "stabbing the [faculty] in the back" and "strongly counselled complete inaction on the part of the Faculty." [34] Moreover, Seligman tried to placate angry colleagues by leading the Committee of Nine, from which John Dewey had resigned after the recommendations of this committee in the cases of Cattell and Dana had been ignored, to endorse a new tribunal, to be headed by Butler—Dr. Alexander Mackintosh Butcher, Randolph Bourne called him—and to be composed of nominees from the faculty appointed by the deans. The new body was to hear all evidence in "doctrinal controversies." [35] Carol S. Gruber has pointed out that Butler and the trustees could use patriotism as a weapon to accomplish their objectives among the faculty "because the Co-lumbia faculty, with few exceptions, agreed that Cattell and Dana as well, deserved to be fired because his activities were injurious to the university." [36]

Henry R. Mussey, who taught economics at Barnard, was among the few who left Columbia at this time. "I'm resigning," he wrote to Seligman. "Co-lumbia has tipped its hand in the Beard matter. The faculty inaction is wrong, dreadfully, clearly, fundamentally wrong. . . . Your arguments leave me cold and the day will come when true friends of freedom will mourn in sack clothes and ashes." Ellery C. Stowell, an assistant professor of international law and a supporter of the war who was also disgusted by the failure of faculty members to rally for each other's academic freedom, left, and Will Durant was dropped from his post as an extension lecturer after a passionate speech at a rally protesting the circumstances of Beard's resignation. [37]

Beard could afford to leave Columbia financially and psychologically. He was not shedding a needed identity. It was a decision he apparently never regretted, for he had never thought of himself primarily as an academician engaged in producing more academicians. His work at the Bureau of Municipal Research, his writing, and his variety of reform activities were more than enough. Perhaps he remembered his childhood explusion from Spiceland Academy. He had survived that, been rendered acceptable and more.

A dozen years later Beard speculated that, even in the absence of repressive trustees, universities did not provide the best atmosphere for creative thought. The university meant, he mused,

> too many charming friends who must not be offended; too many temporal ne-
> gotiations that call for discreet management; too many lectures to be delivered;
> too many promotions requiring emphasis on the amenities of life rather than on
> its thinking processes; too many alumni eager to apply in 1928 what they learned
> in 1888; too much routine, not enough peace; too much calm, not enough
> passion; above all too many sacred traditions that must be conserved; too many
> theories, not enough theory; too many books, not enough strife of experience;
> too many students, not enough seekers.[38]

"It is certainly a relief," he told an old acquaintance from Indiana, "to be out of Mr. Butler's asylum." To Henry Mussey, who had followed him out of Columbia, Beard wrote a kindly and enthusiastic letter, telling him of his "firm conviction that the drift of the world" was "swift and deep" in the direction they had taken. "Ruling classes everywhere" had attempted "to maintain their power by owning the press, the pulpit, and the university," but they were "beginning to realize," Beard hoped, that they could "save themselves only through justice, discussion, science, and reason applied to our economic and social life." They had been right to resign, to call "for a hearing, for moderation, and for civil instead of lynch law," Beard told Mussey. "If we are wrong," he concluded, "then it matters little anyway, for you and I are not interested in keeping a nicely feathered cot in a doll's house."[39]

It was typical of Beard not to develop a theory to explain intolerance. Rather, he actively combated it. He may have wished not to examine the conflict between his participation during the summer of 1917 in a bureaucratic effort to manipulate public opinion in support of the war and his own rationalist demand for freedom of speech, but probably he believed that his work for the Committee on Public Information involved information and not propaganda.

After he departed from Columbia, Beard campaigned against the suppression of civil liberties on numerous occasions. In December 1917, two months after his resignation, along with John Dewey, Leonora O'Reily of the Women's Trade Union League, and John Boyle, he protested the firing of three teachers at DeWitt Clinton High School in New York City, charging publicly that the school board members, who had ostensibly dismissed the teachers for "holding views subversive of good discipline and of undermining good citizenship," were, in truth, anti-Semites.[40] In June 1918 he publicly decried the postal censorship. That autumn he posted bail for Charles Strangeland, who had been jailed for violating the law against trade with the enemy after a customs officer found letters to his wife, the Danish novelist Karen M. Strangeland, in the luggage of a Swedish army captain bound for Europe.

By October 1918 these actions had made him suspect in the eyes of the United States Army's bureaucracy. Two of his collaborative texts were banned from army training camps. The same month, Beard mocked the government by concentrating, in a review of a three-volume history of the English Constitution, on the thirty pages dealing with domestic hysteria over sedition during the Napoleonic wars: "In reading over this remarkable . . . story of how English liberties have been won, many will find cause for gratification that in our trying age we have escaped the evils which marred the domestic life of England during the Napoleonic wars."[41]

In every period Beard detected "supreme issues." By January 1919, after the armistice, "the supreme issue" was free speech. The time had come, he urged, for freeing political prisoners "whose offense was to retain Mr. Wilson's pacifist views after he abandoned them," for restoring the right of asylum to political refugees, and for releasing American citizens held in the interest of foreign governments because they interpreted President Wilson's "'liberty, self-government, and undictated development' to mean a curtailment of British dominion in some parts of the earth."[42]

A week after this criticism of the government's treatment of dissenters appeared, Beard was cited in the record of a Senate committee investigating German propaganda as one of sixty-two men and women who were part of movements that had hindered the battle against the Central Powers. During testimony on Bolshevism and socialism, the Military Intelligence Service had furnished their names. To Senator Lee S. Overman, chairman of the committee, Beard wrote a passionate letter, published in *The New York Times*, describing his support of intervention from the beginning of the conflict in Europe, his services to the government during American participation, and his position that he had never been "'too proud to fight.'"[43]

Under attack, Beard promoted free inquiry more vigorously. He criticized New York City's Department of Education for publishing a patriotic syllabus of the World War that was hostile to the Russian Revolution and that supported universal military service as a permanent public policy, even though public opinion was far from unanimous on these issues. "Could Daniel Webster Teach in New York's Public Schools?," asked John W. Bradford, alias Charles A. Beard, in the pages of the *Nation* during August 1919, the summer of the "Red Scare." A teacher had been dismissed for allegedly teaching the economic interpretation of history. "It is certain," Beard announced with delighted irony,

> that no less than one year after Marx was born, Daniel [Webster] did deliver two speeches in which he came perilously near that awful doctrine at which Nicholas Murray Butler (wearing a Hohenzollern Red Eagle of the Second Class and an Oxford gown) makes a semi-annual tilt for the edification of his subalterns, if not for the pleasure of some one who might give to Columbia University a new gate, a telescope or another piece of Benjamin Franklin's furniture.[44]

Of the Lusk bills, one requiring public school teachers in New York state to take an oath of loyalty, one denying licenses to private schools in the state whose curriculums had not been approved by the Board of Regents, and a third "empowering the courts to remove from the ballot the name of any party whose ideals did not confirm to those of the United States" (all passed by the New York State Legislature after the famous expulsion of the Socialist members in 1919), Beard wrote that there was "no ground for discouragement." The final result of repression and censorship might be "the same kind of stoppage in the course of thinking that occurred in 1789."[45]

The war-inspired restrictions on civil liberties were a searing experience for Beard. It became for him an *idée fixe* that war and free speech could not coexist, and this was an important reason he did not support American entry into World War II. War meant the death of creative, independent thinking. The Committee on Public Information became in later writings "the grand committee on public mystification." Mary and Charles Beard later analyzed the "immense inquisitorial activities" of the war years as partly a conservative reaction to ideas that had come despite the war. "As in England during the period of the French Revolution, the occasion of the war which called for patriotic duties" had been "seized by emotional conservatives as an opportunity to blacken the character of persons whose opinions they feared and hated."[46]

Studying the "contradiction between the role of disinterested scholars dedicated to the pursuit of truth and that of patriotic citizens committed to supporting their country in a time of grave national crisis," historian Carol S. Gruber concluded that both institutions of higher learning and their faculties were engaged in a "quest for legitimacy." Institutions and men were trying to demonstrate their "'usefulness'" through participation in the war effort. Within the several academic disciplines, professors were looking to end their "uncertainty about the nature and function of knowledge—the relation between facts and values and their articulation with and significance for the realm of social action."[47] This is a compelling model and may well explain the activities of faculty members around the country who served their government and acquiesced in the restrictions many universities placed on academic freedom during the war. But it does not explain the behavior of Charles Beard.

John Dewey, James Harvey Robinson, and Beard were all supporters of the war who believed initially that it would be a force for reform at home, a nationalizing and collectivizing experience that might result in the long-awaited arrival of social democracy. In their view, the forces of reaction had captured the war spirit and used it for their own purposes, but this had not been inevitable. These men were confident people. They cannot be described as "uncertain," and they cannot be described as thinking of themselves as a part of what Gruber has spoken of as "an infantile and insecure profession."[48] Certainly, the key to Beard's behavior was a massive *confidence* in his ability to be useful. He went to Washington offering to raise up an army of farmers for food production in New England! He felt competent, qualified to "be of service." Randolph Bourne captured this quality when he wrote in "Twilight of Idols" that "A high mood of confidence and self-righteousness moves them all, a keen sense of control over events that makes them eligible to discipleship under Professor Dewey's philosophy. They are all hostile to impossibilism, to apathy, to any attitude that is not a cheerful and brisk setting to work to use the emergency to consolidate the gains of democracy."[49]

Gruber points out that to support or not support the war was a political judgment and that one cannot charge the intellectuals with betrayal merely for making a political judgment. But she argues further that even supporters of the war could conceivably have chosen "a posture of critical independence from official policies and positions." Thus they might have provided a socially valuable and "sorely lacking principled defense of the very ideals and freedoms in whose name the war was being fought."[50]

Even though he did offer himself in service to the government and even though he did write for a branch of the Committee on Public Information, it can be argued that Beard attempted, not always successfully, to maintain precisely that posture of critical independence the general absence of which Gruber deplores. Beard did criticize the President's sermonizing and his imperialistic policies in Mexico and the Caribbean; he was active in an independent effort, The League of Free Nations Association, to influence the peace treaty, and, unlike Dewey, in writing and action he was never observed *justifying* intolerance and repression.[51] When Columbia University conformed to the prevailing hysteria against those who were critical of the war, or of aspects of the war such as conscription, Beard left in what might be described as an extreme gesture of "critical independence from official policies and positions." Having made this gesture, he did not abandon the battle against censorship and repression. He continued to defend democracy.

7

Experiments and Conclusions,
1919–1922

T he New School for Social Research was probably the idea of James
Harvey Robinson, although the institution that evolved was quite different from his early dream of "an intellectual club—to which all visitors of
intellectual distinction would repair and toward which all residents of intellectual distinction would gravitate." Like Beard, Robinson was disgusted with
Columbia and, although he was so popular that his classes were being held
in the largest auditorium on campus, he too left after the academic year
1918–1919.[1]

Beard and Robinson had talked during 1918 of forming a "Free School of
Political Science," presumably to furnish an antidote for the unfree state of
the discipline at Columbia. According to Beard, the fundamental purpose
of people trying to raise money for the New School in 1918 was "to establish
an institution of learning at which the social sciences may be as emancipated
from lay interference as the natural sciences." Appointment and dismissal of
faculty was to be entirely in the hands of the teaching staff, and Beard headed
a committee to secure a distinguished faculty. Alvin Johnson and Herbert
Croly of The New Republic were interested, as were Emily James Putnam,
former dean of Barnard College and a member of the faculty of history there,
and Emma Peters Smith, then the graduate adviser at Barnard. In Washington
during the summer of 1918, Alvin Johnson met Wesley Mitchell while the
two were doing economic studies for the government, and Johnson persuaded

Mitchell to join the group planning an innovation in adult education. When John Dewey returned to New York from the Far East in 1920, he too was enthusiastic about the project.[2]

European institutions furnished influential models for the designers of the New School. Croly wanted something like the *École Libre des Sciences Politiques*, adapted to American conditions. He and the others agreed that the New School must not be affiliated with any university. But what function was the new institution to perform? "The war," Croly observed in January 1918, "has helped us to realize at once what enormous resources science has placed at the disposal of the human will and the imminent danger that these resources, if not better subordinated to social purposes," might frustrate rather than promote human progress. Croly envisioned the new center as a training school for social engineers, for "men and women who were capable of dealing practically with problems of labor adjustment" and of working out "successful methods of cooperation between the managers of industry and the rank and file of the laborers." Croly's social engineers would leave the New School seeking to "end that divorce between the plain people and the experts who are capable of working out in detail better methods of social progress."[3]

Alvin Johnson, on the other hand, had more general ideas. He wanted "a true school of advanced adult education" based upon an English model such as the London School of Economics, which was, he noted, "not handicapped by mobs of beef devouring alumni, passionate about football and contemptuous of scholarship." As Johnson pointed out, Croly's theory of leadership "implied finding out what was good for the people and doing it for them. Consent? They might consent after the event." Johnson's premise was that what he called "the 'underlying population'—roughly the farmers, the manual workers, the housewives, the routine white collar workers"— were "sound and endowed with good sense" and that the advanced among them would respond to a reasonable, adult education program; that is, to "an institution for the continued education of the educated."[4]

Beard's hopes for the New School were probably closer to those of Johnson than to the ideas of Croly. However, he wanted to stress research and to take advantage of New York's splendid libraries. Robinson, for his part, was concerned to secure for the students a quantity of first-rate lecturers. There were efforts to incorporate the goals of all the planners. To satisfy Beard, three research fellows were appointed. Mitchell was to develop a research program in economic and social statistics. Croly was to plan with Robert W. Bruére, formerly of the Bureau of Municipal Research, a Labor Research Bureau that, according to Alvin Johnson's memory of it, was "to offer its services to labor unions in return for substantial fees."[5]

All the founders' wishes seemed gratified when the New School opened for the first time in spring 1919. Alvin Johnson described the evening of first registration:

The long, narrow reception room was jammed. I saw there about every liberal I knew, and a lot I had heard of. Miss Smith was writing down registrations in hectic haste, filing bills and checks under paperweights on her desk. From time to time she would jump up, wave a bill over her head, and cry, "Who gave me this twenty-dollar bill?"

A needle in a haystack. They had all been giving her twenty-dollar bills. But it was jolly.[6]

"Preliminary lectures" were offered that spring by Beard, Robinson, Thorstein Veblen, Emily James Putnam, Harold Laski, Wesley Mitchell, and Francis Elis, the literary editor of *The New Republic*. That this marvelous constellation might dim the luster of Columbia's graduate school was appreciated at once by Nicholas Murray Butler, who became the New School's most savage critic, calling the founders "a little bunch of disgruntled liberals setting up a tiny fly-by-night radical counterfeit of education."[7]

Beard was thrilled by this adventure. When Lucy Salmon, a well-known educational innovator and a member of the history department at Vassar, wrote Beard congratulating him on the new endeavor, he replied in high spirits. "I have always rather feared that you regarded me as a man with a six shooter in each boot, especially since I disturbed the calm serenity of old Oxford. Radical action grows out of both wisdom and ignorance, and I am not sure as to the chief source of my inspiration." A few days later, thanking Salmon for a reprint, he added, "I believe the time is about here to crystallize the sentiment that is now below the surface, and [to] unhorse the autocrats who are blocking the advancement of learning in American institutions."[8]

In January 1920, Robinson happily described the atmosphere at the New School in the pages of *School and Society*. For prospective students there was "no other inducement than the proffered opportunities to learn"—no degrees and no diplomas. Only "mankind and his present predicaments . . . public affairs and human organizations" were being studied—and not in separate departments of history, anthropology, psychology, biology, economics, sociology, and public law but in a "common effort." Students could speak their mind, Robinson said, about "our business system, our banks and factories and mines; about the Legion or the I.W.W.; about religion, marriage, and patriotism; about the newspapers; about the Senate and Supreme Court," topics that had riled the trustees of Columbia. The instructors, wrote Robinson, believed that "fundamental social readjustments" were "inevitable," but they were "pledged to no program of reform old or new." In their minds "facts" were "not classified . . . as safe or dangerous; radical or conservative; suitable for the young or adapted only for the old and settled." No academic hierarchy was interfering with the pursuit of disinterested truth. Only one thing was lacking, Robinson observed at the end of his description: "We can no longer refresh ourselves with 'truculent quietism,' that potent bracer upon which our class is accustomed to rely. When we fail we have only ourselves to blame. *L'école, c'est nous.*"[9]

The bright atmosphere described by Robinson was, however, rapidly darkened by disagreements among the stellar faculty. One of the early disputes was over whether or not to adopt "principles of business management" in the affairs of the institution. According to Johnson, Beard and Robinson favored "a hand-to-mouth plan. No endowment." However, an endowment was sought, and the board of trustees, concerning itself though it did only with financing and physical plant, had to seek more students by advertising for them. A "trained publicity secretary" was added to the staff, and Alvin Johnson recorded Beard's reaction when he first saw the ads: "Good God! They are selling us like a new brand of cheese."[10]

Beard was also chagrined by the idea of purchasing and renovating buildings for the school, which was done despite his protests. He had wanted (reported Harry Elmer Barnes, who lectured at the New School during its first year) "to house the New School in humble quarters located over a livery stable, garage or brewery where even the olfactory stigmata of conventional education would be effectively obscured."[11]

In spring 1920 Beard was elected to replace Robinson as chairman of the faculty, in the nonbureaucratic circumstances a post that involved the onerous task of constant negotiation with strong and obstreperous personalities such as Barnes, who was apparently very soon persona non grata to a number of other faculty members, and Veblen, who had proved a disaster as a lecturer. Croly and Robinson, moreover, quarreled openly over the main function of the school. Croly rejected Robinson's *The Mind in the Making,* which he had first offered to the New Republic Press, and Croly, referring pointedly to Robinson's emphasis on the lecture classes, started calling the New School "a mere lecture center, a one-horse Chautauqua."[12]

At the end of the year 1920–1921 the great liberal galaxy dissolved. Croly and his followers left because they thought that the Labor Research Bureau was not getting enough of the available funds. Wesley Mitchell eventually rejoined the faculty at Columbia because he decided that the graduate students there who became professional economists would have more influence on the acceptance of economics as a science than would students of the New School. Seeking an escape from the constant acrimony, Beard and Robinson left together in 1921. Alvin Johnson, the sturdy Viking from Nebraska, as he liked to think of himself, seized the helm of the reeling ship and piloted it successfully for the next quarter-century as an outstanding school of adult education for the relatively affluent. Beard did return to lecture at the New School during the 1930s, when it became the University in Exile for European scholars displaced by the fascist regimes in Germany and Italy.[13]

The New School had been an experiment close to Beard's heart, and its failure to fulfill his hopes hurt him. Albert Nock, the anarchist editor of *The Freeman,* had written a nostalgic editorial in June 1921, bemoaning the fact that the United States lacked any institutions comparable to the great medieval universities "run by the students, with only the loosest and most in-

formal organization, with little property, no examinations, no arbitrary grad-
uations, no money-grubbing president, no ignorant and meddling trustees."[14]
This editorial struck a chord in Beard's mind, and he replied to it in a letter
that is a thinly disguised obituary for his dreams relating to the New School.

Was such a "free university" possible? There was "something alluring," he
admitted "about a picture of teachers and students freely associated, vexed by
no rules for schoolboys, searching far and wide in the kingdom of the spirit."
Doubtless, medieval universities had "attracted some of the ablest minds of
the period" and had managed at the same time "to thrive without trustees or
presidents." However, he added sadly, "trustees" were "not the only limitations on the human spirit . . . when a teacher jumps from the arms of trustees
into the arms of his brethren in learning, his earthly cares are not over."

Still, Beard said, he would like to see "one real experiment in higher education in the United States." A band of teachers and students would meet in
random locations and have neither alumni associations nor "academic red
tape." Teachers would be "free to pick [their] own students from among the
applicants and to dismiss wasters and mediocrities on five minutes notice."
This institution would "necessarily be conservative" since "responsible thinking baffled by the world's complexities, never produced half-baked radicalism."
However, "why dream?" Such an institution was not going to be created in
modern America:

> The mediaeval university has had its day. People with money are practical
> people. They have little faith in the unseen, the immeasurable, and imponder-
> able. Professors are sometimes known to hanker after loaves and fishes. More-
> over, what would become of the students who risked their careers at such a
> school? Without degrees and academic authenticity, they could not find any
> place to make a living in the modern business world.

At the end of this wistful letter Beard described "the true teacher, the
restless searcher-out of things." For this person there was "a greater forum"
than the schoolroom. What this person had to say to the world could be
clothed in type, released in the lightning's flash, and sent "to all climes and
all ages. The voice," he concluded dramatically, "grows old and feeble, and
silence comes with the long night." Immortality would come from the printed
page. Had not "the printing-press, therefore, made the university obsolete for
all except those engaged in cramming candidates for degrees?"[15]

These years, 1920 and 1921, were a time of conclusions in Beard's life. After
this, he would be a prophet of the speech and the printed word: *Charles A.
Beard, Dairy Farmer*, as he was fond of signing himself, a man free to follow
his interests, to speculate, and to act upon his convictions unhampered by
the burdens of institutional life. In this period he ended his decade of work
with the Bureau of Municipal Research. To be director while he took a leave

of absence in spring 1920, perhaps to wrestle with the problems of the New School, he chose his student and friend Luther Gulick. When Beard formally resigned in July 1920, the Board of Directors named Gulick to replace him as director of the Bureau.[16]

According to Jane Dahlberg, historian of the Bureau, Beard left because, due to his reputation as a radical, he was unable to raise money. Because of this reputation he also had difficulties with the board of directors, who had wanted to suppress, as too socialistic, the Bureau's report of 1919 on New York City's transit problem, a piece of painstaking work of which Beard was justifiably proud and in which he had recommended that serious consideration be given to municipal ownership of the city's railways. Beard also believed that Nicholas Murray Butler, after Beard's stormy departure from Columbia, had persuaded the Carnegie Foundation, a major backer of the Bureau, to stop supporting it. Beard had delighted in his work with the Bureau. Once he told Raymand B. Fosdick that "this organization would be significant when all that was left of the New York Central Railroad was two streaks of rust!" However, he must have reasoned that the time had arrived for a person of more moderate reputation to be responsible for the organization's future.[17]

Looking back on his term as director, from 1918 to 1920, Beard could feel pleased at the results of his energetic leadership. He had wrestled with the city's transit problem and with the problem of chaotic food marketing in the city, which as yet did not have a central terminal with cold storage and dehydrating facilities to ensure that consumers had a choice of food in better condition than rot. There had been massive projects to educate the public about the city's budget. Especially significant and useful was the postwar report on reconstruction in New York state, prepared at the request of Governor Al Smith and regarded by most members of the Bureau as its finest product.

Beard and Robert Moses had drafted the "Summary of Recommendations" for the Commission on Reconstruction of State Government, a report calling again for what reformers had been trying to achieve for years in the state of New York: efficiently centralized government and responsible officials. Ringing with language of the Bureau, the report suggested the need for "consolidation of the officers, boards, and commissions into a few great departments," specifically that 187 agencies should be consolidated into 16; that the "power of appointment and removal" of these department heads be vested in the governor (whose term, the report recommended, should be extended to four years); that "a consolidated budget system with accounting control over spending offices" be established. The summary of the Commission's recommendations took 44 closely printed pages and was preceded by 375 pages of detailed analysis in which the governments of every other state were examined, as were each of New York state's 187 agencies. It was indeed a masterpiece of thoroughness and clarity, although, due to what his biographer charitably terms Robert Moses' "proprietary attitude" toward the report, the Bureau did not receive credit for its labors, even in those sections of the report for which it had done all the statistics and charts.[18]

More than ever, after the war Beard had wanted to spread the Bureau's methods and message throughout the nation. During the war, there had been a diversion of the Bureau's recruits into federal service. After the armistice, Beard had projected a role for the Bureau in national affairs. He had attempted unsuccessfully to symbolize the changing orientation of the Bureau by dropping "New York" from its title. Partly, of course, this new departure for the Bureau may have been expedient as a result of the refusal of Tammany mayors after 1918 to cooperate with the Bureau in its citizenly efforts to check on the work of city agencies. In any event, Beard's thinking had always had a national focus, and he probably would have chosen the new path anyway.

"No longer," he had written in 1919, would the Bureau harbor "trade secrets." Its "great questionnaires" would be made freely available, and the city that believed it could survey itself would be "encouraged to do so." The Bureau was embarking on a program of "pamphlets for laymen, handbooks for officials, and short intensive lecture and correspondence courses in special subjects." The Bureau was prepared "to make surveys anywhere on demand or to install its systems of administration."[19]

If, fifty years later, the phrase *systems of administration* is a chilling one, calling to mind the cool, impersonal bureaucratic network that surrounds us on every level, it must have sounded fresh and exciting in 1919. A competent bureaucracy was seen as one of the keys to a decent life for people in industrial society. It was the way to escape from what Beard often spoke of as the "tyranny of the rule-of-thumb." The Bolsheviks had shown, he told Raymond Fosdick in 1922, "that you can have the power of government—the symbols of sovereignty—and have nothing but dust and ashes. The sword won't do the job any more. The social engineer is the fellow. The old talk about sovereignty, rights of man, dictatorship of the proletariat, triumphant democracy and the like is pure bunk. It will not run trains or weave cloth or hold society together."[20]

After he resigned as director, Beard retained a keen interest in the Bureau's progress. As he had hoped, the Bureau and the Training School for Public Service became, in 1921, the National Institute of Public Administration, with a board of directors that included such outstanding diplomats of fund-raising as Charles E. Merriam, Robert S. Brookings, Newton D. Baker, Herbert Hoover, and Frank O. Lowden. Beard continued to regret his own inability to attract money for this institution. "I am," he wrote to Charles Merriam in 1924, "simply no good at raising money. Contact with people of cash gives me no special respect for them or their talents and nothing that I write or say seems to give them any respect for me."[21]

Two decades had elapsed since the Beards' adventures at Ruskin Hall, but they had maintained a continuous enthusiasm for workers' education. The experiment at Ruskin Hall had been an inspiration for the founding of the Rand School of Social Science on New York's Lower East Side in 1906. Rand was, as its advertising proclaimed, "an institution for the teaching of social science from the standpoint of socialism." The money came from the income from a trust donated by Mrs. Carrie Rand, the mother-in-law of the Christian Socialist George D. Herron. Charles Beard served on the original board of directors and donated his services as a lecturer there during the first two terms. Mary Beard became involved in the educational efforts of the Women's Trade Union League. In 1921 the Beards were influential in the establishment of the Workers' Education Bureau of the United States, which, modeled after an English counterpart, was designed to supervise educational work among the membership of trade unions. It was a spark that fell from the New School, where the first Workers' Education Conference was held in April 1921.[22]

As chairman of a "citizens group" supporting the Workers' Education Bureau, Beard donated $2000 to the new agency. Spencer Miller, Jr., one of Beard's students, became secretary of the Bureau, and Beard gave him a "traveling fellowship" so that Miller could study at first hand similar projects in England.[23] In 1924, the unions in the American Federation of Labor voted a per capita tax on their members to support the Bureau. By that year there was a nationwide network of classes with an enrollment of close to 40,000. For the use of these classes Mary and Charles Beard each contributed a title to the "Workers Bookshelf," a series of short, inexpensive volumes on important subjects of broad interest. James Harvey Robinson was the first editor of the series.[24]

Hoping that a labor party would develop in the United States, the Beards saw continuing education for working people as an indispensible preliminary. The Workers' Education Bureau could be, Beard wrote in autumn 1921, "the most powerful adult education movement in the world. Its potentialities" were "simply immeasurable." Mary Beard, in *The American Labor Movement: A Short History* (her title on the Workers Bookshelf), spoke hopefully of the American Labor Party, which had tried unsuccessfully in 1919 and 1920 to make a national impact. In the future, workers' education programs might bring success to such a movement, she speculated, citing Ramsey MacDonald's statement that the English Workers' Education Association had been an important part of the "peaceful revolution" that had given Britain a Labour government in 1924.[25]

It was not necessary, wrote Charles in the *American Federationist* of July 1922, "to go into prophecy." There were some who believed that labor would "play a role in the future comparable to that played in the past by the military caste, the landed aristocracy, and the capitalist class." Although the American Federation of Labor had rejected independent political action, Beard argued that this did not mean that some great future event might not force the politicization of American labor. Recalling the course of the Russian Revolution, Beard urged Federationists to think of historic crises not as man-made but as precipitated by larger forces: "Can we doubt that in the future—in the long sweep of centuries—labor will have to make decisions and take actions more fraught with human destiny than any thus far taken?" Until that day, Beard concluded, worker education would train leaders "to handle the technical and difficult problems that arise in collective bargaining," educate the rank and file on "matters of public policy," and encourage independent thought on "foreign relations, domestic controversies, economic measures, and constitutional changes."[26]

It was almost as if Beard were replying to those who believed, like Herbert Croly, that middle-class social engineers were the vanguard of the twentieth century. Beard did believe in a bureaucracy of "social engineers," but he also believed that The People could understand and control the political decisions that affected their lives. Give The People information, Beard was saying, and then have faith in their independent reasoning. Show people the connection between their material and spiritual lives and foreign policy, domestic laws, and changes in the Constitution and they would then act on that knowledge for their own betterment. It must be said, of course, that Beard's workers were quite abstract. He did not appear to give much thought to the everyday problems in people's lives that might stand in the way of their getting an education. For him, the essence of an education was a critical attitude, an independent judgment. Horace Kallen and Walter Lippmann, for example, expressed concern about cultural antagonisms and irrationality among The People, but Beard always talked as if no one was ever going to be too tired or otherwise encumbered to enjoy the cerebral feast. Speaking to the Federationists, Beard was the prophet of the ideal, rational People. It was the only assumption on which a committed, unflagging zeal for commonwealth against wealth could rest.[27]

In spring 1921, following the organization of the Workers' Education Bureau and Beard's departure from the New School, the family went to Europe. As his father had gone South after the Civil War, so one may suppose that Charles was impelled by curiosity to see with his own eyes the impact of his generation's greatest tragedy. In England he introduced Spencer Miller, of the Workers' Education Bureau, to old friends, and we can catch a glimpse of his mood at that moment in the autobiography of Joseph Freeman, Beard's former student at Columbia as well as an ardent Socialist, then in London as a correspondent for the Chicago *Tribune*. The Beards, with their daughter, Miriam, and Miller were having dinner with Freeman.

"Suddenly," Freeman remembered, "Dr. Beard said: 'What are you doing outside the Chicago *Tribune*?'" Freeman answered "'What does one do at twenty-three? I write verses.'" Beard closed his eyes, wrote Freeman, "as in the old days then he opened them slowly and said with the utmost seriousness, watching closely to see if I understood his full meaning: 'When I was twenty-three, I wrote a book on the industrial revolution.'"[28]

Where they traveled on the Continent, in southern France and northern Italy, Miriam Beard Vagts remembers that there was not much physical evidence of the war. Most women, however, were dressed in black, and there was little food for hungry travelers. The Beards spent hours walking with, looking at, and listening to people on the streets. In Italy they observed the railway strikes and demonstrations that were part of the prelude to Mussolini's coming to power in October 1922. On their return to Paris they wandered among the bookstalls along the Seine. Beard, filled with excitement, "rushed in" and bought "a trunk load of books"—mostly French and German editions of documents from the secret diplomatic archives of the Czars that had been captured and released by the Bolsheviks.[29]

A year after this visit to Europe, Beard summarized his thinking about the relationship between recent history, the war, and the future in a series of lectures delivered at Dartmouth College in June 1922. The published title of these talks, *Crosscurrents in Europe Today*, might easily have been something like *Ambiguities in the Postwar Western World*. Recent diplomatic history; economic, social, and legal results of the Great War; the Russian Revolution; Socialism; and the role of the United States in world affairs—these were the subjects of a discussion Beard presented as "a collection of notes pertinent," he hoped, "to the great case of Mankind vs. Chaos."[30]

Chaos was not a word Beard had customarily used to describe either "reality" or future possibilities. However, during the years of the war and after, he must have glimpsed it more than once—in the hysterical suppressions of civil liberties, in the reports from the battlefields, in the financial aspects of the Treaty of Versailles, and in those crowds of strikers in Italy. Previously Beard had always written as if there were grave problems that were difficult but conquerable obstacles in the path of rather clear and easily discerned lines of progress toward a better future. Evolution, modern science, technology, and, above all, people's supreme ability to use their reasonable faculties had been the touchstones of Beard's credo. Now his vision was more complex. The world was perhaps less amenable to men's and women's attempts at manipulation. There were dangerous crosscurrents in the stream of progress that was history—the guiding metaphor was still indicative of a basic optimism, but what had once been certain had become a matter of personal faith.

The chapters in this small book read well because, unlike many of Beard's earlier volumes, they are not filled with page upon page of quotation from other authorities. The style is that of a tentative and speculative conversation. First, Beard discussed the notorious secret archives, which had given the generation that had fought the Great War an unprecedented and precious opportunity, he wrote, "to compare official theses with official facts and to measure propaganda against reality"—the Pentagon Papers of their day. Beard thought of them, as did many contemporaries, as being "new and marvelous beyond anything" that had happened in Europe since the Armistice on 11 November 1918.[31]

What was the lesson for mankind in the secret archives? "Millions of people had gone forth to die"; millions more had remained at home "to suffer and bear burdens," while only a handful of men in each country "knew by what process the terrible denouement had been brought to pass." All parliaments, Beard regretted, had been kept in ignorance of the "conversations, diplomatic notes and understandings" that had combined the nations for battle; all diplomats had acted on the premise that war was inevitable and had devoted themselves to preparing for the inescapable. Beard asked a central question of twentieth-century diplomacy: "Had the records been open, what would have been the result?"[32]

For the future, Beard argued, "mere institutional changes" would not suffice. The remedy for the dilemma of maintaining a balance between democracy and discretion in the conduct of foreign affairs was the same he had prescribed for so many critical problems: "an ever growing body of enlightened citizens" who did their own thinking and would not be "deceived by official propaganda." Just as an intransigent Supreme Court must respond to public criticism and as the Constitution must change when people view it as a human document, so the bureaucracies who make foreign policy must bend to the will of the intelligent, responsible citizenry, to a public aware of the complexity of issues and of the choices available to the nation. Europe could reject the lessons of the past five years, but, Beard concluded in his introductory lecture, it was "not expedient that America should do so."[33]

Like John M. Keynes in *The Economic Consequences of the Peace*, Beard hoped that someday statesmen would agree that nationalism based on ethnic and geographic considerations had nothing to do with prosperity and that "some sort of economic unit," perhaps "some kind of a general economic constitution," would be the best choice for Europe.

The United States, however, was living in "a glass house." Policies since the war, for example, allowing expansion of overseas investments and banking, building an "immense merchant marine at the expense of the tax payers," turning this merchant fleet over to private companies and then proposing subsidies, using the navy to collect the Caribbean debts of private bankers, and supporting "financial and commercial enterprises everywhere on the face of the earth" seemed to Beard to be inviting a new conflict. The Washington Conference of 1922 had been, said Beard, a "brilliant negotiation" to force England and Japan apart and to secure "the reaffirmation of the open door for China."[34]

The Russian Revolution was a test that fascinated Beard, a real case of the meeting between men possessing a radical, formal ideology and program, the Bolsheviks, and titanic, all-engulfing "forces," the national urge for peace and the desire of the Russian peasantry for land. Writing about the revolutionaries' behavior in the face of internal "'sabotage,'" external war, and foreign invasion by British, Japanese, and American troops, Beard might have been describing himself, so closely did he identify with the leaders of the Revolution: "Prolonged, sustained, high-tension action springs from deep, unshak-able passion. In a period when action is the dominant note, the most pas-sionate, the most radical come to the front."

Lenin, Beard thought, had never been "deceived by the childish phantasy that paper decrees would establish the new heaven and the new earth." Citing a well-known fragment of Lenin's speech of spring 1918, "The Soviets at Work," in which Lenin had stated that "'the possibility of socialism will be determined by our success in combining soviet rule and the soviet organization of management with the latest progressive measures of capitalism,'" Beard argued that this was "not the doctrine of the fanatic" who believed that this system could "be applied" and would "be maintained though the heavens fall." It was, indeed, "the doctrine of the pragmatist" who asked of a system "'Will it work?'" Here was an illustration of the fact, he added, "that even the communist may learn by experience." In 1922 it seemed "fairly safe to guess" that Russia would become "a huge peasant democracy" and that "a form of state capitalism" would "take the place of communism."

In fact, Beard took the whole of postwar European Socialist experience as a giant illustration for a sermon on pragmatism, as a clear verification of his own way of looking at the world. From a millennial point of view, the Russian Revolution had failed. The land had not been socialized, and all capitalist enterprise had not been eliminated. The realities of power had forced, in Germany as well as Russia, a "thoroughgoing reorganization of socialist thought." The "rhetoric of academic philosophy and politics" was giving way to more specific "language of production and management." With great sat-isfaction he announced that the socialists of Europe had "laid Marx on the shelf" and had taken "a course in the Taylor system of efficiency management." They had found out—had come around, Beard thought—to the great truth of his kind of thinking: that "the wrath of man might praise the Creator but could not produce a potato or move a freight engine," that "rhetoric does not build houses," that "party programs do not make plows," and that "logic, philosophy, and Hegelianism do not install power plants." Beard welcomed what he perceived to be a "new note of reality" in socialist literature.[35]

While talking of the revolutionaries and of the evolutionary socialists, Beard was also speaking of himself, of the direction in which his own thinking was going. To his general concern for providing, through his writings and speeches, a catylyst for creative citizenship, Beard was beginning to add a more specific interest in collectivist planning on a national scale. The surveys undertaken by the Bureau of Municipal Research during his last years as di-rector had pointed in this direction. A national approach to social and eco-nomic problems had been a basic premise of some of his earlier writings, such as *American City Government*. However, he realized that planning for a good life for more people, for an equitable distribution of the national wealth, could only occur if Americans had a sense of national priorities—a knowledge of the alternative uses to which the available national resources could be put. As early as 1922 Beard had decided that a disproportionate share of those resources were being squandered in the pursuit of an imperialistic foreign policy. Hence, instead of concluding *Crosscurrents in Europe Today* with a chapter on possible remedies for the problems of Europe, Beard lectured on the United States and the balance of power in the postwar situation.

Beard focused, at last, not on Europe but on what he called the "new America," first among "investing, industrial, commercial, maritime, and naval powers of the earth. . . ." In the search for markets for its agricultural bounty, manufacturers, and surplus capital, the United States was being forced, Beard thought, by the "paralysis of Europe" to place renewed emphasis on the Orient. "The Pacific" had "become the new theatre," and he reminded his hearers that, although the Open Door, since it did not involve actual seizure of territory, sounded ethical to many Americans, European and Japanese diplomats did not "look upon American imperial methods in the Orient as different in any essential respect from those of other powers."[36]

The "'Few General and Tentative Reflections'" at the end of *Crosscurrents* would be elaborated by Beard in many future articles and books. Conditions in Europe, he surmised, were leading to "a return to secret diplomacy and the armed peace, preparatory to a re-enactment of the great drama which we have just witnessed." The United States should not attempt to compel a readjustment of indemnities, debts, tariffs, and currencies. Rather, Europe should be allowed to "set its own house in order under the stress of its own necessities and experiences." "Common decency," he added, "required the United States to refrain from publishing periodical homilies on the place of Russia in Europe's affairs."

What of "the Pacific menaces"? (Beard took the phrase from one of President Harding's speeches.) If the open door was really open, that would mean "intense and active rivalry with England, France, and Japan in the Far East." The "crucial question" was "'Shall the government follow trade and investments?'" Beard drew this question from Frederick C. Howe's anti-imperialistic interpretation of World War I, *Why War?*, written in 1916, before the United States entered the conflict. *Crosscurrents* updated the warnings of this earlier work. Howe had hoped that the United States would profit by the example of Europe and avoid the swamp of financial imperialism, which he had viewed as the cause of the Great War. Beard reiterated that admonition in 1922. Characteristically, he warned against "sneering criticism of our manufacturers and bankers." They were only "following economic opportunities as other men do," and it would be the task of a corps of educated citizens to make sure that "nothing short of the interest of the whole nation should come into the decision upon policy."[37]

What was the national interest, and who should define it? Beard would publish his fuller answer to these questions a decade later. In 1922, rejecting the "policy of positive imperialism, naked and unashamed," as well as the policy of "drift and muddle," he proposed instead a policy he said was called "'Little Americanism'" by its opponents and "continentalism" by him. The fires that had consumed Europe still smoldered. Beard saw the smoke before the Great Depression and the consolidation of fascist regimes. But reason, he hoped, could save the United States from the coming holocaust. Reason could create in America a great and democratic civilization.

Adoption of this continentalist philosophy by the government of the United States would mean, according to Beard, the cessation of "diplomatic or any other" sort of aid to investment bankers making loans abroad. The army or navy would not be used to collect debts owed to private citizens. "The government would feel under no greater obligation to a banker who made a bad loan in Guatemala than it would to a banker who made a bad guess in lending money to a dry goods merchant in Des Moines, Iowa."

The United States would abandon imperialism, seize no more territory or spheres of influence in the Caribbean, grant independence to the Philippines, "draw back upon the Hawaiian base," maintain armed forces and a navy "adequate for the defense of our territories," by conscription if necessary, and perhaps enter a League of Nations, "provided all other countries were prepared to adopt a similar domestic policy." Thus freed from the specter of wars caused by commercial rivalry, the United States of Beard's vision would "bend all national energies and all national genius upon the creation of a civilization which, in power and glory and noble living, would rise above all the achievements of the past."[38]

Crosscurrents was not particularly noticed by Beard's contemporaries. It was reviewed with little comment one way or the other. But in the life of its author it can be seen as the valedictory of a period of great experiments and changes. By the end of the 1930s its themes would form the nucleus of one great perspective on American foreign and domestic policy. War, Beard had seen, was not the path to collectivism of the sort he wanted. His own experiences had taught him that war and civil liberties were no more compatible in modern states than they had been in ancient times. The main hope for the future was always going to be, in Beard's mind, an aroused citizenry willing to weigh alternatives. During these years, the belief was burned into Beard's mind that domestic politics and foreign affairs were inevitably linked and that the purpose of future foreign policy must be to protect the home base from predators, thus to provide security for the creation, still to come, of a democratic society.

Reviewing *Crosscurrents* for *The Nation*, Carl Becker penned a portrait of the Beard of these years. He was

> too intelligent to be taken in by ready-made formulas—radical, liberal, conservative; too sophisticated not to delight in dispelling illusions; yet too humanely sympathetic to fall back into the easy cynicism of one who is content merely to

observe the tragic comedy of existence. He is an exasperated cynic and a warm-hearted friend of suffering humanity. He is a hard-headed idealist, the sworn foe at once of all that is stupid and selfish and disingenuous, and of all that is soft and comforting and merely well-intentioned. . . . Perfectly aware of human folly, he never quite loses faith in human nature.[39]

8

Voyages to the Orient, 1922–1923

In February 1922 Beard was invited to Japan to conduct "an educational campaign" in the universities and among city officials for the modernization of municipal government and services. Yusuki Tsurumi, son-in-law of the mayor of Tokyo, Viscount Shimpei Goto, informed Beard that Tokyo was then establishing a Bureau of Municipal Research with money donated by a multimillionaire who had recently been assassinated. Tsurumi hoped that Beard would be in Japan by mid-September, when the autumn term at the universities began.

The invitation delighted the Beards, who had made many Japanese and Chinese friends at Columbia. Several of their acquaintances, including the Deweys and Frank Goodnow, had spent considerable time in the Far East.[1] Moreover, in 1918, Shimpei Goto had visited the New York Bureau of Municipal Research. Charles and Goto, whom Beard described as "Japan's Statesman of Research," had developed a close friendship. Goto, who was sixty-five in 1922, had had a notable career in the Japanese government. After graduating from the Medical School of Fukushima, he had finished his medical studies at the University of Berlin. He had been director of the Bureau of Health in the Japanese Home Department, Minister of Communications, head of the Imperial Railways, civilian governor of Formosa, president of the South Manchurian Railway, Minister of Home Affairs, Minister of Foreign Affairs, and, at the time of the Beards' arrival in 1922, he was mayor of Tokyo and head of its newly created City Planning Commission.[2]

Tokyo, with a metropolitan population of more than 2.5 million, was getting its first modern sewers and its first efficient public transportation in these years after World War I. Under Goto's leadership, plans were being laid for a total modernization of the capital. Beard wrote admiringly that Goto had "never been a regular party man," but instead had been "noted for his political independence." Goto advocated manhood suffrage to replace the restricted and complicated system based on taxes. He believed, according to Beard, in civilian rather than military government. He loved the Chinese classics, wrote poetry, enjoyed a good joke, and laughed "heartily at all solemn farces." Although Goto's associations with the Japanese bureaucracy had been extensive and although he was an archtypal representative of the connection in Japan between political liberalism and imperialism, Beard declared that Goto was "no bureaucrat," that he was a man who had realized that "the old order of things" had been "shaken to its foundations," and that Goto, like Beard himself, based his hopes upon a "spirit of natural science applied to the problems of human welfare."[3]

Certainly Beard did not wish to be associated in any way with official policies of the Japanese government. He did not go to Japan in any official capacity. He "refused financial payments," Mary Beard told Merle Curti years later, and they "went first as a family of four and paid the entire cost" themselves. Although Beard was invited by Oswald G. Villard, editor of *The Nation,* to write for the publication during his journey, he declined. He was not going to regale the public with first impressions and quick judgments. "If, after I have seen a great deal and am safely home again, the spirit moves me to reflections," he told Villard, I shall remember your letter." Beard detested the idea that he might be seen as some kind of missionary. He appears to have regarded the trip as an educational experience for himself and his family and as a chance to promote municipal research, a field he correctly saw as having worldwide significance.[4]

The Admiral Line steamer *President Jackson,* with nearly a hundred first-class passengers, more than half of whom were "in evangelical or allied work," brought the Beards—Charles and Mary; Miriam, twenty-two; and William, fifteen—to the Yokohama breakwater at daylight on 14 September 1922. Goto met them as they disembarked and drove them to apartments at the barely completed Imperial Hotel, designed by Frank Lloyd Wright and located in the center of Tokyo. Surrounded by reporters, Beard announced with characteristic energy that he was "ready to begin working," adding that he had "long ago learned the American habit of the ten-hour shift." Goto had asked him to assist in a campaign to arouse deeper public interest in municipal government, to analyze the problems facing Tokyo in the area of taxation, assessments, transport and administration, and to supervise the establishment of a library and a technique of research procedure at the new Bureau. Beard wrote that Goto had challenged him "to imagine myself mayor of Tokyo for the time being and to make a report to the citizens on the problems of the city, expressing my opinions freely and without reserve!"[5]

At a large dinner party three days after his arrival, an affair attended by Premier Kato, Minister of Foreign Affairs Uchida, American Ambassador Charles B. Warren, and many distinguished guests, Beard sounded a theme he repeated many times during his time in Japan. "In making changes," he told the Japanese officials, "do not go too fast. Do not adopt our institutions and devices without testing them in the fire of your national genius." Things were not "good merely because they [came] out of the West." In the fields of art, literature, and the study of human nature, Beard told the Japanese, they could "teach the world. Do not crush them under a weight of brick and mortar and steel. Do not," he advised, "drown the sweet voices of Japan in the hum of machinery."[6]

During the remainder of September and for the next two months Beard lectured and gave courses at the universities of Tokyo and Waseda and in the cities of Kyoto, Kobe, Osaka, and Nagoya, all of which had new city planning agencies under a law passed by the Diet in January 1920. It was a heady experience for Beard in his prime. "Everywhere," he wrote, "our party was greeted by large and enthusiastic audiences. The addresses were translated into Japanese and published in the great newspapers, thus given a circulation running into the millions." Late in November he returned to Tokyo to speak at the first city planning conference in modern Japanese history.[7]

At this conference and everywhere he traveled Beard was, he wrote, "deeply impressed by the knowledge and insight displayed by the Japanese officials." Nothing that went on in the Western world, he commented, seemed "to escape their eagle eyes. The latest and technical magazines in French, German, and English are at their disposal and they read them." What American city, he asked, could boast of a bureaucracy versed in several foreign languages, acquainted with municipal government in other countries, and eager to learn newer techniques of budgeting and accounting? In February 1923, Beard delivered a course of lectures at the newly established training school for public service in Tokyo. He described the audience of officials, engineers, professors, and members of the staff of the Tokyo Bureau as "the most remarkable" he had ever faced. "All of them," he exclaimed, "understood English and brought informed and critical minds to bear in the discussions that followed the lectures." It was one thing, he added, "to lecture to college boys and girls; it [was] something else to lecture to adults of long experience in doing the work of city government!" Always the enthusiastic teacher, he loved these avid, educated audiences.[8]

The Beards' delight in their hosts was warmly reciprocated. The family visited many famous homes and gardens. In November 1922 they were invited to a remarkable private garden in Tokyo to sit quietly with a large company in order to observe the perfect moment of the crimson maple leaves for which this spot was well known. In a letter to *The New York Times* written after he returned, Beard observed "There is something very exquisite in the old civilization of Japan, and people who rush around in automobiles at sixty miles an hour are likely to miss it."[9]

William, the Beards' teen-aged son, occupied himself with his camera. Mary and Miriam were befriended by Japanese feminists, and Mary Beard lectured to women at a commercial school on "Women's Share in Civilization," describing the struggle of women in the West to acquire "higher education, economic independence, equality before the law and suffrage." Among the surviving mementos of this trip is a poem composed for Mary Beard by Madame Shimodu, a Confucian scholar and head of a girls' school, "expressing pleasure at meeting a foreigner who wanted to know what an Oriental believed, instead of presuming to have an absolute knowledge."[10]

Charles Beard spent the winter of 1922–1923 preparing a massive report on all aspects of the municipal government of Tokyo. He read translated information on assessments, taxation, population, paving materials, public health, and boundaries; he devised questionnaires for city officials, whose answers were translated back into English. The data were checked and rechecked, and Japanese officials were consulted as each section was written. At the end of six months Beard was convinced that "the difficulties of Tokyo" were not a matter of "lack of knowledge about local needs or about modern methods of meeting those needs." The obstacles to change were, he thought, "the lack of adequate financial and legal powers, occasionally in the lack of actual experience in putting technical theories into practice, and fundamentally, here as elsewhere, in the absence of an adequate public spirit to support intelligent and enthusiastic municipal leaders." Summarizing the motivation of his report, Beard commented that he wanted to contribute to "synthetic thinking about municipal affairs" and "to give independent support to the leaders of Tokyo in the execution of plans they have already made."[11]

Looking at Tokyo as an outsider concerned with efficient, humane city government, Beard drew on the experience of cities around the world in consolidating their metropolitan areas. Most of Tokyo was in the hands of village and town authorities and the rest was controlled by an imperial prefect. Beard suggested consolidation under one powerful city government with jurisdiction over firefighting, taxation, borrowing, public utilities, building regulations, and police. The experience of London, Berlin, Paris, and New York had demonstrated that, when the city did not control the suburbs, it could not compel those who used its streets, transacted business in its offices, wore out its pavement, and enjoyed its benefits to pay their share of the cost of city government. If such a government could not be created, then Beard suggested that representation be sacrificed to efficiency and that self-government be abolished for the capital and the entire administration be vested in a set of imperial officers similar to those of the prefecture of the Seine or the commissioners of the District of Columbia.[12]

Why was Tokyo "backward in many things like sewers, paved streets, and transportation"? Were the reforms Beard suggested politically possible? Beard approached these questions tactfully yet directly in a chapter of his published report, "The Spirit and Practice of Self-Government in Tokyo." Here, he restated his theory of the political process as he had observed it in the United States. Groups of citizens, "not the whole body," were always the core of agitation for reform. Such a nucleus seemed to be developing in Japan, although the proportion of eligible voters—three million in a population of fifty-seven million—was very small. Yet, because the mayor of Tokyo had only slight powers, because the people had "just emerged from a feudal order" and had a habit of unquestioning obedience to authority, because most people had not seen the West, the source of new mechanical and scientific ideas, and because Tokyo was "mainly a collection of villages with a metropolitan centre," Beard forecast that progress would be slow. Furthermore, as Beard saw the situation—and presumably his Japanese co-workers had discussed their problems with him at great length, the absence of "democratic sentiment below" was a great hindrance to reform. Japanese workers were unorganized and voteless; the bureaucracy was entrenched comfortably; the complicated system of suffrage, nomination, and elections did not encourage a concentration of public interest on civic issues; the cost of modern improvements was creating opposition among the groups who would pay for the improvements.[13]

As a foreigner, Beard could make suggestions that democrats in Japan could not make without facing censorship under the press laws. Beard urged more civic education, the formation of an Association for Municipal Improvement, and the adoption of the Western system of personal voter registration and nomination by petition, in order to create public interest in the electoral process and in the issues. There was nothing about universal suffrage that would inherently produce "wise or efficient government," but it appeared to Beard that universal suffrage was an "inevitable concomitant" of modernization. Western experience, he concluded rather optimistically, led to the conclusion that the suppression of ideas by the police created more popular agitation against the ruling orders. He did not recommend free public meetings and an end to censorship of the press, but he did ask the Japanese to examine that question.[14]

Administration and Politics of Tokyo was the magnum opus of Beard's thinking about the problems of administering modern cities. It exemplified his belief that accurate, detailed research on all aspects of complicated issues, such as taxation, was the only basis upon which effective progress could be made. He believed in the work of teams of specialists, in the spreading of civic spirit through rational educational efforts to inform people of the activities of their bureaucracy, and in drawing on the experience of cities around the world with similar problems. A fundamental premise in Beard's work was his confidence that a "scientific" analysis of many problems was possible and that the work of the experts could be understood by the public at large. A summary of his report appeared in the Japanese press on 19 March 1923, in the form of a public letter from Beard to Mayor Goto. At noon on 16 March 1923 the Beards had departed from Kobe on the linear *Shinano Maru*, bound for Taiwan.[15]

The family spent three months in China seeing famous sights and visiting with people who had been students at Columbia by means of the Boxer indemnity funds. To view camphor-extraction works in the jungles of Taiwan, they rode in railroad cars pushed by hand; they met "aborigines" and flew over the Great Wall in a converted World War I bomber; they saw the cities of Guangzhou, Nanjing, Hangzhou, and Beijing. In Guangzhou, a former student was mayor. In Nanjing, another student was a high official at the university, and Beard was invited to lecture. In Beijing, they met many of the foreign colony but preferred to spend most of their time with Chinese friends. No part of their trip was a guided tour. Charles would leave his family, when the time came to move on, and reappear with tickets for a trip upriver or with another way of getting to their next destination. His complete unself-consciousness charmed and attracted people everywhere. Beard was impressed, as many Westerners had been before him, by the contrasts between the opulent life of the wealthy Chinese and foreigners and the many visible poor in the cities. Miriam Beard Vagts remarked that to her father, "always a mediaeval student, this was the middle ages again."[16]

As Beard glimpsed the West through the eyes of his former students and friends, he became convinced that the education of Chinese students in the United States had been a waste of the Boxer indemnities. "I here publicly confess," he wrote some months later, "that, ignorant of China and her needs in the course of many years, I filled the minds of hundreds of Chinese students with facts and ideas no more appropriate to China than to the moon." The Boxer funds would have been better used, he concluded, in the building of "schools of engineering, sanitation, economics, and administration in China." He had also gotten a closer look at the fruits of imperialism. "The great powers," he declared, "refuse to do anything magnificent in China; they also refuse to get out and let those who might accomplish something have the field." With the passing years, America had missed the chance to have an intellectual influence in China. Instead, Beard concluded, "the United States had become more bumptious, more swollen with military power."[17]

Just as the Beards were home again and resting from their long journey word arrived that, on 1 September 1923, a tremendous earthquake and an ensuing fire had destroyed two thirds of Tokyo and had left approximately sixty percent of the two and a half million residents of the city homeless. Goto had been asked by the government to accept the post of Home Minister and president of a Board of Reconstruction with special jurisdiction over the wreckage of Tokyo and Yokohama, and he at once cabled Beard, asking him to return to Japan. Beard's affirmative reply was brief: "Lay out new streets, forbid building within street lines, unify railroad stations."[18]

After arranging to sail from Seattle on 23 September, Beard began to gather data on reconstruction after the San Francisco earthquake of 1906. Asked by an interviewer if he were going to help the Japanese to rebuild their capital along the lines of Washington, D.C., Beard replied testily that he did not believe that "any Western engineers or technicians, no matter how able, could plan a city for the Japanese, owing to the peculiarities, as we view them, of the art, customs and mode of living of the people."[19]

Beard was angered by the view of himself as a missionary carrying Western enlightenment to the benighted Japanese. A few days after this interview appeared, he wrote an indignant letter, "Japan's Problem," to the editor of *The Times*. Many Americans, he pointed out, had the mistaken notion that "the progressive Japanese" were "all or nearly all trained in America," while in reality the opposite was true. Most Japanese scentists and engineers were trained in Japan's own well-equipped universities. His own role in Japan had been "a modest one." The Japanese had had their own physical and administrative plans," and his part had been to bring "the light of American experience to bear upon those plans as prepared." The Japanese, he wrote, "understand their own problems better than any foreigner can, and those who [wanted] to help Japan in this crisis [would] do well to remember this simple fact."[20]

This time, without the children, Charles and Mary embarked for Japan with a tent. Upon arrival they immediately toured the ruins. Looking at the devastated city, Beard announced that this was "the best chance for Tokyo and Yokohama to become modernized big towns."[21] Something of Charles Beard's appeal, of his ability to tread the slender path between laughter and tears, a quality which must have endeared him to Japanese friends, was displayed in a speech delivered shortly after his arrival in Japan. "If the Imperial authorities rise to the great opportunities now presented to them, the whole world will applaud and take heart," he told the audience. "If the Imperial authorities in this crisis fail to rise to great heights, the world will say, 'Well, the Japanese are very much like other people' [Laughter]."[22] It was a prophetic joke.

Goto and Beard agreed that the disaster was an opportunity to redesign the city and not to restore it. Beard's unique contribution was to draw upon the experiences of other great cities in comparable moments of disaster and rebuilding. In his report on reconstruction, prepared at Goto's invitation, Beard recommended that Japanese engineers and architects completely redesign the streets of the old city by making them wider, adjusting them to future safety, zoning, and transportation requirements and leaving ample spaces for fire breaks and parks. This was the moment, he suggested, to replace "the worst slum areas" with municipal housing like that being tried in England and Germany. For adjustment of legal rights, Beard advocated the establishment of a "court of fire judges," as had been done in London after the great fire of 1666. This was done. Beard knew little about the construction and design of buildings, but he had brought with him a digest of engineers' opinions with respect to the effects of the San Francisco earthquake and fire on construction there. He drew in similar fashion upon the experience of other cities when analyzing the financial problems of rebuilding.

At the conclusion of his detailed and skillfully organized report, Beard suggested that considerations of prestige and aesthetics should keep the Japanese from "reproducing here the architecture of third-rate provincial American cities." Thus he returned to a theme stressed during his first trip. "Already," he said bluntly, "there are too many Western monstrosities in Tokyo. The capital of Japan will have distinction only by expressing the artistic genius of the nation."[23]

However, when he left Tokyo at the end of November 1923, Beard was discouraged. The seven billion yen he and Goto had hoped to see budgeted for reconstruction had been pared down to a mere 500 million by the Tokyo Reconstruction Board in its proposal to the Diet. Administration and politics had clashed once more. In an article written after his return, Beard described the political problem:

> The burnt area was only superficially cleared; it was not a clean slate, wax in the hands of the artist. It was still a complex of real and potential interests. The street car tracks extending in every direction and representing an investment of millions were intact . . . the water and gas pipes and other subsurface structures remained implanted in the old network of streets, representing millions more of invested capital . . . the sites of great business houses, historic spots, associated for centuries in the minds of customers with standard wares and commodities still possessed for their owners immense and incalculable values. More than a million homeless people and disestablished businessmen . . . naturally thought . . . of houses and businesses restored, in any way, as quickly as possible. There were thousands of small landowners in Tokyo, each tenacious of his little rights and bent upon holding fast to every inch of his sacred soil.

So, after all, Beard came to understand that in circumstances of terror and turmoil people would cling to their certain traditions and that few saw in disaster the opportunity to sail in new directions and to abolish the old in favor of the "modern." Reconstruction "along the old lines," he observed, seemed inevitable.[24]

Thinking about the planning of cities, and pondering the experience of London, San Francisco, and Tokyo in their periods of disaster, Beard wondered at the end of this article "whether any modern city can be planned except under a dictator!" The days of wand-waving dictators were over, but "hydra-headed democracy or near-democracy" did not seem "ready for the task." Engineering, he thought, was "a thousand years ahead of social sciences" all over the industrial world.[25]

Beard returned from the Far East more than ever convinced of the value of scientific planning and more certain than before that the United States, because it had relatively few traditions, would be the great testing ground for social planning. He had "cast off" all his "lingering suspicion about the value of science," he told a meeting of the Governmental Research Conference at Cambridge in autumn of 1924. It was a "delusion" that science was a failure. He had seen with his own eyes "the failure of many delusions without science," and so he would vote against the philosophers who were "fond of harping on the failures of science and capitalism—as if the two were of necessity inseparable twins." He had seen "handicrafts in the Orient" standing substantially unchanged by the course of centuries, and he told his fellow researchers that he would rather work in any modern factory in the United States than in any handicraft shop in the Far East. His vision of possible progress in the United States had been infinitely strengthened by these trips. Conditions of "life and labor, of clean, healthful, and joyous living" in "the best factories of the West" now appeared "like the kingdom of heaven beside those to be found in most if not all the handicraft shops" he had visited in the Orient.[26]

As his hopes for a democratic commonwealth in the United States were reinforced during these journeys, so were his concerns about the dangers and stupidities of imperialism. The Beards were concerned that rivalry between Japan and the United States for trade and profit in China would eventually lead to war. "I am no pacifist," Beard wrote to Albert Beveridge, choosing words and phrases that would appeal to this ancient warrior for empire, "but I hold it to be a crime to waste any of our blood on empire not to be peopled by our stock but by alien races." Wars for empire were folly, delusion, "treason to our fathers!" There was a vision of China in Beard's mind when he wrote "Let us not fight over a whim, or a bit of pique or a few dollars worth of trade to enrich more idle plutocrats. Land that has two or three hundred people to the square mile is worthless to *us,* no matter if a handful of capitalists get ten per cent of it."[27]

In the Far East, Charles and Mary argued in 1925 and 1926, the Japanese empire was a fact, just as the hegemony of the United States in the Caribbean was a fact. Sympathy for the Chinese, they urged, should not lead to the launching of a "children's crusade" to save "that ancient and honorable people" from "the tender mercies of the imperial Japanese." Americans "bent on freeing the downtrodden from the yoke of power," they remarked sarcastically, could "more easily begin in Haiti, but to the heroic that seems irrelevant." Doubtless, "the young Chinese" who were "trying to free their country from the grip of the foreigner" deserved commiseration. However, the Beards pointed out that among the foreigners the Chinese wished to retire were "the English and the Americans as well as the Japanese." A war to liberate the

Chinese "might prove embarrassing to the capital on the Potomac." Thus the Beards had carried home a dramatic vision of the condescension and cultural blindness that had accompanied both missionary efforts and economic exploitation in the Far East. Sympathy for their many friends in China could not erase from their minds the conclusion that it was a quagmire beset by tremendous problems of poverty and political turmoil. Imperialism was an ugly trap that degraded the subject peoples and demoralized the conquerors.

Perhaps the Beards had seen in Japan what they regarded as the sacrifice of democracy to the pursuit of empire. That this would indeed be the case in the United States they were certain. If there was a war for empire with Japan, they argued in 1925, the United States would be certain to win, since it had twice the population of its rival and since it was not dependent, as was Japan, on imports of iron, steel, and other vital raw materials. But what would be lost? There would be, they projected, "'cost plus' once more, labor boards, and committees of public information"; a few thousand new millionaires would emerge; the jails would be filled with violators of new Alien and Sedition laws; shiploads of aliens would be deported; the Department of Justice would send out another million spies. Most of the holders of foreign bonds would "escape the heat of the day," since the men drafted would be "farmers and unskilled laborers not useful for the lathe or test tube" and "since many thousand Negro boys could be called upon to help carry the white man's burden and hold back the rising tide of color."[28]

Years later Beard wrote to Merle Curti that "after a trip to the Orient an Occidental is never the same, if he is sensitive" and that during his "first visit to Japan and China—both so different from the U[nited] S[tates] and other Western countries—I became a changed person. I have never been the same again!"[29]

Nine thousand miles from home, as they crossed the Pacific on their return from their second trip to Japan, Charles and Mary pondered the relationship between history, technology, and culture. They had a fresh perspective on the United States. It seemed again a New World, unique, traditionless, a place where the plagues of the past might indeed be cast off. Steaming toward home, they sketched on a large piece of foolscap the outline for a monumental work of American history, *The Rise of American Civilization.*[30]

9

History, Civilization, and Abundance

From autumn 1923, when they returned from Japan, until the spring of 1927, Charles and Mary spent many hours on their masterpiece. After *The Rise of American Civilization* was published, Mary Beard wrote privately of her disappointment with the many reviewers who had assumed that "the whole product" was "CA's in spite of the fact that he had never written on cultural themes before." However, she declared, "the cultural side was my hunch—not just women."[1]

On the subject of their collaboration the Beards often joked with inquirers. Their privacy was not to be violated. "We collaborate by yelling," Mary told a reporter. "I'm one of the world's noisiest people. But then, so is Charles. I have to keep up my end of the noise in order to be heard."[2] According to their daughter, Charles usually made the outlines of their collaborative works, but, in the drafting, each worked furiously in a separate study, and every paragraph was drafted and redrafted until both were satisfied.[3] "We worked together," Charles Beard commented. "Every line, every word, we discuss between us. You, as a lawyer," he told the interviewer,

> know how two attorneys work together. You talk everything over. The discussions help clarify points and views. You do not duplicate work in research. One will look up one kind of thing; another, another. Mrs. Beard perhaps does a little more on the aesthetic side while I may do a bit more on the economic and political. But when a book comes out it is pretty hard to tell that any part of it is more the work of one than of the other.[4]

This was true, for *The Rise* is a blending of their personal styles.

Although friends were impressed by the "feeling of great ease between them," Charles and Mary had very distinct personalities. He had a kind of peppery radiance, a zest for storytelling and theoretical discussion, while she was more composed and dignified, and also more in tune with the emotions of people in a conversation. Yet, perhaps reflecting her early training in ladyhood, Mary Beard was seldom direct, either in speech or writing. "As we wrote our book," she told a friend, "I was constantly wanting to wander off into pure philosophy forgetting what we set out to do, namely describe the rise of American society, what ever it is. Philosophy, basic morals, analysis of the good life, human rights are part of the larger view. . . ."[5] Given this tendency to ramble on obliquely without focusing directly on her point, Mary Beard's speeches and articles are often difficult to read, while Charles, trained as a debater, developed his ideas with great simplicity and clarity. Together, her occasionally poetic sparks of imagination and his need to score definite points in a contest produced a narrative that often enchanted. Only the Beards together could have written, for example, this passage on the rhetoric of the American Revolution:

> Statesmen and soldiers, led and taught by lawyers, resorted mainly to charters, laws, prescriptive rights, parchment, and seals for high sanction, thus giving a peculiar cast of thought and ornament to the linguistic devices of the fray. When these weapons broke in their hands, they turned, not to theology, but to another secular armory—nature and the imprescriptible rights written by sunbeams in the hearts of men.[6]

Charles Beard was fond of the German saying *Weltgeschicte ist Weltgericht,* translated by him as "Universal history is the Last Judgment." No one could foresee the final course of history, but in this period many intellectuals agreed that a rendering of the past stressing economic and social forces rather than institutions might enable people intelligently to direct some aspects of the future.[7] Beard admired Henry Adams and saw himself as carrying on Adams' tradition, the tradition of "the scientific historian, the seeker after the key to things." The judge in the great court of Universal History was the historian. Writing about Adams, Beard clearly described himself and his own ambitions. Adams, he noted, had had the background to be a great philosophic historian, possessed as he was of family custom, intelligence, and "that other great necessity for the historian: a goodly store of accumulated wealth bottomed on sound securities." For Adams, as for Beard after he left Columbia in 1917, "there was no board of university trustees to pass upon his restless, disturbing quest for the key—a quest so ruthless with preconceptions of a chauvinistic and theological sort." Adams, like himself, was without political ambitions and "did not fear the savage editors who must earn their daily bread by tossing strong meat to the foaming jowls of party bigots."[8]

Although Beard had never shared Adams' hope that a "law" of historical development equivalent to the law of thermodynamics might be found, his active life outside his study had convinced him that men and women could affect the course of the future if their vision of that future rested on an adequate historical foundation. According to the Beards in *The Rise*, the greatest force in the American past had been the great natural wealth of the country, while the foremost result of that force had been modern industrial civilization.

James Harvey Robinson had said in his lectures at the New School that "to be really creative, ideas have to be worked up and then 'put over,' so that they become a part of man's social heritage."[9] Applying "creative thought" to history, the Beards attempted to make a past for America. They tried to work up a past in which all members of the community would see themselves as somehow among the builders of a unique civilization. In order to proceed as a community, Americans needed a common view of history. This the Beards hoped to furnish: "The history of a civilization, if intelligently conceived, may be an instrument of civilization. . . . If, as claimed, some form of socialism based on machine industry, lies beyond the present regime, it will certainly take a civilized people to operate it."[10]

Beard pictured himself as the lively challenger of a staid and stolid profession in his criticism of Frederick Jackson Turner. Turner had maintained that the necessities of the situation on the frontier had fostered egalitarian attitudes, which had been in turn translated into the system of political democracy. Beard chastised Turner for neglecting the industrial East and the "semi-feudal plantation system" of the South, both of which Beard thought were more important in the course of American history than the presence of free land in the West and the westward advance of settlement. Reviewing Turner's collection of essays, which included his famous paper of 1893 on the significance of the frontier in American history, Beard criticized Turner's conclusions on a number of points.

"Certainly free land and the westward advance of settlement alone" were inadequate pivots for an interpretation of American democracy. Had the frontier created a "composite nationality" among the pioneers? Beard was not sure. No one had gathered data to fortify this assertion. Had the frontier evoked laws that strengthened the power and extended the activities of the national government? Turner, said Beard, had exaggerated this interpretation. He did not agree with Turner that "loose construction" of the Constitution had increased as the nation marched west. The West had "perhaps" promoted the development of political democracy, but "it was coming" anyway. As Beard noted, England had achieved it without a frontier. Turner's great contribution was to write "American history mainly in terms of economic group conflicts." However, the clash of capitalist and democratic pioneer had been supplemented by an antagonism between capitalist and organized labor, to which Turner had paid scant attention. Beard regretted Turner's narrow focus, his neglect of Americans' experience far from the frontier, and his lack of a perspective which compared the United States to other Western democracies.

Beard acknowledged Turner's stimulating effect on the study of American history. But by 1921 he regarded Turner as a part of the entrenched establishment of the American Historical Association, a group determined to ignore industrial civilization and to suppress questions on the relationship between past and present being asked by proponents of the New History. "The tabu," Beard commented at the end of his pioneering essay on Turner, "is almost perfect. The American Historical Association officially is as regular as Louis XVI's court scribes."[11]

The Rise was intended to freshen a stale view of the American past, and Beard's writings during the twenties were sprinkled with hints of his purpose. He would "discard . . . the pontificalia approved by the elder statesmen of the American Historical Association" and "apply to the reputable lore of the middling orders the socratic elenchus"; he would "essay the role of Jeremiah against the Philistines" and dare to "invoke the spirit of Buckle or Darwin." In 1925, reviewing a group of surveys of American history for *The New Republic*, he wrote of his conviction that "the bold outline of the great national myth" was standing "unimpaired, waiting on time."[12] Waiting, perhaps, to be replaced by the sweeping interpretations of *The Rise*, which appeared on the tables of bookstores at the end of April 1927.

America was a land of great material abundance. On this obvious fact, and not upon the pillars of ideological, institutional, or racial characteristics unique to Anglo-Saxons, the Beards rested their synthesis in *The Rise of American Civilization*. Indeed, they adopted and elaborated the suggestions of J. Franklin Jameson, whose *The American Revolution Considered as a Social Movement* Charles Beard had hailed as "the definitive close of the Bancroftian or romantic era" in American history.[13] Jameson had written that "political democracy" had come to the United States "as the result of economic democracy" and that America had come "to be marked by political institutions of a democratic type because it had, still earlier, come to be characterized in its economic life by democratic arrangements and practices."[14] Jameson, the Beards acknowledged, was the artist who had prepared a "sketch . . . for a synthetic view of American origins."[15]

According to the Beards, the history of national politics in America had been one extended debate over differing uses of this abundance by Southern planters, Northern merchants, and industrial capitalists. Seeing political conflicts as struggles among wealthy elites was consistent with Charles Beard's earlier histories. A new aspect of *The Rise* was the hypothesis that there had always been enough wealth, first in the form of land and then in the form of industrial growth, for the forms of political democracy to co-exist with gross inequities in the distribution of wealth. Potentially dissatisfied workers in nineteenth-century factories, the Beards argued, following Frederick Jackson Turner, and been lured away from socialism by the promise of free land. In the twentieth century, technology promised unlimited industrial expansion and offered exhiliarating wonders, the automobile and the radio, as plums for dull, routine work.

The Beards handed a special rebuke to young critics of the "deadly uniformity" of modern America. Writers such as Sinclair Lewis and H. L. Mencken had exaggerated the flexibility of older societies. Monotony, the Beards argued, had always been a fact of life for those who performed the hard labor in every society. "As a matter of chill reality," they wrote, recalling their recent travels, "all previous societies had been standardized at some level of poverty or wealth, none more rigidly, save for a fortunate few, than those of the ancient world or of modern China." Contemporary critics of American society who wondered "in the mood of Matthew Arnold" whether "it would not be better to have again peasant villages, manor houses, and Gothic churches, whether middle-class persons of moderate incomes were not crushed . . . by prosperous mechanics and dictatorial servants, whether the fairly good peaches and apples and autos available to working people atoned for the lack of the finest wines found on the best tables in Europe" were wrong. Despairing "utterly of general improvement," making fun of "the mob," and retiring with "'the civilized minority'" to "a new kind of established church," the censors of American culture were mistaken about the tide of history.[16]

Those who bemoaned American materialism, as well as the racist prophets of "'the rising tide of color,'" who equated American civilization with "nordic" survival, had missed the significance of the material basis of American society. It was the richness of land, natural resources, and now technology that would enable American society to go beyond materialism. To the Beards it appeared indeed that "America of the machine age offered material subsistence for a life of the mind more varied and more lucrative, both relatively and absolutely, than any nation that had flourished since the beginnings of civilization in the Nile Valley." The "poignant specialists" who were pessimistic about American life and culture in the third decade of the twentieth century were a minority, the Beards affirmed. Most people, they argued, combined a "belief in unlimited progress" with "an invulnerable faith in democracy" and a confidence in "the ability of the undistinguished masses, as contrasted with heroes and classes" to meet the issues of the time "by reasonably competent methods." The Beards intended to inspire that feeling of competence.[17]

In stressing that material abundance had determined America's peculiar destiny from the colonial period onward the Beards made artful use of the tool of comparative history. They constantly juxtaposed the uniqueness of the American experience against a European standard. During the colonial period the largest social grouping had been the "freeholders," "composed of industrious and ambitious men and women" who "continued to fight their way upward from poverty in a determined quest for comfort, security, and influence. Aided by abundant natural resources," the freeholders had risen "higher and faster in the New World than in the Old" and had thus prepared the way for the American Revolution. That "clash of metropolis and colony" had come, according to the Beards, because "such a position of provincial subordination, diverting riches and power to London" had been "unbearable, impossible" for "a young and energetic people, full of spirit, with the wide sea before them and immense natural resources at their command."[18]

Continuing their comparative perspective, the Beards described the United States of the Middle Period, the nineteenth century before the Civil War, as "the most dynamic society in the world." In accounts of traditional historians, "the politician" had continually occupied "the center of the historical stage, in spite of the fact that he had always been "the shadow rather than the substance of things." The true significance of a political event such as the Civil War was as a symbol of great material transformations, of the dynamic evolution of the United States from primarily an agrarian society, ruled by elites of the agrarian class, especially Southern planters, to an industrial society ruled by wealthy businessmen through their lawyer-agents. The Civil War— in the Beards' brilliant phrase, the "'Second American Revolution'"—had been "merely the culmination of the deep-running transformation that shifted the center of gravity in American society between the inauguration of Jackson and the election of Lincoln."[19]

American inventors and "captains of industry" had effected the transformation in a society without feudal traditions. In the North—a sectional distinction the Beards were careful to make—"no entrenched clergy or nobility overshadowed them in national life or branded their labors," as in European history, "with the stamp of contempt. Available for every kind of manufactures were unparalleled natural resources—timber, coal, iron, lead, and copper. . . ." Recruited to the mills, mines, and industries were not only "the sons and daughters of American farmers" but also a growing number of European immigrants, attracted by the economic promise.[20]

By mid-century, in the Beards' scenario, "American businessmen . . . the Abbots, Lawrences, Astors, Browns, Forbeses, Vanderbilts, and Brookses" were prepared

> in numbers, in wealth, and political acumen to meet in the arena of law or war the staunchest spokesmen of the planting aristocracy. For every southern master commanding an army of bondmen in the field, there was now a northern captain of steam and steel surrounded by legions of working people. If many a planter could boast of a thousand slaves, many a captain of industry could pride himself on his thousand free laborers. On down the scale ran parallel the structures of the two economies, ending at the petty boss with two or three apprentices and the master with two or three slaves.

Each group was "ably led, well informed about the processes of government, and equally alive to the protection of their interests as they conceived them."[21]

As for the political representation of these interests, there was one great difference between them: "the planters frequently sent members of their own order to represent them, whereas the captains of industry relied mainly on lawyers to speak for them in the legislative chambers." By the end of the Middle Period, "the sovereignty of King Cotton and the authority of his politicians were rudely shaken." The process, argued the Beards had been "inexorable"; the "drift could not be reversed." The planters were limited by nature in their expansion, while the amount of captial, the variety of machines, and the number of workers who could be supported by manufacturing "had no limits discernible to the human mind." Though contemporaries did not know it, the "supreme question was whether the political revolution foreshadowed by the economic flux was to proceed peacefully or by violence."[22]

Historians had recorded conflicts between agriculture and capitalism. However, in the Beards' view, the situation of the United States in 1860 was unique. Europe afforded no examples of any country possessed of "a highly developed group of capitalists," the North, "a large body of independent farmers," the West, "and a powerful landed aristocracy," the South, each remarkably "segregated into a fairly definite geographical area." No European nation had ever had "gigantic industries battling for the possession of the domestic trade and at the same time a highly specialized branch of agriculture, like cotton raising," mostly depending for its profits upon a foreign market.[23]

Social wars in the Old World, the Beards thought, had usually resulted from "horizontal rather than from vertical divisions; that is, from the antagonism of classes dwelling together." However, the Civil War in the United States had resulted, they wrote, from "the friction of economic groups localized in separate districts." Furthermore, the great wealth of land and natural resources had given to American politics a peculiar cast, for no modern European country had ever "possessed an immense domain of virgin land available for distribution among the populace by political methods and viewed as a means of commanding party majorities requisite for other ends."[24]

In his earlier histories, *An Economic Interpretation of the Constitution* and *Economic Origins of Jeffersonian Democracy*, Charles Beard had perceived a link between wealth and power in American history. Wealthy men, he thought, had always ruled, though they had differed in the particular focus of their economic interests. In his pioneering early books, written as part of a scholarly debate over the origins of the public law in America, Beard had never satisfactorily explained how the political process worked; that is, how the rhetoric of democracy had resulted in the elevation of wealthy merchants and planters to the position of political authorities without "the masses" at some point recognizing that their own interests might not be identical to the interests of those in power. In *The Rise* this question is answered. Here the Beards assumed that abundance had greased the wheels of the political process.

The Beards constantly recognized that the rise had taken its toll in victims, but they displayed no conspicuous sympathy for those who might not have shared in the economic promise of America. Their audience, white middle-class men and women with enough leisure to read big books and to think about public affairs, had benefited from the largesse of this land, and this was their history. The effect of America on the more recent immigrants or their impact on the country, except as an impersonal economic "force," did not concern the Beards.

Their treatment of Native Americans exemplifies this lack of tenderness. "In the same relentless economic process that destroyed the free cattle range," they wrote, "the wild Indian at last disappeared," although "the aborigines" had been "redoubtable foes of the white invasion." "Even the recorder with no illusions about 'the noble savage' had to draw a black border" around the pages in American history dealing with the white conquest of the Far West. Nevertheless, the Beards asserted, it was "not exactly correct . . . to speak of the 'extermination' of the red man. Indeed, [it was] doubtful whether the arms and whisky of his white competitor were more destructive than his own diseases, such a smallpox, his tribal wars, his clannish jealousies." They were not apologizing, they added, for the cruelties of white people on the frontier, for the government's policy of "security and no responsibility," or for the sins of liquor dealers. But some things "seem to be deeply rooted in the very constitution of the universe." [25]

Although Charles Beard had sometimes used phrases in his writing that would be termed racist fifty years later, Charles and Mary in *The Rise*, as they analyzed the plight of the Southern freedmen after the Civil War, yielded nothing to prophets of "race suicide" and the eugenicists. Once more a comparison between the American and the European experience pointed to the uniqueness of conditions in the New World. The "servile bondmen" of America were not comparable to European serfs, who had been "as a rule as white as their masters." Although "branded with social inferiority," they had been "separated by no indelible color line from the ruling orders." The Southern freedmen carried "the seal of color . . . go where they might they could not escape the ancient sign of servitude." European serfs, moreover, "had always been accustomed to the ownership of personal property and to the management of fields and gardens"; their offspring had "sometimes escaped from bondage," risen in the church or through marriage, and had served at the courts of kings. Serfs, when freed, had been in many cases granted ownership of land, "a stake in the country of their birth." By constrast, American blacks in slavery had not been "used to holding property, working for wages, or managing anything directly." Emancipation had come, the Beards argued, as a "result of no potent striving on their part but as the by-product of a war which broke the power of their masters." When freed, they had "stood emptyhanded, without property, without tools, without homes, hardly the possessors of the clothes on their backs." Therefore, the Beards concluded, it had been "impossible for the Negroes to strike out boldly in the white man's world, especially as their hope for free land" had been "dashed by the federal government." [26]

The Beards took notice of a problem that would again command the attention of historians in the 1960s and 1970s. Since blacks were "seldom rich in worldy goods," they wrote, these people "also suffered the disabilities of the poor in the courts, high and low, receiving as a rule dubious justice from judges and jurors everywhere and often terrible punishment under lynch law for alleged offenses against the white community." Thus, the Beards surmised, blacks had "lost most of the power for social improvement that may inhere in the processes of politics."[27]

The political purpose of *The Rise* was revealed in the Beards' definition of the term *social democracy* as "the idea that the power of the state belonged to the majority of the people and that it could be avowedly employed to control, within certain limits, the distribution of wealth among the masses."[28] The United States had advanced "toward" that goal, but it had not yet been achieved in 1927, although the "projects for direct government," the legislation regulating railroad rates and the uses of the national domain, the currency, banking and income tax laws of the Progressive period had represented an unfocused series of efforts by a larger public, including discontented farmers and organized labor, to change the system of "acquisition and enjoyment" of economic and social power by the wealthy businessmen and financiers of the Gilded Age.[29]

Again and again the Beards made the point, as have many of their successors, that the United States had lacked unifying ideologies. Changes, such as railroad regulation, the income tax, and the federal reserve system, had been accompanied by a cacophony of "trading, bartering, and huckstering as well as fighting." But no president or political leader had "conceived the minor adjustments"—the adjective *minor* is notable—"in terms of a larger whole." No elected official had foreseen "the trend of destiny; no political party could claim credit for results or escape responsibility for the outcome."[30]

The characteristic theme in this analysis of recent American political history was "drift." In attempting to explain the political events of the era of populism and prewar progressivism, the Beards reverted at times to a rhythmic but unsatisfying mystical idealism. "Hegel's theory of history," they informed readers, had been illustrated again as the "system of acquisition and enjoyment" had called into being "its own antithesis—forces that challenged its authority and conditions that required a reconsideration of its laws and ethics." "Factors" had "thrust themselves upward in bursts of power which could not be ignored" by men of affairs.

> Physical realities, always vivid enough to those who worked in shop, factory, and mine, swam at last into the ken of those whose business it was to understand the intricacies of modern society and to proclaim the right and wrong of things. Ideas born in the evolving clash of mind and matter altered the range of America's "intellectual climate," made obsolete phrases that had once contained

substance and driving energy, and in due time shook themselves down into divergent patterns of thought. "Is there nothing eternal in the world?" cried a distinguished educator of the age. "Nothing except change," replied one of his colleagues.[31]

"Factors" thrust themselves upward? Ideas "shook themselves down"? Under such slipshod rhetoric did there lurk an explanation of change?

There had been, the Beards argued—and no one could disagree—"a profound movement of social forces" which had finally ruptured the social philosophy of laissez faire, the businessmen's motto, "Let us alone." Yet, according to the Beards, "that movement as a whole had represented no articulate social theory; the varied measures thrown up by it fitted into no political mosaic." Then why had change occurred? If ideology explained nothing, what was the connection between economic power and events? In all the magnificent torrent of description, in all the mass of the Beards' mighty effort, by way of explanation there appeared finally only a tautology: change occurs; change itself explains change in a society based upon a fantastic natural abundance and lacking prophets able to divine the drift of the future.[32] The ideas of "restive agitators" in the flux—Greenbackers, Populists, Socialists—had acquired respectability through a "course of gradual seepage."[33]

The Beards were ambiguous. For their conclusions, often stunning, they offered no theoretical justification. However, they appear to have had what might be termed a semipluralistic idea of the nature of power in the United States. An elite of wealthy persons or their agents had consistently dominated politics, making the fundamental decisions respecting the distribution of wealth. The conflict in Charles Beard's books and the Beards' joint efforts, historiographical lore to the contrary, was usually conflict among wealthy elites, sometimes within alliances that included poorer people. Certainly this was the interpretation implicit in their descriptions of the American Revolution, the Middle Period, and the Gilded Age. Yet, as they approached their own time, this explanation became clogged with mystical references to ill-defined "social forces" opposed to "a few high beneficiaries who under varied forms and phrases ruled the country."[34] In their picture of events, the elite ruling group was assaulted by various groups of outsiders, but the question of what these skirmishes had meant in terms of the sharing of social and economic power was left unanswered.

There had never been, the Beards implied, a truly "liberal" state, a bureaucracy staffed by persons committed to the public interest above all and operating on a widely shared social theory of a democratically distributed national wealth. The state had never been a fair arbiter of the power of wealth and the needed guardian of the mass of people who increasingly had no stake in the society in the form of landed property and who depended on large corporations for their future well-being. However, the Beards did think that

American history had been characterized by a large degree of social mobility and that mobility or the hope of mobility had blotted out the true facts of social and economic power.

In recent times, they pointed out, the numbers of millionaires and middle-class professionals were increasing. Through the ownership of stock, profit-sharing, savings banks and insurance companies, the large middle class had become "part owners, usually absentee, of the enterprises managed by captains of finance." Marx had not forseen this turn of affairs. His prediction that "the middle class would be ground to pieces between the plutocracy and the pro-letariat" had been "so far unrealized in the United States."[35]

"Filaments of interest and enjoyment," the Beards argued, had bridged the chasms between plutocrats, the middle class, and the poorer "laboring and farming groups"—all ill-defined but agreed by common sense to exist. Auto-mobiles, telephones, radios, labor-saving implements, and "other commodi-ties, classed in more sparing societies as luxuries" had forestalled the conflict of interests in America of the machine age. Doubtless "there were dark sides to the picture" of working-class life in the United States, "but the area of grueling poverty was relatively so limited," they maintained, "that revolu-tionary calls to working people to shed their chains" had met with small response.[36]

Thus, reading the Beards, one sees them come so often close to class anal-ysis, only to pull back, relying instead on "conflict of interests." Why, given Charles Beard's connection between wealth and power, did the Beards in their masterpiece deny themselves the clarity of class analysis? After all, Charles Beard was clear on intraclass struggles, which others had called "contradictions in the ruling class." Surely his attribution of American abundance—"lux-uries"—as the mollifier of conflict touches on the great historical problem of mystification of class interest and hence on alienation.

Two obvious answers to this question are, first, that the Beards did not wish to be identified as Marxists; that is, that they wished to develop a uniquely American view of history, one which could not be denounced by xenophobes as unsuitably foreign; and second that in their history, they were true to their own life experiences. They could not write meaningfully of the lives and attitudes of people who were not part of the urban and rural middle class. But there was a more subtle abstraction in their work. It was assumed that only those with leisure, those with the chance for a college education, would read this book. In that sense it was not a history of the American people. In its pages, the people—even, one could argue, those among the select intended audience—could not really see themselves acting in this impersonal pan-orama.

So the Beards celebrated American abundance and the technology that kept the horn of plenty full enough to prevent social conflict over the mal-distributed wealth of the country. Yet, through all the pages describing the achievements of science in creating a mass culture by electricity, internal combustion engines, wireless radios, and the airplane there ran a question as to the wisdom of allowing the quest for private profit to direct the national future. The shadows of imperialism and the wars resulting from the search for markets and profitable investments darkened the Beards' luminous pages. The World War had been, they wrote, an upsurge of "primitive force." It had frightfully demonstrated the fragility of "law and order" and the Frankenstein-ian side of technology. The Beards noted that some scientists worried about the future. Some had warned that "unless the American mind could be made over by fearless research and by a baptism of freedom, it could never catch up with the industrial machine" and tame its "huge organizations, its mass move-ments, its international belligerency." The alternative to "a more desperate effort at thinking" was "ruin."[37]

The Beards wanted to shape a national consensus on the forces that had molded the American past. By understanding those forces people could enter history, control it, and prevent a breakdown in the future. The Beards in-tended for readers to conclude that the future should not be managed by those who had traditionally determined public policy. The unstated premise of *The Rise* was that, if the great masses of the people of America had understood their society in the past, had observed the transformations wrought by machine industry and technology from a point outside their own lives, then possibly those disastrous conflicts of the past could have been avoided or, at least, might have taken different forms.

Avoiding all questions of psychology raised by irrational behavior, the Beards argued that most political behavior could be explained by people's eternal search for economic security. Technology, as a rational, unbiased "force," could be, they thought, captured and used for humane ends. The hope of rationality was Science—which was, they argued naively, "itself dem-ocratic" because "it spurned nothing low or commonplace in its re-searches. . . . Nothing was sacred to its relentless inquiry. Before it there was neither prerogative nor privilege." With Science as the lamp of policy, thoughtful citizens could close the gap between social knowledge and social reality.[38] Taming the industrial monster would be an enormous but not im-possible task.

In the meantime, riding the tide of abundance without agreement on social goals was costly indeed. Imperial rivalries in the Far East meant that the public was paying for a large merchant marine while American farmers languished in depression. "Considered realistically," the 1920s were "an age of paradox." Many questions should disturb the complacent: "Could the United States continue to supply unlimited streams of farm produce and manfactures to the world except in the guise of credits? And if in the form of credits, would there not come a time when the burden of interest and installment payments must result either in imports ruinous to American business and agriculture or in repudiations ruinous to American investors?"[39] Would there not arise another of those great battles among members of the ruling class, "a terrific struggle between the American banking interests engaged in foreign financing on the one side and American businessmen engaged in manufacturing on the other"? The pathway of normalcy" was brightly lighted, but "shadows lurked there also."[40]

Like all of Charles Beard's books, *The Rise* was intended to inspire public policy. To those citizens who might unite in pursuit of the redistribution of wealth (that is, in an effort to achieve social democracy commensurate with political democracy) the Beards offered their work as an attempt to posit "some kind of benchmark or point of assertion visible to adepts engrossed in specialties" and as an effort that might "aid in that process of drawing together . . . contributing powerfully to the enrichment of civilization."[41] Democracy in its political, economic, and social forms did not arise from ideology, was not inherent in certain sacred forms and institutions. It had been possible because of the presence of a unique material base. The future depended on who controlled the mechanism of abundance, of new technology, and for what ends.

Reviewers were generally enthusiastic about *The Rise*. It captured the front pages of book sections, and the Beards' pictures were widely published. The regular edition sold 70,000 copies. Another 62,000 were distributed as Book-of-the-Month-Club selections. An observer of the mailing of *The Rise* by Book-of-the Month remembered later that, as truckloads of it filled the side streets, it looked as though New York City would be "buried in the fall-out."[42] Lewis Mumford, a younger friend of the Beards, described *The Rise* in *The New Republic* as "the high-water mark of modern historic presentation in America" and compared it to an early landscape by Monet in which the blemishes in the urban vista were diminished by a pleasing fog. "Whenever the darker spots threatened to spoil the even luminosity of their canvas," he wrote,

> Mr. and Mrs. Beard are inclined to offset the effect by an irrelevant flood of light from a foreign source. Instead of describing in any detail housing conditions of the industrial cities, they mention the existence of similar conditions in imperial Rome, London, Berlin; when they discuss the evils of megalopolitan standardization, they add—it seems to me gratuitously—that similar conditions have existed in other civilizations. The effect of these allusions is that of unconscious apology. . . .[43]

In later years Mumford was to become increasingly disgusted by what he regarded as Charles Beard's overly optimistic view of the United States. The Beards' in *The Rise* had not been sufficiently critical, he thought, of American problems.

Historians generally praised *The Rise*. J . P. Bretz in the *American Historical Review* expressed delight, while Carl Becker likened it to a "gust of fresh air" in the placid field that was American history. The most critical comment by a historian came from Ralph Henry Gabriel of Yale, who attacked not the substance of any single interpretation but rather the tone, described by him as "that persistent flavor of sarcasm and cynicism which is a serious blemish on the work of the Beards."[44] Forty years later, Richard Hofstadter recalled his youthful excitement as he read *The Rise* for the first time in 1934, "when all American history seemed to dance to Beard's tune."[45]

In *The Rise* Mary and Charles Beard looked at America from a mountaintop and tried to find some unities in the view. Turner had seen only the Western frontier. Earlier synthesizers James Ford Rhoads and William Ellery Channing had emphasized politics and had done so from a conservative perspective. Others had not challenged the national myth that all good proceeded from the Anglo-American institutions of democracy. Behind the Beards' eyes were scenes of Europe and an experiential knowledge of the significance of class, vistas of the construction of buildings in Tokyo by hand labor, and images of working conditions and unrelieved poverty in China that had made American factories appear ages ahead. They could not understand the "lost generation" that denounced the materialism of American society as somehow evil. To the Beards, this economic abundance, first in land, then in natural resources, and now in technology, was the key to American development in the past and would be the means to a planned future that could assure the continuation of economic security for most American people, a form of security from hunger and deprivation unattainable for most other people in the world.

Their view of applied science and technology as "inherently democratic" now appears excessively optimistic, but this belief was an understandable result of the changes they had experienced in their half-century on earth. As children they had been transported by their own feet and by horses and trains. They had done their reading for twenty-five years by the light of kerosene or gas lamps. They had seen the skyline of New York sprout fingers and spires undreamed of in 1901. Those magnificent buildings of the twentieth century, they wrote, clothed "cubist dreams in metal and concrete" and "overwhelmed beholders with the sense of power and Gargantuan beauty made manifest."[46] As reformers they had rejoiced in such "fruits" of scientific inquiry as sewers and clean milk, cost accounting and modern budgeting.

Nevertheless they were not complacent, and their work had a prophetic realism. Technology, they argued, must be controlled in the interest of commonwealth. American problems of depression, as in agriculture, and poverty, rural and urban, remained to be solved. Racism and exploitation existed. Planning was a necessity, not a choice, if the future was to include social as well as political democracy. Imperialism and war had meant the decline of many rising civilizations, and American uniqueness would be preserved to the extent that the people rejected these avenues in favor of redistributing the national wealth at home.

10

An Intellectual Dairy Farmer's Public Life

T he Beards were moderately wealthy. In the spring of 1923 they had moved into what Beard fondly called his "beautiful studio apartment," the top two floors of the Hotel des Artistes at 27 West 67th Street. Built in 1916, the building had a mixture of Gothic and Tudoresque detail, two-story living rooms, squash courts, a swimming pool, theater, ballroom, restaurant, and a communal kitchen wherein a chef used to stand by to cook tenants' dinners and send them up via the dumbwaiter. In 1941, Beard recalled about this apartment that he had paid rent of $5000 a year in "flush days" before he bought it, adding that, in those days, his "books were selling about 1/4 million a year."[1]

This figure was an understatement. With collaborators, Beard had completed in 1920, 1921, and 1922 five texts for students from grade school through college, each of which sold more than a quarter of a million copies in various editions during the twenties.[2] These schoolbooks, along with some investments and his farms, provided Beard with luxurious comfort and a freedom from financial anxieties. During the early thirties Beard purchased, with money from the sale of some weak securities, another dairy farm at Sherman, Connecticut. "I bought the farm," he told Matthew Josephson, "because I have learned to mistrust all forms of *paper wealth* . . . I like to be able to see my investments with my own eyes, and if the Depression goes on, if worst comes to worst, at least I can *eat* my investments too."[3]

In the Beards' view, wealth implied an obligation to the larger society, a duty to use good fortune to promote the general welfare. Those who deserted their concern for social welfare after they became richer earned the Beards' sarcastic contempt. In 1926, Beard was among the guests at a dinner party honoring his former colleague of Columbia days, Leon Fraser, who had since abandoned his socialist-pacifist principles in favor of life as a consultant on European investments to American banking and industrial firms. At the moment, Fraser was the general counsel for the Dawes Plan, and he had recently left the law firm of Frederic R. Coudert, Senior, one of the board of trustees who had been critical of Beard and who had obtained Fraser's dismissal from Columbia's faculty. After he was introduced, Beard rose and turned to Leon Fraser. "Leon," he asked, "do you remember the old days when you and I used to sit in Hamilton Hall with our feet up on the desk, damning the world up and down? Do you remember what we used to say was the funniest thing in the world? It was one stuffed shirt telling another how good he is."[4]

Reluctantly, Beard had accepted the presidency of the American Political Science Association in 1926. Earlier he had written to Raymond Moley that he was busy writing *The Rise* and that Moley's suggestion that he might be elected president of the Association gave him "chills." He was, he told Moley, "deeply touched by signs of affection" from his "old boys."

> But really and truly, I do not care for the titles and glories of this world—or the next. They add nothing to one's stature. Work alone, good work, honest as possible work may do that. So please call off the boys. Instead, let us have a dollar dinner somewhere and discuss what t'hell is the matter with bare bones legalistic poly sci.[5]

Nevertheless, the honor was bestowed and accepted. In his presidential address to the profession, Beard chided his fellow political scientists for not being activists and questioned whether the university could ever be a significant source of creative social thought.

What was the task of political scientists? A few years earlier Beard had criticized Charles E. Merriam, his predecessor as president of the association, for writing a useless compendium of American political ideas with no historical context. How, he had asked, could Merriam waste time with such trivial books? The work of political science in society was to "help us in trying to discover the social utility of an excess profits tax or the wisest policy to pursue in the Pacific." Judgments on the present had to be based on judgments about the past, and only a "realistic" historical background could provide the illumination needed for issues of public law and policy.[6]

Beard questioned whether colleges and universities could foster creative thought at all, for they were conservative and their faculty underfinanced in research and overworked in teaching, with little time for reflection. Furthermore, the structure of promotion within the institution encouraged faculty members to narrow their vision in order to publish monographs on minute subjects which were "the gateway to the profession." Instead of spending a lifetime within the academic cloister, Beard urged his colleagues to examine the lives of great thinkers in the field—Aristotle, Machiavelli, and the authors of *The Federalist*—and to think about the fact that "every one of these creative workers acquired his knowledge and insight not only through books, but also through first-hand contact with government as a going concern." Put aside your fright and fear of failure, he told them, "daring to be wrong in something important rather than right in some meticulous banality."[7]

Beard delighted in tweaking the noses of academic snobs and in reminding them that much of what passed for achievement in academia was of no use to anybody. In his view, political science should be oriented toward the active present, toward public law and policy. It made him "quiver with pleasure," he told Thomas Reed Powell on another occasion, "to see political scientists running around shirtless with their hairy bosoms and scrawny legs glistening in the winter sun."[8]

In the autumn of 1927, after publication of *The Rise*, Charles Beard accepted an invitation from the American Yugoslav Society to visit the new country of Yugoslavia and to analyze its administrative problems. Once again, the Beards traveled as private citizens, paying their own way. Having studied the chaotic political conditions, glimpsed the rough countryside of peasants, donkeys, and impassable roads, and taken stock of the turmoil of European intellectuals, Charles Beard returned home more confident than ever that America was the place where technology and the scientific method had the best chance of making a good life possible for most people.

On their way to Yugoslavia they spent a few weeks in Germany with their new son-in-law, Alfred Vagts, and their daughter Miriam. Vagts was on the staff of the Institut für Auswärtige Politik in Hamburg. During these weeks Beard conversed with a number of professors, including the economist Werner Sombart, historian Albrecht Mendelssohn Bartholdy, and the agronomist Max Sering. Years later, Alfred Vagts remembered that his father-in-law had been "appalled by the *Weltfremdheit* [otherworldliness], part of it expressed in their utter obsession with the *Kriegschuldfrage* [question of war guilt]—to them a matter of national shame, to the outside observer betraying uneasiness about their own share in German imperialism, their share in Germany's ideological and other unpreparedness in and before 1914."[9]

At Vienna in December 1927 the Beards joined George Radin, a Serbian-American lawyer and executive secretary of the American-Yugoslav Society, who served as their interpreter and guide as they drove in a leisurely fashion toward Belgrade through Hungary and the upper Balkans.[10] For the next four months Beard and Radin examined documents in Belgrade, interviewed officials, attended sessions of the parliament of Yugoslavia, and toured the countryside near and far. Their report, *The Balkan Pivot*, was published in 1929, although it had been outdated to a great extent by the overthrow of the parliamentary system and the establishment by King Alexander of a dictatorship shortly after Beard's departure in 1928. Perhaps because Radin was Serbian and perhaps because Beard and Radin hoped that the existence of the country as a fait accompli would overcome ethnic rivalries, the two analysts did not stress in their report the great gulf between Croats, Serbs, Slovenes, and Macedonians that many commentators before and after have considered the outstanding problem of the country. "What the results of a national vote [on unification] would have been," they wrote, "no one could say."[11] And they did not speculate.

Notably, Beard did spend some time with Stephen Raditch, the famous Croatian nationalist, before he was assassinated by a Montegegrin nationalist, and he did visit Zagreb, the capital of Croatia. However, in their report on the problems of Yugoslavian administration and politics, Beard and Radin, rather than dwelling on the tumult created by ethnically inspired demands for recognition and autonomy, proceeded along lines familiar to students of Beard's thinking in the 1920s.

The main hope for Yugoslavia, according to Beard and Radin, lay in its becoming a more urban, industrial country. Yugoslavia in 1927 remained in a state of "somewhat primitive handicrafts and agriculture." Because necessary land reforms had not been undertaken the peasantry, 80 percent of the population, was not represented in the parliament. Hope for a normal politics would exist when an urban party, based on industry and commerce, could do battle with an agrarian party.[12]

Most of the existing "national cement" in Yugoslavia came, Beard and Radin thought, from industry and commerce. The "supreme economic task of Yugoslav statecraft" was, they felt, the attraction of "Western capital" to "develop the natural resources of the country." Yugoslavia had the national wealth to become a democracy. Lacking the finances or engineers to "develop" their country on a socialistic basis, the government should try to attract foreign capital without sacrificing national rights and property and without arousing the hostility of the peasantry.[13]

Conditions in Yugoslavia raised the obvious question of just what conditions of public life were conducive to democratic government. Again, the authors' answer to this question, in a chapter on public opinion, reflected Beard's view of the public foundation of democracy in the United States:

> . . . a wide liberty for the press, a generous freedom of speech, association and meeting, an electorate not only literate but also well enough educated to take part in political discussions, a keen intellectual interest outside the sphere of partisanship, and the continuous development of economic and political liter-

ature in books and periodicals. The active participation of women in public affairs. . . ."[14]

Conditions in Yugoslavia, where not more than half of the people were literate, did not remotely approximate this description of some necessary conditions for a flourishing democracy. Yet readers were assured by the authors that "machinery, science, education and the press" would "work remorselessly against tradition."[15]

On their way home, the Beards visited Montenegro, Albania, and Greece. "The sharp scenic contrasts in the world" were, Mary Beard wrote, "molders of opinions about life in known and strange places. For [Charles] Beard, unburdened by diplomatic demands, freedom to meditate was his privilege."[16] And the results of these meditations appeared with frequency in Beard's writings during the late twenties. More stark than ever before was the contrast in his mind between urban and rural civilizations. The forces of light were those of technology, science, cities, and industry. The powers of darkness and repression were those of agrarian feudalism and backward-looking idealizations of a village economy doomed to pass away. In his writing after his trip, Beard gave reactionary agrarians a larger role in the coming of the World War, and, in assessing the chances for future peace, he speculated in the manner of such Marxist revisionists as Karl Kautsky and Eduard Bernstein that international capitalism, by encouraging the growth of industry and thus of technologically oriented societies in the agrarian regions of Europe, might be promoting world peace, setting the stage for a future in which men and women would prevail over the material circumstances of their previous defeats.[17]

"Urbanism," Beard wrote in 1929, "is a short term which I apply for convenience to capitalism, science, and the machine," as opposed to "'traditional agriculture.'" Capitalistic production, he argued, was "carried on for the purpose of making profits in contradistinction to historic agriculture"—granting that American cotton production was an exception—"which was carried on for the production of goods principally for use." Capitalism encouraged rationality; agriculture was "mystical and lyrical." Capitalism could exist only "by the use of scientific processes." It admitted "no mysteries, no unknown potentialities." Science, urbanism, and capitalism were opposed to agrarian "evil spirits and priest's blessings." In the great cities of the world, all races met and dogmatism could not thrive. Urbanism was "cosmopolitan"; agriculture was "provincial." Capitalism knew no boundaries, and its inevitable result, the city, was the "center of the press, science, invention, the arts and literature." Outcast classes, Beard wrote, could not exist forever in modern cities. "The slum proletariat" might be "economically depressed" and "relatively ignorant," but it was "not insulated from the ideas" circulating "among the other classes." Instead of Jefferson's virtuous agrarian, Beard promoted the virtuous urbanite of the twentieth century.[18]

Warren I. Cohen suggested in his book on the American revisionists that "Beard was being impish in contending that his expectations of peace rested upon his faith in international bankers."[19] This characterization of Beard's view ignores a distinction he made between international investment in the countries of Western Europe and international investment in the culturally distinct areas of Asia, Africa, and the Middle East. The latter he saw as wasteful and dangerous financial imperialism, while the former was seen as a way of encouraging the demise of feudal agriculture, with its aristocratic classes ruling over inert masses. In the wake of industrialization in areas such as Eastern Europe would come democracy—and with democracy, in Beard's mind, came the possibility that enlightened public opinion would demand leadership more responsive to public desires for peace. International bankers would promote the development of "machine civilization," linked in Beard's thinking with the coming of social democracy in Europe. And social democracies did not war. Thus he could and did argue that international bankers were definitely promoting peace.[20]

At this point in his life, Beard was in constant demand as an author and speaker. He reported to Thomas Reed Powell that in 1931 he could "get from ten to twenty cents a word" for his writings and noted with a chuckle at the end of the letter: "I figger the above as containing $15.20 worth of words not counting your name or mine or the name of this hotel." However, he could grow weary of the many appeals to share his persona. "For some strange reason," he told Arthur Schlesinger, Sr.,

> I get a sheaf of letters every day from people who want me to speak or write or pray or contribute or serve on committees or attend dinners. . . . So I just decided to stop all public speaking in order to get time to think and write. . . . It seems to me that in an age of printing it is a waste of my time to spend days on trains going to lecture halls. Besides the years are slipping—not many are left and there is much work to do. The deafness makes me shrink from contacts which make a strain on my nerves.[21]

These resolutions made in periods of fatigue never lasted long. Although he spent his summers in the large gray house on the mountaintop in New Milford, he and Mary Beard were seldom alone. Matthew Josephson, one of the Beard's young neighbors in Sherman, recalled his first sight of Beard in 1930, at "a square dance . . . his very tall, lean figure vigorously bobbing up and down to the tune of 'Turkey in the Straw.'" On summer Sundays, the Beards held celebrated luncheons, with "visitors arriving from points as far removed as San Francisco, Tokyo, or Berlin," along with some of "the Connecticut illuminati." After lunch, Josephson remembered,

> Mary Beard (always called Jane by her husband) would lead the way to the living room and, before anyone could resume the light chatter of the luncheon table,

she would announce firmly: 'Dr. M——, former cabinet minister, who has just arrived from Europe, will now tell us about the crisis in his country.' . . . Charles Beard, noticing the serious mien we put on, exclaimed on one such occasion, with a twinkle in his sharp blue eyes: 'I see that Jane means to *improve* us.'[22]

It was during the 1920s that Beard began calling for national social values that would be appropriate to the needs of industrial society. Contrary to some interpretations, Beard was not being more conservative in looking for a new morality to fill the need of Science, nor was his quest to define social values a response to totalitarianism.[23] His emphasis on the importance of devotion to "abstract" ideas or values arose from having observed the limits of technocratic rationalism in the 1920s and from having seen other societies with less material abundance than the United States. In the 1920s, before the advent of the great depression and of Hitler, he urged the development of a national vision as an inspiration to peacetime planning, as a moral equivalent to war, which he now knew did not lead to reform.

Speaking to a conference of governmental researchers in 1926, he had concluded that it often seemed "as if George F. Babbit were rich, all dressed up, in possession of . . . a wife, a kid, and a Cadillac—and with no place to go—efficient, fed, and poverty stricken." Beard did not believe that "any truly great work" could be done, "any truly magnificent civilization" be constructed, "with reference to ends merely material and numerical." It was in "the higher realm of the spirit—of imagination—that we must seek for the ideas and purposes that can alone kindle human work with divine fire."[24] Science told no one what to do "in any large human situation." Science furnished no guide for "what is most valuable, what is most worth doing."[25] Babbitt was "an organizer and an administrator in a machine age, not a warrior or priest in a feudal age," and hope lay "in introducing sincerity, thought, beauty, and greatness of spirit into his own work . . . the business of building, making, and distributing." In 1928, which he described as America's "hour of visceral fullness," Beard inquired of Babbitt whether he could imagine Americans sacrificing profit to "high constructive purposes," such as reconstructing the "industrial wilderness, wiping out slums and jungles, and making a city over with a view to beauty and the good life—instead of the unearned increment and a full stomach?" Could middle-class Americans imagine, Beard asked, "great collective effort for any purpose other than war or exploitation?" If the answer was yes, then Babbitt, "full enough of husks and wind," might become civilized.[26]

Obviously, Beard did not abandon his prewar faith in the possibility of a democratic, rational public opinion. He did not share Walter Lippmann's pessimistic view of the people as only a "phantom public" that mistook images for realities, accepted any facade thrown up before them, and thought only in superficial generalities and stereotypes. A great deal of his writing and speaking was directed to the liberal professionals and intellectuals who communed through the pages of *The Nation* and *The New Republic*. However, Beard also addressed himself to teachers at all levels and hoped, through the fostering of critical thinking in the public schools, to gain a wider hearing for his ideas. The gains in social democracy had come, he wrote, because of "the activities of millions of men and women, most of them unknown to the pages of written history," men and women who had "thought, written, spoken, and dared." If freedom of thought were allowed and encouraged, words would have power. They would not be lost in a sea of irrationality. "A word, an article, a phamplet, a speech, or a book" might "set in train forces of incalculable moment."[27]

Ever the activist, Beard sought to create a national consensus in pursuit of "the good life" of mind and body. Technology would be the means for achieving this goal, with its instrument of rationality, the scientific method. It was thus neither any abstract "threat of totalitarianism" nor the shadow of depression that made him appreciative of the role of ideas in history. It was rather his practical dealing with the issues raised by national planning in a world made enormously complex by industrialization and urbanization. Although America lacked the shared social values that would inspire national effort to plan for the good life, it was rich in human, technological, and material resources. Beard had seen the contrasts offered by other parts of the world. The World War and his trips aboard had prepared him for the disillusion and despair of the 1930s. The decade of depression and consolidated totalitarianism only made his previous thinking seem more relevant than ever.

During the summer of 1930 Beard was preoccupied with compiling a book on government in the age of machines, which he co-authored with his twenty-three-year-old son William, a recent graduate of the Massachusetts Institute of Technology. Beard had always combined an interest in the development of a competent bureaucracy with a concern that bureaucrats might become unresponsive to the public interest. Although *The American Leviathan* was a textbook, it was also intended for general readers. Its 824 pages described and analyzed the functioning of the federal bureaucracy in the age of steam, electricity, and machinery. Public servants in the machine age not only had to distribute the mails, set standards and specifications for hundreds of items, run coastal lighthouses, care for public lands, and develop policies for regulation of radio waves; they also had to deal with new perils— falling aircraft, the pollution of streams, dangerous explosives, and new forms of criminality such as safe-blowing, machine-gun banditry, wiretapping, and submarine smuggling. Norman Thomas probably drew a conclusion intended by the Beards when he wrote that the book had increased his "confidence in the degree to which government [was] already a public servant"

as well as his certainty of "the far greater degree to which" it could be
expected to "become a public servant" once "a philosophy and program of
government better adapted to the needs of a machine age" were put into
practice.[28]

Did government by experts mean that the government must be removed
from the people? The Beards affirmed their belief in a rational public.
The familiar critics of democracy—Federalists, Fascists, Bolsheviks, and
even those "intelligence testers" who were claiming that intelligence was
hereditary and confined to a fortunate few—were paraded and disparaged.
A fact of the machine age ignored by those proposing that democratic
government be replaced by a government of "competence groups" was that
people could no longer be easily divided into the wise and the foolish or
even into definite economic and technical groups. Such divisions were
fleeting, "soon [to] be smashed by the flooding cross-currents of our rapidly
changing industrial processes." Confronted by an "intricate question respecting the hydraulics of river improvement, the physics of hull design
and water resistance or the strength of materials, the most intelligent and
highly educated lawyer or editor in America [was] almost as helpless as
the most ignorant laborer," yet no one would argue that the former's
voices should not be heard on the larger goals of particular technical
policies.[29]

By 1930, the heterodoxies of his Columbia days—Beard's views on the
Constitution—were no longer shocking, but they remained a vital part of
his hope that people would develop and maintain a lively interest in what
the government was doing. The Constitution could not be understood by
studying its language and the history of its past development. It was "what
the government and the people who count in public affairs" recognized and
respected, what they thought it was at the present moment. The Constitution
was "always becoming something else," and Franklin Goodnow had been
right when he had urged that "those who criticize [the Constitution] and
the acts done under it, as well as those who praise, help to make it what it
will be tomorrow."[30] Commenting on this chapter of *The American Leviathan*,
Felix Frankfurter wrote that it was not just that the times had caught up
with Beard but that he had "helped to make the times, thus achieving the
ultimate success of every thinker in politics, namely, to rob his ideas of
novelty."[31]

Throughout the twenties Charles Beard had been saying that the plight of
farmers and the blight of cities necessitated national planning. In *The American Leviathan* Beard and son noted that the recent "business depression" had
made the need for planning even more obvious. The necessities of the crisis
were clear: "get the facts, draw conclusions, make designs to specific ends,
and execute accordingly." Technology and the "scientific method" would
substitute "system, forecast, and control for chaos and rule of thumb; law for

chance." Herbert Hoover, they argued optimistically, appeared to be proceeding "on the theory of planned national economy."[32]

Some of the articles that flowed from Beard's pen in the years between 1927
and 1932 could have appeared at almost any stage in his scholarly career, so
familiar were the themes. In "The Fiction of Majority Rule" Beard wondered
"just where civilization would now stand if people of ideas, ideals, inventive-
ness and superior intelligence had always refused to act on their convictions"
until they had won a clear majority of their fellow citizens over to their views.
In "The Dear Old Constitution" he attacked again the ritualistic study of the
language and formal history of that document. In "The Myth of Rugged American Individualism" Beard argued that there existed not a single instance of
government regulation of business that had not been supported by one or more
business interests, and in "Teutonic Origins of Representative Government"
he debunked the theory that governmental institutions had anything to do
with "'the innate structure of human nature.'" All of these pieces came readily
from the hand of a man who had been attacking stereotypical thinking about
government for a quarter of a century.[33] During the depression, the old causes
still made sense. There were still people seeking to prevent progress by dragging
out honorable clichés praising the sacred essence of the Constitution and
ranting about the Bolshevist nature of all talk of a planned economy.

Beard had seen the election of 1928 as a departure from one of the patterns
he had constructed for American history. Neither candidate had, he thought,
really represented the agrarian interest. Hoover, he pointed out, had run as
an engineer and not as a son of Iowa farmers, while Smith was the big city
personified.[34] Both men were examples of the revolution wrought by technology. And, after Hoover took office, Beard had a decidedly greater interest
in events in Washington. He was perhaps hopeful that Hoover would lead
the nation down the inevitable path toward a managed economy, beyond
individualism and capitalism.

When it early appeared that Hoover was not exerting himself to lead the
Congress, Beard urged him to be energetic. Hoover, he pointed out, had a
choice of traditions. There was the negativism of Coolidge or the stormy but
more successful route of Theodore Roosevelt. The Constitution, Beard advised
the President, offered no guidance on presidential leadership.[35]

When the general depression began to present Congress with problems of
unusal scope and tenacity, Beard began to argue that the administrative tasks
of congressmen were too many, that their time was taken up with small bills
of no general significance, while measures of national importance were not
given the sustained thought and attention they deserved. Speaking to a Conference on Return to Representative Government in Washington, D.C., in
June 1930, Beard stated that in every Congress there were usually not more
than eight or ten measures "of high significance." Within this class in the

Seventy-first Congress, he suggested, were "Muscle Shoals, the federal farm loan system, branch banking, unemployment. . . ."[36]

Looking once more to the British example, Beard proposed that the thousands of petty bills which plagued Congress could be entrusted to executive departments, as was done in the British Parliament. Cabinet officers, he suggested, should sit on the floor of Congress, thus ending what Beard called "squirt-gun government. . . . Congress squirts ink at the executive officers and they squirt ink at Congress." Under this plan, important policy measures would be discussed in open sessions of Congress with responsible cabinet officers present to state their own views and to answer questions. To overcome the "executive usurpation" that might result from the technical character of modern legislation, Beard recommended that laws be made more explicit, thus leaving less room for dangerous executive discretion. And for the purpose of scrutinizing the work of executive departments engaged in lawmaking, Congress "could create a grand joint committee, fairly representing its membership, to sit continuously during sessions and between sessions." Beard urged Congress to watch "federal agents at the other end of the Avenue." Even presidents, he noted, were "not infallible." To advise the Congress on economic measures, Beard suggested the creation of a "national economic council."[37]

Meanwhile, Beard also concerned himself with the issue of money spent in congressional campaigns and with the cause, advanced by Senator Bronson Cutting of New Mexico and others, of amending loopholes in the federal legislation defining corrupt practices. During the twenties, there had been scandals of major proportions involving violations of existing federal limits on the amount to be spent in Congressional campaigns. In 1928 and 1929, two men had been refused seats in the Senate because of such violations. Getting elected required a large purse, and it was here, Beard wrote, that "the American theory of democratic equality absolutely breaks down in fact."

In 1930, no federal laws regulated expenditures in primary elections—which, in many states dominated by one party, were the main elections. There were no limits on the amount allowable for letters, telegrams, and circulars. Friends and supporters of candidates could spend freely without accounting for the amount. Political committees could overcome deficits after the election by soliciting funds from lobbies. Provisions for enforcing the existing law were weak and carelessly administered.[38] During 1931 Beard came to Washington to testify in favor of a new national act regulating the money spent in elections.[39] However, reform in this area was not destined to occur in his lifetime. The economic questions raised by the depression soon eclipsed other issues.

As a member of the American Political Science Association's Committee on Civic Education by Radio, Beard summed up the issues of domestic policy in an election year on 24 May 1932, in a speech for the National Broadcasting Company. The "outstanding" political issue of 1932 was, he said, "the stabilization of industry at a high level of production" at a time when "articulate masses" were challenging "the whole capitalist order." What had caused the depression? Beard answered that the origins of disaster lay in "fierce, unrestrained competition in industry and in the unbalanced distribution of wealth" which had forced "too much money into investment or plant extension" and had provided "too little for wages or buying power." This was the commonly held "purchasing power thesis" of the depression.[40] Beard advised voters in the coming election not to look to Democrats and Republicans for clarification of the issues, but rather to think for themselves about national questions so that they could demand from candidates of all parties "plain answers to plain questions."[41]

Thus, during the early years of the depression Beard continued on a national level to advocate all reforms necessary to close the fissure between democratic ideology and reality, between the achievements of pure science and the achievements of science as applied to society, between the dream of an abundant life for most Americans and the real misery of millions during a period of economic disaster. *Use imagination, not adding machines* was his advice to social scientists, and he proceeded to set an example by publishing a sheaf of articles attacking again the old clichés of formalistic thought about government, proposing specific reforms to ease the many burdens of congressmen and Senators, urging national planning of the economy, and calling for an ethical center around which all Americans could rally in the storm and which would be both a standard for all policies and a guide to the future.

11

The Great Depression
Modern Analysis and
Victorian Politics

More than twenty years ago William Appleman Williams wrote a thoughtful essay describing Beard as a "Tory-Radical," a man torn between concern for his fellow men and a personal and philosophic commitment to private property. Beard, Williams argued, did not "launch any frontal attack on private property," although he had "radical insights into the malfunctioning of the existing system." Speaking of Franklin Roosevelt and Beard, Williams concluded that "neither of them looked forward to socialism."[1]

It would seem certain that Beard did *indeed* look forward to the end of the profit system and that the programs he proposed during the Great Depression involved fundamental changes in the American system of government and economy. Yet he was not a Marxist. His understanding of the economic system was gained through absorbing the perspective of Thorstein Veblen, who saw the twentieth-century economy as a mechanical structure awaiting the corps of engineers who would run it in the public interest. Like Veblen, Beard did not see the state as a mere broker between capital and labor. In his view, the ideal state should convert the profit system into a means for producing goods not for profit but for use. Beard knew what he wanted—a decentralized socialism without a deadening state bureaucracy. In a narrow sense, he was attached to personal ownership where it did not threaten the goal of a high standard of living for most Americans, but his proposals went beyond a simple corporatism. He saw early that the programs of the New

Deal were not a reform of the profit system. He was disappointed in Roosevelt's "bread and circuses." His own proposals were more than an effort to patch up wounded capitalism.

The flaw in Beard's radicalism was his conception of politics. He illustrated the persistence of what might be called Victorian modes of thought into the twentieth century. Instead of analyzing the troubling questions of power, the interests of businessmen and bureaucrats in the present system, he relied on notions of "character" and enlightenment to achieve a national consensus in favor of planning. Because he believed in the transforming capacity of reason, he hoped to inspire the powerful to transcend crude self-interest. For himself he had a model: the ideal of the Victorian intellectual, a popular figure, blessed with talent and education and using those gifts in the service of the people as prophet and critic of society but also as a reminder of its best inner tendencies. Although his cultural values were conservative, Beard did propose an alternative to the American system of privately managed enterprise that used and still uses the state for its own advantage. He wished to end the expansion of state-supported capitalism into the competitive markets of the world, to relinquish the empire and colonies, and to create an essentially self-contained domestic economy. Because he did not advocate an unthinking "statism" or a reign of "experts" removed from popular scrutiny, and because his ultimate vision was a decentralized economy and state, Beard is accurately described as a "radical."

Also like Veblen, Beard was not attracted by the study of economic theory. He framed his questions in ethical and institutional terms, and thus he saw economics as a tool: the final answers were human opinions, not scientific "truths." If there is a central motif in his writing on national planning, it is the great Victorian idea that economic goals must be formed within a scheme of ethics. Manchesterism, he urged, was dead; "a timid reformism" was insufficient; planning must rest on a national ethical consensus that would "take the good life as its centre." The capitalist quest for profit ignored this standard, and Beard argued that profit-seeking had to be replaced by a national standard which distinguished "between money getting' and wealth creating." Society, he believed, was ready for the change. The engineering skills available needed only to be mobilized and institutionalized in a plan for commonwealth instead of profit.[2] He wished "to insert a sacrificial sense of responsibility into the calculations of trade, and [to] demand of the merchant the heroic spirit of the soldier," who must sacrifice profit to a better society. Although the passage of half a century has dimmed the appeal of Beard's exhortations to businessnen, he did see further than most New Dealers, progressives, and reformers. He knew that historic capitalism should yield to a new system.[3]

Beard's appeal to a higher morality, his language of moral exhortation, was not appreciated by a younger generation of intellectuals. Thus Edmund Wilson in *The New Republic* wrote that Beard "tells us that about all we can do is fall back on a 'philosophy of ethical reconciliation'—which the old master of social actualities then proceeds to adumbrate in a void from which the social actualities of the present have been completely swept away." In Wilson's view, people like Beard who refused to join a political movement and who devised "planned economies' . . . to preserve the capitalist system while eliminating some of its worst features," were minimizing the realities of power. Suppose, Wilson speculated in February 1932, Franklin Roosevelt were elected and he paid attention to some of the liberal proposals: "It would be the capitalists, not the liberals, who would do the planning; and they would plan to save their own skins at the expense of whoever had to bleed."[4]

Wilson perhaps foresaw the outcome of the New Deal before it was launched, but was his characterization of Beard's position fair? What sort of "collectivism" did Beard want? In what context did he propose to see an ethically inspired, constantly scrutinized bureaucracy operating? What sacrifices would "collectivism" entail, and for whom? These were the questions Beard asked himself, and his answers were conclusive. He clearly proposed an alternative to the preservation of historic capitalism.

Of the many proponents of planning, Beard was one of the few who urged that the Russian experience was worth examining and adapting to American conditions.[5] The details of his "Five-Year Plan" of 1931 are too numerous to be of concern here, but the basic idea was to make the "fundamental industries" of the United States—transportation, communications, fuel, iron and steel, lumber and building materials, electrical utilities, textiles, and food processing—into "national public service enterprises subject to the principles of prudent investment and fair returns." A "kind of economic convention, like that of 1787," would, he hoped, draw up a program that, in contrast to the Soviet Union's plan, would be submitted to the people for discussion and approval. Antitrust laws would be erased, but the industries would be restricted to the economic goals of the plan: increasing wages and production and reducing prices.

His Five-Year Plan, Beard argued, was not utopian; it was simply accelerating the process of concentration described by Gardiner Means. Two hundred corporations, under about 2000 managers, already controlled between 35 and 45 percent of the business wealth of the country. Beard wanted these giants to become "public service corporations" with true public utility status and entrepreneurial dividends limited to the interest on bonds. Property, in the narrow sense of physical facilities, would not be confiscated. But returns to the manager would be limited to a fixed rate of return on bonds.[6]

Beard did not write about prices, wages, investment, taxes, public spending, or distribution of income in any but the most general way. Nor did he grapple with the issue of the politics of planning, with the question of power, of how it was to be divided in his system, of the possible struggles the concept of a profit "limited" by the goal of a decent and uniform standard of living for all of the people would surely have entailed. Beyond expressing a pious hope that labor and capital would avoid "cavemen methods," he said nothing about who was going to control the planned economy.

Explaining to a friend why he had more or less ignored the financial aspects of national planning, he said: "Money plans nothing. Inflation, of course, is an old delusion. Who is to direct finances? And according to what plan are they likely to direct the stream of credit? No, the heart of the matter, as I see it, is the profit-taking system, which diverts to excess capital goods and luxuries wealth that should go to consumers' buying power."[7]

Beard did not want to save capitalism, but rather to go beyond it to a new system that socialized the profits of key industries and some property—for example, agricultural lands in blighted regions. Yet he did not like to be labeled a spokesman for the abolition of private property. This was not what he advocated, except in certain cases, and he was afraid of losing the audience he imagined existed for his proposals. In his public writings, Beard often sounded less radical than he was in private because he believed that people would gradually accept his changes if, over time, they were linked with specifically American precedents. The "abolition of private property" sounded un-American, and Beard did not believe that the American people would adopt it as a goal. When George Counts, Beard's ambitious young friend who had authored an enthusiastic account of Soviet schools and who was active with Beard in the movement to restructure American education around the goal of a collectivist society, asked him to write an article in 1934 in support of the abolition of private property, Beard replied testily. "You," he told Counts,

> use the clichés of communism . . . in effect call for the abolition of capitalism and point to the perfection of Soviet Russia. In short, who [sic] put on a red coat, jump up on the ramparts and say to the American Legion, the D.A.R., and every school board in America: "Here am I, a grand Red; shoot me." Personally, I think such clichés are damned nonsense and the use of Russia irrelevant to our purposes. American ideals are enough. If not, there is no hope. . . . Your idea that I should write on "the abolition of private property" betrays the kind of simple thinking that ignores realities and tells the enemy exactly where and whom to shoot at sunrise. Dead men do no work.[8]

And, though Beard shared John Dewey's view that the economic crisis demanded more than piecemeal adjustments, he did not respond to Dewey's call for a third party, perhaps because he thought that the structure of American politics denied third parties electoral success, due to the arrangement of single-member congressional districts and the winner-take-all electoral vote, and also because he thought of himself as an independent intellectual-politician who could influence the powerful without committing himself to partisanship. In 1931 he broached the third-party issue at a conference of Progressives called to outline legislative proposals for the Seventy-Second Congress. "My friend John Dewey," he told the group, "believes that we need a new party. Some thirty years ago I believed that myself. Now I believe that we need *ideas* and more thinking, and then parties will take care of themselves."[9]

Believing that "planning was the secret of the hope" and that it was due for a hearing, Beard welcomed the election of Franklin Roosevelt.[10] He had approved Roosevelt's record as governor of New York and expected him to lead America toward collectivism. *The Idea of National Interest* and *The Open Door at Home*, both published in 1934, were Beard's major efforts to influence public policy in the early years of the New Deal.

Since the early twenties, Beard had argued that the separation of domestic and foreign policy was impossible, and in *The Idea of National Interest*, which fell somewhere between an intellectual and a political history of the foreign policies of the United States up to 1933, Beard established that historically there had been no single concept of national interest. In most cases, it had been simply the most powerful private interest of the moment. What had happened, particularly in the twentieth century, was that the federal bureaucracy was increasingly staffed by men who came from the ranks of the businessmen with whom they would be dealing. Prominent businessmen or their representatives who sought to influence the decisions of the government were thus greeted by sympathetic government officials who shared their preconceptions, their ideology, that made private profit the standard for national interest.[11]

The Depression was severely testing not only this method of policy-making but also traditional capitalist theories of the national interest. Were low tariffs a solution to the economic crisis? Britain had not recovered after 1920, despite low duties. Beard questioned whether any tariff policy made at the behest of special interests would eliminate the "internal contradictions" of a system that facilitated "periodical expansions and explosions." Had foreign loans and other capital export encouraged under this system helped the American people? No. The results had been disastrous. The "Eastern Empire"—the Philippines—had introduced into the American market commodities that had "slashed into the already depressed economy of agriculture" during the 1920s and created unwelcome competition between cheaper overseas labor and more highly paid workers in the United States. Moreover, imperial competition with Japan in the Far East was a drain on the defenses of the continental United States.[12]

In October 1933, when *The Idea of National Interest* went to press, Franklin Roosevelt appeared to be leading the country toward what Beard termed a "non-imperialistic nationalism." Beard approved the President's refusal to support the gold-bloc countries at the London Economic Conference. He was hopeful that Roosevelt would not follow the advice of people who believed in recovery through the expansion of foreign markets. In *The Idea of National Interest* he applauded the national programs for farm and industry (Agricultural Adjustment Act and National Industrial Recovery Act) as efforts to balance productivity and to achieve a more equitable distribution of wealth.[13]

Privately, however, Beard commented that the President was disappointingly unsystematic, that Roosevelt was without clear goals, and that he was stumbling from one expedient to another. "Where he is drifting, God only knows," he told George Smith. "The London Conference showed up his muddle-headedness from the start. What a mess. No policy, backing and filling, jumping and snorting." To another friend Beard described the New Deal in August 1933 as the "new shuffle."[14]

Beard's collaborator on these books was George Smith, a lawyer who was also an assistant in the government department at Yale. For *The Idea of National Interest,* Smith did two crucial chapters itemizing the direct investments of United States capital in foreign countries, the portfolio investments, and the war debts. Only recently had the federal government begun to keep statistics on foreign trade, and Beard and Smith were among the first to use these numbers. They were enormously impressed to discover that, except for the years of war, and although exports had increased in absolute volume and value, their ratio to the total national product remained the same. Exports had not exceeded 10 per cent of domestic production, no matter what policy the government had pursued. Ninety per cent of all movable commodities were consumed at home in the American market, and there had been a consistent excess of exports over imports. To Beard and Smith this was definitive proof that exports did *not* make the difference between prosperity and depression. It was the linchpin of their argument for an economy based on a semiautarchic trade policy and against a policy of recovery through increased exports, which was the policy being advocated by spokesmen within the administration such as Secretary of Agriculture Henry Wallace and Secretary of State Cordell Hull.[15]

Beard intended the book on the national interest, which was published in late February 1934, to be "coldly factual throughout." Unfortunately, this desire to be dispassionate affected the style, and *The Idea of National Interest* is surely one of the dullest tomes Beard ever produced. By contrast, *The Open Door at Home,* the programmatic volume in the set, was to be a "treatise on political economy," an argument persuasively grounded in history in the manner of Adam Smith and Karl Marx.[16] While working on this second book, in October 1933, Beard had dinner at the White House and was apparently both charmed, like many people, by the President's warmth and persuaded that Roosevelt, then going in many conflicting directions without central goals, might be convinced to follow a path outlined by a daring political economist.[17]

A year later, in November 1934, Beard published *The Open Door at Home*, his own recovery program. Unlike its predecessor, it was and is a zestful book, full of sweeping speculation in the grand manner. After World War I Beard had perceived that the twentieth-century state, a polity controlled by the most powerful economic interests and without a set of national goals, could easily become a warfare state, and that such a choice imperiled the possibility of social security with civil liberties for the masses at home.[18] In Beard's view, the Depression was the ultimate proof that unplanned drift, subject to pressures of private conceptions of national interest, led only to disaster. Consumption and production had to be adjusted in the interest of the whole society, and traditional methods of seeking expanded foreign markets while maintaining elaborate controls on imports were bankrupt.

In *The Open Door at Home*, along with a domestic program based on a "standard of life budget" for eliminating unemployment and redistributing wealth, Beard recommended federal control of all exports and imports. He urged the liquidation of distant territorial holdings, tabulation of needed imports, and restriction of exports to those goods sufficient to pay for essential imports. Thus he predicted the end of enormous naval expenditures, since private interests would no longer use the government to involve themselves with the economies of other nations. The position of America in the world would be "shaped with reference to domestic security. . . ."[19]

Nothing better represents Beard's political approach than the centerpiece of *The Open Door at Home*, the only chapter he later reprinted, "The Ethical Roots of Policy." He addressed it directly to Franklin Roosevelt, "the statesman . . . the socially-minded, public personality engrossed in the public interest." Beard himself spoke as a "scholar conscious of his role . . . a statesman, without portfolio, to be sure, but with a kindred sense of public responsibility." Beard would here attempt to be Machiavelli to Roosevelt's Prince, and he urged the President to look to Western history for inspiration and to frame "an idealized conception of American society" to which choices of policy and action would be referred. Beard reminded the President of a mythical past, before "the rise of the value-free system of mechanistic economics," a time when labor had been "honorable as well as necessary, a source of virtue as well as wealth." People had not always existed in the minds of statesmen as producers of material wealth; instead, policy had been founded on the notion that production existed for the sake of man. Beard regretted that the New Dealers had not made the concrete proposals necessary to implement their bolder social goals. He hoped that the President would draw up a courageous plan for security and stability, submit it to the people for discussion, and battle for the necessary legislation.[20]

At no time in his life did Beard embrace a theory of politics based entirely on material interest. He did argue that power was largely a function of material interest but he was consistent in believing that ideas could affect the future direction of policy. The masses—a term he eschewed—in Beardian thought are not a Marxist proletariat. Rather, they are people aspiring to the good middle-class life—rational people who, when they had enough to eat, would be honest, reasonable, and loyal to cooperative ideals.

As he and Mary Beard had done in *The Rise of American Civilization*, Beard argued in *The Open Door* that the United States had a unique heritage, a set of circumstances which would permit the planning of a great bourgeois civilization without class struggle. The rich material endowment, the lack of any traditional state-supported church, military castes, ruling family, or sharp marks between classes, "despite marked economic divisions and group conflicts," made it possible "to say that, in theory, America has one class—the petty bourgeoisie—despite proletarian and plutocratic elements which cannot come under that classification, and that the American social ideal most widely expressed is the *embourgoisement* of the whole society—a universality of comfort, convenience, security, leisure, standard possessions of food, clothing, and shelter."[21]

Beardian "progress," however, was not only material but also moral, and it was this moral emphasis, this optimistic belief that even those in power could be converted, educated to see and to act on behalf of the common good, even to the point of giving up the "lust for profit" that prevented Beard from really following the insights derived from Max Weber and Karl Mannheim into the process of bureaucratic decision-making. "That the essence of government in the final analysis is compulsion cannot be denied," he wrote in *The Open Door at Home*, "but compulsion without a high degree of desire, consent, and cooperation on the part of large groups and classes is out of the question."[22]

Beard wanted new institutions, but he had too much faith in the men who ran the old ones. As he did not lend his talents to the creation of a "new politics," the amount of influence he might have had must be a matter of speculation. Politics, he said during the 1930s, was after all "a competition of visions." And his vision remained remarkably similar to Edward Bellamy's in *Looking Backward;* that is, commitment to a democracy of consumption based on a theory of common interests rather than on a theory of class struggle or perpetual economic warfare.[23]

Although Beard later wrote that "American continentalism" (as he came to refer to his conception of the national interest) had been the dominant policy from 1933 to 1935, it may be doubted that his particular continental plan, dependent as it was on the restriction of foreign trade, was ever seriously considered by anyone in the administration. The Trade Agreements Act of June 1934 was based on the opposite philosophy that increasing foreign trade through reciprocal agreements would alleviate the economic crisis. *The Open Door at Home* appeared six months after this bill had been passed. President

Roosevelt was thought to have read and enjoyed Beard's book, but its influence on public policy appears to have been nonexistent.[24]

In his review of *The Open Door at Home*, Secretary of Agriculture Henry Wallace, whose free trade sympathies Beard had lamented, commended Beard's "intelligent patriotism" and his denunciation of imperialism. Wallace nevertheless firmly renounced Beard's idea that a domestic market could be created for agricultural surpluses in a relatively short time or that the end of most export trade would not have a serious effect on domestic industry. Wallace thought Beard had neglected to deal vigorously with the "political resistance to the very real degree of so-called regimentation, external or internal," that would accompany "careful planning" as opposed to "the experimental approach" of the Roosevelt administration. "The heart thrills to all of this," Wallace admitted, "but I fear that Beard has not seen the whole problem."[25]

Although Wallace was accusing Beard of a dogmatism that would lead in some vague way to totalitarianism, he was illustrating the point Beard was making about the New Deal. The New Dealers refused to examine the means that would achieve the goals they shared with more radical people like Beard. As Theodore Rosenof has pointed out, the New Dealers were themselves dogmatic about potential programs that seemed "contrary to the given 'capitalist system.'"[26]

On the other hand, Thomas Cochran, reviewing *The Open Door at Home* in the independent Marxist journal *Modern Monthly*, called Beard's book "a labored defense of intellectual liberalism and progress through humanitarian enlightenment." Beard's belief that the standard-of-life budget and the sacrifice on the part of wealthy and powerful interests necessary for its enactment would be accepted as a reasonable alternative to the present chaos represented for Cochran "the complete lack of reality of non-Marxian democratic idealism applied to the industrial state."[27]

This sort of criticism from the left was more discouraging than other sorts to Beard, and he was provoked enough to scold those he referred to as "medicine men of the Sure-Fire School." He reiterated his faith that an economy of abundance could be realized and that "inherited capitalistic practices . . . must give way to any extent required to fulfill the law of mass-production economy." He imagined his younger critics on the left reading his words and saying:

> "That's all very well, but *how* are you going to carry these ideas into effect? You must make the proletariat class-conscious, organize a third, fourth, or fifth party, or splinter. You must rush into every strike or disturbance, no matter who started it or what are the ends of the immediate leaders. You must slam the capitalists and wage verbal war on Frances Perkins and Jane Addams. For God's sake *do* something!" [Italics in original.]

In riposte to this distortion of his leftist critics' well-supported position that he erred by not considering the struggles for power which would accompany the inauguration of a planned economy, Beard cited Marx's reply to the minority of the Communist League, the hot revolutionaries of 1850:

> "The minority has a dogmatic outlook instead of a critical one, an idealistic outlook instead of a materialist one. It makes will the motive force of the revolution, instead of actual relations. . . . You, on the other hand, say to the workers: 'We must attain power at once, or else we may just as well go to sleep.' . . . Just as the democrats have sanctified the word 'people,' so you sanctify the word 'proletariat.' Like the democrats, you subordinate revolutionary development to revolutionary phrase-making."[28]

The first ellipsis in this quotation is crucial. Beard *omitted* Marx's revolutionary point, his assertion that "Whilst we tell the workers that they must go through fifteen, twenty, perhaps even fifty years of war and civil war, not only in order to alter existing conditions, but even to make themselves fit to take over political power, you on the other hand [etc.]. . . ."[29] By leaving out this passage referring to war and civil war, Beard placed the emphasis in the statement where Marx had not intended it, on the phrase *revolutionary development,* and made it appear that Marx had used the word *revolutionary* in a gradualist, nonviolent sense. In his admiration for Marx as "a scholar of the first order," Beard wished to assimilate him into the pantheon of evolutionary radicalism.

Beard had expressed in *The Open Door at Home* his customary and sincere admiration of Marx's scholarship and had observed that, while Marx's writing could not be reduced to a neatly "closed and logical system," his seventy-five-year-old predictions appeared fulfilled "in some respects." Capitalistic industrialism had expanded over the world; there had been "crisis after crisis, renewal after renewal, in the course of expansion"; there had been "wars over commerce and empire . . . culminating in the grand calamity of the World War"; there had been a revolution in Russia. Nevertheless, Beard pointed out that, in his concern for the forces leading to revolution and freedom, Marx had neglected to give "any specifications for the operation of a socialist society to be employed by statesmen. . . ." Marx had been "even less specific in matters of trade and exchange among societies founded on socialist principles."[30]

Moreover, in earlier writings Beard had discussed the inappropriateness of Marx's mechanism of class struggle to political change in the United States. Abundance, he had argued, had fostered an optimistic attitude toward the possibility of social mobility, creating a dream that had weakened class consciousness. Thus Beard rejected a politics based on class struggle, favoring instead an intensive eduation of people everywhere on social and economic issues. Beard combined this educational emphasis with an individual political appeal predicated on his faith in the power of intellectuals to persuade those in power to use means beyond the stitching up of tattered capitalism to achieve socially beneficial goals.

Beard was on sounder ground when he stated that the problem for radicals was "How to give the most expeditious effect to the idea of bringing great technology into full use in providing the posited standard of life for the American people." Problems had to be stated, Beard told his Marxist friends, in language that the American people could hear. Ideas for dramatic change in American circumstances must "be formulated so realistically and with such ethical power, in relation to the objective social order of the United States, and presented so strategically" that they would grip the imagination of "that part of the American people which has the capacity to think, to resolve and to govern."[31]

In 1936 the Beard family produced another discussion of central planning accompanied by yet another proposal. *Create the Wealth* was a product of joint effort by Charles and William Beard, though Charles was anxious for his son to get the credit for the book. William drafted the book after Beard sent an outline to the publisher.[32]

Create the Wealth proposed that problems of operating the American economy could be overcome by the creation of a dual system of public and private enterprise. Here was a concept of the public sector that went beyond the "public utility" idea of Charles Beard's Five-Year Plan of 1931. The public system was "to step in to take over the sector where capitalism had proved to be a failure, namely in meeting the needs of men and women below the median standard of living." Unlike the New Deal or the Marxist proposals, this plan was based on the truly pragmatic concept that "what works efficiently" to produce a high standard of living for most people was "acceptable" rather than "on any mere theory that either capitalism or socialism could provide capacity production."[33]

The pages of *Create the Wealth* reiterated a theme found in many of Beard's writings on the temporary expedients that constituted much of the immediate program of the New Deal: There was a severe danger to the financial stability of the United States posed by the adoption of measures such as public works, loans to public and private bodies for construction, loans to large corporations in financial difficulty, and doles for direct relief of the unemployed. Not only were such measures inadequate to meet the long-range goal of creating wealth, but they were also a threat to "the one great bulwark against hunger and rioting left—the financial stability of the government of the United States."[34] The Beards argued that these piecemeal and inadequate programs had resulted from the fact that President Roosevelt shared with his critics on the right a vision of capitalism returning to "normal." This would never happen, *Create the Wealth* argued, since "normal" capitalism had never solved (and never would) the problems of those victims of technological unemployment, dependent children of unemployed persons, older workers, and those who had "lost their skill during months, if not years of idleness." In 1936, "general belt-tightening by those on relief, and 'normal' business recovery" seemed inadequate approaches to a relief problem which threatened to become permanent. Charles and William Beard recognized that both Republicans and Democrats wanted to help the unemployed and destitute millions of America, but the means tried thus far had only skimmed the surface of "the problem of idleness," unemployed workers and unemployed productive capacity. The "public economy" suggested in *Create the Wealth* offered a means that made a "fundamental attack on the roots" of the dilemma posed by poverty amid plenty.[35]

At the end of the thirties, when Charles and Mary Beard evaluated the New Deal, they thought that even though the National Industrial Recovery Act had not achieved national planning, it had in theory departed from the "philosophy of antitrust individualism" and had "reflected conceptions that had been associated with the apparently inexorable concentration of control in industrial economy." Along with other laws of the New Deal, it had "marked a general surrender of the doctrine that poverty and unemployment come only from the improvidence of the poor and that the persons affected must take the consequences of their futile and evil lives." In its analysis, if not in its programs, the New Deal had recognized the existence of an industrial system separate from individuals.[36]

After the demise of NRA, Beard had advocated trying the ideas of Mordecai Ezekiel, an economist in the Department of Agriculture who proposed a wider application of coercive taxation, the processing tax of the first Agricultural Adjustment Act, to American industry. When Representative Thomas Amlie of Wisconsin introduced a measure for industrial expansion in 1937, a plan that resurrected the National Recovery Administration but added a 25 percent tax on the value added by manufacture to the goods of corporations that underproduced or refused to cooperate with planning, Beard supported it. Amlie's proposal relied on the existing corporate structure yet compelled it to produce, on the assumption that unemployment and underconsumption would thus be eliminated. Beard deeply regretted the fact that Amlie and his fellow leftist Democrats Maury Maverick, Jerry Voorhis, and Robert G. Allen had "made no material impression upon members of the House of Representatives busy piling up debts and deficits, paying farmers for not producing wealth, and voting doles to the ten or twelve million derelicts of capitalism regnant and triumphant."[37]

Ever hopeful that the administration of Franklin Roosevelt would escape from what he had early perceived to be a course of muddle and drift, of "bread and circuses," Beard had continually urged "drastic readjustments in the productive system."[38] In 1937 he strongly advocated federal licensing of corporations. Instead of using its undoubted powers to set federal standards for incorporating, as it had during the nineteenth century in the case of the Bank of the United States, the federal government, Beard argued, had allowed a free hand to states and thus "to professional gamblers in other people's money." In effect, he told a congressional committee, the government was saying: "Create all the corporations you like. Give them blanket powers of marque and reprisal to rob the public and concentrate control over wealth.'"

Beard did not suggest any specific federal standards that might be used to trim the wings of the "corporate vultures" gnawing the body politic, but he saw that such a law had a great future as a way of introducing national planning. Again, the emphasis of his argument was a moral appeal to a sense of national social responsibility for corporate abuses.[39]

Of course, since Beard had long believed that, within the capitalist system, large units were more efficient and offered better standards for workers, he firmly opposed the administration's flurry of "trust-busting" after the recession of 1937. This kind of expedient, he wrote, was a "throwback" to the "flexible price" theory of laissez-faire economics. Veblen had long ago pointed out that "so-called competitive capitalism" had never been prosperous except in wartime or during periods of great speculation by financiers. And both types of prosperity had always been followed by inflation and a ruinous collapse. History could not be reversed. Only genuine national cooperative planning could deal with "the problem of raising our production of wealth to the highest possible level."[40]

Beard was extremely reluctant to commit himself to any systematic analysis of political problems. He understood and condemned a system of "production for profit" rather than "production for use." He indicated that he was willing to accept a lower standard of living himself so that all might enjoy economic security, but he did not want to analyze the political way to this goal.

In Beard's dialogue with his critics, as well as with those he hoped to influence, a key phrase was *ethical power.* Clearly, he awaited the end of the corrupt and despised "plutocracy." The New Deal was a failure, not because it represented predatory plutocrats but rather because New Dealers had accepted the traditional profit system and had linked it with the survival of democracy. Cordell Hull expressed this fear of true pragmatism in 1938, when he argued against Beard that a country which chose "to rely solely upon the material and intellectual resources confined within its own frontiers" would doom its people "to an inescapable lowering of all standards of civilized existence," to "inescapable regimentation and deterioration of the domestic economy."[41]

In 1939, Charles and Mary Beard looked back at the failure of national planning and called it a failure of vision and will. In their self-styled "memoir" of the thirties, *America in Mid-Passage,* the Beards summed up their disappointment:

> Nowhere dominant was there a program of concerted and defensible unity, inspired by strong resolve and informed by realistic knowledge, to continue, expand, and apply effectively, the recognition accorded to the collective character of American economy. Nowhere available was there a scheme of tested thought and moral principle to sustain such a program. Nowhere available was there a body of tried, trained, and loyal public servants to fill all the top positions of administration required to discharge skillfully the functions so suddenly imposed upon the Government of the United States. Nor did the President seem able, during the uproar and haste of the time, to draw together all the duties so suddenly assumed, assure efficiency, and explain to the nation the fullness of the designs taking shape in Washington.

Political action had been characterized by "bustle and improvisation . . . the devices adopted by the administration began to disintegrate," and the "acquisitive instinct" had "seized upon its opportunities for satisfaction, individualists, called 'chislers'" had fallen upon "the spoils, and the 'spontaneous spiritual uprising' of March, 1933, had dissolved."[42]

In defending the constitutionality of the social legislation of the 1930s, in presenting his own "plans" for America, in supporting measures with genuine coercive teeth such as the Industrial Expansion Bill, which the New Dealers in general were not inclined to sanction, Beard performed the duty of an activist, independent intellectual, as he conceived the task. He presented his ideas, such as semiautarchy, with full confidence and expected them to be taken seriously. His great fault was that his institutional analyses were not accompanied by a political analysis of the failure of moral appeals. His great strength was that he was not wearing capitalist blinders. While rejecting the dogmatism of both right and left, he sought to be truly experimental, to find means outside capitalism yet within American tradition, for reaching the humanitarian goals he shared with those New Dealers and progressives less willing to contemplate radical methods.

Also, he could see that central planning might result in a state capitalism remote from the people. He understood that democratic humanism was grounded in the ability of people to control the decisions that affect their own lives. Challenged to write about "The World as I Want It," Beard described his ideal world as "a workers' republic . . . without the degradation of poverty and unemployment on the one side or the degradation of luxury, rivalry and conspicuous waste on the other." Industry would be "widely decentralized," and "factories and fields" would "be united in new relations." The entire United States would become "one vast park" with "decentralized communities" and "irrigated deserts." Schools would inspire workers for the commonwealth and would explore the achievements and beauties of all cultures. Realizing this dream, he wrote, was a problem "of making the best of the best now in existence, of applying and realizing on a large scale that which has been applied and realized sporadically."[43]

Returning to William A. Williams' comments on Beard, it is clear that Beard was *not*, as Williams maintained, bedeviled by a "disparity between radical analysis and conservative preference and program." His own programmatic suggestions and those of others he supported were clearly to the left of the New Deal. He possessed a radical analysis; he proposed public alternatives to private property; what he lacked was a radical politics to implement his ideas. This was a task he left to others.

In 1940, Beard sympathized with the reasons for young John Chamberlain's turn to the right in *The American Stakes*. Beard also did not want "to see every piece of property, every opportunity to make a living, every privilege of education and publishing, turned over to a bureaucratic State run by a crowd of desperate politicians." Nevertheless, in turning away from socialism, Chamberlain was turning away as well, Beard noted, from the problems that had called it forth—farm tenancy and indebtedness, unemployment, a mounting public debt, miles of bankrupt railroads, and rising expenditures on armaments. People must get a grip on their fears and go ahead with more radical solutions. "Can we escape," Beard asked, "meeting this crisis by any of the thimble-rigging devices that have as yet been proposed? I doubt it. There is history yet to be made and, as was said long ago, only the strong can endure it or the thought of it."[44]

12

Science, Relativity, and Faith

M any who wrote during the 1950s and 1960s about Beard's relativism dismissed his writings on this subject as full of contradictions, as displaying an ignorance of the German writers he cited, and as, somehow, an early warning of what many liberal historians then regarded as unjustified criticism of Franklin Roosevelt in Beard's last books. Beard was called a gadfly who had shouldered a "historiographical chip."[1] Richard Hofstadter found no reason in 1968 to disagree with "most of the philosophers and historians who have written about his work on the problem of historical knowledge" and who had "judged it to be not only derivative but fragmentary, obscure, and sometimes contradictory." Summarizing the judgment of the profession, Hofstadter wrote that, in the first place, Beard "in the early and middle 1930s" had undergone an "intellectual conversion from a firm adherence to the economic interpretation of history to a form of historical relativism that proved impossible to square with his earlier views," and second, that at the time Beard wrote on the subject, "the belief in scientific history had not yet been closely re-examined."[2]

On the contrary, when the context as well as the content of Beard's relativism is examined, it is obvious that he was not philosophically unsophisticated. Beard wrote at a time of great controversy, when the philosophical foundations of positivism in both natural and social science had been reduced to unintelligible rubble and when the sociology of knowledge was just emerging as a solution to the limitations of people's ability to think meaningfully about their history, their present, and their future. His particular and carefully considered thought on the problem of historical knowledge was not the product of a hasty conversion. "What I have tried to say so that it can be understood," he wrote in 1938, "is that no historian can describe the past *as it actually* was and that every historian's work—that is, his selection of facts, his emphasis, his omissions, his organizations, and his methods of presentation—bears a relation to his own personality and to the age and circumstances in which he lives. This is relativism as I understand it."[3]

Striking premonitions of this conclusion are found in Beard's outlook during his days at Columbia as a New Historian. During the 1920s, when students of social thought were shaken by the uncertain universe being described by the New Physics and when European historians were conducting an ongoing revision of Rankean historicism, the relativism implicit in the New History was given a new and stronger philosophic foundation. With greater intensity in the late 1920s and during the 1930s, Beard called attention not only to the relativity but also to the inevitably political nature of modern history. It involves judgments of value; it informs the makers of public policy; it is, he once said, the "crystal" through which the eyes of all men and women perceive the world. All action, he knew, is based on some estimate of the past and on some vision of the future.[4]

The New History, although lacking an organized and theoretical attack on positivism, had invited historians to select their facts according to some present standard of relevance.[5] Notwithstanding Beard's hopes, early in his scholarly career, that a "more scientific theory of causation in politics" would be discovered, there is no evidence that he ever believed in any sort of deterministic rule or principle of causation for political science or history. "Written history," he had declared in 1908, "like every other intellectual product, has itself a long history; from generation to generation it takes on new form and content, as the interests and intellectual preoccupations of mankind change. . . ."[6]

Before World War I, James Harvey Robinson had spoken in satisfied tones of "long lines of progress, reaching back as far as we have the patience or means to follow them." Yet, Robinson too anticipated the theoretical formulations of relativism. Sources for written history were limited. This, and the fact that the historian seldom experiences the event of which he or she writes, made it clear to Robinson in 1908 that history could "never become a science in the sense that physics, chemistry, physiology, or even anthropology, is a science. "The complexity of the phenomena is appalling and we have no way of artificially analyzing and of experimenting with our facts . . . students have moreover become keenly aware of the 'psychological operations' which separate them from the objective facts of the past.""[7]

Robinson was groping toward the distinction between interpretation and fact that would become fundamental in Beard's version of relativism.

Although the New Historians believed that "facts" could be objectively ascertained, "absolute truth" in the form of a historical generalization purporting to "explain" the "facts" was unattainable in their view. Former students of Beard at Columbia remembered the emphasis in his lectures on the fickle and mutable nature of truth. The historian's "best equipment," he had often said, "was to consider at all times that the very opposite of accepted faith may be true." Others among his favorite litanies, repeated countless times in speeches, letters, and writings were "We see what is behind our eyes"; Bossuet's warning that "men do other than they intend"; and Beard's own conclusion that it was not possible for historians "to force the iron gates of the future."[8] Before the Great War or the Great Depression, the New Historians, cautious and skeptical of positivism, showed an awareness of what Graham Wallas named the "paradox of unintended consequences."

In his condemnation at Columbia of formal, institutional history, of history written with no reference to "instant business," Beard was arriving at a distinction between history and chronicle similar to the distinction being made in Italy by Benedetto Croce in 1912 and 1913. Enamored of pragmatism in those prewar years, Croce was writing his famous dictum: "History is living chronicle; chronicle is dead history; history is contemporary history, chronicle is past history." Beard had said a few years earlier that "history which does not emerge into the living present is therefore, sterile, when viewed from the standpoint of public need, however diverting it may be as a subject of interested speculation on the part of private persons." During the 1920s, when he read the translation of Croce's prewar essays, Beard surely recognized a kindred spirit in the Italian master's arch and sarcastic style, used in withering attacks on institutional chroniclers, romantic narrativists, Darwinian geneticists, and Marxists. The greatest resonance, however, would have come from the familiarity of Croce's contention that "all history is contemporary history." Here was a striking reaffirmation of a prominent strain in the New History.[9]

Further support for a subjective theory of historical knowledge, as opposed to a positivist theory of knowledge based on laws of historical development, came from startling changes after 1900 in the natural sciences, particularly in physics. By the 1920s, the implications for classical physics contained in the developing quantum theory were becoming well known; during that decade a number of books, most of them written by scientists, popularized and explained the "new physics" of Albert Einstein, Niels Bohr, Max Born, Werner Heisenberg, and others to an academic audience eager to understand the revised vision of the universe. Inevitably, the popularizers and their readers discussed the wider implications of these discoveries for social thought.

What had previously been a "psychological" insight of the New Historians, a poetic and pragmatic affirmation of common sense, became with the dramatic explorations of relativity and the quantum theory a "scientific" view of the world.

Looking at the universe of the atom and discovering that it was not a Copernican universe, the great theoretical physicists, philosopher-scientists, were increasingly skeptical of "objectivity" in the commonsensical meaning of the term. There was to be an end to finality, to finiteness and determinism. Between 1905 and 1908 Einstein and others had spectacularly revised the Newtonian concepts of time and space. The same "facts" appeared to vary with the position and the time frame of the observer in space. Between 1913 and 1918 Niels Bohr had developed a theory of the atom which broke directly with classical physics by incorporating a quantum jump that could not be visualized—that is, a set of a priori possibilities that renounced from the start any knowledge of the cause of observed phenomena. Classical physics had been based on a deterministic law of causality in which, given its initial position and momentum, a particle's future path could presumably be predicted with absolute certainty. Classical physics depended on an absence of discontinuities. The new atomic physics was based on a theory of indeterminate and discontinuous motion of particles. As Heisenberg explained it, in the case of "the strong formulation of the causal law: 'if we know the present, exactly, then we can calculate the future,' it is not the consequent that is false but the presupposition." During the 1920s, Heisenberg measured electrons using the quantum theory and found that measurements of their position and velocity could only be expressed in indeterminate relations, since the measuring instrument itself influenced the position or velocity of the electrons to be measured.[10]

Western social thought has often responded to the "science" of the times, be it the witches of St. Augustine or the evolution of Darwin. The ripples of uncertainty produced by the New Physics proved it also no exception to this generalization. As word of the indeterminate universe crept into intellectual circles during the 1920s, the honorable ideal of social knowledge as a series of statements of "brute fact" was further weakened, if not finally destroyed, in the view of many thoughtful people.

Beard was aware of these developments. In his presidential address to the American Political Science Association in 1926, he referred to time itself as a creation of the Western mind. The universe of the French mathematician Henri Poincaré, in which millions of facts appeared in each arbitrary interval of time, might have suggested to Beard his specific condemnation of historians for their lack of boldness in "seeking any clue to what William James called the big, buzzing, booming confusion of this universe." Historians, he told the group, actually selected only a few facts from the multitudes that had "by chance merely found a pale record on the pages of books and manuscripts and papers," and any selection constituted "an interpretation." Even the denial of a desire to interpret was an unconscious philosophical assertion, "namely, a confession that there is not even a discoverable fringe of order in the universe."[11] On another occasion, reviewing the much-disputed origins of the World War, Beard chose as his metaphor for complexity Einstein's theory of relativity.[12]

While Beard's speeches and writings showed traces of the influence of the New Physics, a strong controversy was emerging in academic ranks over the possible impact of relativity in the physical world on thought in the social sciences.[13] William B. Munro, who succeeded Beard as president of the political scientists, spoke the following year (1927) on the implications of relativity in physics for knowledge in political science.[14] Carl Stephenson wrote an article in 1928 outlining the division among historians over whether or not history could aspire to "scientific" status. On the side of "law," he noted Edward P. Cheyney, who had told the American Historical Association in 1923 that "immutable self-existent law" in history was possible and desirable. On the other side Stephenson saw Carl Becker, who since 1910 had been questioning the possibility of writing "detached" history. Stephenson himself reiterated the battle cry of positivism: "No fact, no history!"[15]

In 1929, Beard contributed an essay to a volume dedicated to James Harvey Robinson by a group of historians who were his former students. Two of the other contributors discussed the relationship of history to the natural sciences and reached opposite conclusions. Preserved Smith maintained that "the action of man is exactly like the action of atoms or bees, unpredictable in the individual but nearly constant in the mass," while Joseph Swain anticipated Carl Becker's "everyman" address by holding that there could be no science of society since "history is mythology, save for the fact that we believe it to be true."[16] Thus, well before Beard blew his own trumpet in the 1930s, the battle lines between "scientists" and "relativists" were clearly drawn.

Echoing the instrumentalist outlook of the New History and compatible with the newer ideas on the nature of the universe were the writings of Benedetto Croce, whose essays of 1912 and 1913 on the theory and practice of history appeared in English in 1920.[17] Croce himself had been keenly interested in the new scientific discoveries of the early twentieth century and in their implications for a theory of knowledge. He recognized that relativity in physics offered support for a subjective view of historical knowledge. He had written about the philosophical and mathematical controversy between Poincaré and Alfred North Whitehead, in which Poincaré had argued that "facts" were only "concepts" in the mind of the observer while Whitehead had maintained that the "facts" had an existence independent of their perception by the human mind. Croce had defended the Poincaré position, and this view of "facts" was the starting point of Croce's writings on the philosophy of history.

He was an absolute relativist.[18] *History: Its Theory and Practice* was one of only a few of Croce's dozens of volumes translated before the late 1930s. From it most historians in the United States derived, and perhaps still derive, their impressions of his thinking. Croce's position on the subjective nature of all facts and values—in short, of all knowledge—represented the extreme conclusion drawn from the great scientific debate getting underway in 1912 and 1913. Croce wrote that "the 'sensations' upon which the whole truth of knowledge is based are not themselves knowledge save to the extent that they assume the form of affirmation—that is to say, in so far as they are history." For Croce, the ancient duality between "facts" and "ideas" had been "superseded," and all "closed systems, like universal histories," were mere "cosmological romances." Croce's "methodical doubt" suggested that "brute facts" were "a *presupposition* that had *not been proved*," and that attempting proof of their existence—an argument Croce did not pause to elaborate—led to the conclusion that *"those facts really do not exist."*[19]

If facts are subjective—that is, exist only in the consciousness of the observer—judgments of ethical value would also be subjective, and Croce did not hesitate in following this line of thought to the conclusion "that every fact has its reason and that no individual is completely wrong." Individual consciousness was the only reality. "True history" was "the history of the individual" insofar as he "was universal and of the universal in so far as individual."[20]

Robert Livingston Schuyler, then at Columbia, was one of the first historians to link the New Physics with Croce's philosophy of absolute immanence and to denounce them both as guides for historians. Schuyler, who had at first been attracted to relativism but who was alarmed, perhaps, by Becker's endorsement of Croce's extreme subjectivism, denounced Croce and all "'current-eventists'" in the spring of 1932; Schuyler refused to countenance "the indignity that astronomy has heaped upon us" by "adopting the metaphysics of subjective idealism, which makes the very existence of the cosmos dependent upon consciousness."[21]

"Confidentially," Conyers Read told Becker as they planned the program for the American Historical Association's annual gathering in 1933, Beard was "a bit hipped on Croce."[22] But Beard's admiration for Croce, his enthusiastic suggestion that this great contemporary be invited to come to the United States personally to speak to the assembled profession, and his many references to Croce's writings did not mean that Beard accepted the solipsistic position of Croce's relativism. Although Beard appreciated Croce's robust style and cited his conclusions on some points, he was careful not to follow Croce over the abyss to solipsism. Beard took from Croce's thought only those aspects that vindicated and strengthened the relativistic stance already apparent in the New History. Croce had written that "only an interest in the life of the present can move one to investigate past fact. Therefore, this past fact does not answer to a past interest, but to a present interest, in so far as it is unified with an interest in the present life. . . ." This was nothing more than the common sense of the New History, and one could endorse it (which Beard did) without taking Croce's extreme position on the subjective nature of facts. Moreover, one could take a different view of the nature of fact and still agree with Croce's conclusions on choice and periodization. Beard was in complete agreement with Croce's position, first, that the historian's selection of facts as well as his periodization were shaped by problems of his contemporary life, and second, that the facts did not present themselves to the mind of the historian bearing an interpretation.[23]

The limits of Beard's adaptation of Croce's philosophy of history and the sources of Beard's own vital distinction between fact and interpretation were made clear in his presidential address to the Middle States Council for the Social Studies in 1930. Here he pondered the attempts of three well-known scientists to come to philosophical terms with an indeterminate, infinite universe. What, he asked, could historians learn from the speculations of Sir James Jeans, Arthur S. Eddington, and Alfred North Whitehead?

Jeans held that the universe appeared "to have been designed by a pure mathematician"; Eddington postulated "a universal Mind or Logos"; while Whitehead spoke directly of God as "the ground for concrete actuality."[24] The "poor historian, who knows nothing of relativity, electrons, and symbolic logic," could only be amused by these theological differences, but for practical purposes, Beard emphasized, there was a crucial single point of agreement among the three interpreters of the new physics. They agreed "on the doctrine of realism . . . the doctrine that beneath all the appearances of life there is an underlying reality." A "real" world of facts *did* exist outside the consciousness of the observer.[25]

In a "quest for light" on the nature of this nonsubjective world, the "presiding discipline" was, of course, history, "but history *as* philosophy," wrote Beard citing Croce. Unless intellectuals were to be blind people feeling the elephant and finding only "partial and transitory truths," then they must gaze into "this perfect crystal," history. But, was it to be the crystal of Croce, an individual mind containing both fact and interpretation, or the crystal of Whitehead, mind arranging external and objective existent facts? Beard replied: "Perhaps it may be, as Goethe says, that when we look we see only our own souls in which the past is mirrored; if so, that itself is more startling than any of the revelations of physical science; history reveals itself looking at itself, for the human mind is an historical product, not a *deus ex machina.*" Rejecting Croce's position, Beard declared that "with the physicist, the student of history can safely say there is also something outside of themselves at which we are looking" and added: "All that is in the crystal is not in the mind of the observer."[26]

Beard noted that Hegel, Marx, and Croce had all "searched for the clue to actuality," Croce "with perhaps indifferent success." Each had seen only part of the elephant. When Beard spoke of "history-as-actuality," later defining it to include "all that has been done, said, felt, and thought by human beings on this planet since humanity began its long career," he was using *actuality* in precisely the manner of Arthur Eddington. In his chapter on reality, Eddington had used *actuality* to mean the world as potentially "knowable," though not known. "We can scarcely describe the beauty of a landscape as nonexistent when there is no conscious being to witness it," Eddington had written, "but it is through consciousness

> that we can attribute a meaning to it. And so it is with the actuality of the world. The less stress we lay on the accident of parts of the world being known at the present era to particular minds, the more stress we must lay on the *potentiality* of being known to mind as a fundamentally objective property of matter, giving it the status of actuality whether individual consciousness is taking note of it or not.[27]

Applying this insight to history, Beard concluded that fact, "history-as-actuality," existed outside the observer's mind as the potentially knowable basis for the subjective activity of interpretation. Hence one could agree—as Beard certainly did—with Croce's proclamation that history was "contemporary thought about the past" while rejecting Croce's conclusion that "every particular form, individual, action, institution, work, thought, is destined to perish. . . . Finally, truth itself perishes, particular and determined truth, because it is not rethinkable."[28]

Thus was it possible to marry instrumentalism and relativism. By halting at the abyss of solipsism and joining the idealistic scientists—Jeans, Whitehead, Eddington, and also Ernest W. Hobson—in their "objective" posture toward the external world of fact, Beard left room for the possibility that "history-as-actuality" might be developmental, might embrace both chance and choice, and just possibly could encompass "the concept of plan."[29] Beard's philosophical position was in accord with the "objective position" outlined by Whitehead:

> This creed is that the actual elements perceived by our senses are *in themselves* the elements of a common world; and that this world is a complex of things, including indeed our acts of cognition, but transcending them. According to this point of view the things experienced are to be distinguished from our knowledge of them. So far as there is dependence, the *things* pave the way for the *cognition*, rather than *vice versa*. But the point is that the actual things experienced enter into a common world which transcends knowledge, though it includes knowledge.[30]

When he entitled his presidential address "Written History as an Act of Faith" Beard recorded his agreement with Whitehead's conclusion that there was a "deeper faith" which could not be justified by inductive generalization, which sprang "from direct inspection of the nature of things as disclosed in our immediate present experience." "There is no parting from your own shadow," Whitehead had written, "to experience this faith is to know that in being ourselves we are more than ourselves, to know that our experience, dim and fragmentary as it is, yet sounds the utmost depths of reality."[31]

The relativistic theory of historical knowledge defended by Beard in the 1930s had been nourished by the pragmatic common sense of the New History; by Croce's more explicit formulation of the subjective nature of hypotheses; and by the endorsement, arising from speculation on the indeterminate universe of the quantum theory, of a philosophical position predicated on the existence of an "actuality," a "real" world of fact outside the mind of the observer, by a number of those scientists who wrote popular books. A fourth source, compatible with the others, was Karl Mannheim's social theory of knowledge. Mannheim's articles had appeared in German scholarly journals throughout the 1920s; a number of them were collected and published in 1929 as *Ideologie und Utopie*, which was enthusiastically received in the United States. Writing to Malcolm Cowley and Bernard Smith, who were editing a collection of essays on the most influential books of the twentieth century, Beard argued that Mannheim's work and Croce's should both be included.[32]

Beard took up Mannheim at a time when other scholars were also beginning to use his insights. One such scholar. was the venerable and witty socialist historian Vladimir Simkhovitch, who combined the terminology of the new physics with Mannheim's view that the origins of knowledge are social. Speaking of the historian as a "world-view artist" who performed the great philosophical task of correlating all knowledge, Simkhovitch wrote that "We have been framed," not only in space but also "in our mental operations." Seeing history with philosophers' eyes, said Simkhovitch, "We can look at it as progressive truth, as the truth that the times are capable of grasping. The historian is then but an intellectual representative of his own times." The genetic attitude in historical writing, he argued, was contrary to "our existential way of seeing things. This existential way of seeing life is based on the sum total of our life's experience, human, racial and personal, with which we are endowed and with which we meet problems of our own life and understand the problems of others."[33] Simkhovitch's magnificent articles were part of the context of Beard's conclusions on relativism and the sociology of knowledge.

Beard's declaration of 1933, however, more directly reflected the observations of another political scientist—Charles W. Cole. The terms Beard would later use in all of his philosophical writings on history appeared in an article by Cole six months before Beard addressed the American Historical Association. Cole, like Beard, saw three principles emerging from theoretical physics: first, relativity, by which Einstein and his followers meant (according to Cole) that "in themselves the fundamental concepts of time and distance involved in motion and the physical facts of measurement have no meaning" and "take on significance only when related to some frame of reference";

second, "indeterminism," which had replaced the Newtonian idea that an adequate knowledge of circumstances could provide a basis for predicting the future behavior of any physical system; and, third, "discontinuity," which hypothesized that the processes of nature were "jerky" and uneven.[34]

As Croce and Beard had already done, Cole argued that the selection, ordering, and relating of facts in written history were an essentially subjective process. A historical judgment "at its best," wrote Cole, was "what the historian thinks of what someone else thinks he saw or said he did or heard." The Rankean ideal of written history as it really was was impossible. Yet, Cole argued, "frames of reference" could clothe facts in new meaning even though the historian could see that "cause" and "contunuity" came from his or her mind. Cole hoped that "the new point of view based on hints from the recent work in physical sciences" would make theories more respectable in American historical writing. Theories would no longer "cringe and cower like handmaidens before the queenly 'facts.'" Instead, they would be tested by the pragmatic "criteria of what significance, connection and continuity they gave to the facts and by their compatibility with theories in other fields."[35]

Thus when Beard wrote about the philosophy of history, he did not write in a lonely desert populated only by Croce and Becker, and he was not abandoning the New History. He was entering a warm argument over the implications for work in the social sciences of a subjective view of knowledge. At stake, as he clearly saw, was the vindication of the life of a reasonable man of action.

In the 1920s Beard had worried that imagination among social scientists was declining, that specialization would kill creativity, and that a humanitarian ethic for the social sciences was disappearing.[36] Increasingly he became more specific about these concerns. Amid an atmosphere in which even the existence of "facts" was questioned, in which all values were seen as relative to particular circumstances, he sought a clear path, a way to reason for himself through the paralysis or drift that might result from a hopeless relativism. In the works of the idealistic physicists—especially Whitehead—he found a faith in the crucial distinction between the observer and the observed. From the New Physics came the idea of "history as actuality" and the concept of "frames of reference" as well as the company of fellow believers in a world outside the individual's consciousness. From Mannheim came a way to reason about relative knowledge itself. The "socially unattached" and self-conscious intellectual could rise above circumstances of birth and class, analyze the reigning ideology, and project his own utopia. Mannheim shared Beard's commitment to a world outside the observer's mind. Like Beard, he urged action to shape coming history. Opposing what he termed the "vague, ill-considered, and sterile form of relativism with regard to scientific knowledge," Mannheim spoke of a "creative skepticism" that would dare to act on the basis of some vision of the future.[37] Mannheim's viewpoint was a vindication of Beard's entire active life.

In "Written History as an Act of Faith" Beard expressed a paradox still at the core of our perception of the human condition: we appear to be conditioned by place, time, class, material circumstance and yet to be moral and responsible actors; we are caught in a net of limiting circumstances and yet have the sense that we act freely to affect our future. Like others, Beard resolved this paradox with an "act of faith," the only leap into freedom possible in the twentieth century.

Consciousness of the historical relativity of all values was the ultimate liberation from dogmatic absolutes—from belief in Hegelian rational spirits, in the inexorable determination of history by forces of production, and in the destruction of "civilization" through the working of irrevocable cycles of destiny. These were only interpretations, hypotheses arising from socially determined frames of reference. Even "the apostle of relativity," in the logic of contemporary criticism, was "destined to be destroyed by the child of his own brain"; when absolutes in history are rejected the absolutism of relativity is also rejected and "the skeptic of relativity will disappear in due course, beneath the ever-tossing waves of changing relativities." Freed from the determinisms of theology, physics, and biology, the historian confronted "the absolute in his field—the absolute totality of all historical occurrences past, present, and becoming to the end of things." Surrounded by this indeterminate web, the historian could choose to act with a free and creative will, not by evading the issues of contemporary thought but by proceeding "to examine his own frame of reference," clarifying and enlarging it "by acquiring knowledge of greater areas of thought and events," and by giving to it "consistency of structure by a deliberate conjecture respecting the nature or direction of the vast movements of ideas and interests called world history." Historical relativity thus became, in Beard's view, the corollary to human freedom. This was also the position of Mannheim. Knowledge, he had written, was not to be regarded "as a passive contemplation but as critical self-examination, and in this sense prepares the road for political action."[38]

Through reading, traveling, and the influence of the historian Alfred Vagts, his son-in-law, Beard was intimately acquainted with the great twentieth-century revision of German historicism begun under Wilhelm Dilthey and continued by such historians and sociologists as Ernst Troeltsch, Max Weber, George Simmel, and Heinrich Rickert. This avalanche of writing critical of historicism, along with the New History, the New Physics, the neo-Hegelianism of Croce, and Mannheim's sociology of knowledge, provided a fifth significant impetus for Beard's writings on the philosophy of history. He tried, not always tactfully, to bring this revision to the attention of American scholars, many of whom still hoped to write history as it actually had been, still assumed "a definite position with respect to the age-long objective-subjective problem," remained convinced "that a thoroughgoing organization of great historical events in an all-embracing coherence was possible," clung to the idea of continuous evolution," and limited history "to the world of the recorded and observable." Beard repeatedly urged his colleagues to read works of historiography such as Karl Heussi's *Die Krisis Des Historismus* (1932), which was a scholarly summary of developments in German historiography, particularly in the period from 1919 to 1929.[39]

Beard spoke in 1933 as the president of a professional group whose commitment to a science of history had already been questioned during the late twenties. In the debate about the question of history as an objective or subjective field of inquiry, Becker had captivated the audience at the 1931 convention by concluding that historians were members "of that ancient and honorable company of wise men of the tribe, of bards and story-tellers and minstrels, of soothsayers and priests, to whom in successive ages has been entrusted the keeping of the useful myths."[40] Becker's charming and extreme subjectivism finds no echo in the writings of Beard. What Beard urged was less esoteric: the replacement of the laboratory approach to history, based on a positivist conception of natural science, with a sociological approach grounded in an understanding of the recently revealed uncertainties and discontinuities of the scientific universe.

Although Beard was a skilled orchestrator, the themes he announced were not new or original, and he never claimed they were. The idea of the relativity of historical knowledge was, he noted, "obvious and commmonplace." His well-known statement of his epistemological position in 1933 was an amalgam of the writings of many contemporaries, and he was generous in citing his sources. In contrast to a history as it really had been, he maintained (following Croce) that written history was really "contemporary thought about the past"; that "any selection and arrangement of facts pertaining to any large area of history" was "controlled inexorably by the frame of reference in the mind of the selector and arranger" and that "the supreme issue" before the historian was the "determination of his attitude to contemporary thought." European critics of historicism had demonstrated, Beard concluded, that "the assumption that any historian can be a disembodied spirit as coldly neutral to human affairs as the engineer to an automobile" had to be rejected. It was time, he announced, to put the Rankean formula away in a museum of antiquities.[41]

Did this mean that "the scientific method"—rallying point of positivists and New Historians alike—was also doomed as an instrument in the hands of historians? In his negative reply to this question, Beard reiterated a distinction that was essential to his own position as distinguished from the purer skepticism of Becker and Croce. The scientific method was "the only method that can be employed in obtaining *accurate knowledge* of historical facts, personalities, situations, and movements." The scientific method alone could "disclose conditions that made possible what happened." In a democracy, this "inquiring spirit of science" was "the chief safeguard against the tyranny of authority, bureaucracy, and brute power."[42] Beard's historians were clearly to be more than "keepers of useful myths."

Recapitulating the German critics of historicism, Beard pointed out that the scientific method must be distinguished from its metaphysical counterpart, the belief in some ultimate law of human development. There were "objective realities," but the arrangement of these objective facts into meaningful sequence is a subjective process controlled by the historian's particular frame of reference—including, Beard supposed, "things deemed necessary, things deemed possible, and things deemed desirable."[43]

Mannheim had written that the future presented itself only in the form of "possibility." It remained "an impenetrable medium, and unyielding wall."

> When our attempts to see through it are repulsed [he concluded], we first become aware of the necessity of willfully choosing our course and, in close connection with it, the need for an imperative (a utopia) to drive us onward. Only when we know what are the interests and imperatives involved are we in a position to inquire into the possibilities of the present situation, and thus to gain our first insight into history. Here, finally, we see why no interpretation of history can exist except in so far as it is guided by interest and purposeful striving. . . . We could change the whole of society tomorrow if everybody could agree. The real obstacle is that every individual is bound into a system of established relationships that hamper his will. . . . The task, therefore, is to remove that source of difficulty by unveiling the hidden motives behind the individual's decision, thus putting him in a position really to choose. Then, and only then, would his decisions *really* lie with him.[44]

The tone of urgency in Beard's writings on the philosophy of history arose from this position that history was central to all knowledge, that it was either consciously or unconsciously goal-oriented—that is, political—and that part of the historian's task was to ask what he or she intended as an ultimate outcome of his or her own time. "Does the world move," asked Beard, "and, if so, in what direction?" Would the historian offer to inquiring minds "the pessimism of chaos" or forward movement "to some other arrangement which can be only dimly divined—a capitalist dictatorship, a proletarian dictatorship, or a collectivist democracy?" The last was his "own guess, founded on a study of long trends and on a faith in the indomitable spirit of mankind." The historian who could never know or explain the totality of history-as-actuality, could still help by writing history "to make history, petty or grand."[45]

On a later occasion, speaking to a standing-room-only crowd at the Association's convention in 1937, Beard cited Mannheim's *Ideology and Utopia* as a work of "great skill and detachment" and defended his membership in the school of historians who stressed material factors in their interpretations of events: "In everyday language, it is by looking calmly at ourselves as well as others, by discovering the affiliation of personalities and ideas with interests, by recognizing frankly and with good humor that we stand somewhere—it is by doing this that we can approach, but never reach, that ideal of objectivity which the Ranke school claimed to have attained."[46]

Thus, when Beard exhorted his colleagues to cast off their "servitude to the assumptions of natural science," to give up trying to turn "the Newtonian trick" by formulating physical laws or using biological analogies in their writing, he was not (as Chester Destler perceived him some twenty years later) acting as an "aggressive subjective relativist."[47] He was not abandoning himself to intuitive idealism, nor was he rejecting the wisdom science might offer to the study of humanity by historians. He was not an apostle blinded on the road to Damascus who suddenly rejected his past intellectual positions. His "act of faith" as to the possibility of order and movement in human affairs should be seen in the context of his understanding of the discontinuous and indeterminate picture of the physical world arising from the New Physics of the first decades of the twentieth century. Conceivably, some historian of the later twentieth century will speak of the implications of "black holes" for theories of human destiny. The very terms used by Beard and other relativists—"frames of reference," history as "actuality"—and even the rejection of solipsism and utter skepticism were characteristic of those scientists turned philosophers, such as Hobson, Whitehead, Eddington, and Jeans, who sought to relate the discoveries of the New Physics in laypeople's terms and to connect these discoveries to the larger questions of human existence.

Beard's 1933 address was not, as some have charged, a "sudden iconoclasm," a "vicious assault on the idol before which all the new historians had prostrated themselves," and a "suicidal lunge at the New History." Rather than rejecting a scientific approach, Beard was following theoretical science into the wilderness of uncertainty where, as Eddington put it, "It is a consequence of the advent of the quantum theory that *physics is no longer pledged to a scheme of deterministic law*. Determinism has dropped out altogether in the latest formulations of theoretical physics and it is at least open to doubt whether it will ever be brought back."[48]

While the New Physics ended its commitment to determinism, the great flowering of creativity in the social sciences in Weimar Germany produced a critique of historicism and a theory of knowledge that were compatible with this revised vision of the universe. Beard's purpose in calling the attention of historians in the United States to the revision of historicism taking place in Europe was *not* to urge others to adopt his own eclectic relativism but instead to focus on the great fallacy of historicism: the idea that the historian stood outside the *Zeitgeist*, a scholar without politics, a neutral mind at work reflecting the connections in a mass of facts. It was Charles Beard's grand ambition that scholars in the United States should join in the effort to formulate a humanism appropriate to conditions in the twentieth century.

Beard's version of the crisis in contemporary thought and the path he had chosen for himself provoked an indiscriminate rage in some historians. C. H. McIlwain, a distinguished historian of English law, directed his 1936 presidential address to the Association to Beard personally. Beard and his ilk were a crowd of "defeatists" who were arguing that, because a completely accurate reconstruction of the past could never be done, "it should not be attempted at all." Ignoring Beard's careful distinction between fact and opinion, McIlwain exhorted his audience in emotional terms: "Now we are told . . . let us rest content with the subjective. It is all that we can ever reach, all that can have any truth or value for us. Objective truth is a chimera. History is only an 'act of faith.' This intellectual weariness is no new thing in the world. Plato spent his life combating it among the Sophists."[49]

Several other colleagues, among them Theodore C. Smith and Allan Nevins, accused Beard of advocating "propagandist history." Nevins combined an anti-intellectual attack on the issues Beard was raising (which he referred to as "that pseudo-philosophic jargon upon Historismus, frames of reference, patterns of culture, and cyclical phases of causation, which I no more understand than do most of its users") with the suggestion that Beard was abetting fascism.[50]

According to Nevins, Beard had invited historians to commit themselves "to a philosophy in accordance with which [they would] deliberately write." He was not trying to reduce the "role of assumption" but to enlarge and emphasize it. The implication, Nevins argued, was that "one set of assumptions would be chosen as sounder than another set, and an effort would be made to organize historical writing on this set of preconceptions." This was "the doctrine to which historical writing [had] bowed under state pressure in Nazi Germany and Fascist Italy." Those who held a "higher ideal of truth," Nevins vowed, would "never give up the attempt" to attain it.[51]

Beard's point, so repellant to his attackers, was that history is always written with a present purpose. But his further conclusion—that recognizing the sociological basis of all knowledge, of all hypotheses explaining facts, would make people more aware of as well as more critical of the purposes for which history was written—was ignored in the furor over the basic relativist position.[52] Replying to Nevins, Beard noted that he had never said that "because knowledge of the whole and the absolute truth" was impossible, that historians "should not search for all the truths we can find with unremitting energies. To admit that one is not God may be defeatism, but it is a confession that has the appearance of 'truth.'"

How, asked Beard, could urging scholars to be aware of their preconceptions "lend any sanction to fascism"? The fascists, with their "preposterous preconceptions" were forbidding "the exploration of any, even their own."[53]

Shortly after this exchange with Nevins, Beard received a kindly note from Becker: "What they can't forgive you for is for saying . . . that history is an act of faith. . . . You are casting doubt on the absolute value & truth of their studies—that's why they call you a defeatist. Don't mind—as I know you don't. . . . In these last days there is a terrific pressure on everyone to be *loyal* to some cause or group or individual. You are expected to join something and hate in unison."[54]

In his writing Beard consistently stressed the political nature of history, the fact that, because public policies were founded on conceptions of history, historians had an inevitable "public responsibility." It was not, as so many of his critics maintained, that history *should* be propaganda, but rather that it *could* be propaganda. In Beard's lexicon, the words *duty* and *responsibility* applied especially to historians, who were statesmen and women without portfolio. The scientific method and the rejection of any absolutist interpretation of events, coupled with a self-consciousness about one's own biases, could only produce greater freedom of choice within democracy and an escape from the totalitarian shadow lurking in what Mannheim, referring to Sorel, had spoken of as the "intellectual twilight" of the twentieth century.[55]

Philosophers soon joined the dispute over relativistic theories of knowledge. Maurice Mandelbaum, a brilliant and bold young philosopher at Yale, prepared as his doctoral thesis in 1938 *The Problem of Historical Knowledge: An Answer to Relativism.* Stridently opposing the relativism of Dilthey, Croce, and Mannheim, Mandelbaum was dismayed that their arguments were being espoused in America by such influential figures as Beard and Becker. In Mandelbaum's view, European scholars such as George Simmel, Heinrich Rickert, Max Scheler, and Ernst Troeltsch who had grappled with relativism had not successfully refuted it: "In this set of failures one lesson should be clear: that unless we go back to the usual view of objectivity and say that historical objectivity resides in the historian's ability to portray the real character and relations of historical events, we shall find no escape from relativism."[56]

Denying Beard's idea of a "limited relativity," Mandelbaum maintained that "once it is held that the validity of knowledge must be understood and estimated with reference to the conditions under which it was formed, complete relativism is unavoidable." It was obvious, said Mandelbaum—making the classic critique of the relativist position—that the truth of a statement was not necessarily (that is, logically) related to its origin.[57]

For Beard's distinction between fact and opinion Mandelbaum substituted the terms *statement* and *judgment.* In his view, the problem of "valid knowledge" was "a problem of the truth of the statements given" and was "not concerned with the judgments out of which those statements originated." But what of the "tendency of historians to go beyond their statements of fact to statements of value?" This was the essential difference between Mandelbaum and his adversaries: "Those who maintain that valuational elements enter into the actual constitution of historical accounts," he stated correctly, "believe that it is only through some unrecognized valuational judgments that the historian orders and arranges his facts." This conclusion was false, argued Mandelbaum, for the reason that all facts occurred in some context, "and in that context the fact itself leads on to further facts without any intermediation or selection based upon the historian's valuational attitudes, class interests, or the like."

On the other hand, if relativists were right in their assumptions, "we should have to appeal to our knowledge of the historian himself or to some general cultural value to determine how one fact is related to another in his historical account."[58] "Of course!" a relativist might have commented on reading this passage, but Mandelbaum continued: "That we do not do this, but consider the concrete facts as themselves possessing a definite meaning, significance and order, testifies to the non-valuational character of that which binds the facts into a historical account."[59]

Philosophies of history such as Beard's teleological view of history as progress toward some distant, receding goal, since they depended on metaphysical assertions rather than on empirical evidence, were, Mandelbaum concluded, "a form of apologetics" with which "the historian, as historian, need not be concerned."[60]

Mandelbaum's axe had been sharp, but the tree refused to fall. Reviewing Mandelbaum's book, Beard contended that his adversary had created a straw man. "I do not hold," Beard wrote, "that historical 'truth' is relative but that the facts chosen, the spirit, and the arrangement of every historical work are relative. Mr. Mandelbaum has missed the whole point of the business." Mandelbaum had not, of course, missed the point. He had simply refused to accept Beard's bifurcation of fact and interpretation.[61]

The coming of World War II strengthened the hand of the empiricists against the relativists. "Truth" did seem absolute and visible and it did appear to be all on one side. Yet Beard remained adamantly committed to the philosophical positions he had elaborated in the 1930s. The final collective project of his life was membership on the Social Science Research Council's Committee on Historiography. In 1946 the committee produced a pamphlet, *Theory and Practice in Historical Study*, that reflected Beard's dominant crusading on the committee. In his introductory essay he again urged, on familiar grounds, a reconsideration of historiography by historians in the United States. Historians who ignored the grounding of public policy in historical interpretation would fail in meeting "one of the supreme intellectual challenges of our time."[62]

For Beard, theory and action had to be intimately connected. Recognition of the relativity of all historical judgments freed the historian to use his knowledge in a self-conscious way in the formation of public policy. During his last years Beard was increasingly attracted to the notion of "fictions," taken from the work of the German philosopher Hans Vaihinger. Examples of fictions are "democracy," "justice," "political man," "economic man," and so forth. "Great thinkers," Beard noted, used these "abstractions drawn from knowledge of history-as-actuality" to analyze, select, and order their data. These abstractions were not true hypotheses, but they furnished guides for thought and action. The abstraction that was always central in Beard's thought was "democracy," thoughtful people participating in the decisions that affected their lives. One had to write, and speak, and act, as if it were going on. Vaihinger, Beard remarked, had warned of the "deadly peril that immediately besets us when thought is separated from action and theoretical thinking is made an end in itself."[63]

Beard was no philosopher, but he was extremely sensitive to philosophical issues, and he was an early participant in a debate that has waxed and waned between proponents of social science based on empirical models and proponents of normative theory.[75] He had started out as a young positivist who entertained Mary Ritter by reading her passages from Fustel de Coulanges and ended by taking a position exactly the opposite of what would come to be labeled "mainstream social science." The social scientist not only collected facts, described, and explained them but also advocated a clear and open set of values, his or her own "frame of reference." A social science without values could not exist, he argued. "As a result of much study and reflection," he told the American Political Science Association in 1948 in his last public appearance before his death, "I have come to the conviction that we have no justification whatever for regarding our universe as a unified process under law and hence reducible to an exact science, either physical or political. . . ."[64]

The seeds of Beard's later questioning of scientific history were planted during his years as a New Historian at Columbia and his own limited relativism was based on an understanding of the implications of the theory of relativity in physics for traditional ideas of causation, on a firm grasp of the subjective neo-Hegelianism of Benedetto Croce, and on an appreciation of Mannheim's and others' efforts to overcome the skepticism that resulted from a view that made even "facts" a creation of the individual mind. He formulated and expressed his views on these questions at a time many other historians and social scientists were doing the same. As in so many instances in his career, Beard was the curious and far-ranging scholar, reading many books, asking many questions, and beckoning others to awaken and follow him onto the main road of contemporary philosophical thought. "When I come to the end," he once told a young historian, "my mind will still be beating its wings against the bars of thought's prison."[66]

13

Battle for Nonintervention, 1935–1941

E arly in 1935, Beard predicted war in the Pacific. Noting that the New Deal had not distributed wealth more generally and that the United States possessed its largest peacetime navy, Beard warned that another war might divert the nation from tasks illuminated by the depression. He was not saying, he added,

> that President Roosevelt will deliberately plunge the country into a Pacific war in his efforts to escape the economic crisis. There will be an "incident," a "provocation." Incidents and provocations are of almost daily occurrence. Any government can quickly magnify one of them into a "just cause for war." . . . The Jeffersonian party gave the nation the War of 1812, the Mexican War, and its participation in the World War. The Pacific War awaits.[1]

During the 1920s Beard had repeatedly recalled the suppression of free speech during World War I. He had consistently campaigned against an American overseas empire. He had urged the development of a "consistent theory of national defense" and a retreat from formal and informal empire.[2] Although he steered away from the controversy over a revisionist interpretation of the causes of World War I, Beard constantly reminded his listeners and readers of its disastrous results.[3]

As military encounters erupted in Asia and Europe during the 1930s, Beard remained optimistic that America could stay at peace. For him, no worthwhile

American interest was imperiled by war. American involvement in these foreign quarrels would mean defending European and American imperialism, debasing democracy, further distancing decision-making from the people and their representatives, and further enhancing the powers of the executive and bureaucratic experts. Unlike many liberals, he never saw the totalitarian evil abroad as a threat remotely comparable to the unsolved economic crisis at home. The latter remained his foremost consideration. "National Defense," he noted regretfully in 1940, was "the only effective motive force which [the New Dealers] appear to have developed with a view to compelling concentrated industrial ownership to produce."[4]

While reviewing Beard's role in the debates over foreign policy in the 1930s, this chapter will emphasize both his concern for the democratic process in the United States and the fact that the struggle, as he viewed it, was also a conflict over the question of whether the American economy was to be directed by private interests or by representatives of planning in the interest of economic democracy.

Beard had enormous sympathy for the victims of fascism in Europe, and, as he demonstrated in some polemics during the thirties, he was a sturdy foe of fascist racist propaganda.[5] He also recommended many displaced foreign scholars for positions in the United States, promoted the establishment of the University in Exile at the New School for Social Research, and helped the Frankfurt Institute of Social Research to find a new home at Columbia after 1934.[6]

In 1936, as honorary chairman of the International Relief Association, a group devoted to aiding political exiles and prisoners, he wrote to *The New York Times* in support of a Nobel Prize for the imprisoned German pacifist Carl von Ossietzky.[7] In 1941, he solicited funds for an organization aiding the escape of antifascists from France.[8]

Actively sympathetic with the Loyalists in the Spanish Civil War, he opposed Franklin Roosevelt's use of the Neutrality Act to block aid to the Loyalists. To Beard, the President's Spanish policy revealed the hypocrisy of Roosevelt's rhetorical sallies against fascism as well as his willingness to abandon traditional methods of diplomacy at the behest of conservative governments in England and France.[9]

Those interventionists who accused Beard of being indifferent to the fate of millions of people in Europe and Asia were wrong. He did condemn the conduct of the governments of Germany, Italy, and Japan as "in most respects barbaric, indecent, cruel, and inhuman. What I do say," he added in 1939, "is that the underlying issues accompanying their conduct cannot be reduced to a single issue: democracy against despotism, humanity against inhumanity." Furthermore, "the business of preventing German and Italian domination in Europe" was "the business of the powers immediately and directly interested,"

and they had "the men, money, and materials to do the work" if that was
what they really wanted to accomplish. [10]

An independent activist, Beard customarily did not lend his name to political organizations. An exception was his acceptance in 1938 of the honorary
chairmanship of the Non-Partisan Committee to Re-elect Senator Gerald P.
Nye. [11] And in 1938 he was briefly associated with the Keep America Out of
War Committee, although his contribution was limited to allowing some of
his statements to be used in pamphlets. This group shared Beard's view of the
primacy of domestic recovery and reform as well as his fears of the threat to
civil liberties posed by war. [12] Beard was never a member of John Flynn's New
York Chapter of America First, and he never met Charles Lindberg before
1945. Although he sympathized with America First's goals, and although his
books were recommended reading for its members, he did not lend his name
to any newspaper advertising sponsored by the Committee. "It [America First]
believes," he told a reporter on 8 September 1940, "that the foreign policy of
the United States should be directed to the preservation of the peace and
security of this nation in its continental zone of interests." [13] As a radical,
Beard could never have belonged to an organization that was backed by the
wealthy interests he had consistently opposed. When their position coincided
with his own on foreign policy, however, he was willing to publicize the fact.

Generally, he wrote and spoke on behalf of himself and his own larger
dream of continentalism, repeating these themes: in the Orient, American
imperialism clashed with Japanese imperialism; in Europe, the so-called "democracies," England and France, governments unrepresentative of the working people and devoted to empire in Asia and Africa, were selling out the
democratic government of Loyalist Spain; in America, people were expecting
war, and the Roosevelt administration had avoided candid discussion of the
issues, the costs, and its goals. Again and again Beard asked how the government, which was unable to bring security to most Americans, could leap on
to the task of planning for the security of the world. And in President Roosevelt's foreign policy Beard detected the same random, experimental uncertainty that had characterized the President's leadership in domestic affairs.

According to Beard, American continentalism had reached its "zenith" with
passage of the neutrality resolutions of August 1935, 1936, and 1937, laws he
described as "a triumph for the plain people who do the fighting and bear the
hardships of war." [14] The neutrality resolutions were steps toward the planned
economy of *The Open Door at Home,* and Beard deeply regretted that they
were "whittled away" by a President and State Department devoted to the
opposite view, collective internationalism. This policy was founded, as Beard
saw things, on "international capitalism . . . increasing world trade through
the free exchange of raw materials and finished products," on "gold as the
basis of a uniform international monetary system," on a "conception of a

unified, automatically regulated world economy," and on "the doctrine that any event anywhere, threatening international peace, law, and order, is a direct threat to all nations which are to act collectively against the peace breaker." Beard's program rested on analysis of the domestic needs of the country, President Roosevelt's policy on a "'world system'" of unreformed international capitalism.[15]

In 1936, at the conclusion of the Senate hearings conducted by Gerald Nye on the role of the munitions industry in World War I, Beard argued against the vulgar interpretation of the war: it was not caused by the evil schemes of bankers and profit-hungry armaments manufacturers. Rather, it was the product of capitalism, its surpluses, and its need for expansion. Before World War I, said Beard, the German submarine attacks on neutral ships of the United States were not only a matter of honor but also a question of lost profits for the domestic economy. Politicians had responded to the pressure of bankers who wanted to loan money to the Allies, and the United States had become enmeshed in the Allied cause. Mounting purchases by the Allies involved millions of people and dollars: "If the war stopped, American business would slow down from prosperity to dullness, if not calamity. If the Allies were defeated, things would be worse. American millions were at stake." The war involved less the honor and virtue of politicians and more the system within which they operated.[16]

Thus mandatory neutrality legislation was a way, as Beard saw it, of amending the capitalist system by shifting responsibility for economic decisions from private parties to representatives of the people. Did we want, Beard inquired, "discussions and decisions of this character to be carried on secretly behind closed doors or openly in the Congress of the United States? In fine, are bans on loans, credits, and sales to belligerents to be raised clandestinely in huddled conferences of bankers and politicians or publicly by the representatives of the American people in Congress assembled?"[17] Beard concluded that mandatory neutrality would doubtless involve "many drastic changes in [American] capitalism," and he preferred "any changes that [might] be required in it to the frightful prospects of American involvement in a war in Europe or Asia." Urging an embargo on the sale of munitions and the extension of credits to belligerents as well as prohibitions on sales to neutrals engaged in reselling to belligerents, he joined the opponents of every effort to modify the neutrality legislation.[18]

Beard's head was not in the sand. He saw the same events as others. But he shunned the belief that "collective internationalism" was a good solution to the problem of expansionist dictatorships—first, because it assumed an unmodified, unplanned capitalist economy, and second, because it depended on the executive and administrative branches of the government to conduct foreign policy and thus violated what Beard deemed the hallmark of democracy, rational public discussion of alternative policies. "If we go to war," he noted, admitting the possibility, "let us go to war for some grand national and human advantage openly discussed and deliberately arrived at, and not to bail out farmers, bankers and capitalists or to save politicians from the pain of dealing with a domestic crisis."[19]

Neither Roosevelt's press conferences nor his homely analogies were regarded by Beard as proper stimulants to informed public discussion. He wanted a probing dialogue and candid analysis, not evasion. "Of all the crazy institutions ever established in the United States," he complained, "the press conference on foreign relations is the worst . . . it is preposterous for the President of the United States or the Secretary of State to allow himself to be heckled by 25 or 30 newshawks bent on snatching sensations even out of burning homes and new-made graves." Instead of holding these conferences, the President should write a public commentary on the pressing issues and give it to all newspapers. If the President believed peace was impossible, then Beard urged that he "should formulate his case, lay it before Congress, and call for action," even for war if he deemed it necessary. "Any other procedure" was "both undignified and dangerous."[20]

When President Roosevelt, in October 1937, used what Beard considered an ill-chosen and condescending analogy, labeling Germany, Italy, and Japan as sick countries that needed to be "quarantined," Beard replied sharply at an Armistice Day commemoration (11 November 1937) at Syracuse University. He was again the fierce debater, passionately challenging the President's implication that he was an expert. ("Remember," the President had said on 12 October, "that from 1913 to 1921 I personally was fairly close to world events, and in that period, while I learned much of what to do, I also learned much of what not to do.")[21]

This stance of the expert infuriated Beard: "[T]he President tells us that he knows and insinuates that the rest of us, who were not fairly close to world affairs between 1913 and 1921, will do well to accept his guidance." But how much, Beard asked, did the experts—President Wilson, Colonel E. M. House, Walter Hines Page, William J. Bryan, and Robert Lansing—really know about world affairs? Did they know of "the network of secret negotiations, treaties, and agreements which controlled world events?" Did President Wilson "really know? . . . Did the then assistant Secretary of the Navy? It may be suspected that even he did not."[22]

By 1938 Beard viewed the President as "more or less obsessed by the universal philanthropy of Woodrow Wilson." According to Beard, Roosevelt, like Wilson before him, believed that America was "morally bound to do good everywhere" and he imagined "himself able to know the good in each and every case." Publicly, Beard urged that through his choices in foreign policy the President was jeopardizing his unique place in American history as the president who had discussed with the people more fundamental problems of American life and society than all other presidents combined.[23] Privately, he described Washington early in 1938 as "a mad house" in which Roosevelt rattled "on domestic policies like a mad man in a fog, and nobody can make head or tail of him, it, or she. All social talk," he noted, "turns on the coming war and the administration is making a drive to stir war psychology."[24]

In these days of peculiar alliances and stormy rallies, Beard relished verbal jousts. In a public debate with Earl Browder, a leading Communist politician who supported Roosevelt's call for "quarantining the aggressors" through an embargo by the United States, France, Britain, and the Soviet Union, Beard replied by questioning whether the other 90 percent of the world, in Africa and Asia, would welcome "peaceful collaboration" between imperialists against "aggressors." In the case of a war for democracy, he asked, would "the democratic powers . . . favor the institution of democratic government among the ten percent and elsewhere?" Imperialism gave cause to suspect such slogans. British and French working people did not control their governments, and these governments, with whom Browder urged collaboration, had been deaf to the appeals of Loyalist Spain. Recalling the intervention of Allied troops in the Russian Revolution, Beard twisted the knife by questioning the premise that war ever advanced the cause of democracy. Finally, he returned to his standard theme: there was "enough to do at home."[25]

In February 1938 Beard again challenged the President. Testifying before the house Naval Affairs Committee, Beard opposed Roosevelt's request for a larger naval budget. A sound domestic economy should have the highest priority, Beard declared, warning that the President's "quarantine" message clearly signaled the abandonment of this goal. Now, since the President was also urging laws to prevent profiteering, to equalize "'the burdens of war,'" and to mobilize the army and navy, Beard asked that the issue of war be "submitted to the country in a direct form, not as an inference in an appropriation bill." It was a question, he emphasized, of who should control the direction of foreign policy.[26]

Unlike the pacifists, Beard believed in planning (but by civilians) for national defense. He predicted that, in the future, planning for the army and navy would be combined, and he called for a combination of members of the House, naval and army officers, and civilians to survey "the whole business of defending Admiral Leahy's line, from the Aleutians to Hawaii and Panama, from the Virgin Islands up to the Coast of Maine." He did not want this vital task to be monopolized by the executive branch or by the armed services.[27]

When the naval bill moved on to the Senate, Oswald G. Villard urged Beard to testify again but Beard declined, although he heartily sympathized with Villard's desire to add some fire to the "old crowd" of "regular peace people." Beard felt that he had "labored in vain for years to get the peace people to study naval warfare and history." However, they had found it easier to remain ignorant of the world and were sure to be fried on Fred Vinson's "gridiron."[28]

Although nothing concrete emerged from their talk, Beard and Villard hoped to have a private committee inquire into the "actual feasibility of the invasion of the United States." Beard also wanted the proposed commission to investigate the utility of battleships in modern warfare of any kind, defensive or aggressive.[29]

In the summer of 1939 Beard published *Giddy Minds and Foreign Quarrels,* in which he suggested that President Roosevelt was following Shakespeare's rendition of Henry IV's advice to his son:

> I . . . had a purpose now
> To lead out many to the Holy Land,
> Lest rest and living still might make them look
> Too near unto my state. Therefore, my Harry,
> Be it thy course, to busy giddy minds
> With foreign quarrels; that action, hence borne out,
> May waste the memory of the former days.

Beard did not follow this bitter suggestion with a charge that President Roosevelt was plotting to take the country to war. On the contrary, Beard emphasized the erratic and contradictory nature of Rooseveltian policy during the thirties: no theory of national interest guided policy beyond the President's "quixotic and dangerous" desire to cooperate with Britain and France and to maintain the Open Door in China.[30]

The process of American policymaking appeared irrational, and the issues were not being clearly formulated. For example, Beard wondered why the administration felt it necessary to cover the worthy undertaking of hemispheric defense with a blanket of rhetoric about the defense of democracy.[31] Policies for both Asia and Europe seemed planless.

In the Far East, the Philippines had been promised independence. But the lingering question of naval bases and the fortification of Guam indicated to Beard "that someone in the Capitol" was "toying with the idea of transforming our obvious liability in the Western Pacific into what is euphoneously called 'an asset of naval power'—for exerting pressure in Asiatic affairs." It was a well-known fact, Beard pointed out, that American trade with China was "relatively insignificant . . . of no vital importance to the United States." Why then, he asked, was the administration laboring hard at taking the Open Door delusion seriously? Japan was the largest American customer in the Pacific. The inclusion of Japan among the enemies of the United States in the President's speeches seemed to ignore this reality.[32]

In regard to Europe, American policy appeared even more contradictory. On the one hand, the administration had actively intervened in the Spanish Civil War, violated its Treaty of 1902 (a year's notice was to be given before changing trading arrangements), and procured an extension of the neutrality laws to civil wars. International law had thus been ignored, and the way had been smoothed for Hitler and Mussolini to arm the fascists.

On the other hand, the violation of neutrality in Spain had been followed in October 1937 by the "Quarantine Speech" and by the President's message of January 1938 urging more armaments and battleships and calling for a mobilization bill. Since Admiral Leahy himself had previously testified that the navy was prepared to defend the Western Hemisphere, the President's call for more battleships appeared to Beard to be part of an unexplained *world* strategy.[33] Appealing for peace in the wake of Hitler's invasion of Czechoslovakia in the spring of 1939, the President had also urged revision of the neutrality law to give him greater discretion in the application of an embargo. Meanwhile, "the Tory government in Great Britain and the reactionary government in France were playing with Hitler and Mussolini and aiding in the destruction of the Spanish Republic."

Although the President had not explained his course of action, Beard proposed now to explain it for him: he was intending to pursue active collaboration with Great Britain and France "in their everlasting wrangle with Germany, Italy, and Japan," and he wanted "to wring from Congress the power to throw the whole weight of the United States" on their side in negotiations and also in war if they managed "to bungle the game." Roosevelt did not seem to understand that the United States had limited power, that a permanent peace could not be constructed and forced upon other nations. Finally, his foreign policy was based on the questionable assumption that the democracy and the economy of the United States were healthy and secure. Given the economic and military circumstances of the United States, Beard announced that "the very idea of world economic pacification" was a "dream of Sancho Panza."[34]

People of his persuasion, Beard concluded, were not advocating isolation. They did not seek withdrawal from the world. Rather, they were "deal[ing] with the world as it is and not as romantic propagandists picture it." The United States, he argued, should "promote commerce, but force 'nothing,'" "steer clear of hates and loves," keep "correct and formal relations with all established governments without respect to their forms or their religions," maintain the anti-imperialist aspects of the Monroe Doctrine, defend our continental zone, and concentrate on the defects in our own economic and social system.[35]

Giddy Minds appeared in September 1939, just as the German invasion of Poland forced form England and France a declaration of war in Europe. Partly because it was a reprinting of an article in *Harper's*, the book received few notices. However, the interventionist *New York Times* thought it worthy of a sarcastic editorial,[36] and a group of interventionist academicians—Clarence A. Berdahl of the University of Illinois, Kenneth Colgrove of Northwestern, Walter Rice Sharp of the University of Wisconsin, and Quincy Wright of the University of Chicago—published a six-column letter to the editors of *The Times* in November 1939 rebutting Beard's position.

Their rebuttal ran: Trade with China was significant and its protection important; Roosevelt and his followers in academia were not diverting giddy minds from domestic problems. The United States, they argued, did have a tradition of intervention in Latin America and the Far East; and no responsible person was proposing "wholesale interference with foreign quarrels and disturbances."[37] However, the professors ignored Beard's most salient points: the erratic process of decision-making in foreign policy, the limits of American power to shape history in other areas, and the continuing malaise of the American domestic economy.

The debate continued as Beard addressed the geopolitical argument against his continentalism with his "memorandum," *A Foreign Policy for America*, published in May 1940, on the eve of the fall of France to the German armies. Point by point, he restated the case for a continental policy of defense and neutrality. His policy, he argued, was clearly the choice of the majority of American people. The "internationalist" intellectuals, he charged, preferred to live with abstractions, not to work with the people on controversial problems:

> To such intellects, matters of fiscal reform, checking deficits, putting ten million unemployed to work, housing a third of a nation, conserving the soil of a hundred million acres . . . might seem piddling in comparison with planning a world order and taking part in the councils of world conferences. Great ardor displayed in conflicts at home over civil liberties, industrial relations, the plight of share croppers, the distempers of the unemployed, and other domestic agitations could readily lead to ruined reputations, damaged careers, and personal distresses.[38]

Simultaneously with *A Foreign Policy for America*, Knopf published a rebuttal of Beard's arguments, *Isolated America* by Raymond Leslie Buell, director of the Foreign Policy Association and editor of *Fortune* magazine's "Roundtable." In a scholarly manner, Buell took on Beard's arguments in full panoply, beginning by questioning the basis of Beard's nationalistic plan for a domestic economy insulated from global shocks by a largely restricted foreign trade. Like Cordell Hull, Buell argued that economic nationalism had in fact brought Hitler to power. Barriers to trade in postwar Europe had increased the cost of living and had resulted in the adoption of rearmament as a solution to the problem of unemployment. Granting, with Beard, that exports consumed only about 10 percent of the national production, Buell maintained that it was a percentage which prevented the emergence of a regimented state capitalism that would deprive its citizenry of "innumerable delicacies imported from abroad" and rob its industries of rubber, tin, nickel, manganese, chrome, tungsten, and platinum. A competitive, free-enterprise captalist economy would no longer exist, Buell said, if Beard's plan for national self-sufficiency were adopted. Even if American industries succeeded in developing alternatives to raw materials currently imported, Buell argued that this success "in developing new and better products" should only open to "the American system of free and efficient enterprise" the chance "of selling such products to countries which have not yet developed them." Moreover, certain "mass-production industries" exported significant percentages of their product: typewriters (41%), agricultural machinery (25%), locomotives (21%), automobiles (11%), machine tools (50%), airplanes (33%). In agriculture, too, a self-contained, planned economy would wreck havoc. "The farmer, in fact," Buell wrote, "needs more than the American market."[39]

Had Beard proved that "with the industrialization of backward areas the basis for international trade [would] disappear?" Not so, said Buell. Trade in 1940 between the United States and Great Britain was twice as great as trade between the heavily industrialized United States and the mostly non-industrial countries of Latin America. "The industrialization of the world," Buell thought, would "change the nature of international trade, once trade barriers are reduced, but should increase its value."[40]

"Equally unfounded" was Beard's warning against foreign investments. According to Buell, the return from foreign investments, linked by Beard with an outmoded imperialism, "despite widespread defaults, due in part to the mistakes in foreign lending, and to our unwillingness to receive sufficient goods and services," had been "surprisingly good."[41]

Summing up his position, Buell proclaimed:

> If America should adopt a policy of self-containment in the hope of escaping from world responsibilities, its standard of living is bound to suffer, new internal maladjustments will certainly arise which will demand new measures of government intervention to take care of the workers displaced from the export and import trade, and America itself will become even more the object of envy, and of hate, to the totalitarian powers. Self-containment would thus turn out to be a form of State capitalism, giving rise to new international dangers.[42]

Buell shared some of Beard's concerns but drew opposite conclusions. He too was worried about a dangerous concentration of power in the executive branch of the federal government and, like Beard, he supported the idea of a citizen's committee to investigate the formulation of foreign policy. However, unlike Beard, Buell believed that free speech and civil liberties could not survive in a nationalist America with a planned economy surrounded by hostile coalitions. "To escape from the tendencies pushing it into State capitalism," Buell urged a foreign trade policy based on the Reciprocal Trade Agreements Act. In the style of Woodrow Wilson, he defined the essential American tradition as a moral tradition, and, in direct opposition to Beard, he called for an ideological foreign policy grounded in the belief that American power was supreme in the world and was capable of affecting the course of world events and of restructuring the world in a manner more satisfactory to what he maintained were the prime American interests: a healthy capitalist economy of competitive free enterprise promoting the welfare of all citizens in an atmosphere of civil freedom.[43]

Critics of Beard's continentalism throughout the thirties, men such as Henry Wallace, Cordell Hull, and Buell, linked it with unacceptable changes in the capitalist system. For them the assertion of American power in the world was concomitant with a healthy capitalism. National planning such as Beard proposed, with its corollary of international neutrality, pointed the way to what they perceived as a grim, regimented "State capitalism." In making this argument, however, they did exactly what Beard had criticized: they announced a moral position in international affairs: they asked questions about "good" and "evil", questions they refused to ask about the domestic system. For Beard the country had no higher task than the pursuit of its own national interest, which he defined as an adequate standard of living for all the people. But "America First," lamented Buell, "will doom the country to a system of power politics which has afflicted the European continent for centuries—a system which has repeatedly sacrificed principles for a national 'interest.'"[44] This was the rhetoric of liberal capitalist internationalism.

Critics on both right and left blasted Beard for refusing to see a moral necessity to war against barbaric Germany and ruthless Japan. Beard, said Reinhold Neibhur, did not obscure the "moral indifferentism" of his position. As early as 1937 Allan Nevins had described Beard's philosophical relativism as an aid to Hitler. In May 1940, reviewing *A Foreign Policy for America* in *The New York Times*, Nevins castigated Beard for writing "a great deal of very bad and misleading history" and for making "no appeal to any motive more elevated than self-interest or more inspiring than national prosperity." Nevins despised what he termed Beard's "frigid indifference to moral considerations." The "democratic world," he wrote with passion, "is slipping into dissolution and despair. Men are dying under bombs and machine guns to save part of it. They speak the language we speak, they hold our faith. But Mr. Beard turns away. . . ."[45]

Beard often responded that he did not see the moral issue quite so clearly, given the fact of British and French imperialism in Africa and Asia, to say nothing of the atrocities attributed to Belgium in the Congo. On the issues of imperialism, Beard's critics took various positions. Buell frankly thought that American power could force potential allies to grant independence to their imperial subjects while Lewis Mumford argued that "capitalist imperialism," though evil and cruel, was at least subject to question in England and France and that, because the democratic process provided for criticism and thus for change, America should defend those countries.[46]

There were some younger left-liberals among Beard's critics who hoped, even as Beard himself had hoped during World War I, that the unity of battle would bring unity on radical domestic reforms. "War never solves any problems," wrote Max Lerner, "but war often removes the obstacles which stand in the path of their solution. . . . [As in England] social catastrophe of any sort may have a cleansing and unifying effect, and for intellectuals to shut their eyes to these facts is for them to shut their eyes to history and politics." Beard must have experienced a sense of *deja vu* as he read these words.

In these debates among left-liberals over foreign policy before World War II was developed the rhetoric of liberal members of the Democratic Party for the next twenty-eight years. "America must assume world leadership," Lerner wrote. It was possible to make "a heroic collective effort to grapple with the problem of unemployment and insecurity through a program of government spending for living standards as well as for armaments, and through new strategic controls of the economic system." War might succeed where the New Deal had failed.[47]

Most bitter among Beard's detractors was Lewis Mumford. During the twenties he had sat at Beard's feet but had gradually become disenchanted with Beard's persistent optimism.[48] "Like the sun-dial," Mumford said of Beard's faith, "it cannot tell time on a stormy day." Utilitarian, pragmatic, tolerant liberalism had "flatly betrayed ideal liberalism." Even though left-liberals of Beard's stripe had been moved by the destruction of the Spanish Republic, Mumford condemned what he thought was their collective indifference to the fate of the Czechs, Jews, Poles, Finns, French, English, and Chinese. "In their deliberate withholding of themselves from the plight of humanity they have even betrayed their own narrow values," Mumford exclaimed, "for they are witnessing the dissolution of those world-wide cooperations upon which the growth of science, technics and industrial wealth depends. This corruption has bitten deep into pragmatic liberalism. The isolationism of a Charles Beard, of a Stuart Chase or a Quincy Howe, is indeed almost as much a sign of barbarism as the doctrines of a Rosenberg or a Gottfried Feder."[49]

Even as Mumford and Neibhur gave sermons on human depravity, Beard clung to the idea that people were basically good and that war against evil would only bring more evil. Lacking evidence of a humane essence in those days of slaughter and rape, he turned to myth:

> Does the evil in human nature outweigh the good in substance and in practice? The question is unanswerable, no matter what assertions are made under that head. Yet good there is, and advocates of freedom who hold their ground without taking on the airs of omniscience lay emphasis on the good; and by so doing doubtless aid in bringing forth the good in creating the reality asserted by their belief. Nothing is more clearly established in historical experience than the fact that even a myth may help to create the very substance of things hoped for and dreamed of.[50]

In April 1940 Beard skirmished with an articulate fellow noninterventionist who was not concerned about civil liberties, Arthur Krock of the Washington bureau of *The New York Times*. Krock had recently defended J. Edgar Hoover and the Federal Bureau of Investigation against what he thought were efforts to "smear" Hoover. It was "distressing," Beard wrote, "to find Mr. Krock apparently treating all criticism of Mr. Hoover as unworthy in motive." Surely Krock would agree that, "with the frightful example of what has happened to civil liberty in Europe before us, we should err, if at all, on the side of emphasizing too much, rather than too little, the right of persons under the law." Recalling the days of A. Mitchell Palmer in 1918 and 1919, Beard suggested that before Hoover began "to round up progressives and other independent citizens as 'possibly detrimental to the internal security of the United States'"the Judiciary Committee of the Senate should investigate the FBI.[51]

Apparently believing that the government might be spying on him, Beard told Bernard Knollenberg, the librarian at Yale, that he was thankful that his own deafness prevented him and Mary Beard from having a phone which "world savers" might have tapped.[52]

During the winter of 1940–1941 Beard went to Johns Hopkins as Visting Professor of American History, invited to assist in reorganizing graduate studies. There are indications in his correspondence that this interlude was not particularly happy.

Baltimore, he complained, was racist and conservative. And at the university he was embattled because of his unrelenting noninterventionism. After his testimony against the Lend-Lease bill in February 1941, Arthur Lovejoy, on behalf of fifteen other members of the faulty at Johns Hopkins, publicly denounced Beard's views.[53] Beard replied acrimoniously, pointing out that Lovejoy could not possibly have read the testimony he denounced, since available transcripts postdated his comments, and implying that Lovejoy had thus violated the code of "a gentleman and a scholar." This forced from Lovejoy the admission that, indeed, his comments had been based on a news summary of Beard's testimony but that Beard had never impugned its accuracy.[54] It was a sour exchange and provoked similar feelings.

"I worked hard last winter to get some concentration on American history," Beard wrote to an old friend the following autumn, "but was treated as a mere damned patriot, immoral and criminal, as neglecting my solemn duty to save the world. So my plan busted and I am back here in the woods, working in my own way and here, God helping me, I intend to stay."[55] In the same letter Beard declined to come to Syracuse and participate in a panel discussion on the war in Europe and Asia:

> My answer to the invitation is No. For several years academic associations, committed by professions to the idea of scholarship, science, and rationality, have asked me to participate in round tables and meetings and then packed the meetings, three to one or ten to two against me in favor of saving the world by talk and war. Several times I have been caught, that is, used to show that the manipulators are "balanced" in their views of their obligations to scholarship and science. But, God helping me, I shall be caught no more. The meeting to which I am invited is already packed by having Coyle, an Army officer, Ber-

nadotte Schmitt, and Lord Halifax. Let them get Colonel Knox and Wrong-Horse Harry Stimson, and make it unanimous, thus displaying their true colors—the banners of war. I do not play that game. Thanks.[56]

That winter (in February 1941) when Beard had gone from Baltimore over to Washington to appear as an individual, unattached citizen opposed to the Lend-Lease bill, it had been one of his most striking public moments. As David Lilienthal described Beard at this time, he was a "grand-looking man, with a mobile face that at times is gentle even to the point of seeming 'harmless,' an impression that is heightened by his deafness and age. His eyes will darken and sharpen, his brows tighten, and a lowering hawklike expression takes over; and then he can lay on the whip in a way that is a joy to see."[57]

Accounts of Beard's statements to the Senate Foreign Relations Committee often neglect his contention that there was no question of either sympathy for or aid to Britain. He agreed with the nation on that issue. The bone of contention was whether the Lend-Lease bill was a form of aid for Britain consistent with security and liberty for the American people and whether a grant of such extensive powers to the President was wise. His answer to both queries was no.

Under Section 2 of the bill, Beard argued that the rubric of "national defense" was an effort to "subject all labor energies and all wealth of the United States to the President's personal orders issued at his discretion." Beard also speculated that, without convoys, the supplies of ships and munitions intended for Britain would not reach their destination and that because of the likely possibility that German submarines would attack the convoys, Lend-Lease was, despite the administration's contention that it was an antiwar measure, "a bill for waging an undeclared war."[58]

The "nation in counsel," he urged, should discuss the alternative policies with respect to the empires of Britain and France, the conquests of Russia in Finland and Poland, the Japanese presence as well as the civil war of China, the costs of intervention, and the inevitable postwar disorders and debts. The "business of Congress" was "to decide now, in voting on this bill, whether it is prepared on a showdown, to stay out to the last ditch and preserve one stronghold of order and sanity even against the gates of hell."[59]

At the end of his negation of the Lend-Lease scheme, Beard proposed a congressionally controlled program of aid to Britain, an extension of credit "generously above a careful estimate of British needs" and "immediately available—within 48 hours." Thus the power to make war would stay in the Congress, where Beard argued it belonged "under the Constitution" and "under every decent, patriotic conception of American democracy." Conserving its power and energy, the United States then might "competently offer" its services to "a shattered postwar world."[60]

Before the war came to America on 7 December 1941, Beard did sympathize with the plight of Britain in Europe. Hence he had proposed a program of aid controlled by Congress instead of the Lend-Lease project with its broad grant of power to the executive. In the case of the Far East, he had remained consistently opposed to a war against Japan. Here he thought that the making of policy was even further removed from the vital process of democratic discussion.

In October 1940, after the Japanese occupation of French Indo-China (in July), the simultaneous announcement of the Tripartite Pact between Germany, Italy, and Japan, the American embargo on exports of scrap iron to Japan (in September), and the announcement of another loan of twenty-five million dollars to China (September), Beard wrote that "an armed action in the Orient would involve the desiderata of imperalism, that is, raw materials, investments, commerce, possessions, and spheres of interest. Declarations that the intention is to strengthen democracy in China or Europe, however sincerely and passionately made, would not obscure in the minds of informed persons the more material ends also put at stake."[61]

Were rational public discussions of what was at stake in the Far East to take place, Beard suggested, the American people would "not take kindly to the thought of spilling the blood of our soldiers in the Far East . . . in aid of commercial profits or 'our little brown brothers.' " But over executive orders for embargoes and loans, there was no debate. The future of policy in the Far East was "no longer in the hands of the people or of Congress, despite the provision in the Constitution that vests in Congress the power to declare war. In fact," Beard concluded sadly, "wars are no longer declared. Situations exist or are created. Actions are taken by authorities in a position to act. The people wait for their portion."[62]

Beard saw, before many others, the limits of American power, the hollowness of the dream of an "American Century." He sensed and described the process by which rational debate among patriotic, intelligent, well-informed citizens was replaced as an ideal toward which a functioning democracy must strive by the goal of a manipulated "public opinion," developed by the use of simplistic and condescending analogies, and accompanied by distorted versions of events and executive secrecy. While supporting the domestic reforms of the New Deal, he encouraged a movement farther to the left. Positive and optimistic, he waited for history to follow his path. When the great choices came to be made between preparing for war abroad and preparing for war on poverty and inequality at home, he took to the hustings against the perversion of his dream of a continental commonwealth. The fact that Beard and others of his persuasion lost the battle to keep the United States out of World War II has not diminished the sharpness of many of his comments on the costs of such a course of action.

14

"The Old Isolationist"

Describing an incident that undoubtedly had occurred at a wartime social gathering, Charles Beard recorded the following dialogue in *The Republic*:

> The Professor, who teaches international relations at Berwick University, greeted me a little boisterously and victoriously with: "How's the old isolationist?" To which his wife added, with a smile intended to be devastating: "A bit confused *now*, I suspect?"
>
> As I was not selling groceries or peddling intellectual wares at a price, I could express my sentiments freely, and I said: "Confused as ever, Mrs. Tempey. I confess that I never have been able to reduce the world and universal history to a simple miniature with no blurred lines in it."[1]

Beard never regretted his prewar noninterventionism. During the war he did not become less radical than he had been in the 1930s. On the contrary, his defense of the democratic process and the Constitution against usurpation by a powerful president, Roosevelt, appears in recent times as a remarkable example of prescience and courage in an age when so many of his contemporaries reviled him as the betrayer of American liberalism. Now we will concentrate on Charles Beard's concern with the process of democracy, on Charles and Mary Beard's final joint effort to create an American history, and on Charles' wartime writings, particularly *The Republic* (1943), which presented themes developed at great length in his final books on Franklin Roosevelt and the conduct of American diplomacy.

These were years when Charles, as an aging patriot prophet, received many honors. But he continued as usual to be delighted more by controversy than by laurels. "What I fear most of all," he told a friend in 1944, "is becoming respectable. I love best the people who are not respectable, such as Francis of A[ssisi] or Thomas à Kempis or Gene Debs or Marcus Aurelius. So if you hear that my stock is going up with the respectables, please jump on it, unload, sell it short, and call it a false alarm."[2]

In 1958, Beard's son-in-law Alfred Vagts wrote that "Roosevelt took us into the war deliberately, there can be no question on this. The question is: Was it necessary for the U[nited] S[tates] to go into the war?" According to Vagts, Beard had "resented deeply that discussion, before and after Pearl [Harbor] was not centered on this point which I often brought up in family talks, being myself convinced that with a man like Hitler you would have to go to war in time. . . . CB would then insist that the discussion must be turning around this point. Myself: I am afraid democracy is constitutionally unable to discuss a rational entry into war, a deliberate one."[3]

As a well-educated, active citizen outside the government, Beard resented as much the terms of the discussion before American entry into World War II as the going to war itself. The first chapter of *President Roosevelt and the Coming of the War, 1941* (1948) is devoted to the hypocritical campaign oratory of 1940, to the President's promises that America would participate in no foreign wars "except in case of attack," as the Democratic platform had it, to promises which Beard labeled "covenants" made by the President with an anxious public.[4]

Supporters of Roosevelt, who believed that his lying to the public was necessary under the circumstances, since the people at large did not seem to see that going to war was in the best long-range interests of the country, have criticized Beard for having a naive view of democratic processes. American political campaigns, they argue, have not traditionally involved rational discussion of issues at hand. There has always been a large quota of malarkey; Roosevelt's promises of peace fall under this rubric. Summarizing this argument, Robert Dallek writes: "In light of the national unwillingness to face up fully to the international dangers confronting the country, it is difficult to fault Roosevelt for building a consensus by devious means." There was, in 1940–1941, Dallek argues, a "need to mislead the country in its own interest."[5]

Warren Kimball, the most recent student of the legislative history of Lend-Lease and a sensitive defender of the President's policy, has concluded about the campaign of 1940:

> As much as one sympathizes with Roosevelt's dilemma, the national election is the one time every four years when the President should be obligated by his own conscience and the nature of the American political system to be totally honest and candid with the public. In that sense, democracy may be a *suicide pact*, which by its nature requires honesty regardless of the possible consequences. [Italics added.][6]

On the issue of Lend-Lease itself and on the President's lack of candor during the development of the legislation, Kimball argues in essence that our system imposes on the majority and the president no responsibility to be candid. "In a democratic society," Kimball asserts, "it is the responsibility of the loyal opposition to point out to the public what it believes to be misguided actions on the part of "the majority party. To expect the majority to make predictions that would, by their utterance jeopardize their program is like demanding that a guilty man plead guilty in a court of law."[7] Of Roosevelt's foreign policy during the prewar period, Kimball asks "must the leader in a democratic society first convince the public of the wisdom of his policies by open and above-board methods, or may he embark on a course of action and face the consequences at the next election? Do we trust our elected officials or must they stand for election on *every new policy decision?*" (Italics added.)[8]

As Beard saw the issues before the country in 1940 and 1941, they could not be described blandly as a "new policy decision." The main issue was war. "In short," he wrote in 1947, "unless deceiving the people in matters of life and death is to be regarded as a proper feature of the democratic politics and popular decisions at the polls are to be treated as chimeras, President Roosevelt's peace pledges of 1940 were imperatives for him in 1941. . . ."[9] Exceptions to "this principle of representative government" were allowable, in Beard's view, "where a drastic and unexpected alteration in the posture of affairs calls for a change of policy after the election." Yet, in such a case, the president had a duty to inform the public. If Roosevelt had concluded in 1941 "that his earlier antiwar commitments of 1940 had been rendered obsolete by changed circumstances in 1941 and that the United States should engage in war," then, according to Beard, "he was under constitutional and moral obligations to explain to the country the grounds and nature of a reversal in policy."[10]

However, instead of a series of state papers arguing the necessity of his policies and explaining their relationship to a conception of national interest, Roosevelt had infuriated many citizens by joking that the occupation of Greenland was "news" to him and by saying, for example, that Lend-Lease gave him the power to stand on his head, but that did not mean he intended to do it.[11]

Beard thought that war was the policy above all that demanded fidelity to the processes of democracy. The terms in which he viewed this process did not involve particular personalities sacrificing themselves on the alter of political candor in fulfillment of a "suicide pact" with a backward and irrational public. Beard continued to believe that the United States contained a large group of patriotic and rational citizens who wanted to understand and discuss the policies of the government and who, in fact, had a constitutional responsibility to do so.

Writing in September 1942 to introduce a volume of public documents of the year 1941, he emphasized the private citizen's crucial role in the democratic process.

All the interests of the American people are at stake; and *under the constitu-tional system* [Beard's italics] of the United States they are called upon to gain knowledge, form opinions and make resolutions of will respecting the nature, objectives, and course of the war. To them, so summoned to the bar of universal history and put to supreme tests, every piece of authentic information bearing upon the events of 1941 becomes useful and necessary in *the discharge* of their *responsibilities,* in *their* quest for a triumphant outcome in the war and in the settlement to follow.[12]

In *The American Spirit* (1942) the Beards sought in the past of the United States an ideology, a world view, that supported the humane collectivist nationalism they advocated. "Having attempted," wrote Mary Beard, "to tell the story . . . of action . . . which brings us to the great conflict between domestic improvement and foreign escape, we fell under obligation to offer our readers, if any continue to exist, a report on the American mind as it has concerned itself with the idea of civilization in America."[13] The idea of civilization meant a "conception of history as a struggle of human beings in the world for individual and social perfection . . . against ignorance, disease, and harshness of physical nature, the forces of barbarism in individuals and society."[14] In support of their definition the Beards marshaled page after page of quotations, including Europeans such as Condorcet and Guizot along with Jefferson, Lucretia Mott, Elizabeth Cady Stanton, Henry George, Edward Bellamy, John Dewey, and hundreds of others. With few exceptions, the examples of "creative intelligence" chosen by the Beards as carriers of civilization's banner were neither politicians nor academicians.

With relish but in less detail, the enemies of the struggle for individual and social perfection were also described: Catholicism, as embodied in the reactionary *Syllabus of Errors* of 1864; individualism, as expounded by William Graham Sumner at Yale from 1872 to 1910; Teutonic racism, as found in the teachings of John Burgess at Columbia; imperialism, as preached by Albert Beveridge and as elaborated in the writings of Alfred T. Mahan; foreign critics, who denounced the materialism of America and exhaulted the spirituality of Europe; and "general internationalism," whose exponents promoted for America a "world mission under arms."[15] In the rather banal way in which they occasionally dealt with abstractions such as capitalism, the Beards personified civilization as "caught in the clash between empiricism and absolutism" and yielding to neither.[16]

As the history of an idea, *The American Spirit* is weak. It is the least readable volume of *The Rise.* "Civilization" as an organizing theme was too amorphous and elusive to be illuminating. Richard Hofstadter, then a young novice, made this point when he wrote of the book that "the fact that [Wendell Phillips, John C. Calhoun, William G. Sumner, and Edward Bellamy] all invoked 'civilization' seems little more revealing than that they all accepted monogamy; perhaps less so, for the meaning of monogamy is generally understood."[17]

Yet, as an autobiographical account of the inspiration for the Beards' nationalism, as a source of intellectual history, *The American Spirit* has redeeming virtues. It was their final effort to create a history meaningful to all of the American people, the capstone of *The Rise,* an attempt to give a past to the diverse peoples of America. What a "civilization" needed, in the Beards' view, and what was lacking in America was a tradition that embodied a social imperative and a humanist ethical perspective. The "progress" of a nation had to be moral as well as material. Sensing as they did that America was *not* "a nation" but "many nations" and choosing *not* to endorse cultural pluralism, which they regarded as a retrogressive ideal fostered by "professional promoters of divisive forces" who gained prestige and profit by keeping alive "separate presses, schools, customs, and predilections as against the tendency of American civilization to uniformity," the Beards attempted in their histories to make a universally meaningful story where, perhaps, there was none.[18] In order to foster the collectivist nationalism of the future, various groups were to be denied their unique history in favor of a more "progressive" vision.

The Beards were aware that there was no vital cultural center of American history. And it is this consciousness of a problem that distinguishes their work from that of other efforts to describe "the American mind" as if no problem existed. They were aware that their perspective was not universal, but they hoped that it would be chosen. *The American Spirit* was an effort to overcome the lack of values perceived by Lucien Romier, a French critic whom the Beards compared favorably to Toqueville. "In truth," Romier had written,

> to understand America we must always bear this fact in mind: that the social structure of the United States does not compose a unified historical nation, nor a body politic; it is a community of purely economic origin. The principle of getting rich and getting-rich-quick establishes the whole scale of values and affects even the daily speech and imagination of the average American. . . . It is for such reasons that America represents completely that type of civilization . . . called the *quantity* civilization. [Italics in original.][19]

The American Spirit can be regarded as an attempt to formulate a socialist ethical tradition. The development of ethnic studies during the sixties and seventies has made the Beards' effort appear narrow and shallow. But it was not dishonest and arrogant. And the problem, the fragmentation of history, the question of its larger social purpose, remains.

In *The American Spirit* Charles Beard's long dialogue with Marx is ended. During the 1930s he had always separated Marx from the Marxists and the Communists. His Marx had been a brilliant scholar and not necessarily an advocate of violent change. Gone now from these pages are the admiring glances at Lenin and the respectful tributes to Marx, the wide-ranging student of human affairs. Now Marx is identified with communism. Apparently this was the message Beard derived from recent history—the trials of party members in Moscow in 1936 and after, the assassination of Trotsky, the pact between Stalin and Hitler in 1939, the shifting position of the Communist Party in the United States from advocacy of collective security in 1937–1938 to pacifism after the Nazi–Soviet pact. Such absolute and religious devotion had always been questioned by the Beards. The inner light could not function in an ideological lamp controlled from afar.

Did Marxism inherently lead to the excesses of Stalinism? In *The American Spirit,* Charles and Mary answered "yes" and cited with approval the bitter words of Benedetto Croce:

> Marx was nearer than one imagines to Prussianism and to its cult of brutal force. . . . Communism is constrained, even against the intentions of its authors, to enter upon the beaten trace which every absolutism, every despotism, every tyranny has always entered upon.[20]

In *America in Mid-Passage* (1939), the failure of basic reform in the 1930s had been attributed to the lack of a collectivist morality that might have inspired planners and downed selfishness. Now the Beards turned their fire on American Communists, who, they argued, had distracted people's attention from native reformers. An indigenous radicalism had remained less developed because of the attraction of a foreign ideology. Communism had "slashed into the idea of civilization. . . . Often it [had] diverted American talents and affections from concentration on tasks clearly within the scope of American capacities and opportunities. . . . It diverted them to romantic enthusiasms for designs remote and obscure, or to an equally romantic pessimism respecting the future of civilization in the United States."[21] This was different, indeed, from the usual attacks on Communists for being "romantic optimists."

Marx himself was now associated by the Beards with the errors of classical economics, with a destructive "pure urbanism" that denigrated the role of agrarians in social change, with the repudiation of a free press, liberty of conscience, personal rights, and rationality. In contrast to the nonviolent Marx of Charles Beard's 1935 essay "The Promise of American Life," the Marx of 1942 did advocate civil war. "By its very origin and nature as an interpretation of history," they proclaimed, "the Marxian invention called dialectical materialism clashed with the idea of civilization. . . . It had close kinship with the mentality of the old Prussian drill sergeant." Neither foreign-born nor native Marxists, they asserted, had "produced any significant contributions to thought in relation to American history or economy."[22]

Placing the Beards on any sort of political spectrum has always been difficult, and it is to this conundrum that their later attitude toward Marx, Marxists, and Communists may offer some clues. They did not write from the perspective of a Max Eastman suddenly become anticommunist and shifting at once to the right to defend capitalism in America. Neither were they in the mode of John Chamberlain, who had undergone a similar transformation. They did not identify liberty with unfettered capitalism. They did not bemoan oppressive bureaucracy and regimentation. The "managerial revolution" Beard thought impossible; the managers were not bright enough.[23] The Beards certainly considered themselves independent radicals, to the left of the Communists, never more so than in the era of the Popular Front.

Charles and Mary Beard promoted a collectivist nationalism down a revisionist road of nonviolent gradualism. Marxist internationalism, especially the internationalism of the Popular Front, was anathema to them. Here was the so-called left making common cause with what they termed the "general internationalism" of Franklin Roosevelt, Cordell Hull, and Henry Wallace. Members of the Communist Party had espoused the abstractions of the Popular Front and turned away from the hard questions of reform at home. They chose war for reasons that seemed utterly fallacious to the Beards.

> Marxists called openly or covertly for a revolution in this country and for American aid to communists waging war anywhere in the world. General internationalists [Roosevelt, Hull, et. al.] demanded American participation in every war among nations which, in their opinion, menaced "world order." Thus, in formulation and application, the idea of Marxian communism and the idea of general internationalism presented to the idea of civilization . . . the most thoroughgoing opposition which it had ever met. . . .[24]

As Charles Beard described it, the honor that gave him the most "solid satisfaction" of his life was the invitation to deliver the commemorative address at Monticello and the University of Virginia on the two-hundredth anniversary of Thomas Jefferson's birth.[25] Standing before the crowds on 13 April 1943, Beard's eyes filled with tears and his voice trembled. Jefferson had been a man of great complexity, now reduced to a symbol in the battle among contending political parties. He had denied equality to women and had practiced human slavery. He was not a "demi-god," was neither Democrat nor democrat. Yet, for people at war in the twentieth century, Jefferson did have a message, as Beard saw it. His "faith in liberty of inquiry, thought and expression" were never more appropriate than "in the midst of a flaming world-war involving the issue of liberty and authority, everywhere . . . during a period in which our own legislatures, federal and local, are prone to suppress objectionable ideas as crimes against the State."[26]

Jefferson, though not a democrat, had been the prophet of the democratic process, Beard's central theme in his last writings. Jefferson had called the people, as Beard beckoned them also, to uphold the processes of republican government, "freedom of inquiry, freedom of expression, freedom of discussion, and freedom of decision by 'the common reason of society.'" As he ended with a peroration common to thousands of Protestant ears, the tall, passionate old man with the fiery glance became again the young positivist preaching the social gospel to miners in England, again the powerful professor renouncing his academic garb and the hypocrisy of censorship at Columbia, again the glowering citizen lecturing President Roosevelt on the lessons of experience:

> We shall do well to follow [the sign of liberty], unafraid, with steadfast assurance that in so doing we shall justly celebrate [Jefferson's] memory, make ourselves worthy of it, and strengthen our country for storms ahead. . . .[27]

During the war, as Beard did not seem to be rallying unquestioningly to Roosevelt's leadership, he was subjected to many blasts of scholarly disapproval. The reception of his final books was anticipated. His reviews and comments on public affairs were no longer welcome on the pages of *The New Republic* and *The Nation*. Sometimes he was bemused, noting at one point that Joseph Dorfman's *Economic Mind in America* had been advertised as an "'antidote' to Parrington and Beard." Not having read it yet, he wrote that he was "not sure which of my many poisons and diseases needs an antidote."[28] "What is back of the savage attack on me?" he asked Merle Curti, replying that he suspected that it was "due to the fact that I refuse to take the world-saving business at face value and think that Churchill and Stalin are less concerned with world saving than with saving the British Empire and building a new and bigger Russian empire. However, history to come will pass judgement on them and me!"[29]

The "savage attack" came from many directions, and the theme of the song was clear. In March 1944 Bruce Bliven, editor of *The New Republic*, had denounced Beard, Oswald G. Villard, Norman Thomas, and others as well as *The Progressive* magazine, all "in theory well to the left," for "'sitting out' this war." These people and their segment of the press, said Bliven, were "spiritual saboteurs, the hang back boys." How, asked Bliven, could "large numbers of Americans" claiming to be "progressive" be "constantly fighting an administration which, despite all its faults, comes closer to being genuinely progressive and humanitarian than any other in our history?" The group of hangers back did not seem to believe, even after Pearl Harbor, that "this country was in mortal danger from Germany and Japan"; they continued to talk about "the wickedness of the Russian government"; they refused "take any real part in the struggle between fascism and democracy"; they were, Bliven argued, thus deliberately cutting themselves off "from the two great centers of dynamic energy in the world today"—"the Roosevelt administration" and Russia. Perhaps, he speculated facetiously, they were being dispassionate in an effort "to keep the torch of truth alive." But there was no "room for ivory towers in a world wide struggle. . . . The calmness and aloofness . . . become about as pleasant as similar qualities in someone who stands disinterested on the bank of a stream where women and children are drowning."[30]

In 1943 Beard had written his favorite book, *The Republic*. Published in October 1943, it went through five printings in six months. About this book

Beard expressed more intense feeling than about any of his other writings. Perhaps it was a substitute for his long years of jousting with opponents in *The Nation* and *The New Republic*. Denied these outlets, he had carried on the discussion as in prewar days, although now full of anxiety that no one would be listening. His theme: "If we cannot govern ourselves decently, what else matters or can be accomplished?" Why plan for an American century in the world if the problems at home remained unconquered.[31] "I attempted the experiment with trepidation," he told Thomas Reed Powell, "with poignant awareness of the terrible things happening

> to popular government, civil liberties, and human decencies throughout large portions of the earth. I wrote the book at white heat and then tried to revise and smooth it out under the light of such cold reason and knowledge as I could command. When at last I released the page proofs, I felt numb with doubt and unable to tell whether it was a mess or had some merit.[32]

Written as a series of twenty-one dialogues, *The Republic* presents in the form of Robert and Susan Smyth, Beard's imaginary neighbors, the prototypical concerned citizens he always assumed existed in healthy numbers. Robert is a medical doctor who combines a private practice with industrial medicine. Susan is employed at home as the mother of four children and also works as a volunteer on community projects. They are white Protestants with a keen interest in public affairs. They read Spengler, Freud, Mencken, and, occasionally, a new book of history. They resent being part of a passive audience constantly exposed to "*selected* facts strung on hidden opinions" in the speeches of public officials and in the radio news. They ask Beard for a "kind of elementary course on current issues in government and democracy." As Reed Powell put it, they are "intelligent and well-meaning worthy people whose unreflecting partialities are without emotional barriers against corrective enlightenment."[33]

Using the Smyths and assorted other characters as foils, Beard again and again asserted his faith in the people's citizenly qualities. "Here we are," he tells Dr. Smyth, who has referred to the American people as "an incoherent and distracted mass," "about 135,000,000 of us, of many races and nationalities, varying degrees of intelligence and ignorance, characters good, bad and indifferent . . . most of us, I think, industrious and eager to accomplish something good for ourselves and our country."[34] Issues of class, race, and economic position could be transcended through participation in the viable republic. The constitutional system provided for "permanence with provisions for progress" within a framework of "civilian as distinguished from military methods." In the context of the war, when people were being urged to look away from America, Beard thought that these self-evident propositions needed reasserting.[35]

A strong theme of the book is that the system itself stood in danger, not from fascist enemies abroad but from abuses of power within. To the author of *An Economic Interpretation of the Constitution,* history appeared different in 1943 than it had in 1913. In 1943 there was an orthodox interpretation of the origins of the Constitution that portrayed it as resulting from "a conflict between radical or agrarian forces on the one side and the forces of conservative or capitalistic reaction on the other." However, Beard now argued that "there were three parties to the struggle" over the Constitution, the third party being "an influential group on the extreme right of the conservatives" who were ready, especially after Shays's Rebellion, to resort to a military dictatorship.[36]

Franklin Roosevelt does not appear in the pages of *The Republic,* but the intended comparison is obvious. Washington's glory came from his refusal to countenance dictatorial schemes, Jefferson's from his "great faith in the people, in freedom of discussion, in education for citizenship, in 'the common reason of society.'" Lincoln, despite his resort to "some measures of dubious constitutionality," did not set aside the Constitution, "did not suppress Congress or try to purge it of opposition members," "did not expell from his cabinet men who were intriguing against him," and did not "seriously interfere with freedom of the press." The greatest presidents, Beard urged, had accepted limits on the power of the executive.[37]

In these chats, one authentic "voice" comes from all mouths, that of Beard himself. As he had for years, he promotes reform of the organization and procedure of Congress and regularization and institutionalization of relations between Congress and the executive. He defends and encourages national planning, federal incorporation laws, independent, progressive, and radical politicians, from whom "new ideas . . . for the improvement of the individual and society" were to be expected. He warns that "no people have any rights in fact except the rights which they have sense enough and competence enough to bring into being, uphold, and enforce in fact. . . ."[38]

Most lively in the series was the dialogue Beard invented between himself and those "choice members of the intelligentsia" who believed, as he had Mrs. Smyth say it, that "the supreme object of American foreign policy ought to be to bring permanent, or lasting, peace to the nations of the earth." In contrast, Beard argued that "the supreme object of American foreign policy should be to protect and promote the interests, spiritual and material, of the American people . . . to protect and advance American civilization on this continent, the firm earthly basis of our economic and military power, with due reference to relevant international responsibilities." This was a restatement of his position during the 1930s. He did favor, he said, "pushing the war against Germany, Japan, and Italy to a successful conclusion," but he refused to agree with the member of the party who called it a "righteous war against war." Describing himself as favoring "an effort to hold the United Nations together on practical issues," he urged abandonment of all nonsense about "world federalism" among "fifty or more independent nations of the earth so utterly diverse in race, history, sentiments, and economy." He wanted a peace without "an elaborate world constitution full of vague phrases that could be, and probably would be, twisted and turned by governments competing for power" and suggested the desirability of a "brief and simple treaty," perhaps limited to "ten years or more, subject to renewal" and binding the signers "to refrain from resorting to violence during that period." This program would more likely realize the aspirations of Americans and other peoples of the world than "grandiose plans for settling everything and everybody all at once and for all time and for trying to hold millions of people down by police and propaganda."[39]

Beard's final session with the Smyths concerned his "large historical philosophy." Did the study of history "necessarily lead to pessimism"? At a time when many liberals were beginning to view the world through Niebhurian lenses and were accepting the war and its inherent dictatorial tendencies as a lesser evil to be embraced in the cause of extinguishing a greater evil, fascism, the question was important. History led, Beard asserted, neither to optimism nor to pessimism about the fate of humankind. Optimism and pessimism were matters of personal temperament and thus not susceptible of philosophical or historical proof. Those who were pessimists, who thought compromise with evil necessary, since the world offered no other options, could easily become paralyzed and inactive. Beard saw this very clearly, and he asked people to join him in the belief that "our universe is not all fate" and that "we have some freedom in it," freedom to work in America "for the good, the true, the useful, and the beautiful." This was the task of intellectuals and citizens. Action was to be the last end of thinking.[40]

The reception accorded this book in some quarters disappointed Beard. Sidney Hook, whom he admired and respected, noted that Beard's "constitutional piety" could be "twisted" to make him "a Hamiltonian *pur sang,*" while Max Lerner announced that Beard had "become a conservative."[41] Certainly, these critics were correct in asserting that Beard was unwilling to bring about the birth of reform by performing a Caesarean operation on the Constitution. It is also true that, in discussing the issue of liberty versus authority in a constitutional system, Beard had argued quite consistently, not only in *The Republic* but also throughout his career, that abuses of authority against liberty, by which he always meant liberty to speak, write, and have decent food and shelter, would be mitigated in the American system by "men of character" who would patriotically rise above their own circumstances to think of the good of the nation.

This was not, of course, a "modern" point of view. It disgusted Marxists, revisionists, behaviorists, and liberals such as Lerner. The view that "character" was important was in the tradition of Beard's spacious and generous upbringing in rural Indiana. As Bertrand Russell once said of Joseph Conrad, a pessimist by nature, so one might say of Beard, the optimist by temperament: "[He] adhered to the older tradition, that discipline should come from within. He despised indiscipline, and hated discipline that was merely external."[42]

Throughout his life Beard clung to this notion of "character." "The conduct of constitutional government," he said to the Smyths, "calls for character," by which he meant the ability on the part of citizens and public officials to be reasonable, humane, dispassionate, and able to subordinate personal antipathies and interests to some larger conception of the public good, a conception founded on "such grand ideas as justice, mercy, truth, beauty, and goodness, and the sentiments associated with them."[43]

All of these arguments could be viewed as tending toward conservatism. Nevertheless, seen in the context of what Beard regarded as the greatest threat to the United States—the unrestrained use of presidential power upsetting the process of democracy and rendering "self-government" null—his defense of constitutionalism appears radically appropriate. It was not that he feared the power of capitalism less than he had in the 1930s, but rather that he had come to appreciate the "irrational" uses to which great executive power could be put. He had devoted a lifetime to urging citizen participation in the democratic process, which he defined as "the constitutional process of proposal, discussion, and adoption or rejection." In basic matters of life and death, the people had been held in contempt by a president who lied and who refused to conduct an open discussion of such vital issues.

Beard did not agree that the United States had been a passive country forced by external events into the war. He thought that choices had been made, that other choices had been possible, that war was the enemy of all democratic change, and that the defense of the constitutional process was the duty of the intellectual in wartime. The war powers of the president, he wrote, were "the unexplored and dark continent of American government," powers limited mainly by "the character of the President, the alertness and firmness of Congress, and the good sense of the people." As he wrote *The Republic*, the war was the supreme reality, and Beard's eyes were, as always, fixed on America. In *The Republic*, he urged people not to give up to the civilian and military bureaucrats the management of the war: "again and again in war, civilians have had to interfere with technicians to save their country from folly if not ruin."[44]

Yet, in reading Beard, one always comes to the same double disappointment: a lack of ability to evoke real people and the absence of a hypothesis explaining how the governing system works. The Olympian approach meant that he never really entered the crowd. Although urban streets and fields of cotton appear in the panorama of his histories and commentaries, the reader is never taken into them. As there is no smell of cologne or sweat in the congressional cloakroom, neither—and more important—is there any sociological analysis of the way power is distributed in a bureaucratic state. In this way, Beard was always a completely "intellectual" person. The emphasis on character enabled him to avoid entirely all questions of personality or of the way systems of decision-making may channel the approaches to action. He approached his fellows in this world of complexities entirely in terms of their ideas. In dealing with the democratic process he neglected to develop a theory of power.

The Republic exemplifies his ideal of the intellectual as teacher, moral guide, and member of a broadly literate community of genteel men and women. The moral authority of the teacher rested not on his gown and degrees but rather on his display of knowledge and on his sympathies arising from experience among the people. Beard rejected "professionalism" as a form of authority and power and urged his fellow citizens to be enraged with him by the notion that ideas about what was good for American society had somehow to be "certified" by academic social science. Writing to a friend about *The Republic,* Beard said that he had tried to be "helpful to all and sundry in their efforts to think about our government and our history and acquire workable knowledge of civil utility."[45]

Scattered in letters to friends in late 1943 and in 1944 are indications that Beard was tired and depressed, willing but unable to carry on the old battles. He remained delighted to "have a jaw" with old friends in New York. "Still," he told Lindsay Rodgers in the summer of 1943, "what in God's name can be said now that will not soon be silly—made silly by events over which we have no more influence than a gnat? 60 years of it are too many!"[46]

After Rodgers, a professor of political science at Columbia, had reviewed *The Republic,* quoting the Smyths to the effect that it might all be taken either as "'well-reasoned optimism'" or as "'well-seasoned pessimism,'" Beard sent him some lines from Diderot: "'On Croit, et tous les jours on se conduit comme si l'on ne croyait pas. Et sans croire, on se conduit a peu pres comme si l'on croyait,'" adding "Comment: God, how true!"[47]

As he groused with Villard about Walter Lippmann, in his eyes Dean of the World Savers, Beard said in the autumn of 1943 that he was anxious to "take a whack" at "the Wilson–F.D. mythology" but "I simply haven't the time or strength. [John] Flynn can do a good job & I hope he does."[48]

However, Beard's flagging spirits did not lead to a cessation of work. Aside from *The Republic,* 1943 was the year in which he and Mary completed *A Basic History of The United States,* and he himself did a ninth edition of his *American Government and Politics,* which had first been published in 1910.

To Merle Curti he railed against the "progressive degeneration" marking the study of history at Columbia—where, he thought, "saving the world and the Pope seems to be the major interest that engages the attention of 'objective historians.'"[49] Working with Curti and others on a bulletin on historiography for the Social Science Research Council, he thought of taking "it as a starter and [working] out a bigger book on the subject. . . . I have a lot of trash for it on hand," he wrote, but added that he was "tired, dog tired and I think that it is more than temporary weariness of the flesh."[50] "When I look over my old tripe and read the tripe that appears daily in the name of history," he told Curti, "I am overwhelmed and moved to retire to a cave in Bull Mountain nearby, which I own in all its small majesty."[51] Speculating on the election of 1944, he scorned Dewey, "the Peanut of Pawling" (a small town in New York just across the state line from New Milford) and said he "might vote for Norman Thomas in protest" but for the fact that he was "a world saver too," adding "I may fish. . . ."[52]

When the Beards' last collaboration, *A Basic History,* appeared in August 1944, it was greeted with a critical rumble its modest and rather colorless retelling of "the rise of American civilization" did not merit. Attacks centered on the final chapter, "Global War and Home Front." The Beards very dryly and succinctly had written an interpretation of the coming of the war in Europe and Asia that emphasized the inability of the British and French, rejoicing as they had in the fascist suppression of communism, to perceive the threat from Hitler and Mussolini and to take united action in the face of it. In dealing with the Japanese, the American State Department had been intransigent and inflexible, in their view. Readers had been reminded that many questions could be asked about the granting of executive power to complete, for example, the destroyers-for-bases agreement of September 1940. They had been treated to a brief sample of Roosevelt's promises of peace during the campaign of 1940.[53]

Sales of *A Basic History* proved the reviewers powerless, and Beard was gratified that people were still reading his books. "Americans," he told Curti cheerfully, "are interested as never before in their history."[54]

But such popularity only aggravated those of opposing views. Henry Seidel Canby devoted a warm editorial in the *Saturday Review of Literature* to the denunciation of the "dangerous and delusive pages" of the History's final chapter. A correspondent of the same journal suggested that the timing of the book (August 1944) made it likely that this book with its "dangerous warp" of isolationism had been intended as a "presidential campaign document."[55] Two weeks later Lewis Mumford wrote another of his scurrile letters in a now familiar tone: "[Beard] has become a passive—no, active—abetter of tyranny, sadism, and human defilement."[56] To Oswald Villard Beard commented that though "the Sat. Lit. Rev. performances" were "shocking," he was "used to it now."[57] When elected to the American Academy of Arts and Letters, he remarked smilingly, "How an abettor of sadism got there is among the seven wonders of divine Providence."[58]

Near the time of Beard's seventieth birthday in 1944, the young historian Eric Goldman drove to New Milford to interview him. Reflecting on that encounter, Goldman voiced the discomfort experienced by younger liberals when confronted by Beard during the war. Beard had, distressingly, remained a relativist. He still had many questions and few certainties. He appeared dispassionate and coldly uninvolved in the antifascist cause abroad. "The great social danger" of this sort of relativism, Goldman thought, was that for good or bad, men do not seem to be able to charge their actions with much emotion unless they believe that they are acting on *the* truth and *the* right. Before the war, liberal groups, especially groups of younger liberals, showed traces of the debilitating effects of relativism. War increased the psychological difficulty a thousand-fold, for war admits of no relativism. There is only our side, which is good, and the other side, which is bad.

Before the war, progressives had been accustomed to say "that men and nations are, after all, what society makes them, that ethics are an expression of particular property interests, that democracy is identified with the needs of the middle classes." Then, as Goldman put it, they "found themselves sheepishly unable to give emotion to a war they wanted to fight." They "followed gladly when Archibald MacLeish included Charles Beard"—wrongly—"among 'The Irresponsibles.'"[59]

15

Lessons of Pearl Harbor

During late winter and early spring of 1945 Beard was close to death from pneumonia in a hospital in New York City. Writing to a friend, he described his desire to get out of the city, to return to the country, there to touch again the sources of optimism and hope. Lying in bed, he reflected impatiently on the state of the world, on his life, and on what was left to be done:

> Now after 70 years of it the big world, the big people, and the big clatter (soon to be covered by oblivion) seem dull & common place, if not worse. Only a few dear personal friends seem precious. As Henry Adams feared in 1894 the pessimism of Petersburg, Berlin, Paris and London has conquered the U.S. (Look at Dumbarton and Yalta!) and I seem to be about the only fragment of an optimist left.[1]

From a room at the Hotel Commodore, where he had to stay during most of March 1945, Beard eagerly followed the public discussion about Yalta and Dumbarton Oaks and fumed over the fact that Franklin Roosevelt had underwritten unilateral arrangements in Eastern Europe while speaking to the American people of putting an end to unilateral action.[2] As for the United Nations, Beard suggested that it was a "bauble" not worth opposing. The American people would never be satisfied until they had joined some sort of world organization. "It [the proposed United Nations] gives Russia, Britain, and the United States a veto on everything they do not like," he told Edwin Borchard. "How people with any knowledge and intelligence can be taken in by it passes my understanding."[3]

This illness was the nadir of a period of low spirits, and Beard emerged from his ordeal with the feeling that death was coming closer, that time was now precious as never before. While recovering, he planned his books on Roosevelt's foreign policy. By June, his customary pep was returning and he wrote to Curti that he was "coming up hill again. . . . I am collecting materials on how Mr. Roosevelt conducted diplomatic affairs from 1933 to 1941. And believe me a lot of neglected and unpublished materials are available to me now. I have several things that will take the hair off your head."[4]

In September 1945 *The Progressive*, which had maintained an independent and critical attitude toward American policy throughout the war, published Beard's synopsis of the issues raised by the catastrophe at Pearl Harbor on 7 December 1941.[5] He had hoped to see it in print before the election of 1944, when some Republicans, notably Thomas Dewey, were threatening to raise questions about Pearl Harbor during the campaign. However, two long talks with publisher Henry Luce could not persuade him to bring it out during the war.[6]

To Beard, Pearl Harbor symbolized the problems that resulted when the democratic process of debate and discussion was ignored in the formulation of foreign policy. Pearl Harbor was a test of responsibility for policy in a democracy and a test of whether the American people were truly informed on the consequences that would result from actions taken by the president and the Department of State. It was also a measure of the "character" of the civilian leadership in Washington, who had seemed in haste to condemn Admiral Husband E. Kimmel and General Walter C. Short, the military commanders in Hawaii, "whose honor and devotion to duty," Beard noted, had "been under a cloud."[7]

Beard had called the Pearl Habor issue a "challenge to the Republic." While *The Progressive* was not a widely circulated journal, having only a few thousand subscribers, Allan Nevins thought Beard's article troublesome enough to warrant a reply, "'A Challenge to Historic Truth,'" which was published in *The New York Times* in December 1945.

In contrast to Beard, Nevins was a militant internationalist. He had written at the end of 1944 that "the true [postwar] policy" should be "a policy of collective action for security, with world control over such bases and war-potentials as are not in the hands of peace-loving powers, a world police, and the systematic inculcation of a world tradition of disarmament and the peaceable adjustment conflicting interests."[8]

Those who had attacked American policy before Pearl Harbor, said Nevins in 1945, were now trying to put a "stigma upon a national course which both in detail and in its larger bearings" had "been more completely justified by events than any great line of action since our Government committed itself to the destruction of chattel slavery."[9] Intimating that the Japanese had been encouraged in their prewar expansion by "men who loudly proclaimed that what Japan did in Asia was no affair of ours," Nevins lamented the continuation of such "moral myopia" in 1945. "It was," he concluded, "for the future of America and of all civilization that we fought this mightiest of wars. . . ."[10]

Nevins' article ignited other fires, some of them rather highly placed. Secretary of War Robert P. Patterson clipped Nevins' piece and sent it, along with a worried note, to his special assistant in the Historical Division of the Army, Troyer S. Anderson. Recalling the revisionist histories which had appeared after World War I and which had given "our younger people . . . a feeling that our part in World War I was a disgraceful business, and the less said about it the better," Patterson detected "the beginnings of the same kind of thinking . . . already becoming evident." It was "of utmost importance," he told Anderson, "that people should not fall into the trap again. I hope that something can be done to see to it that there is sound scholarship put into the writing of recent history. . . ."[11]

Anderson replied with a sympathetic note agreeing that the struggle against new "'revisionism'" was one of tremendous import. In January 1946 he sent word to Patterson that he and Nevins had discussed the possibility of having, at the end of the Pearl Harbor inquiry,

> a small group of historians with established reputations go over the testimony of the hearing and prepare an analysis of it which would serve to dispel the notion that this country was pushed or tricked into war by its own government. This would, of course, be a strictly private venture, but Professor Nevins thinks he can get two or three outstanding scholars to join us in the task.[12]

While working on his last books, Beard suspected that the authorities in Washington were trying to influence the histories of the war yet to be written. He tried to start a public debate on the issue of equal access by all citizens to available public documents of the United States Government and to the papers of Franklin D. Roosevelt. "Who's to Write the History of the War?" he asked in *The Saturday Evening Post* of 4 October 1947.

This editorial was inspired by the preface to William L. Langer's recently published *Our Vichy Gamble*. Langer related that his book's publication had been authorized by the Department of State, by the War Department, and by the director of the former Office of Strategic Services. He revealed that Secretary Hull had "requested" him to make a detailed, independent study and that he had been given full access to the records of the Office of Strategic Services, his own employer during the war, as well as "a detailed digest of such military records as had political importance," and some of Admiral Leahy's papers. On completion of the draft of his book during the summer of 1944, Langer recorded that Hull, Leahy, and numerous other concerned officials had read it and that President Roosevelt had offered to help and had, in fact, had "such of his papers as bore on the problem" abstracted for Langer.[13]

After this introduction, Langer's assertion that *Our Vichy Gamble* was "an altogether independent analysis" that "in no sense" reflected or recorded "official opinion or judgment" might well be questioned.[14] The Chicago *Tribune's* epithet "a hired liar" certainly exaggerated the case, but Beard's comment that "subsidized histories of this kind, prepared to serve a fixed purpose in advance" were "more likely to perpetuate errors than to eliminate them" was entirely warranted. "Official archives," Beard insisted, "must be open to all citizens on equal terms, with special privileges for none; inquiries must be wide and deep as well as uncensored; and the competition of ideas in the forum of public opinion must be free from political interests or restraints."[15]

Beard had cause to be personally angry with the government policy, although that was not his reason for raising the issue of access. On 27 August 1945 he had written to the Secretary of State inquiring about the existence of correspondence between President Roosevelt and Winston Churchill before the latter became prime minister, between September 1939 and May 1940. Seven weeks later William Benton, Assistant Secretary of State, replied to Beard's letter without answering his question, referring to it in fact as an "allegation" and saying that the Roosevelt papers being made available to the congressional committee investigating Pearl Harbor might have the answer.[16]

On 1 May 1946 a search room for the use of scholars had been opened at the Roosevelt Library at Hyde Park, and in September 1946 Beard had written to Fred W. Shipman, director of the Roosevelt Library, asking to see copies of the President's press conferences for 1941, 1944, and 1945. Shipman had refused the request.[17] "That seems about the limit," Beard protested to George Smith, his former collaborator. "Why should the taxpayers support a library for trustees picked by Roosevelt to run [it] as they please?"[18]

When a friend, Clarence B. Hewes, a former diplomat, wrote at Beard's request to Harry S. Truman in January 1947, inquiring about the policy of the National Archives toward the admission of scholars to recent materials in the possession of the government, Truman did not reply.[19] Beard himself asked about access to the Roosevelt papers in a letter to the Archivist of the United States, Solon J. Buck, in January 1947. Buck replied that "some of these" were "now available for use by qualified scholars, but not all of them" and that he did not believe that Shipman had "made any discrimination among qualified scholars."[20]

Why were the press conferences unavailable? In March 1947 another of Beard's acquaintances, Senator Homer Ferguson (Republican, Michigan), obtained the answer when Fred Shipman appeared at a congressional hearing:

> *Senator Ferguson.* Have you ruled, now, that they [the press conferences] are limited-access papers?
> *Mr. Shipman.* By a negative rule, yes; that they are not open.
> *Senator Ferguson.* Why did you rule so?
> *Mr. Shipman.* Because there are many things which have been said by the President informally to the press which have been off the record, and I just am questioning the wisdom of making such things available.[21]

One aspect of the controversy over access to recent documents involved, by Shipman's criteria, the character of the documents themselves. However, as Beard had commented to Hewes, the minutes of the President's press conferences were not "state secrets"; they were "notes of what President Roosevelt said to journalists, presumably for the benefit of the American public," and it did indeed seem absurd that they were not again available to the public after the war.[22]

The central issue of access was not, however, *which documents* could be seen, but rather *which scholars* could do the looking. According to Solon J. Buck, the joint resolution establishing the Roosevelt Library had given "to the Archivist authority to make regulations for the use of the materials in the custody of the library."[23] Asked by Senator Ferguson in March 1947 if he assumed that the statute allowed the archivist "to determine that certain material cannot be seen or . . . who may see it," Buck replied that that was his view of the law.

> *Senator Ferguson.* In other words, if one man wants to write a history, you can say, "you can see it." And if another man wants to write a history, you can say, "You cannot see it."
>
> *Mr. Buck.* Well, actually, Senator, I have directed, instructed the director informally that no distinction whatever should be made between reputable scholars who wish to consult materials, and I am sure no such distinctions have been made.
>
> *Senator Ferguson.* Who is going to determine who is reputable? . . .
>
> *Mr. Buck.* Well, the law does not use the term "reputable" at all. I simply have the general authority to make regulations.[24]

In May 1947, the Department of State echoed the position of the National Archivist by issuing a series of regulations governing the use of original records. Unpublished files prior to 1 January 1922 were, with some exceptions, available to the general public at the National Archives. Files and records between 1922 and 1 January 1933 were open with some restrictions to such persons as "lawyers, publicists, and qualified scholars," if approved by the Chief of the Division of Historical Policy Research, at this time Bernard Noble, and if the applicant submitted to Noble "all notes, copies of documents and the like, which he has made." Unpublished records dated later than 1 January 1933 were to be made available to persons outside the government *"only on the grounds that the interests of national policy are served thereby,"* and access would be decided by "a Committee on the Use of Departmental Files, consisting of the Security Officer of the Department, the Chief of the Division of Historical Policy Research . . . and a representative of the offices responsible for the political and/or economic policy involved."[25]

These regulations, the hearings in March 1947, Beard's failure to elicit meaningful responses from the Department of State, even on so simple a question as the *existence* of certain correspondence, the reluctance of the director of the Roosevelt Library to grant access even to the stenographic records of the late president's press meetings, and finally Langer's preface revealing that, indeed, people with privileged connections were scrutinizing documents unavailable to other members of the public all form the background to Beard's editorial blast of October 1947.

In an effort to demonstrate that Beard was a petty and bitter man, Thomas Kennedy has argued that Beard either "unwittingly or unjustly" conveyed the "impression that he had been denied such access," while individuals close to Roosevelt such as Ernest K. Lindley, Herbert Feis, Samuel Eliot Morison, and William L. Langer had been granted privileged access to unpublished materials of the government. In Kennedy's scenario, Beard is the man who complained about the difficulties of getting access but who never applied. In fact, Kennedy maintains, Beard's sour grapes were tasted for nothing because the revisionist historian Charles C. Tansill gained access to the records of the State Department *"before* Beard *published his charges in the Saturday Evening Post"* (italics in original). By taking a narrow view of the issue, Kennedy portrays Beard as an irrational, unreasonable, and uninformed troublemaker.[26]

However, Kennedy overlooks the fact that Beard had a sound reason for not applying to the State Department. Beard refused to be a party to a process whereby a group of self-styled experts decided who was a "qualified scholar" and who was not. His position was that all unclassified materials should be available to all members of the public on an equal basis without discrimination, and his view was echoed by such newspapers as *The Washington Post* and *The Christian Science Monitor.*[27]

In an angry letter to the editor of *The Washington Post,* a letter replying to Beard's *Saturday Evening Post* commentary on his preface, Langer referred, without citing the explicit regulations, to the State Department's *Bulletin* of 25 May 1947 and argued mistakenly that the State Department had never "suggested that the use of its records was conditional upon its approval of the results of such use."[28]

Before Langer's letter was published Beard had asked William L. Neumann, a young historian then in Washington, D.C., to inquire at the Department of State as to whether some recent materials after 1933 were being made available to scholars authorized by a board of review to examine them.[29] Neumann wrote to Bernard Noble, Chief of the Division of Historical Policy Research, and Noble replied with a copy of the regulations of 25 May 1947 and this comment: "The files from January 1, 1933 to the present are closed, though in exceptional circumstances they may be open for special purposes if such as in line with the *national interest.* The Committee on the Use of Departmental Files has been established to make decisions in such cases." (Italics in original.)[30]

When Neumann sent him the results of his inquiry, Beard replied, "Of the many fine weasel words, 'National Interest' must be regarded as among the loveliest. It doth seem that Professor Langer stretched his imagination when he said, in reply to me, that the Department was opening up the secret papers."[31] In these circumstances, Beard did not care to validate an undemocratic process by applying for access to unpublished government materials. He chose instead to arouse citizens to ponder the dangers inherent in the policy of sifting scholars as well as documents.

American Foreign Policy in the Making, 1932–1940 (1946) and *President Roosevelt and the Coming of the War, 1941: A Study in Appearances and Realities* (1948) were Beard's last works of political science. They were political landscapes laid carefully before the people to instruct them and to inspire an informed assault on the dangers posed for the Republic by the unclear definition of the president's powers. In these works Beard returned to a distinction, important also to the understanding of his early books, between the political science of pure thought and the political science of action. His most significant books—*An Economic Interpretation of the Constitution* (1913) and *The Open Door at Home* (1934)—had been entries in debates on the direction of public policy. His last books are of the same kind. The argument is historical in nature, but the purpose is to guide action in the present moment.

Events of the thirties, particularly the example of great power wielded by dictators and presidents in modern industrial states, had led Beard to widen his focus, to admit in his later books that history could be shaped by incomprehensible currents of irrationality. "There certainly is something in economic determinism, more than most people suspect, but there is a lot of sheer, damned folly in the world, that is no-sense or chaos" he confided to Merle Curti in 1943.[32]

The political science of action was still connected to an analysis of material factors. "With economics left out of account," he wrote, "political science cannot rise much above the level of astrology."[33] However, the impact of the last twenty years was evident in his final revision of *The Economic Basis of Politics* (1945). Here, for the first time, Beard emphasized the role of the military as an independent interest commanding power in the modern state. To Marx's "economic man" and to Aristotle's "political man" he would add "'the military man' and 'military force'" which would "play an increasing role in the public affairs of the United States as well as in the affairs of other countries."[34] Universal Military Training, he warned, would mean an immense growth in the number of persons with careers in the armed services. It was not that these military men were necessarily "more warlike than civilians," but rather that "military men have, necessarily, a set of values which differ in many respects from civilian values." With great prescience Beard admonished that the "man of war," with his insatiable demand for materials, "would be even more than ever dependent on economic production" and that this would be the "economic underwriting" of the modern state.[35]

Once more Beard pointed out that Marx and Engels had offered no guidance to these modern dilemmas, for neither had "substantially qualified his 'economic man' by reference to the role of the military man in universal history." Capitalism had spread throughout the world, but the state, far from shrinking, was becoming a military bureaucracy.[36] In his last books, Beard looked at democracy in America and found authoritarian shadows. Their substance was the very dramatic accretion of power to the executive during the years of Roosevelt's presidency.

Sent to the printer in January 1946, *American Foreign Policy in the Making, 1932–1940* was published in August 1946. By driving his "reluctant body," Beard had completed the book in six months during 1945. At first he had promised the manuscript to Macmillan, but Edwin Borchard had contacted the Yale University Press, which had promised to bring it out sooner, and Beard had decided to give it to them. The royalties were not as important to him as early publication, he wrote Borchard, for that "would make it reasonably certain that I may be able to see the proofs through the press."[37] Sending the manuscript to Borchard for his inspection in December 1945, Beard commented that "the lack of strength & the brevity of the days oppresses me, but I want to leave at least a memorandum on these years."[38]

Beard's intention was not to write a history of American foreign relations. It was to give the public a grasp of the ways that the President and others in his administration had abused the democratic process in the pursuit of a foreign policy which had not been honestly discussed. What, he asked, could an active citizen have known about American foreign policy between 1933 and 1941 if he or she had followed the public explanations of that policy given by the administration in Washington?

As he assembled the record of pronouncements on policy, the evidence appeared to contradict those writers who had sought during the war to present a picture of the administration as having perceived danger throughout the thirties, as having repeatedly warned the people but as regretfully having to resort to some deception when people failed to respond to numerous warnings of impending danger. As a responsible citizen, Beard was enraged by efforts to change official records to conform with this view of history. He was angered by attempts to blame the senators who had refused to support American entrance into the League of Nations for the coming of the war and by endeavors to portray the mass of the American people as naive isolationists who had had to be deceived into taking action.

Beard devoted his early chapters in this book to outlining and documenting current assumptions, which he challenged, about responsibility for the coming of war. One such common theory was that "obstructionists" in the United States Senate in 1919 and 1920, had, by preventing the United States from ratifying the Treaty of Versailles, been somehow responsible for the instability of the peace. Along with Senator Claude Pepper (Democrat, Florida), Thomas

Connally (Democrat, Texas), and "T.R.B." of *The New Republic*, Beard regarded Thomas A. Bailey, an influential and respected young historian, as a chief propagator of this view, especially in his book *Woodrow Wilson and the Great Betrayal*. While praising Bailey's careful research and noting that his first twenty-one chapters were critical of Wilson and left open the issue of who was at fault, Beard was indignant that Bailey had implied in his final chapter that "Senator Lodge and the 'bitter-enders'" were "at least to be regarded as among the culprits in the 'great betrayal' which brought World War II upon humanity."[39]

Along with the "presuppositions so commonly taken for granted without analysis, namely that the contest in the United States over the League of Nations was a 'partisan' strife; that it was a struggle between idealists who were realists and alleged realists who did not know what they were doing," Beard found a further argument commonly associated with the others. In *How War Came: An American White Paper* (1942) by Forrest Davis and Ernest K. Lindley, two journalists with solid connections to the White House, and in the anonymous introduction to the State Department's *Peace and War: United States Foreign Policy, 1931–1941* (July 1943), appeared the generalization that "the American people, or at least a dominant portion of them, were afflicted with smugness and ignorance in matters of foreign policy," that President Roosevelt had been hampered by the people in pursuing his own wiser policy, and thus that the people "were responsible for the catastrophe that marked the opening of the all-out war for Americans at Pearl Harbor."[40]

Beard's lens was closely fixed on the contention in the State Department's volume of documents that public opinion during much of the period from 1931 to 1941 differed from the opinion of the President and Secretary of State Hull. Roosevelt and Hull, the State Department claimed, had "'early become convinced that the aggressive policies of the Axis powers were directed toward an ultimate attack on the United States and that, therefore, our foreign relations should be so conducted as to give all possible support to the nations endeavoring to check the march of axis aggression.'"[41]

"When," Beard asked, "was this great, indeed revolutionary decision reached by the President and Secretary Hull?" In 1934, or 1937, or 1940? When did they "present to the country their fateful decision and their outline of a foreign policy adverse to isolation, neutrality, and peace for the United States?"[42]

The remainder of the book led inevitably to the conclusion that defenders of the foreign policy of the Roosevelt administration who made it a consistently internationalist program, hampered only by the burden of a neutralist public opinion and by the constraints imposed by the circumstances of democracy, could conduct their defense only by distorting and falsifying the historical record. And Beard implied that Roosevelt had attempted to do precisely this by omitting from his *Public Papers and Addresses* his early repudiation of internationalism and the League of Nations.[43] The Roosevelt administration, Beard maintained, had publicly supported neutrality and non-intervention through 1936, and even the famous "quarantine speech" of October 1937 had not resulted in a public definition and explanation of a new departure in American policy. Publicly, the administration's discussions of foreign policy had emphasized neutrality, peace, and nonintervention up to and including the campaign of 1940. The administration, the historians, the journalists, and others who blamed an ignorant public for the disastrous beginning of the war were ignoring the fact that the leadership had not conducted a realistic dialogue with the public, a dialogue that clearly set forth the reasons for decisions. Instead of a foreign policy developed by democratic discussion of the larger issues and assumptions, the President had thrown dust in people's eyes at his enigmatic press conferences and had never informed the people of his change of heart—of his view that the United States was indeed on the road to war.

By the time of the Democratic convention in July 1940, Beard noted, France had fallen; the British had been driven off the Continent; and the triumph of the Axis powers in Europe seemed imminent. But, aside from a few derisive remarks about "American ostriches," the President had not seized the opportunity to proclaim a policy of preparation for war. His campaign speeches of 1940 had repeated "peace promises," most of which Beard reprinted seriatum in his last chapter.[44] The obvious conclusion was that President Roosevelt had left the people to guess the nature of his policy, as indeed many had been able to do. However, Beard was asking, why should serious citizens, honest patriots, have to tolerate such vapid hypocrisy and cant in a democratic system? Were people to shrug and laugh at campaign rhetoric, meanwhile leaving important questions of national destiny to leaders who had access to more information than the person in the street?

During 1946, as he worked on his book on 1941, Beard corresponded with George H. Smith, his collaborator during the thirties who was then Secretary of the Minority Steering Committee of the Senate. Smith had previously furnished Beard with copies of the State Department's press releases from 1932 to 1941. Now that Beard had completed his first manuscript, Smith suggested that he read the transcripts of the hearings of the joint congressional committee which was investigating the disaster at Pearl Harbor and that he prepare "a report that could be used officially."[45]

Although deeply interested in Pearl Harbor, Beard was not enthusiastic about doing an anonymous memorandum that might be used by Republican politicians. He was, he told Smith "no partisan but a student of history desirous of reviewing the evidence with care and drawing the conclusions warranted by the evidence in such a form that they will stand the test of critical scholarship on all sides." As a nonpartisan, Beard said he was willing to write something for the whole committee, and in characteristic rational fashion he urged a nonpartisan approach to the problem, beginning with an agreement on terms.[46] Finally, at Smith's urging, Beard sent a set of questions to the committee, but he refused to write the larger report Smith wanted. Remembering Henry Luce's rejection of his first "memorandum" on Pearl Harbor in 1944 and expressing suspicion of Smith's motives, Beard wrote that "working in a dark room for men whose plans, desires, and intentions I know nothing about seems to offer no advantages to any cause." To mollify Smith, Beard agreed to see anybody from the committee who wanted to talk to him at New Milford in April.[47]

Although Beard was unenthusiastic about Senator Homer Ferguson's record as an interventionist in prewar days, he conferred with him on the preparation of the minority report of the joint committee, once in April 1946 and again in June.[48] Before the minority report was published Smith sent Beard two copies for his corrections.[49] Returning the proofs to Smith, Beard expressed his disappointment with the report as Ferguson and Owen Brewster (Republican, Maine) had presented it. Ferguson and Brewster had concluded that President Roosevelt, Secretary of War Henry L. Stimson, Secretary of the Navy Frank Knox, General George C. Marshall, Admiral Harold R. Stark, and Major General Leonard T. Gerow had had sufficient information indicating that war was imminent by December 6 and that they had failed in the crucial responsibility of delivering to their field commanders a full war alert. However, the minority report had not cleared Admiral Kimmel and General Short of the charge of "dereliction of duty" made by the Roberts Commission in January 1942. In Beard's mind, this had been the "supreme issue before the Committee. . . . For, if Short and Kimmel, despite their orders from Washington, were *'left with sufficient responsibility'* (galley 47, last line), then," Beard argued, "they were bound to be prepared for the Japanese attack and to blast it—so there would have been no Pearl Harbor affair." Furthermore, Beard maintained, clearing the two officers of the charge of dereliction did "not clear them of errors of judgment and lack of efficiency and alertness," though in his opinion "they were befuddled by the kind of orders they received." If Ferguson and Brewster did not dispose of this issue, Beard concluded, then the whole report would be "a flop."[50]

Beard's plea was ignored. The offending words were not removed from the minority report, and, in *President Roosevelt and the Coming of War, 1941,* Beard excoriated the minority for leaving Kimmel and Short "under the stigma put upon them by the Roberts Report" and "the subsequent action of President Roosevelt," who through his press secretary, Stephen Early, had intimated that the two commanders deserved to be court-martialed.[51]

In apportioning the greatest responsibility for Pearl Harbor to high civilian and military authorities in Washington, the minority report *was* very direct. President Roosevelt, it said had "failed to take that quick and instant executive action which was required by the occasion and by the responsibility for watchfulness rightly associated in law and practice with his high office."[52] Thus Beard might have appeared to be, as he put it himself, *"quibbling over words."*[53] However, from his perspective, this was the central issue. Roosevelt's effort to avoid any responsibility for the carnage and wreckage at Pearl Harbor aroused Beard's deepest moral instincts. It was a matter of "character" and integrity, a test of these virtues the President had failed ignominiously. Always outraged by hypocrisy and betrayal on the part of those in a position of leadership and trust, Beard had felt a similar contempt for Nicholas Murray Butler when Butler had acquiesced in the firing by the trustees of a former protégé at Columbia in 1917. This time the moral derelict was no mere president of a university.

Yet "the real issue," as Beard later described his intention in doing the book about 1941, was "not Mr. Roosevelt's personal virtue or lack of it but whether his major performances squared with his major promises and whether his conduct squared with the first principles of the constitutional and 'democratic' government."[54] While Beard loathed Roosevelt's willingness to shift responsibility, he did not focus on personalities, and Richard Hofstadter's contention that Beard had a "profound animating hatred of F.D.R." and a "conspiratorial view of historical events"[55] is supported neither by the great majority of his surviving letters nor by the restrained conclusions—accompanied, it is true, by many sarcastic questions in his last book. It is fairer to say that he sought controversy and encouraged the questioning of the mystique of power surrounding the presidency. Spending two years, 1946 and 1947, he produced a vivid, thoroughly documented, nonpartisan account of President Roosevelt's methods in the conduct of foreign policy in 1941. After all, he told Smith, he was "no damned committee or corpus of three or four incapable of going after the truth and unwilling for political reasons to tell it."[56]

Letters written while he worked on the book indicate that Beard changed his mind a number of times as he sifted through the available evidence on the coming of war. In January 1942, writing to Robert M. La Follette, Jr., who had questioned the conclusions of the Roberts Report that Kimmel and Short bore the major responsibility for Pearl Harbor, Beard surmised that "whatever blame" was "to be attached to the local officers, the fundamental responsibility" rested on others—"the President, Stimson, and Knox, and on members of Congress, especially the chairmen of the military affairs and naval affairs committees of the two houses." Members of Congress had been warned for years against "voting money blindly to the Army and Navy and urged to considered [sic] the whole armament program as a unity and a relation to the foreign policy pursued by the President." They had, he wrote, "been warned against trusting to monster battleships and ignoring the growing power of airplanes."[57]

"I wonder and wonder," he confided to Edwin Borchard in 1945, a few months after Roosevelt's death, "what kind of man F.D. was, above all why he was not ready at Pearl Harbor. He baffles me more than any character I have met in history."[58]

Usually, when Beard entered a controversy he was not alone. In 1913, when he had questioned the formalistic approach to the study of constitutional history, others had preceded him. In the 1930s, he was one of a legion of exponents of national planning. After World War II there were also other people asking questions about the coming of war.

Following the revelations of the army and navy inquiries into Pearl Harbor in late August 1945, which documented for the first time that the government had broken the Japanese diplomatic code, "Magic", before the beginning of hostilities, John T. Flynn published an article in the *Chicago Tribune* on 2 September 1945. He concluded that Roosevelt had decided on war with Japan by 1 January 1941 but that the President had been unwilling to take the offensive because he had promised during his campaign for re-election that America would not go to war unless attacked. Hence, according to Flynn, Roosevelt had provoked the Japanese assault. In November he had handed the Japanese "an ultimatum which he knew [from reading the messages sent to Japanese ambassadors in the secret code] they dared not comply with." However, Flynn argued, the President was certain that the attack would be against Singapore, the Phillipines, or Guam and definitely not Pearl Harbor. Roosevelt had "completely miscalculated," had ignored military advice to seek a modus vivendi, and had disregarded the coded message that had spelled out the very hour of the attack. After the attack, wrote Flynn, the President "maneuvered to lay the blame upon Kimmel and Short. To prevent them from proving their innocence he refused them a trial." When the case was investigated in 1944 by two naval and army boards, "he suppressed the reports."[59]

After he read Flynn's article, Beard commented that he disagreed with Flynn's conclusion that "F.D. was actually surprised on December 7," adding, however, that he did "not claim to know the secret of the mystery" but that he did "not think that F.D. was surprised. That explanation seems to me to be too 'rational.'"[60]

A few months later Beard changed his mind again. Perhaps, he thought, it was Hull who had taken the fateful steps to war. He wrote to Smith urging him to press Senator Ferguson to confront former Secretary of State Cordell Hull with this question at the hearings on Pearl Harbor:

> Why did Hull throw overboard the modus vivendi which had been arrived at and send the message of November 26 which as he said, put the business in the hands of the Army and Navy?[61]

Suggesting that Hull had drafted the memorandum of 26 November without consulting the President, Beard noted that "F.D.'s pencil memo in the photostat" he had "was a sensible proposal for a real settlement with Japan." Complaining to Smith, Beard remarked that he was "struck by the low grade of competence shown by the whole crowd: Army Navy & Civilians involved in the mess that resulted in the disaster. There doesn't seem to have been enough sense to plan anything."[62] In a similar vein, he wrote to Borchard that it was "ridiculous for anyone to imagine that the inquiry would turn up documentary evidence that President Roosevelt planned to induce a Japanese attack on Hawaii and to let Kimmel and Short sit in darkness unprepared." The business was "highly complicated."[63]

Beard thus did not begin with the intention of writing a personal attack on the dead President. Though he came to despise the methods of diplomacy utilized by Franklin Roosevelt—the secrecy, the dissimulation, the indirect presentation of issues to the public, the exploitation of incidents in order to overcome the public's apparent reluctance to go to war—he was wary of assigning absolute responsibility for history. Studying stacks of documents from 1945 to 1947, he described himself as trying to keep his mind open and free from prejudgments.[64]

While Beard was completing his volume on 1941, George Morgenstern, a young man on the editorial staff of the *Chicago Tribune*, published (in January 1947) his *Pearl Harbor: The Story of the Secret War*. Beard had read the book in manuscript and had allowed an endorsement from him to be printed on the dust jacket. Morgenstern's book was polemical, as many good books are, but it was also a work of considerable documentation, a historical account of the coming of Pearl Harbor based on evidence available in the transcripts of the hearings of the joint committee. Aside from Flynn's articles, it was the first scholarly attack on the myth that a Japanese attack was unexpected and that the administration had been, at the moment of the attack, seriously seeking peace.

Morgenstern took firm positions on the large questions. In his view, the secret diplomatic messages decoded by American intelligence pointed clearly to an attack on Pearl Harbor on 7 December.[65] During many months before Pearl Harbor, the high civilian and military officials in Washington, in Morgenstern's view, had "had almost as good a knowledge of Japanese plans and intentions as if they had been occupying seats in the war councils of Tokyo."[66] After the attack, leaders of the administration had been "frantically scurrying about proving their surprise and injury" and had made sure that the first investigation, conducted by Justice Owen Roberts (who was denied knowledge of the deciphered code messages), placed the blame on Admiral Kimmel and General Short. In reality, said Morgenstern, it was the President who had kept the fleet at Oahu, overruling military advice to the contrary and acting as a "one-man general staff working through intuition."[67] Roosevelt's main interest had been in the European theater, which he "schemed" to enter through the "back door" of the Pacific when sufficient "incidents" could not be found in the Atlantic.[68] According to Morgenstern, "diplomacy failed in 1941 because diplomacy was not employed to avert war, but to make certain its coming."[69] Morgenstern carefully documented the preoccupation of the administration with the possibility of a Japanese attack in South East Asia. However, he also thought that an attack on Pearl Harbor could have been reasonably inferred from history and from the evidence available at the time to the administration. Although Morgenstern did not explicitly say that President Roosevelt knew that the attack on Peark Harbor was coming and when, he did accuse the "war hawks of the Roosevelt Administration of wanting a Pearl Harbor or something very much like it to push this country into war."[70] In his view, there was "good reason to believe that Stimson knew not only that war was coming, but that he knew it would break out at Pearl Harbor."[71] Morgenstern speculated that Roosevelt and the men around him probably had diverse motives for "warping the nation into war in 1941":

> Desire for glory and enhanced status could have contributed to it. Men in the regular establishments of the Army and Navy who saw the vision of spectacular commands and stars upon their shoulders. . . . All of them were enlisted, long before Pearl Harbor, in Roosevelt's conspiracy to fight an unacknowledged and unconstitutional war in the Atlantic. All of them were parties, before December 7, 1941, in his secret war alliance with the British and Dutch in the Pacific.[72]

Even if one rejected his analysis and interpretation of events, Morgenstern concluded that the administration could still be faulted for acting dishonorably in failing to warn the men in the field. "When the price of silence proved to be 2,326 lives, it was necessary to add two more victims to the list—Admiral Kimmel and General Short."[73]

The fact that Beard welcomed Morgenstern's contribution to the historical debate about the origins of the war did not necessarily mean that he agreed with Morgenstern's version of the tale. Morgenstern, he told Harry Elmer Barnes, "goes too far in some of his conclusions. . . . I find no evidence to traduce any of his conclusions based on circumstantial evidence but I think he does not realize how utterly senseless Roosevelt could be at times."[74] Indeed, since Morgenstern and Beard are often lumped together as irresponsible critics of Roosevelt's prewar policy, it is instructive to view their books together, for, in that situation, Beard's purpose—to write a documented tract on the wrong way to conduct foreign policy in a democracy—sharply contrasts with Morgenstern's desire, to write a history of the incident at Pearl Harbor.

Beard's book was much broader than Morgenstern's, and many more questions were asked than were answered. As the subtitle, *A Study in Appearances and Realities,* suggests, the first part of the book documented the President's fundamentally dishonest, or, as a friendly historian later wrote, his "watchfully indirect" expalnations to the American people of the Lend-Lease Act, of whether or not convoys, prohibited by that law, were being used, of the incidents in the Atlantic involving the USS *Greer* and the USS *Kearney,* and of the negotiations with Japan both before and after the Atlantic Conference in August 1941. Beard ended the first part of his book where Morgenstern had begun, with the official explanation of the tragedy at Pearl Harbor.[75]

Roosevelt, Beard recalled, had "characterized the Japanese attack as a sudden, unexpected treacherous act committed while relations between the two countries were peaceful." On 26 November, according to the President, the

Japanese had been "handed a clear-cut plan for a broad but simple settlement," but "we did not know then as we know now that they had ordered and were even then carrying out their plan for a treacherous attack upon us."[76] Secretary Hull, echoing the President, had said that Japan's attack was utterly unprovoked.[77] The report of the Roberts Commission, completed in January 1942, had "exculpated high officials in Washington," and had charged the Hawaiian commanders with "derelictions of duty and errors of judgment" that were "'the effective causes for the success of the attack.'"[78]

In the second portion of the book, "Unveiling Realities," Beard contrasted what knowledgeable citizens were told about the coming of war in 1941 with what the hearings before the joint committee and other information released after the war had so far revealed about events in 1941. His main interest was in showing up the discrepancy between what a person seeking information could have found out at the time and what had actually transpired. He was not writing a diplomatic history but rather a commentary on the methods of conducting public policy. Although "much was publicly known about warlike activities in the Atlantic between June and November, 1941," concerned citizens could only know that "the origins and nature of these activities were obscure, at least as officially explained."[79]

In Beard's rendering, the realities were not so clear as they had been for Morgenstern. For example, Morgenstern had boldly theorized that, before the war had begun, Roosevelt had consummated "secret war alliances" with the British, Dutch, and Canadians during the Anglo-American military and naval conferences in 1941.[80] Like Morgenstern, Beard was interested in the question of whether or not "contingent war plans" constituted an "alliance," but he refused to go beyond the evidence and there was, when he wrote, no evidence of such a military alliance. Beard's main point was that the Japanese knew, if not the precise nature of the plans, at least "that the United States and Great Britain were cooperating in the making of military plans, as well as in the application of economic sanctions and diplomatic pressures." According to Beard, the plans, not revealed to the public for many months, were more evidence of the hypocrisy of Roosevelt's claim to have been surprised when war came.[81]

How much should the people have known? Beard's answer was that, in a democracy, those citizens who have an interest in issues of life and death should be able always to inform themselves of the facts on which the issues of life and death depend. Roosevelt's record in this respect was lamentable.

> Concerning the course of specific transactions in official relations between the United States and Japan from the opening of the Atlantic Conference until December 7, 1941, the American people knew little at the time. Those who read the newspapers learned from reports of the President's meetings with representatives of the press that, at the Atlantic Conference, no new commitments had been made, that the country was no closer to war, that arrangements for operations under the Lend-Lease Act had been developed, that a list of grand

principles, soon known as the Atlantic Charter . . . had been promulgated over the names of the President and the Prime Minister, and that relations with Japan were dangerously strained. From the President's quip that he and Mr. Churchill had discussed affairs in all the continents of the earth, newspaper readers possessed of the slightest imagination could conclude that affairs in the Far East had in some manner been reviewed at the Atlantic Conference.[82]

Some critics later faulted Beard for suggesting that Roosevelt had deliberately kept secret the negotiations between 17 August and 16 October 1941 over a possible meeting in the Pacific between the President and the Japanese Prime Minister, Prince Konoye. In reality, the secrecy had been requested by Prince Konoye himself, who had wished to keep news of such a meeting from reaching the military people in his own government.[83] But this criticism does nothing to the logic of Beard's argument, which was that, after the fall of the Konoye government on 16 October 1941, when secrecy was no longer an issue, the administration neither made public the negotiations nor offered an explanation of why the idea of a Pacific meeting had been rejected.

Having driven home his view that the negotiations should not have been kept secret, Beard was cautious on the narrower historical issues raised by the proposed meeting in the Pacific. It was, he said, at present impossible to tell what parts President Roosevelt and Secretary Hull had played in the final decision to reject the Konoye proposal. Nor was it possible, Beard admitted, "now to discover whether, if the Pacific conference had been held, Premier Konoye could have carried out his intentions as communicated to the President and Secretary Hull." A solution to "this insoluble 'problem,'" Beard wrote, lay outside the purposes and limitations of his inquiry.[84]

On the other great question that has always troubled historians of the coming of war with Japan, the issue of the rejection of a modus vivendi presented by Japan on 20 November 1941 and the issuing instead of the famous memorandum of 26 November demanding that Japan withdraw all military forces from Indo-China and China and support only the Nationalist government in China, Beard was more direct: "Did [Hull and Roosevelt] believe that their action would lead to a break in negotiations, if not immediate war? If they made this crucial decision with reference to such consequences, why did they resort to ultimative action in the Pacific rather than in the Atlantic?"[85]

In reply, he suggested that the failure to rouse Congress to declare war by claiming that America had been attacked in the *Greer* and *Kearney* cases, as well as the long tussle in Congress over modifying the Neutrality Act, had led Roosevelt and Hull to decide on the memorandum of 26 November. They knew, Beard noted, from intercepted code messages that the memorandum was certain to be rejected.[86]

Yet Beard hesitated. This interpretation of the origins of the memorandum of 26 November was only a "conjecture of circumstances," and without Roosevelt's private papers, which had been denied to the minority of the joint committee and to historians, many questions remained. "Beyond question," however, "according to the evidence produced by the Congressional Committee, the President and the Secretary, before, on, and after making the decision *were expecting if not actively seeking war;* and having this expectation they continued to 'maneuver' the Japanese and awaited the denouement, *without calling on Congress for the authority to wage war.*"[87]

Certainly, Beard was ambivalent as to whether or not the President and his advisers were plotting war. This was a historical question on which there was evidence both negative and affirmative. Unlike Morgenstern, Beard could not definitely assume that Roosevelt had been "warping the nation into war," that he had seized on the idea of forcing Japan to attack when his "unconstitutional conspiracy in the Atlantic" had failed.[88]

On the issue of principle—the question of whether or not the *way* Roosevelt had conducted diplomacy had violated, through its secrecy, the process of democracy—Beard was certain. "Was it within the legal and moral competence of President Roosevelt in 1941 so to conduct foreign affairs as to maneuver a foreign country into firing the shot that brought on war—indeed to make war on his own authority?"[89] Secretary Stimson, who had recorded the fateful discussions within the administration on maneuvering the Japanese into firing the first shot, had answered this query in the affirmative. Beard shuddered at the implications. Furthermore, Stimson had argued before the joint committee that the President alone should determine defense policy and how it should best be carried out. According to Stimson, the warmaking power thus belonged completely to the executive.[90]

In an epilogue Beard took the opportunity to reply to Stimson and to throw a few punches at critics of his first volume on 1933 to 1940. There were, he began, discrepancies between official versions of foreign policy and official realities in the conduct of foreign affairs. Referring to Morgenstern's book, he noted that these discrepancies could be "formulated into a bill of indictment against President Roosevelt and his Administration." Or, as critics of Beard's first book had done, the facts could be conceded and it could be denied that they made a true case "under superior and overriding principles, taken for granted in advance." Or, speaking of himself, these anomalies might be seen as "precedents material and relevant to the future and fortunes of constitutional and democratic government in the United States."[91]

Many reviewers of Beard's first volume had conceded that Roosevelt had "dissembled" and been indirect and unexplicit in his public discussions of foreign policy, but these critics argued essentially that the end, defeating Japan and Germany, had justified the means Roosevelt chose for conducting policy. Young Arthur M. Schlesinger, Jr., was most direct: "You can prove that any democratic leader was opportunistic. The significant thing is to prove that he was wrong."[92]

Samuel Flagg Bemis, who had never referred to himself as any sort of liberal, wrote:

This reviewer never voted for Mr. Roosevelt upon any of the numerous occasions when he was invited to do so, but he shudders to think what would have happened had we stood by with folded arms and let Hitler and Japan establish their "new orders" in Europe and Asia and then close in on the New World and the United States. To prevent this it was necessary to defend the British Empire in the Pacific as well as in the Atlantic.[93]

Beard had no patience with this argument. "When did the end that justified the means actually come? With the surrender of Italy, Germany and Japan?" How could this be argued when the "noble principles of the Four Freedoms and the Atlantic Charter" had been thrown out the window in Eastern Europe and in the European colonies in Asia? More significant was the fact that the end of the war had meant the "triumph of another totalitarian regime no less despotic than Hitler's system, namely Russia."[94]

And, in American domestic affairs, what had been the meaning of the war? Recalling those who had told him before the war that his continentalism would mean turning "the United States into a kind of armed camp for defense, with . . . a permanent conscript army, multiplied annual outlays for armaments, a huge national debt, and grinding taxes," Beard mused that, obviously, victory over Hitler had not prevented the coming of these "dreadful evils."[95] Conscription was being promoted in the postwar era to secure the fruits of victory; military expenditures in 1947 were many times the annual outlays of prewar years; the annual interest on the national debt in 1947 was enormous; the taxes of 1947 made the taxes of the 1930s look "positively trivial," and prospects for doing business with Stalin were not better than they had been with Hitler.[96]

Indeed, Beard observed that discussions of domestic affairs in 1947 were subordinated to overriding foreign commitments, known and covert, made by Roosevelt and Truman. Beard described the Truman Doctrine as "an unlimited program of underwriting, by money and military 'advice,' poverty-stricken, feeble and unstable governments around the edges of the gigantic and aggressive Slavic Empire." The dreams of a great domestic American economy providing wealth and security for most of the people had become "appendages to an aleatory expedition in the management of the world."[97]

Debating with his critics, Beard wrote that even if one accepted the defeat of Germany and Japan as somehow justifying the means of accomplishment, there remained the question of whether these means were constitutional. It was a matter of power, and certainly, Beard argued, the Constitution had not vested "in the Congress or the President illimitable power secretly to determine the ends of the government in foreign or domestic affairs and secretly to choose and employ any means . . . to achieve those ends."[98] The prewar period was rife with examples of unconstitutional behavior by Roosevelt—his misrepresentation of Lend-Lease, the development of secret war plans, the distortion of the *Greer* and *Kearney* incidents into uninvited attacks on the innocent, his use of convoys in the Atlantic at a time when the law explicitly forbade them, and his aggressive policy toward Japan, "conducted with the knowledge that some incident would occur." But, in Beard's eyes, the "crowning act in the arrogation of authority to himself, without the consent of the Senate" had been his commitment to Churchill at the Atlantic Conference of 1941 August to "'police the world'" after the war. "That is, in the eyes of other governments and peoples policed, to dominate the world."[99]

A. A. Berle, Jr., had remarked of Beard's first book that Beard had, in his haste to indict the President, left out "the Hamlet of the play—the shrinking world, the surmountable oceans, the rise of ideas and implemented intent, monstrous and insane . . . which threatened . . . the peace of the world and the safety of the United States." Unilateral action was impossible, Berle argued, in the circumstances of an integrated moral, physical, and scientific world.[100]

Beard replied to Berle, saying that, while he agreed that the United States was a great power and had obligations as such, he found utterly repugnant the argument that America could somehow manage the course of world history: "The range of [America's] *effective* power supportable by armed forces and economic resources is limited."[101] Also limited was American moral power. The stern Victorian in Beard urged that

> To sensibility, the very idea is repulsive. As ladies and gentlemen who publicly proclaim their own virtues are suspected and resented by self-respecting persons, so the Government and people of the United States, by loudly proclaiming their moral leadership of the world, awaken suspicion and resentment in Great Britain, France, Russia, China, and other countries of the world; and, what may be worse in the long run, contemptuous laughter.[102]

At the end of perhaps the most remarkable of his books, Beard, the independent realist, advised Americans that history had brought them to the point of operating "under the theory that the President of the United States possesses limitless authority publicly to misrepresent and secretly to control foreign policy, foreign affairs, and the war power." Meeting this challenge would be the greatest test of citizenship, for there was, he warned, "no divinity hedging our Republic against Caesar."[103]

Several years after Charles Beard's death Merle Curti asked Mary Beard whether Beard continued to have faith in the years after 1934 that the United States was moving toward a collectivist democracy. Mary Beard answered by referring to the Epilogue to *President Roosevelt*. Here, she wrote, her husband had expressed "a doubt . . . more than a warning and yet a warning." At Columbia, she remembered, Charles had heard John Burgess say over and over again that "Caesar was always in the shadows." As a young man "just turning from his twenties to his thirties," Charles had disagreed. "But after Hitler became a Caesar, using demagogy to incite the people to believe he would give them the welfare they needed and desired," Beard had recalled "Burgess in a new way" and had "understood that youth is 'romantic' by nature." He had begun to think about "the probable Caesar complex as a historic fixture."[104]

"It was Shaw," Beard noted, "who said that a good book goes through four (4) stages: it is against God; it is contrary to the Bible; it violates the Constitution; and finally, everybody knew that anyway."[105] Beard's concern about the possible abuse of constitutional power by American presidents no longer shocks us: We have, perhaps, felt some of his fire in our own reactions to the managed "crisis" of the Cuban missiles, to the official lies told about the incident in the Gulf of Tonkin, to Hubert Humphrey's exuberant proclamations portraying a future of Great American-sponsored societies in Asia. The hearings on the affair of Watergate displayed again the recurrent contempt of the executive branch for the people's representatives, a contempt that Beard was among the first to decry.

Although his last books now seem to be only an anticipation of a recent disillusion, at the time they appeared, to many people who had less respect for the public than Beard, it was as if a supreme traitor had arisen to mislead the citizenry. World events and a heady belief in the power of American military and moral leadership combined in the vision of those who denounced Beard as the fallen angel of American liberalism, "the corroded Beard," as McGeorge Bundy put it.[106] It was an age of absolutes, a time when many intellectuals wished to believe and did believe that somehow American power was power for good, that the American chariot (though Truman gave pause to those who thought about the drivers) was commanded by benevolent experts. Beard pointed to aspects of this vision that many people preferred to forget. Power, he said, had to be defused rather than concentrated, if the democratic process was to be preserved. Democracy became authoritarian when questions of life and death were left to remote experts.

After the war, while Beard questioned the Marshall Plan and deplored the messianic rhetoric of the Truman Doctrine, orthodox historians such as Samuel Flagg Bemis had by 1948 seized upon wartime analogies to argue for new and greater American responsibilities in the world. Defending the shipment of money and arms into Turkey and Greece, Bemis asserted that if "the plug" was "pulled . . . at the Dardanelles," Soviet power would "pour unobstructed through the Near East into Africa, as Japanese power did through the straits of Singapore in 1942. . . ."[107]

Most reviewers of *President Roosevelt* concentrated on Beard's account of Roosevelt's dishonest approach to Congress and the public. Gordon Craig, Arthur Schlesinger, Jr., and Harry Gideonse conceded that Roosevelt had not been honest with the public but said that the "national interest" had demanded a lack of candor. According to Schlesinger, Beard was "confused about the nature of democratic government." Campaign oratory and platforms *were* meaningless; they were not "convenants" with the people, as Beard had maintained. "But certainly," wrote Craig, "no President charged with the protection of the national security and faced with a changing war situation, could admit for a moment such a theory."[108] Perry Miller, calling himself "a child of Beard," chided the master for "vilifying those who cope, however imperfectly with the demonic forces of their time" and ignored Beard's argument that Roosevelt's example posed a threat to the democratic process.[109]

Blair Bolles, director of the Washington bureau of the Foreign Policy Association, acclaimed Beard's last book as "an alarm bell to jar us into serious contemplation of the rights of the public and the duties of officials in the exposition of truth where foreign affairs are concerned." Bolles, although he argued that the war had been inevitable, despised the justifications of postwar foreign policy made in terms of "the free world." He called this "sweet baloney," and Beard appreciated his review.[110] Someone had heard the message.

Beard's latter-day association with George Morgenstern and thus with the *Chicago Tribune* was the basis for wonder in his own time and later. Richard Hofstadter remarked that Beard had been brought "to the verge of allegiances that he must himself have thought strange." Responding to the war, Beard had, in Hofstadter's view, "been pulled steadily toward the right."[111]

Although Morgenstern and Beard never saw each other face to face, in 1947 and 1948 they carried on a vigorous correspondence. The *Tribune* had millions of readers, and the most casual perusal of the Beard–Morgenstern letters demonstrates Beard's effort to influence the *Tribune*'s editorials on foreign policy. Morgenstern recognized Beard's dramatic disagreement with the *Tribune*'s position on domestic policy as a spokesman for big business. "It doth appear," Beard wrote him, "that if you agree with me on Roosevelt, Hull, Stimson, and Co., you must also support my views on virgin birth, marginal utility, infant damnation . . . total immersion, transubstantiation, and compensatory financing. Though an exigent old cuss, I make no such demands upon my friends."[112] Beard wanted an audience. Moreover, he had a long-standing faith in the people's ability to separate chaff from good grain.

To his delight, both books on Roosevelt sold well. Two printings of *American Foreign Policy in the Making* sold immediately, and a third was ordered in February 1947. The week after its publication in April 1948, *President Roosevelt* was in its third printing. "If my own part of the book [the Epilogue] is all 'wet,' as [Walter] M[illis] & S[chlesinger] contend, the documents which I print verbatim are alone enough to show the public how FDR & his associates were operating behind the scenes." When a fifth printing was ordered before the end of April, Beard began to hope that it might influence the election of 1948.[113]

Far from the "crusty and suspicious note" that Hofstadter detected, Beard's later letters appear to be full of the joy of combat. He had begun work on a third volume, which was to discuss appearances and realities through Yalta and Potsdam and, he told Morgenstern, made his "last book seem like a Sunday School Sermon!"[114]

However, Beard knew he was dying. During spring of 1945, his pneumonia had been treated with sulfa, a drug to which he was allergic. The resulting aplastic anemia made him irrevocably ill and weak by late July 1948, and he died on 3 September 1948. To political scientists assembled in convention he gave his last major speech in December 1947. Perhaps speaking of his life, he said, "I close not on a note of admonition but of deep curiosity."[115]

Epilogue

Beard had a magnificent persona. He was tall and commanded crowds
with a rhetorical flair, an actor's sense of timing, that could bring them
cheering and stamping to their feet. He read and listened intensely. He
laughed and wept publicly on occasion. He was, as someone once said of
one of his heroes, the Marquis de Condorcet, a "volcano covered with snow."
His autobiography does not exist, except in the most formal sense, for he
left no diaries, no reams of private personal observations, few choice letters.
He desired to be immortal, if such were possible (and his relativism made
him doubt it), through the durability of his own published works. That they
are not more widely read today is a tribute to the kind of academic practices
he most despised—to specialization—and to the American penchant, true
among many academic historians of the United States as among society at
large, for believing and acting as though (as with cars and deodorants) "newer
books are somehow better books."

Perhaps the ever-tossing waves of relativity will again cast Charles and
Mary Beard's writing before the public eye. To a generation now in their
thirties and forties who studied the history of the United States in books
from whose pages women were absent, the volumes of *The Rise of American
Civilization* come as a pleasant surprise. To a generation of intellectuals seeking
to cast off the partisan affiliations of the post–World War II period, Beard's
admonition to be critical and independent, to doubt the "experts" is bracing
and cheering. Certainly, he asked questions about the policy of the United
States in foreign affairs that revisionists are only beginning to explore. We

honor him as the prophet of our present discontent with secrecy and waste; with subservience of the governments at all levels to large corporations and to their god, profit; with the neglect of domestic priorities in favor of spending on an endless and ever more sophisticated array of armaments.

As the history of the United States has been periodized, the Beards' writings are significant as cultural monuments of each era—the progressive period, the first world war, the twenties and thirties, and the second global conflict. Whoever would understand the twentieth century must be acquainted with the Beards' "memoranda," for they understood, in a way that many intellectuals did not, that the greatness of America was material, not spiritual, and that a transcendent ethical outlook would have to arise, if ever, from the cooperation that could be achieved on this continent.

In Charles and Mary Beard's books one cannot find any measured appreciation of cultural diversity, of the experiences of ethnic groups pursuing wealth and adjusting traditional social patterns in a new environment. Beard did not believe that "a nation" of diverse cultures could exist without serious conflict. He wanted to create "an American nation" by promoting general agreement on a social ethic of cooperation and striving for the common good, which he always defined as decent housing, food, and cultural opportunities for everyone. The common issues arising in the pursuit of economic and social security were the basis for the nationalism he hoped to foster.

Perhaps, also, Charles Beard did not write about the experiences of the many European, Asian, and Latin American immigrants of the nineteenth and twentieth centuries and of the Afro-Americans and Native Americans as such because their perceptions were not his, their lives were not realistically imagined by a wealthy, white Protestant male whose family had been in America since the seventeenth century, and Beard wrote always from his own experience. He was always skeptical about the "science" of psychology. Though full of a genuine and humane sympathy for people of all kinds, he stayed within his own cultural boundaries. He was what he was unabashedly, and those who believe that the freshest writing on history and politics comes from the well of reflection on personal experience will admire his restraint, while appreciating that his picture was and is uniquely his own.

Charles Beard kept a faith in the common sense of ordinary people that should inspire social democrats today. If given the facts, he believed, people would choose life, not the death and hell of war. They would have social justice and commonwealth. The historian's highest function, he once said, is "to ascertain the master current in the age of which he writes." Paradoxically, the master current would reveal itself only "in the crises of the age that follows." Therefore the historian was bound to be "like the poet—a seer as well as a chronicler." Today, as we seem to see the public interest often overwhelmed and defeated by insensitive bureaucracy and the quest for corporate profits, we must keep alive that faith in ordinary people. We must, as Beard did, appeal to reason and keep asking questions.

Notes
Selected Bibliography
Index

Notes

Preface

1. Mary Ritter Beard to Merle Curti, 18 Feb. 1950 and 6 Dec. 1950. Merle Curti Papers, Wisconsin State Historical Society.

2. Charles A. Beard, "Roosevelt's Place in History," *Events* 3 (Feb. 1938), 82.

3. "Professor Beard's Letter of Resignation from Columbia University," *School and Society,* 6 (18 Oct. 1917), 446–47.

4. Herman Melville, *Moby Dick,* vol. 48, Encyclopaedia Britannica Great Books of the Western World (Chicago: Univ. of Chicago, 1952), p. 55.

1. Life in Indiana

1. Charles A. Beard (hereafter abbreviated CAB), Review of *Political Parties* by Robert Michels, *Political Science Quarterly,* 32 (Mar. 1917), 155.

2. CAB to Fred Millett, 23 Feb. 1937, a copy of which was lent to the author by Beard's daughter, Mrs. Alfred Vagts; CAB to Editor, *New York Times,* 20 Jan. 1938 (printed on 23 Jan. 1938); CAB to "friends" (n.d.), 1938, in *Souvenir Booklet of the Spiceland Centennial* (Spiceland, Ind., 1938), 15–17. Copy in Box 10, Folder 14 of Charles A. Beard Collection, DePauw Univ. Archives.

3. CAB to Fred Millet, 23 Feb. 1937. Mary Ritter Beard to Harry Elmer Barnes, 25 Oct. (no year), says that CAB worked "like all the 'hands' on his father's farm" until he was fifteen. Harry Elmer Barnes Papers, Univ. of Wyoming Archive of Contemporary History.

4. CAB, "The American Invasion of Europe," *Harper's Magazine,* 158 (Mar. 1929), 477.

5. CAB to Fred Millet, 23 Feb. 1937; CAB to "friends", *Souvenir;* CAB to Editor, *New York Times,* 23 Jan. 1938. *See also* CAB, *"Turner's The Frontier in American History,"* in Malcom Cowley and Daniel Smith (eds.), *Books That Changed Our Minds* (New York: Kelmscott Editions, 1938), p. 69.

6. *History of Henry County Indiana* (Chicago: Interstate Pub. Co., 1884), pp. 796–98; Mary R. Beard to Harry Elmer Barnes, 25 Oct. (n.d.), Barnes Papers; Mary Ritter Beard, *The Making of Charles A. Beard* (New York: Exposition, 1955), pp. 9–12.

7. Mary R. Beard, *The Making,* p. 12. In 1895, when CAB was preparing to enter college, William Henry Beard became the president of the bank in Spiceland at the request of local residents, who wanted him to reorganize the institution on a sound basis, which he did. Mary Beard to Eric Goldman, 16 May 1952. Merle Curti Papers, Wisconsin State Historical Society.

8. Paul L. Schmunk, "Charles Austin Beard: A Free Spirit" (Ph.D. diss., Univ. of New Mexico, 1957), p. 10. Professor Schmunk's thesis is most useful, and every biographer of Beard will be in his debt. He died of cancer in 1973, while working on a two-volume life of CAB.

9. CAB to Fred Millett, 23 Feb. 1937; Mary R. Beard, *The Making,* p. 12.

10. Mary R. Beard, *The Making,* p. 9; undated newspaper clipping on Caroline Beard in Box 10, Folder 10, Charles A. Beard Collection, DePauw Univ. Archives; CAB to "friends" (n.d.), 1938; *DePauw Palladium,* 28 Mar. 1898. See also Peter A. Sonderbergh, "Charles A. Beard, The Quaker Spirit, and North Carolina," *North Carolina Historical Review,* 46 (Winter 1969), 19–32.

11. CAB to Arthur M. Schlesinger, Sr., 23 Jul. 1917. Arthur M. Schlesinger Papers, Harvard Univ. Archives; CAB to George Morgenstern, 11 Apr. 1948. George Morgenstern Collection, Univ. of Wyoming Archive of Contemporary History.

12. Surviving neighbors, interviewed by Paul L. Schmunk in 1956, remembered Beard's mother a "kindly soul," but noted that her "progressive deafness made social life difficult." Schmunk, *Free Spirit,* p. 12. There is an undated letter from Beard's mother to him on the Beard Microfilm, No. 179, DePauw Univ. Archives, describing the schools in Henry County in the days of early settlement. She died in 1924.

13. These paragraphs are based on an undated manuscript, probably written by CAB in 1942, describing the exploits of Sarah Wilson Payne as one of Indiana's early white residents and recreating her presence and her home. Beard Microfilm, No. 179. Beard also refers enthusiastically to his grandmother in the previously cited letter to the editor of the *New York Times.*

14. Sadie Bacon Hatcher, *A History of Spiceland Academy* (Indianapolis: Indiana Historical Society, 1934), pp. 124–125 *passim,* 152; CAB to "friends," *Souvenir.*

15. Schmunk, *Free Spirit,* p. 18; Loring B. Eiler to Clifton Phillips, 22 Oct. 1958. Box 11, Folder 1, Beard Collection, DePauw Univ. Archives; Sadie B. Symons to Clifton J. Phillips, 8 Apr. 1959. Box 11, Folder 1, Beard Collection; Richard Ratcliffe, "Along the Banks of Brook Bezor: A History of the Spiceland Academy" (n.d.), p. 31, a copy of which is in Box 10, Folder 14, Beard Collection; Miriam Beard Vagts to the author, 8 Sept. 1976. Clifton Phillips, a professor of history at DePauw, conducted a number of interviews by mail with surviving contemporaries of the Beard family during the 1950s, particularly with surviving classmates of CAB at DePauw.

16. Schmunk, *Free Spirit,* pp. 23–24; *Knightstown Banner,* 3 Sept. 1948; Mary R. Beard to Eric Goldman, 16 May 1952, Merle Curti Papers; Clifton J. Phillips, "The

Indiana Education of Charles A. Beard," *Indiana Magazine of History*, 55 (Mar. 1959), 5.

17. Floyd J. Newby to Clifton J. Phillips, 10 Sept. 1957. Box 11, Folder 1, Beard Collection; Mrs. Mary Jackson to Clifton J. Phillips, 7 Jan. 1958. Box 11, Folder 1, Beard Collection. Mary Beard, in *The Making* (p. 14), remarks that her husband was "prodded by an admiring friend."

18. CAB to Fred Millett, 23 Feb. 1937; Mary R. Beard to Harry Elmer Barnes 12 Oct. 1949, Barnes Papers.

19. James T. Farrell, "An Interview with Dr. Charles A. Beard," *Phi Gamma Delta* (Nov. 1939), n.p. Copy on Beard Microfilm, No. 480, DePauw Univ. Archives.

20. *DePauw Palladium*, 18 Oct. 1897. CAB was not the editor of the General News column, which began appearing in the 20 Dec. 1897, issue. On newly elected President McKinley, the writer of this column commented "Never before has there been so great a universal confidence in the chief executive of the nation." In later years CAB himself would edit similar columns dealing with current events for the *Political Science Quarterly* and *Current History*. The style, with its lists of aphorisms interspersed with editorial comments, is reminiscent of CAB's surviving letters, especially of those to another newspaperman, George Morgenstern.

21. *DePauw Palladium*, 20 Dec. 1897, 10 Jan. 1897, 21 Feb. 1898, 28 Feb. 1898, 28 Mar. 1898.

22. *The Mirage* (1899), p. 259.

23. *DePauw Palladium*, 25 Apr. and 2 May 1898; Mary R. Beard, *The Making*, p. 15. Clifton Phillips, "Indiana Education" (p. 13), says that there is no surviving record at the university of Beard's volunteering for service in the war with Spain.

24. Phillips, "Indiana Education," p. 8; R. M. Stephenson to Clifton J. Phillips, 10 Oct. 1957. Box 11, Folder 1, Beard Collection; Josephine Ives to Clifton J. Phillips, 8 Oct. 1957; Raymond J. Wade to C. J. Phillips, 10 Dec. 1957; Floyd J. Newby to Clifton J. Phillips, 18 Sept. 1957; CAB, "Go Easy on the Professors," *New Republic*, 27 (17 Aug. 1921), 328.

25. R. M. Stephenson to Clifton J. Phillips, 10 Oct. 1957. Box 11, Folder 1, Beard Collection. A copy of Cab's courses is in Box 10, Folder 1, Beard Collection. General information on Andrew Stephenson is found in *The Mirage* (1899), pp. 39–40. "Editorial," *DePauw Palladium*, 7 Feb. 1898; CAB, "Neglected Aspects of Political Science," *American Political Science Review*, 42 (April 1948), 222.

26. "Editorial," *DePauw Palladium*, 7 Feb. 1898; "Editorial," *DePauw Palladium*, 17 May 1898.

27. CAB, "The Story of a Race," *DePauw Palladium*, 18 Apr. 1898. See Charles M. Andrews, *The River Towns of Connecticut*, Johns Hopkins Studies in Historical and Political Science (7th Ser., VII–IX [Baltimore, 1889]), and Andrews, "The Theory of the Villiage Community, *Papers of the American Historical Association* (5 [1891] 47–60), in which he argued that comparing New England towns to German towns was arguing a likeness "of the most superficial kind" (p. 50).

CAB's thesis in his senior oration thus reveals his dependence of Stephenson, who presumably rejected the work of Andrews in favor of that of their common mentor at Johns Hopkins, Herbert Baxter Adams, who had written in his famous monograph, *The Germanic Origin of New England Towns* (Johns Hopkins Studies in History and Political Science, 1 [1883], 8–9), that "The town and village life of New England is as truly the reproduction of Old England types as those again are reproductions of the village community system of the ancient Germans." On the Teutonic theroy of American institutions see Thomas F. Gossett, *Race: The History of an Idea in America* (Dallas: Southern Methodist Univ. Pr., 1963), Chapter V, "The Teutonic Origin Theory," pp. 84–122.

28. Andrew Stephenson, general letter, n.d., Box 10, Folder 11, Beard Collection; *Young Oxford*, 1 (Jul. 1900), 40.

29. CAB, it should be noted, was only one of many outstanding orators on his campus. He did not always win the contests, and other members of the debating team were considered as strong or stronger. Beard's comments on Professor Priest's classes appear in *DePauw Palladium*, 28 Feb. 1898. Accounts of the debating team appear in *Greencastle Democrat*, 30 May 1896, and *DePauw Palladium*, 11 Apr. 1898. An excellent discussion of Beard's oratorical pursuits can be found in Clifton J. Phillips, "Indiana Education," pp. 6–10.

For an example of CAB later writing as though he were actually on stage engaged in a debate, see *The Supreme Court and the Constitution* (New York: Macmillan, 1912), p. 117.

30. Merle Curti, "A Great Teacher's Teacher," *Social Education*, 31 (October 1949), 263 passim. The quotations from Weaver are from this article. There is also some information about Weaver in *The Mirage* (1899), p. 34.

31. CAB, *The Nature of the Social Sciences* (New York: Scribner, 1934), pp. 68–69.

32. Eric F. Goldman, "Charles A. Beard: An Impression," in Howard K. Beale (ed.), *Charles A. Beard: An Appraisal* (Lexington: Univ. of Kentucky Pr., 1954), p. 3. See also Hubert Herring, "Charles A. Beard: Free Lance Among the Historians," *Harper's Magazine*, 178 (May 1939), 642.

33. *Greencastle Banner Times*, 13 Aug. 1896, cited in Phillips, "Indiana Education," p. 12; list of fraternity activities of CAB, Box 11, Folder 1, Beard Collection.

34. *DePauw Palladium*, 25 Oct. 1897.

35. Ibid., 7 Mar. 1898.

36. Ibid., 17 May 1898.

2. Sojourn in England

1. Beard penned this description of Oxford, with some account of the town's history, including "the bold Saxon freeman assembling in 'tun' meeting" and striking "the first note of freedom," on 10 Sept. 1898 for the *DePauw Palladium*; it was published on 17 Oct. 1898. Years later, he described his arrival in letters to the Principal of Ruskin College on two separate occasions. See CAB to A. Barrett Brown, 7 Jul. [?] 1940, and CAB to Lionel Elvin, 18 Dec. 1945, both reprinted in Burleigh T. Wilkins (ed.), "Charles A. Beard on the Founding of Ruskin Hall," *Indiana Magazine of History*, 52 (Sept. 1956), 277–284. York Powell's comment is found in Oliver Elton, *Frederick York Powell* (Oxford: Oxford Univ. Pr. 1906), vol. I, p. 314.

2. H. B. Phillips, *Walter Vrooman: Restless Child of Progress* (Ph.D. thesis: Columbia Univ., 1954), pp. 3–255, has some details of Vrooman's early life. See *The New Democracy* (St. Louis: Witt Printing, 1897), the only issue of what was to be a journal,

The Volunteers Quarterly. Vrooman spent a half-million dollars of his wife's considerable fortune, divorced her in 1903 to marry his secretary, and died in 1909 at the age of forty, believing, according to his brother Hiram, that he was God. There is a brief discussion of the founding of Ruskin Hall in Ross E. Paulson, *Radicalism & Reform: The Vrooman Family and American Social Thought, 1837–1937* (Lexington: Univ. of Kentucky Pr., 1968), pp. 147–151.

    3. L. T. Dodd and J. A. Dale, "The Ruskin Hall Movement," *Fortnightly Review,* 73 (June 1900), 328. Phillips, *Vrooman,* p. 225.

    4. Quotations from CAB are in Wilkins and Mary R. Beard, *The Making,* p. 17. Years later, Beard still agreed with Ruskin's "insistence that economics is a branch of morals and that morals is not a mere side issue to economics." CAB, "Ruskin and the Babble of Tongues," *New Republic,* 87 (5 Aug. 1936), 371. Some of Ruskin's beliefs with which Beard probably disagreed were his support of a hereditary aristocracy, his view that the correct place for women was as mothers in the home, and that the solution to "the social problem must proceed chiefly from individual, not from public action." See Chapters 7, 8, and 9 in the work of Ruskin's great systematizer, John Hobson—who, as one contemporary put it, "rescued Ruskin from himself"—*John Ruskin Social Reformer* (London: James Hisbet & Co., 1898). Comment on Hobson's work is in Dodd and Dale, "Ruskin Hall," p. 325. CAB almost certainly read Hobson's work on Ruskin.

    5. Kier Hardie, a leader of the Labour Party, is cited in Harlan B. Phillips, "Charles Beard, Walter Vrooman, and the Founding of Ruskin Hall," *South Atlantic Quarterly,* 50 (Apr. 1951), 189. Phillips, in both his thesis on Vrooman and this article (p. 191) describes CAB as "without question Vrooman's most thoroughgoing convert in England." Certainly, Vrooman had the idea for Ruskin Hall, but it was Amne Vrooman's money and practical eye, combined with CAB's unflagging zest for management and organization, that gave stability to the venture. Walter Vrooman's major contribution to the effort was his supreme ability, as a passionate and exotic American orator, to nail the attention of an audience to the plan. Vrooman's masculine characterization of workers is found in his speech at the Hall's opening, reprinted in "The Opening of Ruskin Hall, Oxford, England," an undated pamphlet in the Papers of Carl Vrooman, Library of Congress, Box. 14.

    During CAB's residence in England, the number of resident male students in the Hall, a large Stuart house, formerly the home of the historian J. R. Green and leased from Balliol by Amne Vrooman, ranged from twenty-five to thirty. A copy of an undated prospectus, "Ruskin Hall, Oxford," giving CAB's name and address to seekers of information is in the Carl Vrooman Papers. In the Ruskin Hall Minute Books of 1900–1902 is an undated fragment of a letter from CAB to Denis Hird, the Warden, which suggests that CAB faced the dilemmas of many a school administrator confronted with a choice between supporting liberty or upholding authority. CAB suggested that one or two of the rebels who wanted to assume control of the house and dispense with the Warden be expelled. After three weeks of controversy, students drew up their own house rules. See Beard Microfilm, No. 480, DePauw Univ. Archives.

    6. "Ruskin Hall, Oxford," Carl Vrooman Papers; Mary R. Beard to Merle Curti, 26 May 1949. Curti Papers, Wisconsin State Historical Society; Vrooman speech in "The Opening of Ruskin Hall, Oxford, England," n.d., Carl Vrooman Papers; *Labour Leader,* 11 Mar. 1899, cited in Schmunk, "Free Spirit," 79; CAB, "Men Who Have Helped Us: William Cobbett," *Young Oxford* 2 (Feb. 1901), 171.

7. CAB, "Ruskin and the Babble of Tongues," 372; Karl Marx and Friedrich Engels, *Basic Writings on Politics and Philosophy*, ed. by Lewis S. Feuer (New York: Anchor, 1959). pp. 35–36.

8. Oliver Elton, *Frederick York Powell: A Life and a Selection from His Writing and Letters* (Oxford: Clarendon Press, 1906), is a fascinating two-volume encomium in the tradition of many English biographies. The quotations are from Vol I, pp. 421, 447, 444, and 413.

9. Elton, *Powell*, pp. 404–405, 406.

10. Ibid. pp. 407–414.

11. Ibid. For a gracefully written account of the intellectual importance of CAB's relationship with York Powell that is strikingly different from the one presented above see Burleigh T. Wilkins, "Frederick York Powell and Charles A. Beard: A Study in Anglo-American Historiography and Social Thought," *American Quarterly*, 11 (Spring 1959), 21–39.

12. Frederick York Powell, "Preface," in Charles A. Beard, *The Industrial Revolution* (London: George Allen & Unwin, 1901), pp. vii–xv.

13. Powell to CAB, 12 Jan. 1901, in Elton, *Powell*, Vol. I, p. 314.

14. CAB, *A Charter for the Social Sciences in the Schools* (New York: Scribner, 1932), pp. 74, 78. See CAB, "Is Babbitt's Case Hopeless?," *Memorah Journal*, 14 (Jan. 1928), 27–28.

15. CAB, "Men Who Have Helped Us: William Cobbett," p. 172.

16. *Young Oxford*, 1 (7 Apr 1900), 5. CAB never discussed this term at Cornell, except to remember Moses Coit Tyler as a wonderful lecturer in "Go Easy on the Professors" and to recall, in 1945, that George Lincoln Burr had made the striking comment in his seminar that " 'It is only through sympathy, never through hatred that we can understand an age or a people.' " Cited in Houston Peters (ed.), *Great Teachers* (New Brunswick, N.J.: Rutgers Univ., Pr., 1946), 177.

17. Author's interview with Miriam Beard Vagts, Sept. 16, 1976; Schmunk, "Free Spirit," p. 58; Beard Microfilm No. 480, Folder 16, DePauw Univ. Archives, contains many clippings and interviews. "Interview with Mary Beard," *Indianapolis Star*, 22 Jul. 1955; Mary R. Beard, "The Twentieth Century Woman: Looking Around and Backward," *Young Oxford*, 1 (Dec. 1900), 100–104, and "The Nineteenth Century Woman: Looking Forward," *Young Oxford*, 2 (Jan. 1901), 119–122. The best biographical study of Mary Beard is "Mary Ritter Beard: An Appraisal of Her Life and Work" by Ann J. Lane in her *Mary Ritter Beard: A Sourcebook* (New York: Schocken, 1977), pp. 1–72.

18. *Young Oxford*, 1 (May 1900), 31.

19. Mary R. Beard, *The Making*, p. 20; letters in Wilkins, "CAB on Ruskin Hall"; CAB, "Ruskin and the Babble of Tongues," 372. Schedules of CAB's visits to surrounding industrial towns were occasionally printed in *Young Oxford*. A small extra fee was charged for "lantern slides" to accompany the lectures. "Notes from the Field," *Young Oxford*, 2 (Jan. 1901), 154.

20. CAB, "Self-Education," *Young Oxford*, 1 (Oct. 1899), 17; CAB, "What Is Worth While in Education," *Young Oxford*, 1 (Dec. 1899), 16. Compare CAB, "Lessons from Science," *Young Oxford*, 2 (Jun. 1901), 341 in which CAB again says that "the grandest, noblest thing that can engage our attention and powers" is the battle against "injustice, oppression, cruelty, ignorance and chaos. . . ." On temperance, see CAB, "Co-operation and the New Century," *Young Oxford*, 2 (Dec. 1900), 98, and CAB, "Ruskin Hall and Temperance Reform," 2 (Mar. 1901), 221; *Macclesfield*

Times, 28 Sept. 1900, clipping on Beard Microfilm, No. 179, DePauw Univ. Archives.

21. CAB, *The Industrial Revolution* (London: George Allen & Unwin, 1902), p. 90. In connection with the publication of his first book, Beard began formally using the middle name Austin so that readers would not confuse him with the famous religious historian Charles Beard. According to Miriam Beard Vagts, the Quaker tradition was to give no middle names, so neither Charles nor his brother Clarence was given one. However, both invented them: Clarence called himself Clarence Herbert, and at first Charles called himself Charles Arthur, after President Chester A. Arthur, whose reform of the civil service he admired. Later he resented the association between Arthur and Tennyson and chose Austin. Miriam Beard Vagts to author, 28 Apr. 1977.

22. "Home and Field Notes," *Young Oxford*, 2 (Feb., 1901), 192.

23. CAB to Howell Wright, 4, Jul. 1942. Miscellaneous Collection, Yale Univ. Archives.

24. CAB, "A Living Empire I," *Young Oxford*, 3 (Oct. 1901), 24–25, and "A Living Empire II" (Nov. 1901), 39.

25. CAB, "A Living Empire II," 39–43.

26. Mary E. Lease, *The Problem of Civilization Solved* (Chicago: Laird & Lee, 1895), pp. 17, 32, 35, 93. According to Lease, the "ryot, negro and coolie" tenants would not be slaves. The white masters would "be bound by oath" to treat their workers justly and equitably, and "planters and tenants" were "to share equally in the products of the land." It was, she concluded, "manifestly . . . our duty and destiny to become the guardian of the inferior races." Along with colonization, she called for enactment of a populist program of nationalized railroads, telegraph, "all labor saving machinery," for free trade with a tariff on "alien products," the initiative and referendum, coinage of silver and gold at 16 to 1 in order to produce "that potent factor of a new era—the abstract dollar." However, the great theme of her book and the one CAB remembered was her scheme of colonization.

Eduard Bernstein, a leader of the German Social Democrats, had written in 1899 in *Die Voraussetzungen des Sozialismus*, a book CAB had certainly read: "But if it is not reprehensible to enjoy the produce of tropical plantations, it cannot be so to cultivate such plantations ourselves. Not the whether but the how is here the decisive point . . . only a conditional right of savages to the land occupied by them can be recognized. The higher civilization ultimately can claim a higher right." Sounding like a Lockean instead of a Marxist, Bernstein concluded that "Not the conquest, but the cultivation of the land gives the historical legal title to its use." This quotation is from Bernstein, *Evolutionary Socialism: A Criticism and Affirmation*, tr. by Edith C. Harvey (New York: Schochen, 1961), pp. 178–179.

27. CAB, "A Living Empire II," p. 42. CAB held on to the idea for a "World's International University." It surfaced in attenuated form in 1916, when CAB, while at Columbia, promoted the founding of a University Center for Higher Education in Washington, D.C., as a place for scholars to work on important social, economic, and political problems. The center was to be financed by annual payments from a consortium of universities. Insufficient financial support for the proposal and the organization of other research groups in this period put an end to the project in 1921. See CAB et. al., "Report of a Conference Held in Cincinnati, December 27, 1916" (American Historical Association *Annual Report*, I [1916]), pp. 271–274, and CAB et. al., "Final Report of a Committee on a University Center for Research in Washington" (American Historical Association *Annual Report*, I [1921]), pp. 72–82.

28. *Young Oxford*, 4 (Apr. 1902), 278.

29. Schmunk, "Free Spirit," p. 82; CAB, "An Ideal Labour College," *Young Oxford*, 4 (Dec. 1901), 79–81. See Peter Kropotkin, "Brain Work and Manual Work," in Collin Ward (ed.), *Fields, Factories and Workshops Tomorrow* (London: George Allen & Unwin, 1974), pp. 169–187.

30. CAB, "Ideal Labour College," p. 81.

31. Miriam Beard Vagts to the author, 8 Sept. 1976.

32. Letter in Wilkins, "CAB on Ruskin Hall," p. 284.

3. At Columbia

1. "Citizenship in the Twentieth Century," *Young Oxford*, 3 (Apr. 1902), 243–246. Though this article was not signed, *Young Oxford*, 3 (Nov. 1901), 76, carried a notice that CAB had delivered this speech to a new extension session at Nelson on 1 Oct. 1901.

2. Miriam Beard Vagts to author, 8 Sept. 1976. Mrs. Vagts describes the neighborhood of the Beards' first New York apartment as "shabby-genteel" but adds that from the beginning the Beards had maids, "immigrant girls, English, Scottish." In 1907, before the birth of William, they moved a few blocks away to a more modern building, with an elevator, just three blocks from CAB's office. On CAB the farmer, see Detlev Vagts, "A Grandson Remembers His Grandfather," in Marvin C. Swanson (ed.), *Charles A. Beard: An Observance of the Centennial of His Birth* (Greencastle, Ind.: DePauw Univ. 1976), p.20. For CAB's view that "outdoor life" was vital to children's well-being, see "Professor Beard Tells Why He Does Not Send His Children to School and Mr. Chubb Describes the Ideal Education," *New York Times*, 10 Oct. 1907, V, p. 4. "It is absolutely impossible to give a child a right bring-up in the city," CAB informed the interviewer. Mary Beard taught the children reading, arithmetic, and geography for a number of years before they were finally sent to school. CAB admitted that his educational theories would not apply to every family, but that "given a home where there are books and where the child hears intelligent conversation," he saw "little necessity for holding a child down to learning a certain number of tasks imposed regardless of individual characteristics."

3. CAB's teachers and his prizes are listed in the *Vita* printed at the back of *The Office of Justice of the Peace in England* (New York: Columbia Univ. Pr., 1904). His first book review, of Beatrice and Sidney Webb's *History of Liquor Licensing in England*, appeared in *Political Science Quarterly*, 19 (Mar. 1904), 152–154.

4. There is much information on John W. Burgess' career as a scholar, administrator, and builder of Columbia's mighty School of Political Science in Ralph G. Hoxie, et. al., *A History of the Faculty of Political Science: Columbia University* (New York: Columbia Univ. Pr., 1955). A sympathetic article on Burgess' views and achievements is William R. Shepherd, "John William Burgess," in Howard W. Odum (ed.), *American Masters of Social Science* (New York: Holt, 1927), pp. 23–57. CAB's own critical discussion of Burgess is found in *The American Spirit* (New York: Macmillian, 1942), pp. 305–310. "Burgess," said CAB of his teacher, who had died in 1930, "stood for Teutonic imperialism in foreign affairs and extreme individualism in domestic affairs.

Imperialism and individualism were to fulfill the law prescribed by Providence, nature, and history—the civilization of nations and the world." By the 1940s, Burgess represented to CAB the epitome of everything he despised—racism, formal institutionalism, laissez-faire individualism, glorification of executive power, fear of legislatures. For a description of Burgess as a "gentleman scholar" with a "turgid" writing style, see Alvin Johnson, *Pioneer's Progress* (New York: Viking, 1952), pp. 122, 155.

5. Edwin R. A. Seligman, *The Economic Interpretation of History* (New York: Columbia Univ. Pr., 1902), pp. 24, 106, 67, 126, 130, 147–149, 153. See F. H. Giddings, *Democracy and Empire, with Studies of Their Psychological, Economic, and Moral Foundations* (New York, 1900), an Anglo-Saxonist tract to which Seligman may have been referring.

6. CAB's writings while at Columbia were sprinkled with references to Seligman's work. For example, he commented in *Political Science Quarterly*, 21 (Mar. 1906), 120, that Seligman had "demonstrated that socialism and the economic interpretation of history" were "entirely different propositions." In Chapter 1 of *An Economic Interpretation of the Constitution of the United States* (New York: Macmillan, 1913), pp. 14–15, CAB compared Madison's statement on the role of various economic interests in the formation of factions in *Federalist* Number 10 with Seligman's "nearly axiomatic" proposition on the role of economic causes in the transformation of social structure. CAB's review of Laski's *Political Thought in England from Locke to Bentham* is in *New Republic*, 24 (17 Nov. 1920), 303–304.

An indispensable survey of CAB's thought by a political scientist who is aware of historical contexts is Bernard C. Borning, *"The Political and Social Thought of Charles A. Beard* (Seattle: Univ. of Washington Pr., 1962).

7. CAB praised Goodnow's teaching in an unpublished obituary dated 16 Nov. 1939, in the Lindsay Rodgers Papers, Columbia University Special Manuscript Collections. His remarks on Goodnow's personality at a luncheon honoring the older man in 1929 are reprinted in Charles G. Haines and Marshall E. Dimock (eds.), *Essays on the Law and Practice of Governmental Administration* (Baltimore: Johns Hopkins Pr., 1935), p. v. On Goodnow's career at Columbia, see Hoxie, et. al., *History of the Faculty*, pp. 35 *passim*.

8. Haines, *Essays on the Law*, p. xiii; Hoxie, *History of the Faculty*, pp. 266; Martin J. Schiesl, *The Politics of Efficiency: Municipal Administration and Reform in America, 1800–1920* (Berkeley: Univ. of California Pr., 1977), p. 3.

9. Schmunk, "Free Spirit," pp. 119–120; CAB, *Syllabus of a Course of Six Lectures on the Expansion of the United States* (New York: Teachers College, Columbia Univ., 1904), p. 2. Included on CAB's list of readings was John Hobson's *Imperialism*, which, he noted, made "short work of many current fallacies." The next spring he taught English history "from the Accession of James I to the Present Time." See CAB, *Syllabus of a Course of Lectures on English History from the Accession of James I to the Present Time* (New York: Teachers College, Columbia Univ., 1905).

10. See the Prefatory Note to this volume, *An Introduction to the English Historians* (New York: Macmillan, 1906), pp. v–vii. According to Miriam Beard Vagts (to the author, 26 Jul. 1976), there are no letters or reports of this visit to England.

11. CAB to Albert Beveridge, 25 Jun. 1924. Box 286, Albert Beveridge Papers, Library of Congress; James Harvey Robinson, "The Spirit of Conservatism," in *The New History: Essays Illustrating the Modern Historical Outlook* (New York: Macmillan, 1912), p. 252; Robinson, "The New Ways of Historians," presidential address before

the American Historical Association, 29 Dec. 1929, *American Historical Review*, 35 (Jan. 1930), 245; Arthur M. Schlesinger, Sr., *In Retrospect: The History of a Historian* (New York: Harcourt, 1963), pp. 34–35.

12. CAB, "A Socialist History of France," *Political Science Quarterly*, 21 (Mar. 1906), 111, 120; James Harvey Robinson, "History," *Columbia University Lectures on Science, Philosophy and Art* (New York: Columbia Univ. Pr., 1908). Alvin Johnson, whose memories are wonderful though sometimes suspect, says in *Pioneer's Progress* (p. 156) that CAB, while a lecturer, brought Jaurès' book to his chief's attention and that this book "awakened Robinson out of his academic slumber and gave us the Robinson all liberals love."

13. James Harvey Robinson and CAB, *The Development of Modern Europe: An Introduction to the Study of Current History* (New York: Ginn, 1908), vol. 2, p. iii; Robinson, "The New Allies of History," in *The New History*, p. 80, n. 1. Robert Allen Skotheim ably discusses the New History in *American Intellectual Histories and Historians* (Princeton, N.J.: Princeton Univ. Pr., 1966), pp. 66–86.

14. CAB, "A Plea for Greater Stress upon the Modern Period," Middle States Council for the Social Studies (Minutes of the 6th Annual Convention, 1908), pp. 13, 15. To the American Historical Association in 1908 CAB proposed the establishment of a journal devoted to contemporary history.

15. Enrollment in Columbia's graduate faculties, the largest in the United States, increased by 68 percent between 1907 and 1912. In 1904, when CAB finished his doctorate, there were 148 graduate students in political science. By 1912 there were 366. In 1912, Columbia College became Columbia University. Hoxie, *History of the Faculty*, pp. 103, 264.

16. "Foreign Events," edited by CAB and Carlton J. H. Hayes, appeared in every issue of the *Political Science Quarterly* from Jun. 1905 to Dec. 1909. In 1914 and 1915, CAB served on the Committee of Management of the *Quarterly*. CAB's activities with the debate team are mentioned by Arthur Macmahon in "Charles Austin Beard as a Teacher," *Political Science Quarterly*, 65 (Mar. 1950), reprinted in Mary R. Beard, *The Making*, pp. 85–104. CAB described the Intercollegiate Civic League in a letter to Robert M. La Follette, Sr., 25 Jan. 1911. La Follette Family Collection, Series B, Box 66, Library of Congress. The "Political Laboratory" was announced in *National Municipal Review*, I (Aug. 1912), 152. His articles "Ballot's Burden" and "The Syndication of the Speakership," the latter with C. R. Atkinson, appeared in *Political Science Quarterly*, 22 (Sept. 1909), 589–614, and 26 (Sept. 1911), 381–414. CAB (ed.), *Loose Leaf Digest of Short Ballot Charters: A Documentary History of the Commission Form of Municipal Government* (New York: The Short Ballot Organization, 1911), 10101. CAB and one of his students from Indiana, Birl E. Schultz, also edited *Documents on the State Wide Initiative, Referendum and Recall* (New York: Macmillan, 1912). CAB, *American Government and Politics* (New York: Macmillan, 1910), pp. v–vi; CAB, *Readings in American Government and Politics* (New York: Macmillan, 1909).

17. *New York Times*, 4 Dec. 1909, p. 6; Irwin Edman, "John Dewey and Others," in Houston Peterson (ed.), *Great Teachers Portrayed by Those Who Studied Under Them* (New Brunswick, N.J.: Rutgers Univ. Pr., 1946), pp. 187–189; Schlesinger, *In Retrospect*, p. 35. CAB and Schlesinger were close friends. Of his thesis, published as *The Colonial Merchants and the American Revolution*, a title suggested by CAB, Schlesinger wrote to CAB that he had been "prompted to take this fresh view of the Revolutionary Period by suggestions and points of view which I got in your courses." CAB to Arthur

M. Schlesinger, 14 May 1917, and Schlesinger to CAB, 31 Jul. 1917, in Arthur M. Schlesinger Correspondence, Widener Library, Harvard Univ.; Arthur Macmahon, "CAB as Teacher," p. 85. CAB's kindnesses were many. The Randolph Bourne Papers contain, for example, a little note from CAB to Bourne telling the young student that CAB has gotten him a job with a "new paper," *The New Republic*, as contributor for "*at least* $1,000 a year." CAB to Randolph S. Bourne, 15 May 1914. Bourne Manuscripts, Columbia Univ. Archives. Wellington Koo, interviewed by *The New Yorker*, 53 (18 Apr. 1977), 32–35, recalled that while a graduate student in 1912, he had been offered a position in the Chinese government. CAB had urged him to take the position, although Koo was concerned because his Ph.D. thesis was not yet completed. "'But I haven't done my index,' I said, 'My wife, Mary, will attend to that,' [CAB] said, 'and now you get yourself to the Trans-Siberian Railroad and go right back home as fast as you can.'" Koo became a diplomat, representing the Republic of China in Washington, at the League of Nations, the United Nations, and on the International Court of Justice.

18. CAB, "The Study and Teaching of Politics," *Columbia University Quarterly*, 12 (Jun. 1910), 269–270.

19. John Erskine, *The Memory of Certain Persons* (New York: Lippincott, 1947), p. 194.

4. Progressivism and Citizenship

1. Author's interview with Miriam Beard Vagts, 16 Sept. 1976.

2. Morris Hillquit, *Loose Leaves from a Busy Life* (New York: Macmillan, 1934), pp. 68– 69. Perhaps the X Club of New York was inspired by English scientist T. H. Huxley's X-Club, which he had called together in London in 1864 to discuss Darwinian science and its implications for theology. See James R. Moore, *The Post-Darwinian Controversies: A Study of the Protestant Struggle to Come to Terms with Darwin in Great Britain and America, 1870–1900* (New York: Cambridge Univ. Pr., 1979), 84.

3. Raymond G. Gettell, Review of *American City Government*, *American Political Science Review*, 7 (May 1913), 319.

4. CAB, *American City Government* (New York: Century, 1912), pp. 7–29. CAB characteristically put stock phrases and clichés in quotation marks.

5. *American City Government*, pp. 81–84, 96, 134, 383, 184–185, 228–229, 245– 250, 308, 311, 324, 358, 386; Richard W. Fox, "The Paradox of 'Progressive' Socialism: The Case of Morris Hillquit, 1901–1914," *American Quarterly*, 26 (May 1974), 127–140.

6. Jane S. Dahlberg, *The New York Bureau of Municipal Research* (New York: New York Univ., 1966), pp. 3–23; Martin J. Schiesl, *The Politics of Efficiency: Municipal Administration and Reform in America: 1880–1920* (Berkeley: Univ. of California Pr., 1977), pp. 114–115.

7. CAB, "Recent Activities of City Clubs," *National Municipal Review*, 1 (Aug. 1912), 431. CAB described the work of the bureau in *American City Government*, pp. 78–79, 150. Dahlberg, *Bureau*, pp. 130–132, relates that CAB was a member of a

Committee on Practical Training for Public Services of the American Political Science Association, which evaluated the available places graduate students could do field work in state and municipal government. After touring the bureau's Training School for Public Service, he wrote an enthusiastic report which recommended that Columbia offer graduate credit toward the Ph.D. in Political Science for work at the school. Following this report, Columbia, the University of Pennsylvania, New York University, and the University of Michigan accredited the Training School. Samuel Haber, *Efficiency and Uplift: Scientific Management in the Progressive Era, 1890–1920* (Chicago: Univ. of Chicago Pr., 1964), is a useful survey, although CAB, as a specific example of such a reformer, belies his conclusion that these reformers were basically elitist and antidemocratic.

8. CAB, "Reconstructing State Government," *New Republic*, Special Supplement, 4 (21 Aug. 1915), 1–16; CAB, "The Budgetary Provisions of the New York Constitution," *Annals of the American Academy*, 62 (Nov. 1915), 65–66; Dahlberg, *Bureau*, p. 96.

9. CAB, "Reconstructing State Government," 7. In his stress on the centrality of budget-making in the achievement of efficient government CAB drew on the teachings of Goodnow and also was much influenced by the thinking of the great French pluralist Léon Duguit. See CAB in *Annals of the American Academy*, 64, and his review of Duguit's *Traité de droit constitutionnel* in *Political Science Quarterly*, 27 (Sept. 1912), 518–519. Schiesel, *Politics of Efficiency*, pp. 88–110, has a useful chapter on budget reform as a national phenomenon.

10. CAB, *The Advancement of Municipal Science* (New York: Bureau of Municipal Research, 1919), p. 16.

11. David M. Ellis, et. al., *A Short History of New York State* (Ithaca: Cornell Univ. Pr., 1967), pp. 390, 400–402. CAB continued to promote the executive budget as "a means for focusing the public attention on the realities of administration—human services and materials" even after this reform had been rejected by the state's voters. See CAB, "What a Budget Should Be," *New Republic*, 10 (17 Feb. 1917), 66–67. Al Smith secured passage of the executive budget in New York in 1927.

12. CAB, "Training for Efficient Public Service," *Annals of the American Academy*, 64 (Mar. 1916), 215, 216, 217; CAB "Human Nature and Administration," *Nation*, 106 (25 Apr. 1918), 502; CAB, Review of *The Need and Purpose of the Measurement of Social Phenomena* by A. L. Bowley, *National Municipal Review*, 5 (Jul. 1916), 518.

13. CAB, "Human Nature and Administration," 502–504; *New York Times*, 9 May 1918, p. 11; Schiesl, *Politics of Efficiency*, p. 119.

14. Dahlberg, *Bureau*, pp. 133, 134–135, 127; Luther Gulick, "Beard and Municipal Reform," in Howard K. Beale (ed.), *Charles A. Beard* (Lexington: Univ. of Kentucky Pr., 1954), p. 49; George A. Graham, *Education for Public Administration* (Chicago: Public Administration Service, 1941), p. 138; CAB, "Methods of Training for Public Service," *School and Society*, 2 (25 Dec. 1915), 904, 910–911. Successful graduates of the school included Raymond Moley and Robert Moses, both of whom studied with CAB.

15. James Fallows, "The Passionless Presidency II," *Atlantic Monthly*, 243 (Jun. 1979), 79. A history that reflects current disillusion and disgust with conservative bureaucracies is Michael B. Katz, *Class, Bureaucracy and Schools: The Illusion of Educational Change in America* (New York: Praeger, 1971). See also the essay by J. R.

Hollingsworth, "Perspectives on Industrializing Societies," in Allan G. Bogue (ed.), *Emerging Theoretical Models in Social and Political History* (Beverly Hills: Sage Publ., 1973), pp. 97–121.

16. Schiesl, *Politics of Efficiency*, p. 195.

17. CAB, *Contemporary American History* (New York: Macmillan, 1914), pp. 254–275, 672–673.

18. Robert M. La Follette, *La Follette's Autobiography: A Personal Narrative of Political Experiences* (Madison: La Follette Co., 1913), pp. 672–673; CAB to Robert M. La Follette, 14 May 1913. La Follette Family Collection, Series B, Box 73, Library of Congress.

19. CAB to La Follette, 14 May 1913. CAB, *Contemporary American History*, pp. 283–307. However, CAB indicted La Follette's National Progressive Republican League for having presented a shallow analysis of contemporary problems in 1912. Demanding only changes in the machinery of government, "on the deeper issues of political economy it was silent," CAB noted, "at least as to positive proposals" (p. 344).

20. CAB, *Contemporary American History*, p. 379.

21. CAB, Review of *The New Freedom* by Woodrow Wilson, *Political Science Quarterly*, 29 (Sept. 1914), 506–507; CAB, "Jefferson and the New Freedom," *New Republic*, 1 (14 Nov. 1915), 18–19.

22. CAB, "The Key to the Mexican Problem," *New Review*, 2 (Jun. 1914), 324.

23. Author's interview with Miriam Beard Vagts, 16 Sept. 1976; Nancy Schrom Dye, "Creating a Feminist Alliance: Sisterhood and Class Conflict in the New York Women's Trade Union League, 1903–1914," *Feminist Studies*, 2 (1975), 24–38; Ann J. Lane, *Mary Ritter Beard: A Sourcebook* (New York: Schocken, 1977), pp. 22–23.

24. CAB and Mary R. Beard, *American Citizenship* (New York: Macmillan, 1914), pp. v–vi.

25. Ibid., pp. 21–23.

26. Ibid., pp. 58–59, 266–267; CAB, "Internationalism in the United States," *New Review*, 3 (1915), 159–160. As chairperson of the South Harlem Neighborhood Association's Parks and Playgrounds Committee, Mary Beard faced the problem of what she called "gangs" that had "appointed the playgrounds to their own exclusive use." See her letter to the *New York Times*, 5 Dec. 1913, p. 10.

27. Mary Beard, "Editorial," *Woman Voter*, II (Sept. 1911), 8; Beard Microfilm, No. 179, Mary Beard File, Part I; Eleanor Flexner, *Century of Struggle* (Cambridge, Mass.: Harvard Univ. Pr., 1975), pp. 272–273; Ronald Schaffer, "The New York City Woman Suffrage Party, 1909–1919," *New York History*, 43 (Jul. 1962), 269–287, has a good general account of the suffragists' activities.

28. "Conversations with Alice Paul," pp. 105–106, Columbia Univ. Oral History Collections; MRB to Margaret S. Grierson, 15 Jul. 1945. Box 1, Mary Beard Papers, Sophia Smith Collection, Smith College.

29. CAB, "Woman Suffrage and Strategy," *New Republic*, 1 (12 Dec. 1914), 22–23; CAB, "Section Four and Suffrage," Ibid., 1 (9 Jan. 1915), 23; CAB, "Historical Woman Suffrage," Ibid., 4 (9 Oct. 1915), Part II, 1–3; Beard Microfilm, No. 179, Mary Beard File, Part I; *New York Times*, 4 Mar. 1914, p. 12; Mary R. Beard, "Letter to the Editor," *New York Times*, 17 Jan. 1915, III, p. 2.

30. *New York Times*, 18 Jan. 1915, p. 6.

31. Ibid., 18 Jul. 1915, IV, p. 10.

32. *New York Times*, 31 Jan. 1916, p. 5; 12 Nov. 1917, p. 1; CAB, "Politics and Education," *Teacher's College Record*, 17 (May 1916), 219–220.

33. Gordon W. Allport, "The Functional Anatomy of Motives," in Chalmers L. Stacey and Manfred F. DeMartino (eds.), *Understanding Human Motivation* (Cleveland: Case Western Reserve Pr., 1958), p. 81. This statement of the problem of treating a collective mind versus the minds of particular individuals responding to particular situations in a rational manner was called to the author's attention by David P. Thelen in his article "Social Tensions and the Origins of Progressivism," *Journal of American History*, 56 (Sept. 1969), 323–341.

34. CAB, "Democracy and Education in the United States," *Social Research*, 4 (Sept. 1937), 395.

5. Wealth and Power

1. CAB, "Politics," *Columbia University Lectures on Science, Philosophy, and Art, 1907–1908* (New York: Columbia Univ. Pr., 1908), p. 10.

2. "Politics," p. 11.

3. "Politics," pp. 14–15; Arthur F. Bentley, *The Process of Government: A Study of Social Pressures* (Chicago: Univ. of Chicago Pr., 1908), pp. 111, 162.

4. CAB, "Politics," pp. 19–20, 23–24.

5. CAB, *Public Policy and the General Welfare* (New York: Farrar and Rinehart, 1941), pp. 141, 143.

6. John W. Burgess, *Reminiscences of an American Scholar* (New York: Columbia Univ. Pr., 1923), pp. 12–13; Burgess, *Political Science and Comparative Constitutional Law*, (Boston: Ginn, 1890), Vol. II, p. 365; Bentley, *Process*, pp. 19, passim.

7. Westel Willoughby, "The Political Theories of Professor John W. Burgess," *Yale Review*, 17 (Winter 1908), 59–84. A useful study of Burgess' political thinking is Bernard Edward Brown, *American Conservatives: The Political Thought of Francis Lieber and John W. Burgess* (New York: Columbia Univ. Pr., 1951).

8. Goodnow's unsuccessful efforts to attain the Ruggles chair are described in Hoxie, *The Faculty*, p. 106. CAB tried to organize support in the department for Goodnow's effort. Author's interview with Miriam Beard Vagts, 16 Sept. 1976. Late in life, CAB wrote another description of Burgess' approach to constitutional questions: "In 1902, a justice of the Supreme Court, in the theory of the classroom, seemed to be a kind of master mechanic. Indeed, as I heard the budding lawyers and judges talk, I was often reminded of a machine once used in the Bank of England to test the coins deposited day by day. When a coin was gently placed on its delicately balanced receptacle, the machine trembled for a second or two and then dropped the coin, right or left, into the proper chest as sound or spurious according to its monetary merits." CAB, "Introduction," in John P. Frank, *Mr. Justice Black* (New York: Knopf, 1949), p. viii.

9. Frank J. Goodnow, *Social Reform and the Constitution* (New York: Macmillan, 1911), pp. 3, 11.

10. Goodnow, pp. 16, 100–145, 300–317. The quotation is from p. 357.

11. At Columbia under Burgess, a great distinction was made between the study of history, defined by Burgess as "the progressive realization of the ideals of the human spirit in all of the objective forms of their manifestation, in language, tradition and literature, in customs, manners, laws and institutions and opinions and beliefs," the study of political science, speculation about the nature of the state, which today would be called political theory, and public law, the study of the state as it is and was, the permanent conditions of its existence. J. D. Bluntschli, whose categories Burgess adopted, said of public law that it asked "whether what is conforms to law. Politics whether the action conforms to the end in view. . . . The highest and purest expression of Public Law is to be found in the Constitution or enacted positive laws: the clearest and most vivid manifestation of Politics is the practical conduct or guidance of the State itself, viz. Government." Brown, *American Conservatives*, pp. 116–120. Bluntschli is cited on 119–120. CAB's studies appear to fit within these definitions of public law and politics.

12. CAB, *The Supreme Court and the Constitution* (New York: Macmillan, 1912), pp. 46, 77, 89–93, 107, 117. CAB summarized his research in "The Supreme Court: Usurper or Grantee?," *Political Science Quarterly*, 27 (Mar. 1912), 1–35.

13. CAB, "Editorial," *DePauw Palladium*, 17 May 1898.

14. CAB, *Economic Origins of Jeffersonian Democracy* (New York: Macmillan, 1915), p. 440, mentioned his intention to write a series of books applying the economic interpretation to American History. He described his reading in *Economic Origins*, p. 464; Schmunk, "Free Spirit," pp. 268–270. Schmunk had in his possession CAB's letters to Lewis Mayers, then a graduate student at Columbia. Schmunk's conjecture on the time it took CAB to research and write these books was based on these letters.

15. CAB, "Preface," *An Economic Interpretation of the Constitution* (New York: Macmillan, 1935), p. vi. All citations are from this edition.

16. CAB to Robert M. La Follette, Sr., 14 May 1913. La Follette Family Collection, Series B, Box 73, Library of Congress.

17. CAB, *An Economic Interpretation*, pp. 1–4, 7–8. Robert E. Brown, *Charles Beard and the Constitution: A Critical Analysis of 'An Economic Interpretation of the Constitution'* (Princeton: Princeton Univ. Pr., 1956), pp. 26–27, in his critique of CAB's first chapter ignores the intellectual context in which the book appeared and appears to believe that CAB was addressing himself to historians alone.

18. CAB, *An Economic Interpretation*, pp. 9–14.

19. Ibid. p. 15.

20. Ibid., pp. 14–15. Douglass Adair, in a lively essay, "The Tenth Federalist Revisited," *William and Mary Quarterly*, 8 (Jan. 1951), 48–67, suggested that it was CAB who made Madison's *Federalist* No. 10 "famous for students of the United States Constitution" (p. 48) and also that CAB re-established "Madison's reputation as a major statesman of the Convention rather than as its mere 'reporter'" after a long period of neglect by historians. Adair does not mention that the *Federalist* No. 10 was used by J. Allen Smith in *The Spirit of American Government*, first published in 1907. See Smith's Chapter VIII, "The Party System," pp. 205–206. (All citations are to the John Harvard Library edition of 1965, edited by Cushing Strout.) Smith took his title from *Federalist* No. 10, specifically the passage: "When a majority is included in a faction, the form of popular government, on the other hand, enables it to sacrifice to

its ruling passion or interest both the public good and the rights of other citizens. To secure the public good and private rights against the danger of such a faction, and at the same time to preserve the spirit and the form of popular government, is then the great object to which our inquiries are directed." (p. 206). CAB did not cite Smith's book in *An Economic Interpretation*, but see his review of it in *Political Science Quarterly*, 23 (Mar. 1908), 136–137. Summarizing Smith's point of view, CAB noted that he saw the constitution as the outcome of a conservative reaction directed by "a strong and intelligent class, possessed of unity and informed by a conscious solidarity of material interests" (p. 136).

21. CAB to Raymond Moley, 29 Aug. 1916. Raymond Moley Papers, Hoover Institute, Stanford, Calif.

22. CAB, *An Economic Interpretation*, p. 24.

23. Brown, *Critical Analysis*, pp. 34-35.

24. CAB, *An Economic Interpretation*, pp. 26 passim, 51.

25. Ibid., pp. 73–151.

26. Ibid., pp. 152, 169–175.

27. Ibid., pp. 189–190.

28. Ibid., p. 218. Burgess, *Political Science*, vol. I, pp. 105, 107–108.

29. *Economic Interpretation*, pp. 239, 290–291, 292 passim.

30. Ibid., p. 323.

31. Ibid., p. 324. See pp. 23, 31, 34, 37, 74, 153, 188, 241–242, 249, 253, 256, 266, 271, 280, 290, and 292 for examples of CAB's calling attention to the incompleteness of his data, the need for more research, and the tentative nature of his own conclusions.

32. Ibid., P. 188.

33. Bentley, *Process of Government*, p. 177.

34. CAB, *An Economic Interpretation*, pp. 100–114.

35. CAB, *Economic Origins of Jeffersonian Democracy*, p. 131.

36. Ibid., p. 429. Richard Hofstadter, in *The Progressive Historians* (New York: Knopf, 1968), p. 216, pointed out that *An Economic Interpretation* could be read "either as an attempt to replace an abstract and rarefied version of the origins of constitutional ideas with an account founded upon economic and sociological realism, or as a crude essay in economic determinism which seeks to reduce statecraft to motives of personal gain . . . and in so doing to cast discredit on the Fathers." My own interpretation stresses the former purpose. Hofstadter was constructing an argument by which he could later explain CAB's attitude toward Franklin Roosevelt. Hence he emphasized what he saw as CAB's "ambiguity" toward the Founding Fathers. Or perhaps he "saw" the "ambiguity" and then "saw" its result. The "ambiguity" becomes less apparent if the two books, *An Economic Interpretation* and *Economic Origins*, intended to complement each other, are considered together. Curiously, Hofstadter inserted eleven pages on the rest of CAB's life, up to his death in 1948, between his lengthy discussion (one fifth of a book devoted to three historians) of the first volume and his brief paragraphs on the second.

37. CAB, *Economic Origins*, pp. 1–43.

38. Ibid., pp. 398–399, 461.

39. Ibid., pp. 437, 440–447, 467.

40. Ibid., pp. 194–195.

41. Ibid., pp. 300, 319.

42. Ibid., pp. 380–382, 387, 391, 446, 456.
43. Ibid., p. 195.
44. CAB to Arthur M. Schlesinger, 30 Jun. 1915. Schlesinger Papers, Harvard Univ. Archives.
45. *Educational Review*, 46 (Sept. 1913), 207.
46. *New York Times*, 14 Dec. 1913, IV, 5. A Copy of the *Ohio Star*'s comment is on Beard Microfilm, No. 179, DePauw Univ. Archives. CAB had written to Lewis Mayers on 13 Aug. 1913, "Taft has read my book on the Constitution and said it deeply wounded his patriotic sensibilities. Too bad." Cited in Schmunk, "Free Spirit," p. 182.
47. CAB, *Economic Origins*, p. 195.
48. *Mississippi Valley Historical Review*, 1 (Jun. 1914), 113–117; *History Teacher's Magazine*, 5 (Feb. 1914), 65–66.
49. CAB, *Economic Origins*, 106.
50. Libby in *Mississippi Valley Historical Review*, pp. 114, 116. Libby reiterated this argument in his review of *Economic Origins* in *Mississippi Valley Historical Review*, 3 (Jun. 1916), 100.
51. *South Atlantic Quarterly*, 12 (Jul. 1913), 269–273.
52. CAB, *Economic Origins*, pp. 464–465.
53. CAB, *Contemporary American History* (New York: Macmillan, 1914), pp. v, 8–9, 18, 24–26.
54. See Mary R. Beard, *Woman's Work in Municipalities* (New York: Appleton, 1915), pp. 182–195, 210–215. Mary Beard's concern about segregation is reflected in her commendation of Mrs. Robert La Follette's speeches against Wilson's segregation orders in Washington. See Mary Beard to Miss Dunn, 12 Jan. 1914. La Follette Family Collection, Series B, Box 75, Library of Congress.
55. Otis L. Graham, Jr., *The Great Campaigns: Reform and War in America, 1900–1928* (Englewood Cliffs, N.J.: Prentice-Hall, 1971), p. 145. Graham's essays are generally splendid. David W. Southern, in his monograph on progressives' racial attitudes, *The Malignant Heritage: Yankee Progressives and the Negro Question, 1901–1914* (Chicago: Loyola Univ. Pr., 1968), pp. 53–54, concluded that most progressive writers "steered sharply around the Negro problem. In fact, they considered the Negro a perpetual lower caste which blighted the 'promise of American life.' The apparent failure of reconstruction and the scientific findings of the time gave credence to the belief that the Negro race was inferior. . . . No social scientists sought to explain that the Negro had a legion of millstones around his social, political, and economic neck. . . ." CAB did not ignore the Negro; neither did he use racist interpretations. However, on a personal level, he probably was unable to shed the pervasive race-consciousness of his times. See the footnote in *An Economic Interpretation*, p. 22, on the "negro attendant at the Treasury" who had "sold a crateload or more of these records to a junk dealer."
56. CAB to Lewis Mayers, 31 Jan. 1913. Cited by Schmunk, "Free Spirit," pp. 295–296.
57. CAB, *Contemporary American History*, pp. 33, 50–89. The last quotation is from p. 53.
58. Ibid., pp. 164, 194–196.
59. Ibid., pp. 199, 202–203.
60. Ibid., pp. 248–250.

61. Ibid., p. 252; Eugene D. Genovese, "Beard's Economic Interpretation of History," in *Charles A. Beard: An Observance of the Centennial of His Birth* (Greencastle: DePauw Univ., 1976), pp. 32–33, 35; Elias Berg, *The Historical Thinking of Charles A. Beard* (Stockholm: Almquist   Wiksell, 1957), pp. 18–30.

62. CAB, *The Economic Basis of Politics* (New York: Knopf, 1922), pp. 86, 87, 88, 89–90, 99.

63. A persuasive discussion of this weakness in the progressive left is Kenneth McNaught, "American Progressives and the Great Society," *Journal of American History*, 53 (Dec. 1969), 504–520.

64. *New Republic*, 31 (9 Aug. 1922), 282–283. See *Public Opinion* (New York: Macmillan, 1922), pp. 180-190, where Lippmann, without mentioning CAB, repeats his argument against what he regarded as "the naive view of self-interest."

65. *New Republic*, 32 (27 Sept. 1922), 128–129.

66. CAB, "Politics," p. 11; CAB, *Economic Origins*, p. 87; CAB, *Contemporary American History*, p. 53.

6. World War

1. CAB to Sen. Lee S. Overman, reprinted in *New York Times*, 26 Jan. 1919, p. 8. Edward Jenks, whom CAB regarded as a "brilliant thinker," had advanced the notion that the state had originated in the conquest of primitive settled communities by a war band and in the regimentation of the conquered by the victorious class. CAB referred to and repeated this idea on numerous occasions. See his review of Stephen Leacock's *Elements of Political Science* in *Education Review*, 35 (Feb. 1908), 202, and CAB, "The Evolution of Democracy," in F. A. Cleveland and Joseph Schafer (eds.), *Democracy in Reconstruction* (Boston: Houghton Miftlin, 1919), p. 490.

James Harvey Robinson shared CAB's antipathy toward the Central Powers from the beginning of the war. See his article, "War and Thinking," *New Republic*, 1 (19 Dec. 1914), 17–18. CAB and Robinson had criticized the unrepresentative nature of the German government in *The Development of Modern Europe* (New York: Ginn, 1908), vol. II. pp. 145–149.

On CAB's early interventionist sentiment, see also CAB's colleague at Columbia, James T. Shotwell, "Reminiscences," Columbia Oral History Collection, pp. 65–66.

2. CAB, "Politics and Education," *Teacher's College Record*, 17 (May 1916), 219. See similar remarks in his "Training for efficient Public Service," *Annals of the American Academy*, 64 (Mar. 1916), 215–216.

3. Joseph Freeman, *An American Testament: A Narrative of Rebels and Romantics* (New York: Farrar and Rinehart, 1936), p. 107.

4. Charles Forcey, *The Crossroads of Liberalism* (New York: Oxford Univ. Pr., 1961), pp. 250–263; CAB, *New York Times*, 26 Jan. 1919, p. 8.

5. *New York Times*, 21 Jan. 1916, p. 9.

6. Ibid., 23 Jan. 1917, p. 2.

7. Ibid., 27 Feb. 1917, p. 2.

8. CAB, "Statement," *Hearings on Production and Conservation of Food Supplies before the Committee on Agriculture and Forestry*. U.S. Senate, 65th Congress, 1st Sess., 507. These hearings were held on 10 May 1917.

9. James R. Mock and Cedrick Larson, *Words That Won the War: The Story of the Committee on Public Information, 1917–1919* (New York: Russell   Russell, 1939), p. 172. Stephen Vaughn, *Holding Fast the Inner Lines: Democracy, Nationalism, and the Committee on Public Information* (Chapel Hill: Univ. of North Carolina Pr., 1980), pp. 23 passim, 238. See also George T. Blakey, *Historians on the Homefront: American Propagandists for the Great War* (Lexington: Univ. Pr., of Kentucky, 1970).

10. CAB, "The Perils of Diplomacy: A Communication," *New Republic*, 11 (June 2, 1917), 136-138.

11. "Perils of Diplomacy."

12. CAB to Frank Tannenbaum, 14 Apr. 1918. Columbia University Special Manuscript Collections.

13. CAB, "The End of the War," *New Republic*, 15 (6 Jul. 1918), 297.

14. *New York Times*, 27 Nov. 1918, p. 12; Charles De Benedetti, *Origins of the Modern American Peace Movement, 1915–1929* (Millwood, N.Y.: KOT Pr., 1978), pp. 6–8.

15. *New York Times*, 2 Dec. 1918, p. 8; De Benedetti, *Origins*, pp. 8–9.

16. *New York Times*, 28 Nov. 1918, p. 16. Selig Adler, in *The Isolationist Impulse: Its Twentieth Century Reaction* (New York: Abelard-Schuman, 1957), pp. 51-52, on which Thomas C. Kennedy's account in *Charles A. Beard and American Foreign Policy* (Gainesville: Univ. of Florida Pr., 1975), p. 36, appears to be based entirely, suggests that the League of Free Nations was a group of "the President's friends," who "sensed the growing liberal unrest and the peril of incipient revolt against Wilsonism." He describes the group, which included, aside from the cluster of Columbia friends, others such as Herbert Croly, Hamilton Holt, Judge Learned Hand, Horace M. Kallen, Frederic C. Howe, Felix Frankfurter, Owen R. Lovejoy, Rose Schneiderman, Harold Stearns, and H. G. Wells, as "liberal rather than conservative internationalists." However, they were not propounding some vague internationalism; their main concern was the very specific issue of imperialism and imperial rivalries at the peace conference. Neither Adler nor Kennedy mentions that their manifesto called for "a new world economic order."

17. *Gesprache mit CAB uber Woodrow Wilson* (from a diary of Alfred Vagts), 1938, Beard Microfilm No. 480, DePauw Univ. Archives. I am indebted to Norman E. Nordhauser for assistance in the translation of this passage. *New Republic* began printing installments of J. M. Keynes' *Economic Consequences of the Peace* in Dec. 1919.

18. CAB, "Political Science in the Crucible," *New Republic*, 13 (17 Nov. 1917), 3–4. On support for the war and optimism about possible social reforms emerging from it, see Charles Hirschfeld, "Nationalist Progressivism and World War I," *Mid-America*, 45 (Jul. 1963), 139–156; Allen F. Davis, "Welfare, Reform and World War I," *American Quarterly*, 19 (Fall 1967), 516–523; Stanley Shapiro, "The Great War and Reform: Liberals and Labor, 1917–19," *Labor History*, 11 (Summer 1971), 323–344; and Alan Cywar, "John Dewey: Toward Domestic Reconstruction, 1915–1920," *Journal of the History of Ideas*, 30 (Jul.–Sept. 1969), 385–400.

19. CAB in F. A. Cleveland and Joseph Schafer (ed.). *Democracy in Reconstruction* (Boston: Houghton Mifflin, 1919), pp. 490–491. Robert E. Thomas, in his "A Reappraisal of Charles A. Beard's *An Economic Interpretation of the Constitution of the United States*," *American Historical Review*, 57 (Jan. 1952), 374, quoted CAB's reference to the Rockefellers, Morgans, Vanderbilts, and Harrimans as "creative pioneers" as part

of his attempt to prove that CAB had a "Federalist orientation." However, he *omitted* CAB's obvious reference to the future socialization of the work of the pioneers.

20. CAB described this affair in "A Statement," *New Republic*, 13 (29 Dec. 1917), 249. In this article he referred to Goodnow as "Professor X," but earlier, in *New Republic*, 13 (17 Nov. 1917), 3, CAB had called Goodnow by name and had reported that Goodnow was "shut out" of the Ruggles chair because of his book on the Constitution and social reform. See Hoxie, *Faculty*, p. 106.

21. "Statement of Facts in the Matter of the Committee of Education of the Board of Trustees of Columbia University and Professor Charles A. Beard," Beard Microfilm, No. 179, DePauw Univ. Archives; *New York World*, 22 Apr. 1916. This clipping and numerous others are on the Beard microfilm.

22. "Statement of Facts," Beard Microfilm No. 179.

23. "Statement of Facts;" CAB, *New Republic* 13 (29 Dec. 1917), 249. A group of CAB's students had written to the *New Republic* defending his speech. See "What Professor Beard Said'" *New Republic*, 7 (6 May 1916), 18, and CAB, "Letter to Editor," Columbia *Spectator*, 26 Apr. 1916; CAB to James M. Cattell, 16 May 1916, James M. Cattell Papers, Box 98, Library of Congress.

24. CAB, "Statement." Dewey had earlier protested the "arbitrary exercise of a legal right based upon the conception of the relation of a factory employer to his employee" by trustees of the University of Pennsylvania, when they had denied reappointment to the radical economist Scott Nearing in Jun. 1915. See Dewey, "Professional Freedom," *New York Times*, 22 Oct. 1915, p. 10.

25. Richard Hofstadter and Walter Metzger, *The Development of Academic Freedom in the United States* (New York: Columbia Univ. Pr., 1955), pp. 498–499; CAB, "Statement," p. 250.

26. CAB, "Statement," p. 250. At the time of CAB's "'To Hell With the Flag'" episode, in Apr. 1916, Fraser had been summoned to the board of trustees to explain his criticism of military training.

27. Butler's commencement speech of Jun. 1917 is found in *Report of the Special Committee Appointed March 5, 1917 to Inquire into the State of Teaching in the University* (New York: Columbia Univ. Pr., 1917). An exemplary and fascinating account of these contests over academic freedom at Columbia, one that emphasizes intrafaculty politics, is Carol S. Gruber, *Mars and Minerva: World War I and the Uses of the Higher Learning in America* (Baton Rouge: Louisiana State Univ. Pr., 1975), pp. 187–206. Her article "Academic Freedom at Columbia University, 1917–1918: The Case of James McKeen Cattell," *Bulletin of the American Association of University Professors*, 58 (Autumn 1972), 297–305, contains some information on CAB that was excluded from her book.

28. Gruber, *Mars and Minerva*, pp. 191–195, 202–204. The quotation on Cattell is from p. 195. *Report of the Special Committee Appointed March 5, 1917* contains Cattell's letter to the House of Representatives as well as an account of the trustees' and Butler's objections to Dana's activities. Cattell had been at Columbia for twenty-six years, and the Committee of Nine had recommended that he be retired on grounds of personal unfittness, *not* on grounds of having committed treason, and that he be given his full pension.

29. CAB, "Statement," p. 250; "The Call to Battle," Columbia *Spectator*, 9 Oct. 1917.

30. *New York Times*, 10 Oct. 1917, p. 10. According to Gruber, *Mars and Minerva*, p. 205, Dewey, Robinson, and Thomas Reed Powell requested an AAUP investigation of the cases of Dana and Cattell. Cattell had a legal right to petition Congress, and the organization to which Dana belonged was not illegal. The AAUP responded weakly in a report that mentioned neither the university's name nor Cattell's and did not discuss the case of Dana.

CAB had refused to join the AAUP after its organization in 1915. In 1917 he described it as "a futile enterprise," without saying why he thought so. See CAB to H. W. Tyler, 16 Jun. 1917, in Seligman Papers, Columbia Univ. Special Manuscript Collection.

31. H. R. S[pencer], "Academic Trusteeship," Ohio State *Lantern*, 29 Oct. 1917. CAB told Arthur Schlesinger that Spencer was "the only man who has written on the matter who sees what I was driving at and the significance of the affair." See CAB to Arthur Schlesinger, 10 Nov. 1917. Arthur Schlesinger Papers, Harvard Univ. Archives.

32. "Professor Beard's Letter of Resignation from Columbia University," *School and Society*, 6 (13 Oct. 1917), 446-447. The letter appeared also in Columbia *Spectator*, 9 Oct. 1917, New York *American*, 9 Oct. 1917, New York *Evening Post*, 10 Oct. 1917, New York *Call*, 9 Oct. 1917.

33. Annie Nathan Meyer, "Letter to the Editor," *New York Times*, 13 Oct. 1917, p. 10.

34. Quotations are from Thomas Reed Powell to E.R.A. Seligman, 13 Nov. 1917, cited by Gruber, "Academic Freedom at Columbia University, 1917–1918," 304.

35. Columbia *Spectator*, 9–12 Oct. 1917; Freeman, *American Testament*, pp. 107–109; New York *Tribune*, 17 Oct. 1917, p. 1; Randolph Bourne, *History of a Literary Radical* (New York: Huebusch, 1920), p. 98.

36. Gruber, *Mars and Minerva*, p. 202.

37. Henry R. Mussey to E. R. A. Seligman, 6 Nov. 1917, Columbia University Special Manuscript Collection; Schmunk, "Free Spirit," pp. 362–363.

38. CAB, "Political Science," in Wilson Gee (ed.), *Research in the Social Sciences* (New York: Macmillan, 1929), pp. 289–290, and similar remarks in CAB, "Conditions Favorable to Creative Work in Political Science," *American Political Science Review*, 24, Supplement (Feb. 1930), 30–31. CAB delighted in his work with the Bureau. See CAB to Arthur M. Schlesinger, 24 Mar. 1917, Schlesinger Papers, and E. R. Seligman to John Burgess, 31 Mar. 1914, Seligman Papers, Columbia Univ. Special Manuscript Collection, in which Seligman expressed concern that CAB would leave Columbia if the Bureau raised his salary.

39. CAB to Henry R. Mussey, n.d. Miscellaneous Manuscripts Collection, Harvard Univ. Archives.

40. *New York Times*, 16 Dec. 1917, I, p. 5.

41. *New York Times*, 20 Jun. 1918, p. 8; CAB to E. R. A. Seligman, 3 Dec. 1918 and 18 Dec. 1918. Columbia Univ. Special Manuscript Collections. Seligman furnished the money for Charles Strangeland's bail bond. Mock and Larson, *Words That Won*, p. 177; CAB, "English Liberty," *New Republic*, 16 (19 Oct. 1918), 350–351. Thomas Kennedy, *Charles A. Beard and American Foreign Policy*, p. 38, was thus in error when he stated "It was not until after World War I ended, however, that Beard publicly registered his private concern about such matters."

42. CAB, "The Supreme Issue," *New Republic*, 17 (18 Jan. 1919), 343.

43. *New York Times*, 25 Jan. 1919, p. 1. Among those listed as belonging to "movements not helping the United States" were Jane Addams, Roger N. Baldwin, Sophonisba P. Breckenridge, Henry Wadsworth Longfellow Dana, Elizabeth Gurley Flynn, Morris Hillquit, Frederick C. Howe, David Starr Jordan, Scott Nearing, Kate Richards O'Hare, Harry A. Overstreet, Vida Scudder, Norman Thomas, Alexander Tractenberg, Oswald G. Villard, Lilian Wald, and Eugene Debs. *New York Times*, 26 Jan. 1919, p. 8.

44. CAB, "Propaganda in the Schools," *The Dial*, 66 (14 Jun. 1919), 598–599; CAB [pseud. J. W. Bradford], "Could Daniel Webster Teach in New York's Schools?," *Nation*, 109 (2 Aug. 1919), 147.

45. David Ellis, et al., *Short History of New York State* (Ithaca: Cornell Univ. Pr., 1967), p. 399; CAB, "On the Advantages of Censorship and Espionage," *New Republic*, 27 (24 Aug. 1921), 350–351.

46. CAB and Mary R. Beard, "Ten Years Back: The American People and the War," *Survey*, 58 (1 Apr. 1927), 51.

47. Gruber, *Mars and Minerva*, pp. 256–257.

48. Gruber, "Academic Freedom at Columbia University, 1917–1918," p. 305. For Dewey's and Robinson's analyses of restrictions of free expression written after CAB's resignation, see John Dewey, "In Explanation of Our Lapse," *New Republic*, 13 (3 Nov. 1917), 17–18, and James Harvey Robinson, "The Threatened Eclipse of Free Speech," *Atlantic*, 120 (Dec. 1917), 811–817.

49. Randolph Bourne, "Twilight of Idols," in Resak (ed.), *War and the Intellectuals*, p. 59.

50. Gruber, *Mars and Minerva*, pp. 254–255.

51. For Dewey's "explanation of our lapse" based on themes of innocence and national adolescence, see *New Republic* (3 Nov. 1917), 17–18.

7. Experiments and Conclusions

1. Three general accounts of the founding of the New School for Social Research are Lucy Sprague Mitchell, *Two Lives: The Story of Wesley Clair Mitchell and Myself* (New York: Simon & Schuster, 1953), pp. 333–343; Alvin Johnson, *Pioneer's Progress* (New York: Viking, 1952), pp. 271–288; Harry Elmer Barnes, "James Harvey Robinson," esp. pp. 339–347, in Howard W. Odum (ed.), *American Masters of Social Science* (New York: Holt, 1927).

2. CAB to Felix Frankfurter, 9 May 1918. Frankfurter Papers, Box 23, Library of Congress. Agnes E. Meyer, who contributed money and taught some classes in psychology at the New School during its early years, says in her autobiography, *Out of These Roots* (Boston: Little, Brown, 1953), p. 100, that Robinson, Beard, and Dewey, whom she aptly described as "empirical idealists," began to talk about "the need for a liberal university" as early as 1915.

3. Herbert Croly, "A School of Social Research," *New Republic*, 15 (8 Jan. 1918), 167–171.

4. Johnson, *Pioneer's Progress*, pp. 272–273, 167.

5. Ibid., p. 276.

6. Ibid., p. 278.

7. An announcement of the organization of the New School and of the first lectures, to be given from Feb. to May 1919, before the school was fully staffed, appeared in *New Republic*, 17 (25 Jan. 1919), p. vii; Johnson, *Pioneer's Progress*, p. 278. Veblen shared Croly's interest in the potential role of engineers as managers of society. *The Engineers and the Price System* (New York: Huebsch, 1921), grew out of discussions at the New School. See William E. Akin, *Technocracy and the American Dream: The Technocrat Movement, 1900–1941* (Berkeley: Univ. of California Pr., 1977), pp. 18–26.

8. CAB to Lucy Salmon, 25 Feb. and 27 Feb. 1919, in Lucy Salmon Papers, Vassar College Library. The founders appear to have thought of themselves, at least the male founders, as like a reckless band of cowboys. Wesley Mitchell described his acceptance of duty in the "Free School" as "like settling moral issues on the spot with a six shooter, after the best tradition of the old west." Mitchell, *Two Lives*, p. 342.

9. James Harvey Robinson, "The New School," *School and Society*, 11 (31 Jan. 1920), pp. 129–132. See also *The Socialist Call*, n.d., clipping on Beard Microfilm, No. 179, for the glowing account by McCallister Coleman, a Columbia student who had followed CAB to the New School.

10. Johnson, *Pioneer's Progress*, p. 279.

11. Miriam Beard Vagts to the author, 8 Oct. 1976; Barnes, "Robinson," pp. 345–346.

12. Johnson, *Pioneer's Progress*, p. 279; CAB to Harry Elmer Barnes, 13 Apr. and 16 Apr. 1920; Harry Elmer Barnes to CAB, 17 Apr. 1920; CAB to Harry Elmer Barnes, 21 Apr. 1920. Harry Elmer Barnes Collection, University of Wyoming Archive of Contemporary History.

13. Johnson, *Pioneer's Progress*, p. 279; Mitchell, *Two Lives*, pp. 342–343; Miriam Beard Vagts to the author, 8 Oct. 1976.

14. Albert Nock, "The Vanished University," *The Freeman*, 3 (29 Jun. 1921), 364.

15. CAB, "Letter to the Editor," *The Freeman*, 3 (20 Jul. 1921), 450–451.

16. See Chapter 4 for a discussion of CAB's earlier career with the Bureau. Jane S. Dahlberg, *The New York Bureau*, p. 30; Luther Gulick, "Beard and Municipal Reform," p. 53.

17. Dahlberg, *The New York Bureau*, pp. 133, 241; CAB to Raymond Fosdick, 19 May 1922. Raymond B. Fosdick Papers, Princeton University Archives.

18. On the traction crisis and the Bureau's remedy, see *New York Times*, 5 Oct. 1919, III, p. 3, and Bureau of Municipal Research, Publication No. 94 (New York, 1919). On food storage and CAB's recommendations, see *New York Times*, 27 May 1918, p. 18. The budget of New York City was analyzed by CAB and David Zuckerman in "Bringing the Budget Home to Everybody," *New York Times*, 12 Oct. 1919, IV, p. 1. CAB, Robert Moses, et. al., *Report of the Reconstruction Commission to Governor Alfred E. Smith on Retrenchment and Reorganization in the State Government*, 10 Oct. 1919 (Albany: J. B. Lyon, 1919), pp. 4–5. Robert Caro, *The Power Broker: Robert Moses and the Fall of New York* (New York: Harper, 1974), pp. 106–108, has a fine summary of the report. Moses apparently wished to claim total responsibility for the report and even went so far as to accuse CAB of plagarizing his work when CAB published an article on reorganization. CAB's article, however, was based on a section of the report he had written. See Caro, pp. 107–108.

19. Miriam Beard Vagts to the author, 8 Oct. 1976; *National Municipal Review,* 8 (Jun. 1919), 271–272.

20. CAB to Raymond Fosdick, 20 May 1922. Fosdick Papers.

21. CAB to Charles E. Merriam, 3 Nov. 1924. Charles E. Merriam Papers, University of Chicago Archives, Box 25, Folder 17; Gulick, "Beard and Reform," pp. 49, 60. Under Gulick the Bureau became, first, the National Institute of Public Administration, and then, in 1928, the Institute of Public Administration affiliated with Columbia. CAB hoped for a period that the League of Nations would establish an international bureau of municipal research. See CAB, "A World Bureau of Municipal Research: Being Considered by the League of Nations," *National Municipal Review,* 14 (Jan. 1925), 1–2.

22. New York *Call,* 30 May 1908, p. 5, 25 Aug. 1908, p. 5. CAB's experience at Ruskin Hall is mentioned as an inspiration for the Rand School by Bertha H. Mailly, "The Rand School of Social Science," in *Workers Education in the United States* (New York: Workers Education Bureau, 1921), p. 25, and by Etta Freedlander, *Education in the Workers' Schools of New York City* (Ph.D. thesis: New School, 1937), p. 150. The papers of William J. Ghent, administrator of the school at its founding, are in the Library of Congress, but they are disappointingly lacking in materials on the beginning of the Rand experiment.

23. George S. Counts, "Charles Beard, The Public Man," p. 241; Workers Education Bureau of America *News Letter,* 10 (Oct. 1948), 1.

24. Luther V. Hendricks, *James Harvey Robinson* (New York: Kings Crown, 1946), p. 26.

25. CAB, Review of *Workers Education in the United States, New Republic,* 28 (9 Nov. 1921), 328; Mary R. Beard, *The American Labor Movement* (New York: Workers Education Bureau, 1924), pp. 197, 163–171.

26. CAB, "The Potency of Labor Education," *American Federationist,* 29 (Jul. 1922), 500–502.

27. See Horace M. Kallen, *Education, The Machine, and The Worker* (New York: New Republic, 1925), and Walter Lippmann, *Public Opinion* (New York: Macmillan, 1922).

28. Joseph Freeman, *An American Testament* (New York: Farrar and Rinehart, 1936), p. 223.

29. Author's interview with Miriam Beard Vagts, 16 Sept. 1976.

30. CAB, "Preface," *Crosscurrents in Europe Today* (Boston: Marshall Jones, 1922).

31. *Crosscurrents,* p. 5.

32. Ibid., pp. 6, 81–82.

33. Ibid., p. 6.

34. Ibid., pp. 97–120, 133–138. See John M. Keynes' proposal for a European "Free Trade Union" in *The Economic Consequences of the Peace* (New York: Harcourt, Brace, 1920), pp. 265–266.

35. *Crosscurrents,* pp. 140–162, 170–174, 176–177, 236–237, 238. Beard and many other pragmatic liberals were probably influenced in their view of the Revolution by the writings of the anarchist journalist Robert Minor, who had visited Russia in 1918 and who had been especially impressed by the evidence he saw of a Russian return to capitalism. See Christopher Lasch, *American Liberals and the Russian Revolution* (New York: Columbia Univ. Pr., 1962), pp. 149–157. This view of revolutions is still

commonplace in the United States. See Alan Riding, "Reality Transforms Nicaragua's Revolutionists into Pragmatists," *New York Times*, 20 Jul. 1980, IV, p. 3.

36. *Crosscurrents*, pp. 239–257.

37. Ibid., pp. 263–266.

38. Ibid. The similarities between Beard's *Crosscurrents* and Howe's *Why War?* (New York: Scribner, 1916) are striking. Howe's book is not included in Beard's bibliography, but many of the themes, especially the economic nature of imperialism and its relationship to the origins of the war, are the same. Howe and Beard had worked together on the League of Free Nations Association's proposal for a peace treaty during the summer of 1918. Compare Howe (p. 4), "Tens of millions of men have been taken from their homes and sent to the trenches for reasons which have not been explained to them or by virtue of secret alliances in whose making and as to whose propriety the people had no voice," with Beard (p. 6), "Out of the millions that went forth to die, out of the millions that stayed at home to suffer and bear burdens, only a handful—a score or more—knew by what process the terrible denouement had been brought to pass." Compare also Beard's concern, in Chapter IX of *Crosscurrents*, that America might continue on the path of financial imperialism, with Chapter VII of Howe's work, "The Flag Follows the Investor" (pp. 83–88).

39. *Nation*, 115 (22 Nov. 1922), 552–553.

8. Voyages to the Orient

1. Beard Microfilm, No. 179, Part 2, Chap. 2, "Trips to the Orient." DePauw Univ. Archives. When CAB resigned from Columbia, a group of Chinese and Japanese graduate students had petitioned Nicholas Murray Butler to reject his resignation. *New York Tribune*, 12 Oct. 1917, p. 1; author's interview with Miriam Beard Vagts, 12 Sept. 1976. Goodnow had been a foreign adviser to the repressive postrevolutionary government of Yuan Shih-K'ai, and CAB had publicly criticized Goodnow's assertion that the Chinese people were at a stage of development which made them unsuited for representative government. See Frank J. Goodnow, "Reform in China," *American Political Science Review*, 9 (May 1915), 209–224, a speech which he gave to the Dec. 1914 meeting of the American Political Science Association. CAB's response in the discussion that followed the speech is mentioned in *American Political Science Review*, 9 (Feb. 1915), 116. On Goodnow's "extaordinary cultural and academic arrogance" in support of Yuan and his dictatorship see Ernest P. Young, *The Presidency of Yuan Shih-k'ai: Liberalism and Dictatorship in Early Republican China* (Ann Arbor: Univ. of Michigan Pr., 1977), pp. 168–176, 220–222. A somewhat kinder view of Goodnow in the role of adviser to the Chinese government, an argument that makes him a dupe of the Chinese monarchists and an intellectual mercenary, is Noel Pugach, "Embarrassed Monarchist: Frank J. Goodnow and Constitutional Development in China, 1913–1915," *Pacific Historical Review*, 42 (Nov. 1973), 499–517. John Dewey had witnessed at first hand the May Fourth Movement of May and June 1919, and he had been greatly impressed by the vigor of the students' political and intellectual protest against the government's acceptance of the Treaty of Versailles, which had recognized Japan's claim to former German concessions in Shantung. Many of the essays Dewey

wrote about China in 1919, 1920, and 1921 are reprinted in *Characters and Events: Popular Essays in Social and Political Philosophy,* ed. Joseph Ratner, 2 vols. (New York: Holt, 1929). On the May Fourth Movement and on Dewey's response, and also for a bibliography of Dewey's writings on China and Japan, see Jerome B. Grieder, *Hu Shih and the Chinese Renaissance: Liberalism in the Chinese Revolution, 1917–1937,* (Cambridge, Mass. Harvard Univ. Pr., 1970).

2. CAB, "Japan's Statesman of Research," *Review of Reviews,* 68 (Sept. 1923), 296–298, and CAB, "Goto and the Rebuilding of Tokyo," *Our World,* 5 (Apr. 1924), 11–21.

3. CAB, "Japan's Statesman of Research"; CAB, "Goto and the Rebuilding of Tokyo."

4. Mary R. Beard to Merle Curti, 26 Mar. 1950. Merle Curti Papers, Wisconsin State Historical Society; Oswald G. Villard to CAB, 18 Jul. 1922; CAB to Oswald G. Villard, 19 Jul. 1922. Villard Papers, Harvard Univ. Archives.

5. *Osaka Mainichi,* 16 Sept. 1922, and *Japan Advertiser,* 15 Sept. 1922. Clippings are found in Beard Microfilm, No. 179. CAB, "Municipal Research in Japan: A Report to American Research Workers," *National Municipal Review,* 12 (Sept. 1923), 520.

6. *Japan Advertiser,* 17 Sept. 1922. See Tokyo *Nichi Nichi* (n.d.) clipping in Beard Microfilm, No. 179. In this speech CAB advised that "true dignity" existed "in the realization in the new Tokyo of the Japanese art and architecture. . . . Most western style buildings in Japan are not worthy of the genius of Japanese artists. They are too commonplace and even awkward." See the same theme in CAB, "For a Greater Tokyo," *Far Eastern Review,* 19 (Apr. 1923), 263–266, 277.

7. CAB, "Municipal Research in Japan: A Report to American Research Workers," p. 521; CAB, *Administration and Politics of Tokyo* (New York: Macmillan, 1923), pp. 2–4. The translations of CAB's speeches into Japanese were done by Dr. Seigo Takahashi, a former student at Columbia.

8. CAB, "Municipal Research in Japan," p. 523; CAB, *Administration and Politics of Tokyo,* p. 9.

9. Beard Microfilm, Nos. 179 and 480; *New York Times,* 17 Sept. 1923, p. 14.

10. Some of William Beard's photographs are included in Miriam Beard, *Realism in Japan; Japan Advertiser,* 3 Dec. 1922, has an account of Mary Beard's speech; the poem is on Beard Microfilm, No. 179.

11. CAB, *Administration and Politics of Tokyo,* pp. 10–14, 25, 16.

12. Ibid., pp. 27, 58–59, passim.

13. Ibid., pp. 137–148.

14. Ibid., pp. 149–160.

15. CAB, "Letter to Mayor Goto," *Japan Times & Mail,* 19 Mar. 1923; *Osaka Mainichi,* 15 Mar. 1923. As he departed, CAB expressed a desire to return to Japan for "two or three years" of continued study.

16. Photographs taken by William Beard during the visit to Taiwan and China are on Beard Microfilm, No. 480. Other information about this trip was furnished by Miriam Beard Vagts to the author, 12 Sept. 1976.

17. CAB, "American Influence on Municipal Government in the Orient,"*National Municipal Review,* 14 (Jan. 1925), 7–11.

18. CAB, "Goto and the Rebuilding of Tokyo," *Our World,* 5 (Apr. 1924), 11, 13–14; CAB, "The Awakening of Japanese Cities," *Review of Reviews,* 69 (May 1924), 523–527; CAB's telegram is cited by Robert S. Schwantes, *Japanese and Americans: A*

Century of Cultural Relations (New York: Harper, 1955), p. 111. A general account of
the destruction wrought by the earthquake and fire is Noel F. Busch, *Two Minutes to
Noon* (New York: Simon & Schuster, 1962).

19. *New York Times*, 13 Sept. 1923, p. 3.

20. Ibid., 17 Sept. 1923, p. 14.

21. Tokyo *Nichi Nichi* (n.d.), clipping on Beard Microfilm. See CAB, "Rebuilding
in Japan," *Review of Reviews*, 68 (Oct. 1923), 373–382.

22. Tokyo *Nichi Nichi*, 10 Nov. 1923.

23. CAB, "Memorandum Relative to the Reconstruction of Tokyo," *Far Eastern
Review*, 21 (June, 1925), 252–256.

24. *New York Times*, 29 Nov. 1923, p. 35; *Tokyo, Capital of Japan—Reconstruction
Work* (Tokyo: Municipal Office, 1930), p. 42; CAB, "Goto and the Rebuilding of
Tokyo," pp. 14, 18.

25. CAB, "Goto and the Rebuilding of Tokyo," p. 21. In the rebuilding of Tokyo,
about 200,000 older buildings were removed and approximately a million persons were
relocated. Four hundred sixty miles of new, wider streets were built, four hundred
bridges constructed, and fifty-four parks newly laid out. See *The Reconstruction of Tokyo*
(Tokyo: Municipal Office, 1933), pp. 378–380, and *Tokyo and Yokohama Rebuilt* (Tokyo: Jiji Shimpo, 1930), p. ix—volumes brought to the author's attention by Miriam
Beard Vagts. After World War II, the Japanese again invited CAB to assist with
planning for reconstruction. See *Chicago Daily Tribune*, 2 Jun. 1948, p. 7.

26. CAB, "Municipal Research Abroad and at Home," *Journal of Social Forces*, 3
Mar. 1925), 495.

27. CAB to Albert Beveridge, 4 Apr. [1925]. Albert Beveridge Collection, Box
286, Library of Congress.

28. CAB and Mary R. Beard, "War with Japan: What Shall We Get Out of It?"
Nation, 120 (25 Mar. 1925), 311–312; CAB and Mary R. Beard, "The Issues of Pacific
Policy," *Survey*, 56 (1 May 1926), 189.

29. CAB to Merle Curti, 15 Apr. 1945; CAB to Merle Curti, n.d. Merle Curti
Papers, Wisconsin State Historical Society.

30. Edwin Sever and Robin McKown, Book-of-the-Month Club Book Information
Service, "Radio Script, No. 180," 11 Sept. 1944. Copy on Beard Microfilm.

9. History, Civilization, and Abundance

1. Mary R. Beard to Florence Kitchelt, 18 May [1929]. Florence Kitchelt Collection,
Elizabeth Schlesinger Library, Radcliffe College.

2. New Bedford, Mass., *Standard Times*, n.d., 1946. Clipping on Beard Microfilm,
No. 480, Part 2.

3. Author's interview with Miriam Beard Vagts, 16 Sept. 1976.

4. James T. Farrell, "An Interview with Dr. Charles A. Beard, '98," *Phi Gamma
Delta* (Nov. 1939), n.p. Copy on Beard Microfilm, No. 480.

5. Author's interview with Marine Leland, 14 Sept. 1976; Mary R. Beard to Elizabeth Gardiner Evans, 25 Jul. 1927. Elizabeth Gardiner Evans Collection, Elizabeth
Schlesinger Library, Radcliffe College. Ann Lane, in her biographical introduction to

Mary Ritter Beard: A Sourcebook (New York: Schocken, Books, 1977), p. 32, notes that Mary Beard "said many things during the course of her lifetime, but on close study, never directly."

6. CAB and Mary R. Beard, *The Rise of American Civilization* (New York: Macmillan, 1927), vol. I, p. 103.

7. CAB often referred to this maxim in reviews. See CAB, Review of *Great Britain and the American Civil War* by Ephraim D. Adams, *New Republic*, 44 (30 Sept. 1925), Part II, 6. In *The Rise of American Civilization*, vol. II, p. 658, CAB and Mary use the phrase to sum up their discussion of the making of the Treaty of Versailles. On the attitude of many intellectuals toward history in this period see Warren I. Susman, "History and the American Intellectual: Uses of a Usable Past," *American Quarterly*, 16 (Summer 1964), 243–263.

8. CAB, Review of *The Degradation of the Democratic Dogma* by Henry Adams, *New Republic*, 22 (31 Mar. 1920), 162–163.

9. James Harvey Robinson, *The Mind in the Making: The Relation of Intelligence to Social Reform* (New York: Harper, 1921), 53.

10. CAB and Mary R. Beard, "Introduction," in *The Rise of American Civilization*, revised one-vol. ed. with new material (New York: Macmillan, 1933), pp. vii–xv.

11. CAB, Review of *The Frontier in American History* by Frederick Jackson Turner, *New Republic*, 25 (16 Feb. 1921), 349–350. Turner wrote to his daughter that he had "enjoyed Beard's review . . . his reactions are interesting and have a real point to them. Only, as you hint, there is something besides the urban side of the case. But at present, (30 or so years after the 1st essay) the capital and labor side has an importance which I think emphasizes the importance of the *ending* of the frontier, while he thinks the movement was all along more important than the frontier. The truth is both are related." Cited in Ray Allen Billington, *The Genesis of the Frontier Thesis: A Study in Historical Creativity* (San Marino, Calif.: Huntington Library, 1971), pp. 271–272, n. 47.

Earlier, CAB had chided other established historians, Edward Channing and James Ford Rhodes, for neglecting to analyze the relationship between wealth and power in the politically active segment of American society. See CAB, "Classical History" (A Review of Channing's *History of the United States, 1789–1812*), *New Republic*, 11 (7 Jul. 1917), 282–283, and CAB, Review of James Ford Rhodes, *History of the United States, 1877–1896*, *New Republic*, 21 (17 Dec. 1919), 82–83. CAB was obviously influencing a generation of younger historians; yet among the ruling powers of the American Historical Association he felt himself an outsider. See *New Republic*, 29 (4 Jan. 1922), 160–161. On CAB's importance to enthusiastic younger teachers at Columbia even after his departure, see Roy F. Nichols, *A Historian's Progress* (New York: Knopf, 1968), pp. 47–49.

12. CAB, "History and History," *Nation*, 111 (13 Oct. 1920), 416–417; CAB, "History and an Antidote," *New Republic*, 44 (11 Nov. 1925), 310–311.

13. CAB, Review of *The American Revolution Considered As A Social Movement* by J. Franklin Jameson, *New Republic* 47 (11 Aug. 1926), 344.

14. J. Franklin Jameson, *The American Revolution Considered as a Social Movement* (Princeton, N.J.: Princeton Univ. Pr., 1926), p. 41. In his review CAB singled out this generalization for special commendation.

15. CAB and Mary R. Beard, *The Rise*, vol. II, p. 764. Carl Becker, a former student of Turner, had made the same point about abundance in an earlier book, *The United*

States: An Experiment in Democracy, a textbook CAB had reviewed enthusiastically in *Nation,* 111 (13 Oct. 1920), 416–417.

16. CAB and Mary R. Beard, *The Rise,* vol. II, pp. 798–799. David Noble has argued forcefully (but wrongly, I believe) in *Historians Against History: The Frontier Thesis and the National Convenant in American Historical Writing Since 1830* (Minneapolis: Univ. of Minnesota Pr., 1965), 118 passim, that CAB was nostalgic for an agrarian utopia of preindustrial years. On the contrary, if CAB had a utopian streak, it was his belief in the power of science and technology to effect social transformations desired by him. See Cushing Strout, "The Twentieth-Century Enlightenment," *American Political Science Review,* 49 (Jun. 1955), 321–339.

17. CAB and Mary R. Beard, *The Rise,* vol. II, pp. 729–730, 798–799, 743, 800.

18. Ibid., vol. I, pp. 130, 225.

19. Ibid., vol. I, pp. 631–632.

20. Ibid., vol. I, pp. 633–634.

21. Ibid.

22. Ibid., pp. 635–636.

23. Ibid., pp. 663–664.

24. Ibid.

25. Ibid., vol. III, pp. 146–147, 148.

26. Ibid., pp. 264–266.

27. Ibid., pp. 266.

28. Ibid., p. 577.

29. Ibid., p. 544.

30. Ibid., pp. 543, 555, 547.

31. Ibid., p. 544.

32. Robert Allen Skotheim, in "Environmental Interpretations of Ideas by Beard, Parrington, and Curti," *Pacific Historical Review,* 33 (Feb. 1964), 35–44, has pointed out that the Beards in *The Rise* (although his article treats *The Rise* as if it were written by CAB alone) tended to see those ideals they disliked as rationalizations of an all-powerful environment while they treated those ideas they favored, such as reformist thought of the late nineteenth century, as in themselves "causes" of historical events.

33. *The Rise,* vol. II, pp. 589, 591.

34. Ibid., p. 591.

35. Ibid., pp. 716–719.

36. Ibid., pp. 719, 720.

37. Ibid., pp. 746, 799.

38. Ibid., vol. I, p. 737.

39. Ibid., vol. II, pp. 710–712.

40. Ibid., p. 711.

41. CAB and Mary R. Beard, "Introduction," in *The Rise of American Civilization,* revised ed. (New York: Macmillan, 1933), pp. vii–xv.

42. Book-of-the-Month Club, Robert K. Haas. Columbia Univ. Oral History Collection. Figures on sales are in Beale, p. 311.

43. Lewis Mumford, "The New History," *New Republic,* 50 (11 May 1927), 338–339.

44. J. P. Bretz, Review of *The Rise of American Civilization, American Historical Review,* 33 (Oct. 1927), 140–142; Carl Becker, "Fresh Air in American History," *Nation,* 124 (18 May 1927), 561–562; Ralph H. Gabriel, Review of *The Rise of Amer-*

ican Civilization, Yale Review, 17 (Jan. 1928), 494–496. For a sharp comment on the Beards' critical vocabulary when they spoke of American writers and other artists, see Alyse Gregory, "Aesthetic Astigmatism," *Dial*, 83 (Oct. 1927), 350–351.

45. Richard Hofstadter, *The Progressive Historians* (New York: Knopf, 1968), p. 299. Surveying CAB's influence on textbooks in American history, Maurice Blinkoff, a graduate student at the Univ. of Buffalo, found in 1935 that the vast majority of college texts had incorporated or given space to CAB's views on the origins of the Constitution and had also adopted the interpretations of the Civil War advanced in *The Rise*. See Blinkoff, *The Influence of Charles A. Beard upon American Historiography* (Buffalo: Univ. of Buffalo Studies, Vol. XII, May 1936). Blinkoff noted, however, that Beardian interpretations were largely, almost entirely, ignored by the authors of texts for elementary and high school students.

46. CAB and Mary R. Beard, *The Rise*, vol. II, p. 787.

10. Public Life

1. CAB to Lindsay Rogers, 31 Oct. 1941, Columbia Univ. Special Manuscript Collections; Paul Goldberger, "Sale of a Regal Triplex Stirs Hotel des Artistes," *New York Times*, 26 Mar. 1974, p. 43; Miriam Beard Vagts to author, 8 Sept. 1976.

2. CAB and William C. Bagley, *A First Book in American History* (Macmillan, 1920; rev. ed., 1924), sold 351,751 copies; Beard and Bagley, *The History of the American People* (Macmillan, 1920; rev. ed., 1923; 2nd rev. ed., 1928) was adopted by all public high schools in California in 1920 and sold 437,865 copies; CAB and Mary R. Beard, *History of the United States* (Macmillan, 1921), sold 360,149 copies; CAB and James Harvey Robinson, *History of Europe in Our Own Times* (Ginn, 1921; rev. ed., 1927), sold 622,000 copies; CAB and Bagley, *Our Old World Background* (Macmillan, 1922; rev. ed., 1925), sold 305,834 copies. William C. Bagley was a member of Teachers College at Columbia Univ. See "Sales of Beard's Histories," in Howard K. Beale (ed.), *Beard*, pp. 310–312.

3. Matthew Josephson, *Infidel in the Temple: A Memoir of the Nineteen-Thirties* (New York: Knopf, 1967), p. 171.

4. Josephson, "The Hat on the Roll-top Desk—II," *New Yorker*, 17 (21 Feb. 1942), 22. This article and its predecessor in *New Yorker*, 17 (14 Feb. 1942), are a profile of Leon Fraser. On the social obligations of more fortunate members of society, see Mary R. Beard to Elizabeth Gardiner Evans, 25 Jul. 1927. Elizabeth Gardiner Evans Collection, Schlesinger Library, Radcliffe College.

5. CAB to Raymond Moley, 15 Jan., n.d. Raymond Moley Papers, Hoover Institute Archives, Standford Univ. This letter was filed with correspondence from 1918, but it cannot be dated 1918 because Beard gives his address as 27 West 67th Street, where he did not live until winter 1923.

6. CAB, "Time, Technology, and the Creative Spirit in Political Science," *American Political Science Review*, 21 (1927), pp. 6–7; CAB, Review of *American Political Ideas, 1865–1917* by Charles E. Merriam, *New Republic*, 25 (19 Feb. 1921), 235–236.

7. CAB, in *American Political Science Review*, 21 (Feb. 1927), 7–11.

8. CAB to Thomas Reed Powell, 21 Feb. 1931. Thomas Reed Powell Papers, Harvard Univ. Law School Archives.

9. Author's interview with Miriam Beard Vagts, 16 Sept. 1976; CAB to Lindsay Rodgers, 22 Dec. 1936. Lindsay Rogers Papers, Special Collections, Columbia Univ.; Mary R. Beard, *The Making of Charles A. Beard: An Interpretation* (New York: Exposition, 1955), pp. 30–31; Alfred Vagts to Cushing Strout, 31 Oct. 1958. Beard Microfilm, No. 179, DePauw Univ. Archives.

10. Mary Beard, *The Making*, 30.

11. George Radin, "Charles A. Beard's Mission to Yugoslavia (1927–1928)," in Mary Beard, *The Making*, pp. 80–81. Although Radin says that they were in Yugoslavia about six months, this is inaccurate. See CAB to Whitney Cross, 26 Apr. 1927. Whitney Cross Papers, Yale Univ. Archives. Copies of the latter correspondence were kindly presented to the author by Miriam Beard Vagts; CAB and George Radin, *The Balkan Pivot* (New York: Macmillan, 1929), p. 53. CAB, "Congress Under Fire," *Yale Review*, 22 (Autumn 1932), 38, contains an unflattering description of the "wind, indecision, trivialty, and incapacity for action" in the Yugoslavian parliament. With twenty-three changes of government between Dec. 1918 and Jul. 1928, the assembly had been unable to develop any cohesive program of legislation for the country.

12. Mary R. Beard, *The Making*, p. 29; CAB, "The Last Years of Stephen Raditch," *Current History*, 29 (Oct. 1928), 82; Beard and Radin, *Balkan Pivot*, 2, 8, 11, 93–94.

13. Ibid., pp. 153–155, 220–221.

14. Ibid., p. 249.

15. Ibid., p. 263.

16. Mary R. Beard, *The Making*, pp. 30–31.

17. For example, see CAB, "Democracy Holds Its Ground: A European Survey," *Harper's Magazine*, 157 (Nov. 1928), 680–691, and CAB, "Prospects for Peace," *Harper's Magazine*, 158 (Jan. 1929), 133–143, and Beard's introductions to two anthologies, *Whither Mankind* (New York: Longmans, Green, 1928) and *Toward Civilization* (New York: Longmans, Green, 1930), which he edited after his return from Europe.

18. CAB, "The Contrast Between Rural and Urban Economy," *University of Georgia Bulletin of the Institute of Public Affairs and International Relations*, 30 (Nov. 1929), 70–73.

19. Warren I. Cohen, *The American Revisionists: The Lessons of Intervention in World War I* (Chicago: Univ. of Chicago Pr., 1967), p. 126.

20. CAB, "The American Invasion of Europe," *Harper's Magazine*, 158 (Mar. 1929), 470–471, 475, and articles cited in notes 18 and 19.

21. CAB to Thomas Reed Powell, 21 Feb. 1931. Thomas Reed Powell Papers. CAB to Arthur M. Schlesinger, 15 Dec. 1928. Arthur M. Schlesinger Papers, Harvard Univ. Archives. Enclosed with this letter was a copy of a printed card sometimes used by CAB to decline appeals for his services: "Mr. Charles A. Beard begs to acknowledge the receipt of your communication of recent date and to say that he regrets his inability to accede to your request. He has been compelled by the pressure of work to discontinue service on committees, public speaking, and general lecturing. This seems to him to be the only way of avoiding unfair discrimination among many worthy causes, especially as every violation of the rule only brings an additional flood of requests. He regrets the

necessity of resorting to this rather formal mode of reply, but finds it the only alternative to spending two or three days every week declining additional engagements." A note on the copy reads: "Dear S. This I use on strangers!"

22. Matthew Josephson, *Infidel*, pp. 38-39. It should be noted that the Josephsons were rather casual acquaintances of the Beards, who were quite surprised to find *The Robber Barons* dedicated to them. See CAB to Oswald G. Villard, 24 May 1934. Oswald G. Villard Papers, Harvard Univ. Archives.

23. Robert Allen Skotheim, *American Intellectual Histories and Historians* (Princeton: Princeton Univ. Pr., 1966), pp. 102–103, argues that CAB's search for social values was a response to totalitarianism, while Robert Lang Davis, *The Search for Values: The American Liberal Climate of Opinion in the 1930's and the Totalitarian Crisis of the Coming of the Second World War as Seen in the Thought of Charles Beard and Archibald Macleish* (Ph.D. thesis, Claremont, 1970), p. 36, argues that CAB, responding to the depression in the 1930s, was "aging, adopting more conservative positions, moving away from economic determinism, searching for values, absolutes, a new morality to fill the gap left by an exclusive concentration on science."

24. CAB, *Government Research Past, Present and Future* (New York: Municipal Administration Service, 1926), 8.

25. CAB, "Conditions Favorable to Creative Work in Political Science," *American Political Science Review*, 24, Supplement (Feb. 1930), 29.

26. CAB, "Is Babbitt's Case Hopeless?," *Menorah Journal*, 14 (Jan. 1928), 24, 27–28.

27. CAB, "Recent Gains in Government," *World Tomorrow*, 10 (Nov. 1927), 441.

28. CAB and William Beard, *The American Leviathan* (New York: Macmillan, 1930), 10 passim. Compare, CAB, "Government by Technologists," *New Republic*, 63 (18 Jun. 1930), 115–120, which was incorporated in the first chapter of *The American Leviathan*; Norman Thomas, Review of *The American Leviathan*, *Columbia Law Review*, 31 (19 May 1931), 906.

29. CAB and William Beard, *American Leviathan*, 16–17.

30. *American Leviathan* p. 25. CAB published this chapter separately as "The Dear Old Constitution," *Harper's Magazine*, 160 (Feb. 1930), 281–291.

31. Felix Frankfurter, Review of *The American Leviathan*, *Harvard Law Review*, 44 (Feb. 1931), 661.

32. CAB and William Beard, *American Leviathan*, pp. 615, 640, 643.

33. CAB, "The Fiction of Majority Rule," *Atlantic Monthly*, 140 (Dec. 1927), 831–836; "The Dear Old Constitution," pp. 281–291; "The Myth of Rugged Individualism," *Harper's Magazine*, 164 (Dec. 1931), 13–22; "Teutonic Origins of Representative Government," 26 (Apr. 1932), 223–240.

34. CAB, *The American Party Battle* (New York: Workers Education Bureau, 1928), pp. 132–134.

35. CAB, "The President and Congress," *Outlook*, 152 (29 May 1929), 179.

36. A draft of this speech is in the Herbert Hoover Papers. Hoover Library, West Branch, Iowa. It was published as "Squirt-gun Politics" in *Harper's Magazine*, 161 (Jul. 1930), 148–151.

37. "Squirt-gun Politics," pp. 151–153; CAB, "Congress Under Fire," *Yale Review*, 22 (Autumn 1932), 35–51. Beard was one of many critics of Congress, few of whom, however, offered practical proposals as he did. See Jordan A. Schwarz, *The Interregnum*

of Despair (Urbana: Univ. of Illinois Pr., 1970), pp. 224–226, for a discussion of some critics of Congress in this period.

38. CAB, "Money in Federal Politics," *New Republic*, 63 (30 Jul. 1930), 305–307.

39. *New York Times*, 6 May 1931, p. 13; *Hearings Before a Select Committee on Senatorial Campaign Expenditures*, U.S. Senate, 72nd Cong.; 4, 5, and 7 May 1931, pp. 53–61. CAB was depressed by revelations of Gerald Nye's investigation—for example, the attempt to defeat Sen. George Norris by conservatives who had placed another George Norris on the same ticket in an effort to confuse voters in the Nebraska primary election of 1930. See CAB, "Conservativism Hits Bottom," *New Republic*, 68 (19 Aug. 1931), 7–11.

40. CAB, "Issues of Domestic Policy," Government Series Lecture No. 8, 24 May 1932, National Broadcasting Company (Chicago: Univ. of Chicago Pr., 1932), pp. 1–2. On the "purchasing power thesis," see Theodore Rosenof, *Dogma, Depression, and the New Deal: The Debate of Political Leaders over Economic Recovery* (Port Washington, N.Y.: Kennikat, 1975), pp. 39–43.

41. CAB, "Issues of Domestic Policy," p. 10.

11. The Great Depression

1. William A. Williams, "Charles Austin Beard: The Intellectual as Tory-Radical," in Williams (ed.), *History as a Way of Learning* (New York: Franklin Watts, 1974), pp. 229–242. Quotations are from pp. 238–239. The essay originally appeared in Harvey Goldberg (ed.), *American Radicals: Some Problems and Personalities* (New York: Monthly Review Pr., 1957).

2. CAB, "Rushlights in Darkness," *Scribner's* 90 (Dec. 1931), 571–578. "Science," Veblen had written in 1906, in an essay reprinted in *The Place of Science in Modern Civilization and Other Essays* (New York: Huebsch, 1919), p. 19, "creates nothing but theories. It knows nothing of policy or utility, of better or worse." CAB agreed with the technocrats that "the capitalist system does not keep our productive and distributive machine running at the highest level of capacity." However, he added, "How its economists can meet that challenge, I do not see." Technocracy was "a stimulating mode of thought," but he could "see no political possibilities in it." See "Twenty-Five on Technocracy," *Common Sense*, 1 (2 Feb. 1933), 8, CAB, "Introduction," to Graham A. Laing, *Towards Technocracy* (Los Angeles: Angelus Pr., 1933), and CAB, Review of *The Chart of Plenty* by Harold Loeb, *New Republic*, 82 (20 Mar. 1935), 164.

On the technocratic movement, see William E. Akin, *Technocracy and the American Dream: The Technocrat Movement, 1900–1941* (Berkely: Univ. of California Pr., 1977).

3. In his attitude toward those in power, CAB perhaps shared with Frederick Howe a difficulty in overcoming the effect of his early education. Howe wrote in *Confessions of a Reformer* (New York: Scribner Sons, 1925), p. 17, "It was with difficulty that realism got lodgment in my mind; early assumptions as to virtue and vice, goodness and evil remained in my mind long after I had tried to discard them. This is, I think, the most characteristic influence of my generation. It explains the nature of our reforms, the regulating legislation in morals and economics, our belief in men rather than institutions and our own messages to other peoples." This passage is cited by Warren

Susman in a provocative article, "The Persistance of American Reform," in Daniel Walden (ed.), *American Reform: The Ambiguous Legacy* (Yellow Springs, Ohio: Ampersand 1976), pp. 94–108, in which Susman suggests that many reformers in the twentieth century before and after World War I "wished to maintain the advantages achieved by the changing systems of economic, technological, and social life while at the same time, they hoped to retain the personal, moral, and social values of the world they knew—or thought they knew—from a previous order"; CAB, "Captains Uncourageous," *Virginia Quarterly Review*, 7 (Oct. 1931), 502. Proof to Beard that such "enlightened" capitalists existed was the operation of the Rocky Mountain Fuel Company under its president, Josephine Roche. See CAB, Review of *Miners and Management* by Mary Van Kleeck, *American Political Science Review*, 28 (Aug. 1934), 699–700.

4. Edmund Wilson, "What Do the Liberals Hope For?," *New Republic*, 69 (10 Feb. 1932), 345–348.

5. The general literature on planning and economic policy in the 1930s is extensive. Particularly useful in preparing this chapter were Otis L. Graham, Jr., "The Planning Ideal and American Reality: The 1930's," in Stanley Elkins and Erick McKitrick (eds.), *The Hofstadter Aegis: A Memorial* (New York: Knopf, 1974), pp. 274-299, the same author's *Toward a Planned Society: From Roosevelt to Nixon* (New York: Oxford Univ. Pr., 1976), David Garson, "Research on Policy Alternatives for America in the 1930's," *Political Inquiry*, 1 (1973), 50–77, James Gilbert, *Designing the Industrial State: The Intellectual Pursuit of Collectivism in America, 1880–1940* (Chicago: Quadrangle, 1972), esp. pp. 7–24, and Chapter II of Richard H. Pells' *Radical Visions and American Dreams: Culture and Social Thought in the Depression Years* (New York: Harper, 1973). Frank A. Warren, "Socialism in the 1930's: Towards a New Perspective," in Daniel Walden (ed.), *American Reform: The Ambiguous Legacy*, pp. 51–71, is thought-provoking, as is R. Alan Lawson, *The Failure of Independent Liberalism, 1930–1941* (New York: Capricorn Books, 1972.) The author is particularly indebted to Theodore Rosenof, *Dogma, Depression, and the New Deal: The Debate of Political Leaders over Economic Recovery* (Port Washington, N.Y.: Kennikat, 1975). L. P. Carpenter's biography of G. D. H. Cole (Cambridge: The Univ. Pr., 1973) afforded many insights into social planning from the perspective of a prominent British intellectual of the left whom CAB admired.

On CAB and planning, see George Soule, "Beard and the Concept of Planning," in Beale, pp. 61–74. Soule notes (p. 64) that *planning* was an "omnibus word" given a different content by various individuals but that "its functional meaning" to its advocates was "opposition to those who advocated letting economic forces take their course." In 1932, CAB published his own plan, cited below, along with a selection of others' proposals in *America Faces the Future* (New York: Macmillan).

6. All quotations are from CAB, "A 'Five-Year Plan' for America," *Forum*, 86 (Jul. 1931), 1–11.

7. CAB to Ralph Flanders, Jul. 4 [1931]. Ralph Flanders Papers, George Arents Research Library at Syracuse Univ. CAB was here paraphrasing John A. Hobson, who had written in *Wealth and Life: A Study in Values* (New York: Macmillan, 1929), p. 289: "No juggling with credit can cure the maladjustment which periodically chokes the channels of industry and stops production. This waste . . . arises directly from a failure of the economic system to put a sufficient proportion of the general income, or purchasing power, into the hands of those who would use it in demanding consumables,

and too large a proportion into the hands of those who, after supplying all their urgent or conventional needs, have a large margin for purchasing capital goods."

8. CAB to George Counts, 5 Aug. 1934. Copy furnished to the author by Miriam Beard Vagts. On CAB and the educational reform movements of the 1930s, see the excellent anthology edited by Raymond A. Ducharme, Jr., *Charles A. Beard and the Social Studies* (New York: Teachers College, Columbia Univ., 1969), Claude A. Bowers, *The Progressive Educator and the Depression* (New York: Random House, 1969), Gerald L. Gutek, *The Educational Theory of George Counts* (Columbus: Ohio State Univ., 1970), and CAB correspondence in the papers of Charles E. Merriam, Univ. of Chicago Archives, A. H. Krey, Univ. of Wisconsin Archives, and George Counts, in the possession of Miriam Vagts.

9. *Proceedings of a Conference of Progressives to Outline Program of Constructive Legislation* (Washington, D.C., 1931), p. 70; CAB, "Are Third Parties Futile?," *Today*, 3 (22 Dec. 1934), 6–7; 24.

10. To his former student, brain-truster Raymond Moley, CAB wrote on 31 Mar. 1933: "Mrs. Beard and I wish to express to you our great joy and satisfaction in the course thus far pursued by the Administration. To have enlightened and humane people in the White House is a privilege to be deeply appreciated." Raymond Moley Papers. Hoover Institution Archives, Standford Univ.

11. CAB and George H. E. Smith, *The Idea of National Interest: An Analytical Study in American Foreign Policy* (New York: Macmillan, 1934), pp. 400, 118–119. CAB's discussion of the federal bureaucracy was heavily influenced by Max Weber, particularly his argument that not only were the civil servants representatives of those they were supposed to regulate in the public interest but that they also constituted a powerful interest in themselves, an interest directed to maintaining their own institutional base of power. See the translation of Weber's chapters on bureaucracy in H. H. Gerth and C. Wright Milles, *From Max Weber: Essays in Sociology* (New York: Oxford Univ. Pr., 1958), pp. 196–244.

12. CAB and Smith, *The Idea of National Interest*, pp. 494–509, 513–518.

13. *The Idea of National Interest*, pp. 541–544.

14. CAB to George H. Smith, 4 Aug. 1933. George H. Smith Papers, Yale Univ. Library; CAB to George Counts, n.d., but probably early Aug. 1933. Copy furnished to author by Miriam Beard Vagts. In *The Idea of National Interest*, pp. 547–548, CAB and Smith did note that Roosevelt's policy of naval construction and the administration's assistance in the overthrow of the regime of Machado in Cuba were indications that "all phases of foreign policy were not assimilated to the implications of the National Recovery Program."

15. In 1921, the Department of Commerce had begun to calculate the balance of payments, and in 1930/1931 the Department published the first statistics of direct investment in foreign countries. CAB and Smith, *The Idea of National Interest*, pp. 196, 245–247, 261, 534.

16. CAB to George H. Smith, 25 Aug. 1933; CAB to George H. Smith, 2 Oct. 1933. George H. Smith Papers.

17. CAB to Franklin D. Roosevelt, 16 Dec. 1933. Franklin D. Roosevelt Papers, Roosevelt Presidential Library, Hyde Park, Presidential Person File, 2039. CAB felt comfortable enough with the President to write him a "thank you" note including an article critical of Hitler written by his daughter, Miriam, a comment on the intelligence of Mr. Saito, the new ambassador from Japan, and a report that he was forwarding to

the President a copy of *The Future Comes* (New York: Macmillan, 1933), an early and hopeful analysis of the New Deal by Smith and himself.

18. CAB, *Cross-Currents in Europe Today:* (Boston: Marshall Jones, 1922), pp. 267–268; CAB, *American Government and Politics* (New York: Macmillan, 1924), p. 351.

19. CAB and George H. Smith, *The Open Door at Home: A Trial Philosophy of National Interest* (New York: Macmillan, 1934), pp. 217–221, 232, 302. CAB had earlier suggested that "the feverish and irrational methods of unloading and dumping goods on foreign countries" might be minimized or possibly "discontinued entirely" and that the Webb–Pomerene Act of 1918, which had created syndicates for export exempt from the antitrust laws, could be extended to cover imports as well. A syndicate for foreign trade, a public corporation, would control the issue of foreign securities in the United States. See "A 'Five Year Plan' for America."

20. *The Open Door at Home*, pp. 137–183, 143–144, 146–148, 153. CAB reprinted this chapter in a book of essays, *Public Policy and the General Welfare* (New York: Farrar and Rinehart, 1941).

21. *Open Door*, p. 197.

22. Ibid., p. 309.

23. CAB, "The World As I Want It," *The Forum and Century*, 91 (Jun. 1934), 334; James Gilbert, *Designing the Industrial State: The Intellectual Pursuit of Collectivism in America, 1880–1940* (Chicago: Quadrangle, 1972), pp. 7–24.

24. CAB and George H. Smith, *The Old Deal and the New* (New York: Macmillan, 1940), pp. 240–243; CAB to George H. Smith, 8 Jan. 1935. George H. Smith Papers. The President's reading of *The Open Door at Home* was also mentioned by Samuel F. Bemis in his review in *American Historical Review*, 40 (Apr. 1935), 543. At this time Bemis was in agreement with CAB's views and reviewed the book enthusiastically. An annotated copy of *The Open Door at Home* is in the Roosevelt library.

25. Henry A. Wallace, "Beard: The Planner," *New Republic*, 81 (2 Jan. 1935), 225–227. Wallace had expressed similar concerns in a letter written when he first heard that CAB was going to do a study of the national interest. See Henry A. Wallace to CAB, 7 Apr. 1932. Henry A. Wallace Papers, Univ. of Iowa Microfilm, Reel 13, Frame 651. Despite their differences over policy, Wallace admired CAB greatly.

26. Theodore Rosenof, *Dogma, Depression, and the New Deal: The Debate of Political Leaders over Economic Recovery* (Port Washington, N.Y.: Kennikat, 1975), pp. 16 passim.

27. T. C. Cochran, Review of *The Open Door at Home*, *Modern Monthly*, 8 (Feb. 1935), 759–760.

28. CAB, "That Promise of American Life," *New Republic*, 81 (6 Feb. 1935), 352.

29. Transcripts of the complete passage can be found in Boris Nicolaievsky (ed.), "Toward a History of 'Communist League,' 1847–1852," *International Review of Socialist History*, 1 (1956), 249, and in Franz Mehring, *Karl Marx: The Story of His Life*, trans. by Edward Fitzgerald (Ann Arbor: Univ. of Michigan Pr., 1962), p. 206. However, since these translations differ slightly in wording from CAB's, it may be supposed that CAB was making his own translation from the German. He owned David Rjazanov (ed.), *Marx–Engels Gesamtausgabe* (Moscow: Marx-Engels Institute, 1927–1932) and was fond of citing chapter and verse. See his review of Mehring's biography of Marx in *Common Sense*, 5 (Jan. 1935), 25.

30. CAB and George H. Smith, *The Open Door at Home,* 103–104. Veblen had also noted that Marx had been vague about the nature of socialist society after the revolution. See his essays on Marx in *The Place of Science in Modern Civilization,* esp. p. 428, where CAB has followed his wording closely.

31. CAB, "That Promise of American Life," p. 352.

32. The genesis of *Create the Wealth* is revealed in CAB to W. W. Norton, 21 Feb. 1935 and 17 Mar. 1935, in which CAB included "a sketch" of the book and suggested to Norton that he send it to William "as a mere suggestive outline of a book that needs doing and inviting him to consider it. . . ." W. W. Norton Papers, Columbia University Special Manuscript Collections. William Beard undoubtedly wrote the book, but it certainly reflected ideas of which his father approved.

33. William Beard, *Create the Wealth* (New York: Norton, 1936), Chapter IX, "An Experimental Program for Creating Wealth," pp. 266–291. As a statistical basis for their argument the Beards used the famous 1935 Brookings Institute studies on America's capacity to produce and consume and also Harold Loeb's popular book, *Chart of Plenty* (1935).

34. *Create the Wealth,* p. 292.

35. Ibid., 302 passim, 280.

36. CAB and Mary R. Beard, *America in Midpassage,* (New York: Macmillan, 1939), vol. I, pp. 248, 250.

37. CAB, "Monopoly in Fact and Fiction," *Events,* 4 (Nov. 1938), 383–387. See also CAB, "The Anti-Trust Racket," *New Republic,* 96 (Sept. 1938), 182–184; CAB, "Realism About Money," *New Republic,* 99 (17 May 1939), 48–49; CAB, "The Next Step for Progressives," *The American Teacher,* 23 (May 1939), 27–28. The Industrial Expansion Bill was introduced in the House of Representatives by Voorhis, Allen, Maverick, and Amlie in June 1937 and again in June 1938. Speeches explaining the bill by Voorhis, Allen, and Amlie can be found in *Appendix to the Congressional Record,* vol. 81, part 10, pp. 1576–1578, 2465–2469, 2429–2434, and vol. 82, part 3, pp. 528–529. Ezekiel's ideas on planning were elaborated by him in two books, *$2500 a Year: From Scarcity to Abundance* (New York: Harcourt, Brace, 1936) and *Jobs for All Through Industrial Expansion* (New York: Knopf, 1939). See the discussion of the Industrial Expansion Proposal in Donald L. Miller, *The New American Radicalism: Alfred M. Bingham and Non-Marxian Insurgency in the New Deal Era* (Port Washington, N.Y.: Kennikat, 1979), pp. 137–141, and also Stuart Weiss, "Thomas Amlie and the New Deal," *Mid-America,* 59 (Jan. 1977), 19–38.

38. CAB, "Behind the New Deal," *Saturday Review of Literature,* 11 (22 Dec. 1934), 383.

39. CAB, "Statement," *Federal Licensing of Corporations: Hearings before a Subcommittee of the National Committee on the Judiciary on Senate Bill No. 10* (Washington, D.C.: Government Printing Office, 1937), Part I, pp. 70, 71, 74. See also CAB, "The Constitution and States Rights," *Virginia Quarterly Review,* 11 (Oct. 1935), 481–495, and CAB, "Forty-Eight Sovereigns," *Today,* 5 (11 Jan. 1936), 3–5.

40. CAB, "America Must Stay Big," *Today,* 4 (14 Sept. 1935), 3–4, 21; CAB, "The Anti-Trust Racket," 182–184.

41. Cordell Hull, "Trade, Prosperity and Peace," Radio Address of 6 Feb. 1938, reprinted in *Hearings before the Committee on Naval Affairs, House of Representatives, on House Resolution 9128 to Establish the Composition of the United States Navy, to*

Authorize the Construction of Certain Naval Vessels and for Other Purposes, 75th Cong. 3d sess., pp. 2102–2106.

42. CAB to George H. Smith, 31 Jan. 1937. George H. Smith Papers. *America in Midpassage* was going to be, he wrote, "a kind of memoir of the time from 2 old birds." CAB and Mary Ritter Beard, *America in Midpassage*, vol. I, p. 255.

43. CAB, "The World As I Want It," pp. 332–334. See also Archibald Macleish, "Preface to an American Manifesto," *The Forum and Century*, 91 (Apr. 1934), 195–198, in which Macleish had issued a challenge to intellectuals to "consider *without reference to* [their] *enemies* the kind of world they would like to bring about." (Italics in original.) The venture of the New Deal which probably came closest to CAB's ultimate vision of planning was the Tennessee Valley Authority, with its effort to develop a regional economy and its public power plants which competed with private utilities.

David E. Lilienthal had attended DePauw some years after CAB, and the two men maintained a cordial friendship after they met in the 1930s. CAB wrote an endorsement of Lilienthal's book, *T.V.A.: Democracy on the March* (New York: Harper, 1944), in which he referred to the Authority as "a great American experiment in the creative use of science and natural resources in the civilization of a vast region." CAB to David Lilienthal, 7 Jan. 1944. David E. Lilienthal Papers, Princeton Univ. Library. See also the Beards' discussion of TVA in *America in Midpassage*, vol. I, pp. 236–238, where they conclude: "In some respects the Tennessee Valley development stood alone. It had its own history. Doubtless it would have come in one form or another had there been no depression emergency."

44. CAB, Review of John Chamberlain, *The American Stakes, Common Sense*, 9 (May 1940), 25.

12. Science, Relativity, and Faith

1. S. E. Morison, "Did Roosevelt Start the War? History Through a Beard," *Atlantic*, 182 (Aug. 1948), 91–97; Chester M. Destler, "Some Observations on Contemporary Historical Theory," *American Historical Review*, 55 (Apr. 1950), 503–529; Whitaker T. Denninger, "The Skepticism and Historical Faith of Charles A. Beard," *Journal of the History of Ideas*, 15 (Oct. 1954), 573–588; Lloyd R. Sorenson, "Charles A. Beard and German Historiographical Thought," *Mississippi Valley Historical Review*, 42 (Sept. 1955), 274–287, and "Historical Currents in America," *American Quarterly*, 7 (Fall 1955), 234–246; Cushing Strout, *The Pragmatic Revolt in American History: Carl Becker and Charles Beard* (Ithaca: Cornell Univ., 1958), pp. 2–3; Richard Hofstadter, *The Progressive Historians* (New York: Vintage, 1970), p. 305. The term *gadfly* apparently originated with Denninger and was also used by Strout and Hofstadter.

2. Hofstadter, Progressive Historians, pp. 304–305.

3. CAB, Review of Maurice Mandelbaum, *The Problem of Historical Knowledge*, in *American Historical Review*, 44 (Apr. 1939), 371–372.

4. CAB, "A Historian's Quest for Light," *Proceedings of the Middle States Council for the Social Studies*, 29 (1931), 17.

5. John Higham, Leonard Krieger, and Felix Gilbert, *History* (Englewood Cliffs, N.J.: Prentice Hall, 1965), p. 120.

6. CAB, "Politics," in *Columbia University Lectures on Science, Philosophy and Art, 1907–1980* (New York: Columbia Univ. Pr., 1908), p. 8.

7. James Harvey Robinson, "History," in *Columbia University Lectures on Science, Philosophy and Art, 1907–1908* (New York: Columbia Univ. Pr., 1908), pp. 16–17, 26.

8. Raymond Moley, *27 Masters of Politics* (New York: Funk & Wagnalls, 1949), p. 15; M. M. Knight, "Introduction to the American Edition," in Henri See, *The Economic Interpretation of History* (New York: Adelphi, 1929), p. 18.

9. Benedetto Croce, *History: Its Theory and Practice*, tr. Douglas Ainslie (New York: Russell & Russell, 1960), p. 19; CAB, "A Plea for Greater Stress upon the Modern Period," *Middle States Council for the Social Studies* (Minutes of the 6th Annual Convention), 1908, p. 12.

10. E. W. Hobson, Chapter XIV, "Einstein's Theory of Relativity," *The Domain of Natural Science* (New York: Macmillan, 1923), pp. 316–343; Arthur S. Eddington, Chapter IX, "The Quantum Theory," *The Nature of the Physical World* (New York: Macmillan, 1929), pp. 179–229. CAB referred to both of these books on numerous occasions. Arthur I. Miller, "Visualization Lost and Regained: The Genesis of the Quantum Theory in the Period, 1913–27," in Judith Wechsler (ed.), *On Aesthetics in Science* (Cambridge, Mass.: MIT Pr., 1978), pp. 73–102, is fascinating intellectual history. The quotation from Heisenberg is on p. 92.

11. CAB, "Time, Technology and the Creative Spirit in Political Science," *American Political Science Review*, 21 (Feb. 1927), 6–7. Compare CAB's view of time with Hobson's (pp. 123–124). "Public time, that which we employ in social life, and in which from the point of view of Science physical processes are regarded as taking place, is a concept constructed by means of intersubjective intercourse."

Two useful articles are Edward Lurie, "Science in American Social Thought," *Journal of World History*, 8 (1964–65), 638–665, which traces developments in the nineteenth century, and especially Hugh J. Rodger's first-rate "Charles A. Beard, the 'New Physics,' and Historical Relativity," *Historian*, 30 (Aug. 1968), 545–560.

12. CAB, Review of Sidney Fay, *Origins of the Great War*, in *Books of The New York Herald Tribune*, 11 Nov. 1928, p. 1. The same year Bertrand Russell considered the implications of the New Physics for social thought in an article, "Science," which he contributed to *Whither Mankind?* (New York: Longmans, Green, 1928), an anthology edited by CAB.

13. Rogers cites numerous articles on relativity that appeared in both scholarly and popular journals during the 1920s.

14. William B. Munro, "Physics and Politics: An Old Analogy Revisited," *American Political Science Review*, 22 (Feb. 1928), 1–11.

15. Carl Stephenson, "Facts in History," *The Historical Outlook*, 19 (Nov. 1928), 313–317. Compare Joseph Wood Krutch, "A New Philosophy of History," *Nation*, 129 (16 Oct. 1929), 423–425.

16. Preserved Smith, "The Place of History Among the Sciences," *Essays in Intellectual History* (New York: Harper, 1929), pp. 209–218; Joseph Ward Swain, "History and the Science of Society," pp. 305–325. Compare Swain and Carl Becker, "Everyman His Own Historian," *American Historical Review*, 37 (Jan. 1932), 221–236.

17. Benedetto Croce, *History: Its Theory and Practice*.

18. For an argument that Croce's was a philosophy of complete immanence, see Maurice Mandelbaum, *The Problem of Historical Knowledge* (New York: Harper Torchbooks, 1967), pp. 39–57. Compare Benedetto Croce, *The Philosophy of the Practical* (New York: Longmans, Green, 1909). See also Edmund Jacobitti, *Revolutionary Humanism and Historicism in Modern Italy* (New Haven. Yale Univ. Pr., 1981). A perceptive contemporary criticism of Croce is found in Angelo Crespi, *Contemporary Thought of Italy* (New York: Knopf, 1926), pp. 67–148. Though CAB never cited this book in support of his differences with Croce, it is conceivable that he read it, since he owned the Library of Contemporary Thought, of which it was a part. Miriam Vagts to the author, 24 Mar. 1978.

19. Croce, *History*, pp. 32, 61–62, 72.

20. Ibid., pp. 101, 107.

21. Robert L. Schuyler, "Some Historical Idols," *Political Science Quarterly*, 47 (Mar. 1932), p. 3 passim. Compare Schuyler's earlier and more favorable article, in which he appeared impressed by the relativists' argument that henceforth historians must be skeptical of terms such as "fundamental cause," "Law and Accident in History," *Political Science Quarterly*, 45 (Jun. 1930), 273–278. Useful, though differing, accounts of Becker's relativism are found in Burleigh Taylor Wilkins' Chapter IX, "The Heavenly City and Historiography: A Nearly Absolute Relativism," in his *Carl Becker: An Intellectual Biography* (Ithaca: Cornell Univ. Pr., 1960), and in Charlotte Watkins Smith's Chapter III, "The Nature of Becker's Relativism," in her *Carl Becker* (Ithaca: Cornell Univ. Pr., 1956).

22. Conyers Read to Carl Becker, 12 May 1933. Papers of the American Historical Association, Box 456, Program Committee File, May–Jun. 1933. Library of Congress.

23. Croce's letter, declining the invitation to speak to the convention in 1933, was printed at the end of CAB's presidential address in *American Historical Review*, 39 (Jan. 1934), 229–230; Croce, *History*, pp. 12, 108–116.

24. CAB, "A Historian's Quest for Light," *Proceedings of the Middle States Council for the Social Studies*, 29 (1931), 13–14. Compare James Jeans, *The Mysterious Universe* (New York: Macmillan, 1930), pp. 140 passim; Eddington, "Quantum Theory," p. 338; Alfred North Whitehead, *Science and the Modern World* (New York: Macmillan, 1925), pp. 275–276.

25. CAB, "A Historian's Quest for Light," pp. 13–14, 15. CAB's terminology bears a marked resemblance to Whitehead, p. 121.

26. CAB, "Quest," pp. 15–17. Compare Croce, *History*, p. 14. In his own copy of Croce's book of essays, beside this passage on the relationship of history to life, CAB had written: "A long-winded way of saying what Goethe said 100 years ago." Miriam Vagts to the author, 25 Mar. 1978.

27. CAB, "Quest," p. 18; CAB, "Written History as An Act of Faith," *American Historical Review*, 39 (Jan. 1934), 219; Eddington, "Quantum Theory," p. 91.

28. Croce, *History*, p. 91.

29. CAB, "Quest," p. 19.

30. Whitehead, *Sciences*, pp. 128–129.

31. Whitehead, p. 27.

32. Malcolm Cowley and Bernard Smith (ed.), *Books That Changed Our Minds* (New York: Kelmscott Editions, 1938), p. 19. CAB also mentioned Brooks Adams' *The Law of Civilization and Decay*, probably because, even though it represented "the thought of the mechanical age of physical science," it was also an example of the sort

of theorizing, of the grabbing of history by the forelock, that CAB admired. See CAB, "Introduction," in Brooks Adams, *The Law of Civilization and Decay* (New York: Knopf, 1943), pp. lix–lxi. For an argument that Brooks Adams was a significant influence on CAB, see William A. Williams, "A Note on Charles Austin Beard's Search for a General Theory of Causation," *American Historical Review*, LXII (Oct. 1956), 59–80.

32. Valdimir G. Simkhovitch, "Approaches to History I," *Political Science Quarterly*, 44 (Dec. 1929), 482–484; the remainder of the series appeared in 45 (Dec. 1930), 481–526; 47 (Sept. 1932), 410–439; 48 (Mar. 1933), 23–61; and 49 (Mar. 1934), 44–83.

34. Charles W. Cole, "The Relativity of History," *Political Science Quarterly*, 48 (Jun. 1933), 162–163. Compare Eddington, *Science*, pp. 12–15, on "frames of space," and Karl Mannheim, *Ideology and Utopia: An Introduction to the Sociology of Knowledge* (New York: Harcourt, Brace, 1936), p. 77, on "frames of reference."

35. Cole, "Relativity," p. 170.

36. These themes are prominent in CAB, *Government Research* (New York: Municipal Administrative Service, 1926); CAB, "Conditions Favorable to Creative Work in Political Science," *American Political Science Review*, 24, Supplement (Feb. 1930), 25–32; CAB, "Political Science," in Wilson Gee (ed.), *Research in the Social Sciences* (New York: Macmillan, 1920), pp. 269–291.

37. Mannheim, *Ideology*, pp. 174, 237, 222.

38. CAB, "Written History as An Act of Faith," pp. 219–231, Mannheim, *Ideology*, p. 171. An excellent essay on this paradox is H. P. Rickman, "General Introduction," *Meaning In History: Wilhelm Dilthey's Thoughts on History and Society* (London: George Allen & Unwin, 1961), pp. 11–63.

39. This evocation of "historicism" is found in CAB and Alfred Vagts, "Currents of Thought in Historiography," *American Historical Review*, 42 (Apr. 1937), 462. Compare the similar definition in CAB, "That Noble Dream," p. 76.

Karl Heussi was not, as Lloyd R. Sorenson contended in "Charles A. Beard and German Historiographical Thought" (p. 277), "one of the first of the Germans whom [Beard] encountered." Before the Nazi period, CAB subscribed to a number of German scholarly periodicals; he reviewed many works of German scholarship while an editor of the *Political Science Quarterly* at Columbia; during the 1920s he demonstrated a thorough familiarity with the works of Oswald Spengler and with the controversy among German historians over the "war-guilt question"; he was a personal friend of the historian Kurt Riezler, whose "Idee und Interesse in der Politischen Geschichte," *Dioskuren* (Munich), III (1924), 1–13, he often cited in support of a dialectical approach to ideas and interests in history. Through his son-in-law, Alfred Vagts, Beard had met and conversed with a number of prominent German scholars during his visit to Germany in 1927. For a criticism of Max Weber's theory of the origins of capitalism in the Protestant Ethic, see CAB, "Individualism and Capitalism," in E. R. A. Seligman and Alvin Johnson (eds.), *Encyclopaedia of the Social Sciences* (New York: Macmillan, 1930), vol. I, pp. 148–149. CAB was one of very few American scholars invited to contribute to the journal of The Institute of Social Research after its members had left Frankfurt and established themselves at Columbia. See CAB, "The Social Sciences in the United States," *Zeitschrift für Sozialforschung*, IV (1935), 61–65, and Martin Jay, *The Dialectical Imagination: A History of the Frankfurt School and the Institute of Social Research* (Boston: Little, Brown, 1973), 114.

40. Carl Becker, "Everyman His Own Historian," p. 231.

41. CAB, ':Written History as an Act of Faith," pp. 220–221, 226–227.
42. Ibid., p. 227.
43. Ibid., p. 228.
44. Mannheim, *Ideology*, pp. 234–235.
45. CAB, "Act of Faith," p. 228.
46. CAB, "Historiography and the Constitution," in Conyers Read (ed.), *The Constitution Reconsidered* (New York: Columbia Univ. Pr., 1938), p. 161.
47. CAB, "Act of Faith," p. 223. Destler, "Some Observations," p. 508, n. 18.
48. Sorenson, "Historical Currents in America," p. 243; Eddington, "Quantum Theory," p. 294. Harry Marks has also argued that CAB was not a complete relativist. Compare his "Ground Under Our Feet: Beard's Relativism," *Journal of the History of Ideas*, 14 (Oct. 1953), 628–633. Although Marks does not discuss the sources of CAB's qualified relativism, his article is a sensitive reading of CAB and some of his critics. A well-argued restatement of the case for the relativity of all hypotheses, a case based on CAB's writings, is J. W. Meiland, "The Historical Relativism of Charles A. Beard," *History and Theory*, 12 (No. 4, 1973), 405–413.
49. C. H. McIlwain, "The Historian's Part in a Changing World," *American Historical Review*, 42 (Jan. 1937), 209–210. See also the critical remarks on CAB by Theodore C. Smith, "The Writing of American History in America, 1884 to 1934," *American Historical Review*, 40 (1935), 445–449, a speech delivered at the Convention of 1934.
50. Smith, "Writing of American History"; Allen Nevins, *The Gateway to History* (New York: Heath, 1938), pp. iii–iv, 43.
51. Nevins, *Gateway*, pp. iii–iv, 43.
52. CAB, "Noble Dream," 76.
53. CAB, "Another Battle of the Books," *Nation*, 147 (24 Sept. 1938), 300–302. CAB's reply to Nevins' remarks was combined with a generous review of *The Gateway to History*.
54. Michael Kammen (ed.), *What Is the Good of History? Selected Letters of Carl Becker, 1900–1945* (Ithaca: Cornell Univ. Pr., 1973), p. 261.
55. CAB, "Written History," 226; CAB, *The Discussion of Human Affairs* (New York: Macmillan, 1936), p. 124.
56. Maurice Mandelbaum, *The Problem of Historical Knowledge: An Answer to Relativism* (New York: Harper Torchbooks, 1967), 174.
57. Mandelbaum, pp. 78–180. Robert K. Merton had made the same criticism of Mannheim in "The Sociology of Knowledge," *Isis*, 27 (Nov. 1937), 493–503. Compare Ernest Nagel, "Some Issues in the Logic of Historical Analysis," *The Scientific Monthly*, 74 (Mar. 1952), 162–169.
58. Mandelbaum, *Problem*, pp. 198, 200, 201.
59. Mandelbaum, p. 201.
60. Mandelbaum, pp. 320–321.
61. CAB, Review of *The Problem of Historical Knowledge* by Maurice Mandelbaum, in *American Historical Review*, 44 (Apr. 1939), 571–572. See Mandelbaum's continuation of his argument, "Causal Analysis in History," *Journal of the History of Ideas*, 3 (Jan. 1942), 30–50. Arthur O. Lovejoy in "Present Standpoints and Past History," *Journal of Philosophy*, 36 (31 Aug. 1939), 477–489, disagreed with CAB and other relativists that their epistomological position represented "a true psychological gen-

eralization." History, he wrote, "demands an effort of self-transcedence." One had either to believe that the effort could be made or accept a "universal skepticism" destructive of all science and all exercise of intelligence. Two supporters of the relativist position among philosophers of history were John H. Randall, Jr., in "On Understanding the History of Philosophy," *Journal of Philosophy*, 36 (17 Aug. 1939), 460–474, and Sterling P. Lamprecht, "Historiography of Philosophy," *Journal of Philosophy*, 36 (17 Aug. 1939), 449–460. Both critics and supporters of the relativist position took CAB seriously and attacked or supported his philosophical position. No one of these contemporaries accused him of misrepresenting or misunderstanding the sources of his ideas.

In this chapter I have not attempted to treat the philosophical criticism of CAB's views made by Arthur C. Danto, since the linchpin of Danto's argument, his assertion that CAB was "a Baconian in the sense that he assumed, not merely that science can, but that science does get on without hypotheses," has been knocked out by an examination of the importance of the New Physics in CAB's reasoning about the structure of empirical knowledge. Danto was a philosopher writing without his historical spectacles. See his *Analytical Philosophy of History* (Cambridge: Cambridge Univ. Pr., 1965), esp. pp. 88–102.

62. CAB, "Grounds for a Reconsideration of Historiography," pp. 3–6.

63. CAB, "Reconsideration," pp. 7–10, 14; CAB, "Neglected Aspects of Political Science," *American Political Science Review*, 42 (Apr. 1948), 213. CAB apparently did not read Vaihinger until the 1940s, or at least did not cite his work until then. The only other citations of Vaihinger's *The Philosophy of 'As If,'* tr. by C. K. Odgen (New York: Harcourt, Brace, 1925), aside from the one in Bulletin 54, occurred in the above-cited article in 1948 and in *The Republic* (New York: Viking, 1943), p. 339. For an argument that Vaihinger was an important influence on CAB's views, see Gerald D. Nash, "Self-education in Historiography: The Case of Charles A. Beard," *Pacific Northwest Quarterly*, Vol. 52, (1961) 112–113.

64. See Richard J. Bernstein, *The Restructuring of Social and Political Theory* (Philadelphia: Univ. of Pennsylvania Pr., 1978) for an excellent discussion of the ongoing modern debate.

65. CAB, "Neglected Aspects," p. 213.

66. Eric F. Goldman, "Charles A. Beard: An Impression," in Beale, p. 7.

13. Battle for Nonintervention

1. CAB, "National Politics and War," *Scribner's Magazine*, 97 (Feb. 1935), 65–70.

2. CAB, *American Government and Politics*, 4th rev. ed. (New York: Macmillan Company, 1924), p. 351.

3. His review of Harry Elmer Barnes' *The Genesis of the World War* appeared in *Current History*, 24 (Aug. 1926), 730–735. He reviewed Sidney Fay's monumental *Origins of the World War* in *Books of the New York Herald Tribune*, 11 Nov. 1928, p. 1. Although he admired the way Barnes rode his "wild steed" of revisionist argument, CAB thought that he came too close to whitewashing the Kaiser, the war party, and the German superpatriots. See CAB to H. E. Barnes, n.d. [1926], Harry Elmer Barnes

Collection, Archive of Contemporary History, Univ. of Wyoming. As Warren Cohen has pointed out in his lucid and well-argued study, *The American Revisionists: The Lessons of Intervention in World War I* (Chicago: Univ. of Chicago Pr., 1967), Beard did not come to view American intervention in World War I as unnecessary until the mid-1930s, when he had already developed an analysis and a program for American foreign policy based on the *results* rather than on the *causes* of that conflict.

4. CAB and George H. Smith, *The Old Deal and the New* (New York: Macmillan, 1940), p. 230.

5. CAB, "Forward," in Alfred D. Rosenberg, *"Mythus" I. The Worship of Race* (London: Friends of Europe, 1936), Publication No. 46. Copy in Hoover Institute Archives; CAB, "Benjamin Franklin Forgery Exposed," (New York: League for Labor Palestine, 1935). This pamphlet reprinted an article that had appeared in *Menorah Journal.* See also CAB, "Spooks—Made in Germany," *New Republic,* 77 (6 Dec. 1933), 97–98; CAB, "Hitlerism and Our Liberties," Speech at the New School for Social Research, Tues. 10 Apr. 1934 (New York, 1934); CAB, "Germany Up to Her Old Tricks," *New Republic,* 80 (24 Oct. 1934), 299–300; and CAB "Education Under the Nazis," *Foreign Affairs,* 14 (Apr. 1936), 437–452. Manfred Jonas, "Pro-Axis Sentiment and American Isolationism," *Historian,* 29 (Feb. 1967), 221–237, is a useful general article.

6. CAB to William E. Dodd, 8 Feb. 1933, Box 9, Folder 2, Department of History Correspondence, Univ. of Chicago Archives; CAB to August Krey, 21 Nov. 1937, August Krey Papers, Univ. of Minnesota; CAB to Alvin Johnson, 14 Aug. 1940, Alvin Johnson Papers, Yale University Archives. Miriam Vagts to author, 8 Oct. 1976; Martin Jay, *The Dialectical Imagination: A History of the Frankfurt School and the Institute of Social Research, 1923–1950* (Boston: Little, Brown, 1973), p. 39.

7. *New York Times,* 20 Jul. 1936, p. 14. See also CAB's letter to Dodd while the latter was ambassador to Germany, urging Dodd to argue with German authorities for the release of Carl Mierendorff, a former Socialist member of the Reichstag, and enclosing a job offer from Dartmouth and a personal offer of financial assistance for Mierendorff: CAB to William E. Dodd, 13 Mar. 1934, William E. Dodd Papers, Box 43, Library of Congress.

8. CAB to Bernard Knollenberg, 24 Apr. 1941, Bernard Knollenberg Papers, Yale University Archives.

9. CAB to Douglas Jacobs, 15 Aug. 1938, Columbia Univ. Archives, Special Manuscript Collection, Spanish Refugee. See CAB to Bishop Francis J. McConnell, 1 Nov. 1938, in which CAB agreed to join in an appeal to the government to lift the embargo on Spain, in Columbia University Archives, and CAB "Will Roosevelt Keep Us Out of War?," *Events,* 2 (Jul. 1937), 1–6; CAB and Earl Browder, "Collective Security—A Debate," *New Republic,* 93 (2 Feb. 1938), 354–359; and CAB, *Giddy Minds and Foreign Quarrels: An Estimate of American Foreign Policy* (New York: Macmillan, 1939), 48–49, for expressions of disgust with the administration's Spanish policy.

10. CAB, "We're Blundering into War," *American Mercury,* 46 (Apr. 1939), 393, 399.

11. CAB et. al., "To Re-elect Senator Nye," *New Republic,* 96 (9 Oct. 1938), 310. See also Oswald G. Villard to CAB, 26 Apr. 1938, Villard Papers. Other members of the committee were William S. Abernathy, Alfred Bingham, Dorothy Detzer, John T. Flynn, Hubert Herring, John Hayes Holmes, Edwin Johnson, and Villard.

12. CAB, "'Collective Security' Begins at Home," in *War—What For* (New York: Keep America Out of War Committee, 1938), p. 3. Copy in Hoover Institute Collections. See also CAB's comment on the betrayal of Republican Spain by British and French "democracies" in "Cooperation—But Not for Foreign War," Keep America Out of War Committee, 1938. However, CAB's name was *not* among the sponsors of the National Anti-War Congress held in Washington, D.C., 28–30 May 1938. See Keep America Out of War Committee, Unlisted Materials, Hoover Institute Collections. On the divisions in the peace movement during the 1930s, see Charles Chatfield, "Alternative Antiwar Strategies of the Thirties," *Journal of American Studies*, 13 (Spring 1972), 81–93, and Justus D. Doenecke, "Non-interventionism of the Left: The Keep America Out of War Congress, 1938–41," *Journal of Contemporary History*, 12 (1977), 221–236.

13. *New York Times*, 9 Sept. 1940; Mary R. Beard to William Neumann, 4 Jun. 1950, in the possession of Mrs. William Neumann; CAB to Robert Douglas Stuart, Jr., 5 Aug. 1940, America First Committee Papers, Box 65, Hoover Institution Archives. Stuart, a student of law at Yale, was an early organizer of America First. For the recommendation of CAB's writings to America Firsters, see the bulletins from various chapters in America First Committee Papers, Box 293. A fine study of the "urbane and stophisticated" Northeastern wing of America First, which included many left-liberal and Socialist members and which was headed by John T. Flynn, is Michele Flynn Stenehjem, *An American First: John T. Flynn and the America First Committee* (New Rochelle, N.Y.: Arlington House, 1976).

14. CAB and Smith, *Old Deal and New*, pp. 247–249.

15. *Old Deal and New*, 251. Many writers, most recently and boldly Ronald Radosh, have noted that CAB's support of neutrality was directly related to his support of the New Deal's domestic programs and to his hopes that there would be a more thorough-going restructuring of the economic system. See Radosh, *Prophets on the Right: Profiles of Conservative Critics of American Globalism* (New York: Simon & Schuster, 1974), who admits, despite his title (p. 64–65), that CAB "cannot so easily be surrendered to the political right wing." See also Robert E. Osgood, *Ideals and Self-Interest in America's Foreign Relations* (Chicago: Univ. of Chicago Pr., 1953), pp. 371–372, who faults CAB for embracing "the comforting theory that domestic reform was a substitute for diplomacy," and who thus missed the connection CAB saw between methods of diplomacy—i.e.—neutrality, and reform of the economic system. The following writers have seen the connection: Fred Harvey Harrington, "Beard's Idea of National Interest and New Interpretations," *American Perspective*, 4 (Fall 1950), 335–345; Cohen, *Revisionists*, pp. 129 passim; Manfred Jonas, *Isolationism in America, 1935–1941* (Ithaca: Cornell Univ. Pr., 1966), p. 98; Bernard Borning, *The Political and Social Thought of Charles A. Beard* (Seattle: Univ. of Washington Pr., 1962), pp. 217 passim; and Thomas C. Kennedy, *Charles A. Beard and American Foreign Policy* (Gainesville: Univ. of Florida Pr., 1975), p. 163.

16. CAB, "Peace for America: The Devil Theory of History and War," *New Republic*, 86 (4 Mar. 1936), 102; CAB, *The Devil Theory of War: An Inquiry into the Nature of History and the Possibility of Keeping Out of War* (New York: Vanguard, 1936), Chapter II, "War Is Our Own Work." Beard's inspiration for this pamphlet came from a book he had inherited from his grandfather, Nathan Beard. It was Daniel Defoe's *History of the Devil*, and Beard thought of his own effort as similar to that of the eighteenth-century narrator, who had concluded: "Thus, good people, I have brought

the history of the Devil down to your own times. . . . If any cunninger men among you think they are able now to lay him again, and so dispose of him . . . that you shall not be troubled . . . go to work. . . . You know things future do not belong to an historian." Miriam Beard Vagts to author, 28 Apr. 1977.

17. *Devil Theory,* p. 103.

18. *Devil Theory,* p. 120; CAB, "In Time of Peace Prepare for Peace," *New Republic,* 86 (18 Mar. 1936), 158–159; Radosh, *Prophets,* pp. 26–30; Cohen, *Revisionists,* pp. 181–187. Neither Radosh nor Cohen agrees with Manfred Jonas (p. 153) and Kennedy (p. 83) that CAB's book, *The Devil Theory,* as Jonas put it, "had the effect of advertising, rather than refuting," the idea that wars are caused by the activities of sinister individuals.

19. CAB, "In Time of Peace Prepare for Peace," p. 159.

20. CAB, "We're Blundering Into War," pp. 393–394.

21. Cited in CAB, "Learning from Experience," unpublished MS in William E. Mosher Papers, Syracuse Univ. Archives.

22. "Learning from Experience."

23. CAB, "Roosevelt's Place in History," *Events,* 3 (Feb. 1938), 85–86. *Events* was a small magazine started in Jan. 1937 by Spencer Brodney, who hoped to finance the venture by subscriptions alone and thus to carry no advertising which might contaminate the reporting on public affairs. CAB donated his services and wrote some of his best brief pieces for this short-lived journal. See CAB to Edwin Borchard, 3 Mar. 1938, Borchard Papers, Yale Univ. Archives.

24. CAB to George H. Smith, 31 Jan. 1938. (Misdated in the Smith Papers.)

25. CAB and Earl Browder, "Debate," pp. 354–355, 356–359. CAB addressed Browder just as he would have spoken to any representative of internationalism. Anticommunism was not one of his interests. He regarded the Communists as belonging to another religion, one whose sectarian quarrels did not appeal to his independent, Quakerish mind. In 1937 he had refused an invitation to be a member of the independent commission of inquiry, headed by John Dewey, that went to Mexico to examine critically the verdict of the Moscow trials of 1936 that Leon Trotsky had betrayed the Revolution of 1917. CAB's refusal was not on political grounds but rather on the basis that the "confessions" heard in Moscow were not "positive proof" of Trotsky's guilt, since there was no corroborating evidence. Hence, applying the rules of American jurisprudence, Trotsky was innocent until other evidence was presented. Furthermore, Beard thought it impossible for Trotsky to prove that he had *not* been involved in a conspiracy. An exchange of letters on the hearing for Trotsky in Mexico City is found in Burleigh T. Wilkins and Harld Kirker, "Beard, Becker and the Trotsky Inquiry," *American Quarterly,* 13 (Winter 1961), 516–525.

CAB in the 1930s certainly regarded himself as to the left of the Communists. And, during 1938, Browder, in his campaign on behalf of the slogan of the Popular Front, "Communism Is Twentieth Century Americanism," supported this judgment and anticipated the historians of the 1950s who criticized CAB for writing history that reduced "the rich pattern and colors of social development to a uniform gray monotone of human greed, unprincipledness, and lust for power, an undifferentiated mass of depravity from which the intelligent student finally turned in revulsion to an all-embracing skepticism or nihilism. No progress at all was possible," Browder maintained, "until we broke out of this blind alley into which Beard had led progressive study of history in the United States." Earl Browder, "American Revolutionary Traditions," *Political Affairs*, 17 (Dec. 1938), 1079–1080.

26. CAB, "Statement," *Hearings before the Committee on Naval Affairs, House of Representatives, on House Resolution 9128*, 75th Cong., 3d sess., 2133–2136.

27. "Statement," pp. 2140–2141. The *New York Times*, 10 Feb. 1938, p. 1, reported CAB's off-the-record remark: "We are told that the Fascist goblins of Europe are about to take South America. . . . This is the new racket created to herd the American people into President Roosevelt's quarantine camp . . . if we had a navy twice as big as that proposed by President Roosevelt, it could not alone impose victory on Japan in Far Eastern waters."

28. Villard to CAB, 21 Feb. 1938; CAB to Villard, 22 Feb. 1938, Villard Papers, Harvard Univ. Archives.

29. CAB to Oswald G. Villard, 22 Feb. 1938; CAB to William E. Borah, 15 Feb. 1938; William E. Borah to CAB, 16 Feb. 1938; CAB to William E. Borah, 19 Feb. 1938, William E. Borah Papers, Box 417 and Box 420, Library of Congress. Borah was reluctant to promote such a committee in the Senate; the Beards were occupied in 1938 with the writing of *America in Midpassage*, and Beard was having severe problems with his eyes. See CAB to George Counts, 6 Mar. 1938, George Counts Papers, Southern Illinois Univ. at Carbondale, and CAB to George H. Smith, 31 Jan. 1938, Smith Papers.

30. CAB, *Giddy Minds and Foreign Quarrels: An Estimate of American Foreign Policy* (New York: Macmillan, 1939), pp. 7, 58.

31. Ibid., p. 29.

32. Ibid., pp. 33–42.

33. Ibid., pp. 46–49.

34. Ibid., pp. 54–64.

35. Ibid., pp. 78–87.

36. *New York Times*, 22 Oct. 1939, IV, p. 8.

37. Clarence Berdahl et. al., "Letter to the Editor," *New York Times*, 12 Nov. 1939, IV, pp. 8–9.

38. CAB, *A Foreign Policy for America* (New York: Knopf, 1940), pp. 27–28.

39. Raymond Leslie Buell, *Isolated America* (New York: Knopf, 1940), pp. 27–28, 229–238, 234, 235.

40. Ibid., p. 237.

41. Ibid.

42. Ibid., pp. 238–239.

43. Ibid., pp. 246, 240, 322, 452. "A moral concern," Buell urged, "is a national interest" (p. 325).

44. Ibid., p. 327.

45. Reinhold Niebhur, *Review of a Foreign Policy for America*, Nation, 150 (25 May 1940), 656–658; Allan Nevins, Review of *A Foreign Policy for America*, *New York Times*, 26 May 1940, VI, p. 1.

46. Buell, *Isolated America*, "Designs for A New World"; Lewis Mumford, *Men Must Act* (New York: Harcourt, Brace, 1939), pp. 64–69. For a similar argument see Albert Vinton, "Imperialism, Old and New," *Nation*, 152 (22 Mar. 1941), 345–348, and Max Lerner, "The War as Revolution II: The Attitude of the Intellectuals," *Nation*, 151 (3 Aug. 1940), 88–92.

47. Lerner, "War," p. 92. See Lerner's contribution, "The State in Wartime," in Willard Waller (ed.), *War in the Twentieth Century* (New York: Random House, 1940), pp. 409–428, and also Stanley High, "The Liberals' War," *Nation*, 152 (22 Mar. 1941), 619–693. A fascinating compendium of information on liberal opinion as expressed in *New Republic*, *Nation*, and *Common Sense* is James J. Martin, *American Liberalism and World Politics, 1931–1941: Liberalism's Press and Spokesmen on the Road Back to War between Mukden and Pearl Harbor* (New York: Devin-Adair, 1964).

48. In 1933, reviewing an anthology edited by CAB, *A Century of Progress*, Mumford had chastized CAB for espousing "the deadest of dead ideas," adding "we who have seen the recurrent poverty, misery and starvations that punctuate the advances of technology, we who have seen the immense irrationality and destruction of the World War, we who have seen barbarous, atavistic modes of feeling and expression rise again in Germany, technically the most advanced country in the world—we cannot comfort ourselves with a naive belief in progress." *New Republic*, 76 (6 Sept. 1933), 106–107.

49. Lewis Mumford, "The Corruption of Liberalism," *New Republic*, 102 (June 1940), 568–573. See Archibald MacLeish's less impassioned and more famous article, "The Irresponsibles," *Nation*, 150 (18 May 1940), 618–623. After the autumn of 1940, the writing of such prominent noninterventionist spokesmen as CAB, John Flynn, Stuart Chase, and Villard was unwelcome in the *Nation* and *New Republic*.

50. CAB, "Freedom in Political Thought," in Ruth Nanda Anshen (ed.), *Freedom: Its Meaning* (New York: Harcourt, Brace, 1940), p. 292.

51. CAB, "Letter to the Editor," *New York Times*, 13 Apr. 1940, p. 22.

52. CAB to Bernard Knollenberg, 4 Jun. 1940, Knollenberg Papers. See *Nation*, 152 (18 Jan. 1941), 74, on the harassment by the FBI of "isolationists without the faintest fifth-column sympathies." Whether or not the FBI had a file on the Beards is unknown at present. His family has applied to see potential files under the Freedom of Information Act, but the results of this inquiry are unknown to the author. For a well-researched discussion of Roosevelt's harassment of his critics, many of whom could not remotely be accused of constituting a "fifth column," see Richard W. Steele, "Franklin D. Roosevelt and His Foreign Policy Critics," *Political Science Quarterly*, 94 (Spring 1979), 15–32.

53. CAB to Merle Curti, 12 Jan. 1941, Curti Papers, Wisconsin State Historical Society; Arthur O. Lovejoy, "Letter to the Editor," *Baltimore Sun*, 7 Feb. 1941, p. 14.

54. CAB, "Letter to the Editor," *Baltimore Sun*, 12 Feb. 1941, p. 12; Arthur O. Lovejoy, "Reply to Beard," *Baltimore Sun*, 15 Feb. 1941, p. 12.

55. CAB to William E. Mosher, 3 Oct. 1941.

56. CAB to Mosher.

57. David E. Lilienthal, *The Journals of David E. Lilienthal* (New York: Harper, 1964), vol. I, p. 156.

58. CAB, "Statement," *Hearings Before the Committee on Foreign Relations, United States Senate, on S. 275, a Bill Further to Promote the Defense of the United States and for Other Purposes*, 77th Cong., 1st sess., 4 Feb. 1941, pp. 307–310.

59. Ibid., p. 312.

60. Ibid., p. 313.

61. CAB, "War with Japan," *Events*, 8 (Nov. 1940), 121–123. This article is dated 21 Oct. 1940.

62. Ibid.

14. "The Old Isolationist"

1. CAB, *The Republic: Conversations on Fundamentals* (New York: Viking, 1944), p. 302.

2. CAB to August Krey, 31 Mar. 1944. Krey Papers, Univ. of Minnesota Archives. In Jan. 1939 CAB had been elected to membership in the National Institue of Arts and Letters. In 1944 Columbia presented him an honorary doctorate of letters. After the war, in 1946, he was elected a member of the National Academy of Arts and Letters, and in 1948 he received the gold medal in history of the National Institute of Arts and Letters, an honor bestowed only once every ten years to an outstanding scholar.

3. Alfred Vagts to Cushing Strout, 31 Oct. 1958. Beard Microfilm, DePauw Univ. Archives.

4. CAB, *President Roosevelt and the Coming of the War, 1941: A Study of Appearances and Realities* (New Haven: Yale Univ. Pr., 1948), p. 4.

5. Robert Dallek, *Franklin Roosevelt and American Foreign Policy, 1932–1945* (New York: Oxford Univ. Pr., 1979), p. 289.

6. Warren F. Kimball, *The Most Unsordid Act: Lend-Lease, 1939–1941* (Baltimore: Johns Hopkins Pr., 1969), p. 235.

7. Ibid., p. 240.

8. Ibid., p. 238.

9. CAB, *Roosevelt*, p. 8.

10. Ibid.

11. Ibid., pp. 16–20.

12. CAB, "Introduction," in Franklin K. Watts (ed.), *Voices of History: Great Speeches and Papers of the Year 1941* (New York: Franklin Watts, 1942), p. x.

13. MRB to Folla La Follette, 4 Sept. 1941. La Follette Papers.

14. CAB and Mary R. Beard, *The American Spirit: A Study of the Idea of Civilization in the United States* (New York: Macmillan, 1942), pp. 580–581.

15. Ibid., esp. chap. 10, "World Mission Under Arms."

16. Ibid., p. 580.

17. Richard Hofstadter, Review of *The American Spirit*, *New Republic*, 108 (4 Jan. 1943), 27–28.

18. *American Spirit*, p. 475.

19. Ibid., pp. 440–441.

20. Ibid., p. 463. See also CAB to Sidney Hook, 27 Sept. 1940: "I have always had contempt for Communists and Communist tactics and certainly do not want to do anything that would lend my countenance to them." Copy furnished to the author by Miriam Beard Vagts.

21. *American Spirit*, p. 420; see CAB and Mary R. Beard, *America in Midpassage* (New York: Macmillan, 1939), vol. I, p. 255.

22. *America in Midpassage*, pp. 458, 49, 461, 464.

23. CAB to David Lilienthal, 12 Sept. 1941. David Lilienthal Papers, Princeton Univ. Library.

24. *American Spirit*, p. 457.

25. CAB to Merle Curti, 1 Feb. 1943. Curti Papers, Wisconsin Historical Society; CAB to Julian Boyd, 6 Feb. 1948, *Virginia Quarterly Review* Correspondence, Collection No. 5708, Alderman Library, Univ. of Virginia.

26. Quotations are from a draft of CAB's ms in Collection No. 1644, Univ. Virginia Archives. The speech was reprinted as "Thomas Jefferson: A Civilized Ma[n]" *Mississippi Valley Historical Review*, 30 (Sept. 1943), 159–170.

27. "Jefferson."

28. CAB to Merle Curti, 24 Dec. 1944. Curti Papers, Wisconsin Historical Socie[ty]. In a review of *The American Spirit* in *American Economic Review*, 33 (Sept. 1943), 64[?]–647, Dorfman had referred to the Beards as Hamiltonian proponents of a "natu[ral] artistocracy" to manage the masses and as advocates of a political economy similar [to] Adam Mueller and Metternicht. While denying that he was "hunting openings," C[AB] did confide to Sidney Hook that some magazines were not receptive to his work. C[AB] to Sidney Hook, 27 Sept. 1940. Copy furnished to the author by Miriam Beard Va[gts].

29. CAB to Merle Curti, 31 Jan. 1945.

30. Bruce Bliven, "The Hang-Back Boys," *New Republic*, 110 (6 Mar. 1944), 3[0]–307.

31. CAB to Mr. Halter, 9 May 1945. *Virginia Quarterly Review*, Miscellaneous Fi[les], Alderman Library, Univ. of Virginia.

32. CAB to Thomas Reed Powell, 14 May 1944. Thomas Reed Powell Pape[rs], Harvard School of Law.

33. CAB, *The Republic*, p. xi; Thomas Reed Powell, Review of *The Republic*, *Harv[ard] Law Review*, 57 (Apr. 1944), 579.

34. CAB, *The Republic*, pp. 11–12.

35. Ibid., pp. 15, 268.

36. Ibid., p. 24.

37. Ibid., chap. IV, "Washington and Jefferson Exemplify Constitutionalism," a[nd] Chapter V, "Lincoln Exemplifies Constitutionalism." See also CAB's address, "Tho[mas] as Jefferson: A Civilized Man," pp. 159–170.

38. CAB, *The Republic*, pp. 256–257, 258, 277–301, 272–273, 296.

39. Ibid., pp. 306, 309, 329, 337–338.

40. Ibid., pp. 339, 342, 343.

41. Sidney Hook, Review of *The Republic*, *Nation*, 157 (23 Oct. 1943), 474–4[?]. Max Lerner, Review of *The Republic*, *American Political Science Review*, 38 (Aug. 194[4], 781–784.

42. Bertrand Russell, *The Autobiography*, (New York: Bantam, 1968), vol. I, 281.

43. CAB, *The Republic*, pp. 42, 47–48, 83.

44. Ibid., pp. 103–104.

45. CAB to Thomas Reed Powell, 14 May 1944.

46. CAB to Lindsay Rodgers, 27 Aug. 1943 (?). Lindsay Rodgers Papers, Colum[bia] Univ. Archives.

47. CAB to Lindsay Rodgers, 21 Oct. 1943. Rodgers' review had appeared in S[at]urday Review of Literature, 26 (9 Oct. 1943), 5–6.

48. CAB to Oswald G. Villard, 25 Nov. 1943. Villard Papers, Harvard Uni[v.] Archives.

49. CAB to Merle Curti, 1 Feb. 1943. Curti Papers, Wisconsin Historical Societ[y].

50. CAB to Merle Curti, May [1944].

51. CAB to Merle Curti, 28 Sept. 1944. A publisher had earlier offered Bear[d] $5000 advance, which he had refused, to do a book on historiography. He said he w[as] "too tired." CAB to Merle Curti, 8 Nov. 1944.

52. CAB to Oswald G. Villard, 20 Oct. 1944.

53. The *Basic History* was the first part of a series of sixty-nine-cent paperbacks designed to reach a mass audience of "drugstore buyers." More expensive editions were to follow the first, including a Doubleday model with gold-edged pages reminiscent of the Bible. The Beards had volunteered to write a cheap edition for the New Home Library because the series had no American history. Many publishers wanted the original edition, but the Beards allowed Lewis Freeman to publish it first at sixty-nine cents. Chip Boutell, "Authors Are Like People," *New York Post*, 27 Jul. 1944, Clipping on Beard Microfilm. Comments denouncing the heresies of the last chapter appeared in Sterling North, Review of *A Basic History*, *New York Post*, 3 Aug. 1944; Adrienne Koch, *New York Times Book Review*, 6 Aug. 1944, p. 1; and Robert S. Fletcher, *American Historical Review*, 50 (Jan. 1945), 400.

54. CAB to Merle Curti, 28 Sept. 1944. Curti Papers.

55. Henry S. Canby, "History of Innuendo," *Saturday Review of Literature*, 27 (11 Nov. 1944), 12; Edmund Fuller, "Letter to Editor," *Saturday Review* (11 Nov. 1944), 13. See the less frenetic review by Dixon Wecter in the issue of 4 Nov. 1944, 7–8.

56. Lewis Mumford, "Letter to the Editor," *Saturday Review of Literature*, 27 (2 Dec. 1944), 27.

57. CAB to Oswald G. Villard, 31 Jan. 1945. Villard Papers.

58. CAB to Merle Curti, n.d., 1946. Curti Papers.

59. Eric F. Goldman, "A Historian at Seventy," *New Republic*, III (27 Nov. 1944), 496–497.

15. Lessons of Pearl Harbor

1. CAB to Lindsay Rodgers, 14 Mar. 1945. Rodgers Papers, Columbia Univ. Special Collections. See CAB to Edwin Borchard, 4 Mar. 1945. "Still weak. Longing for return to Hills!" Borchard Papers, Yale Univ. Archives.

2. CAB to Borchard, 6 Mar. 1945. Borchard Papers.

3. CAB to Borchard, 11 Mar. 1945. Borchard Papers.

4. CAB to Merle Curti, 12 Jun. 1945. Curti Papers, Wisconsin State Historical Society.

5. CAB, "Pearl Harbor: Challenge to the Republic," *Progressive*, 9 (3 Sept. 1945), 1–2.

6. CAB to Oswald G. Villard, 20 Oct. 1944. Villard Papers, Harvard Univ. Archives; CAB to Edwin Borchard, 6 Nov. 1944. Borchard Papers; CAB to George H. Smith, 19 Mar. 1946. Smith Papers, Yale Univ. Archives. On Pearl Harbor as a political issue in 1944, see Martin Melosi, "Political Tremors from a Military Disaster: 'Pearl Harbor' and the Election of 1944," *Diplomatic History*, 1 (Winter 1977), 83-95, and Melosi's book, *The Shadow of Pearl Harbor: Political Controversy over the Surprise Attack, 1941–1946* (College Station: Texas A & M Univ. Pr., 1977), pp. 71–88.

7. CAB, "Pearl Harbor," *Progressive*, 9 (3 Sept. 1945), 1–2.

8. Allan Nevins, Review of *Bases Overseas* by George Welles. *New York Times Book Review*, 16 Dec. 1944, p. 4.

9. Allan Nevins, "'A Challenge to Historic Truth,'" *New York Times*, 16 Dec. 1945, VI, 8.

10. "Challenge" Nevins and CAB, of course, disagreed on more than foreign policy. They had quarreled about relativism during the 1930s, and CAB had attacked Nevins' *John D. Rockefeller and the Heroic Age of American Enterprise* (1941) as a defense of Rockefeller's unscrupulous business practices. See CAB's review of the *Rockefeller* in *American Political Science Review*, 35 (Oct. 1941), 977–980. Noting that he had read "Nevins' diatribe" in the *New York Times*, Beard told George H. Smith that Nevins had "discredited himself in the historical profession by his book on Rockefeller." CAB to George H. Smith, 18 Dec. 1945. Smith Papers.

11. Robert P. Patterson to Troyer S. Anderson, 16 Dec. 1945. Patterson Papers, Library of Congress. I thank Barton Bernstein for bringing these letters to my attention.

12. Troyer S. Anderson to Robert Patterson, 17 Dec. 1945. Patterson Papers.

13. William L. Langer, *Our Vichy Gamble* (New York: Knopf, 1947), pp. vii–viii.

14. *Our Vichy Gamble*, pp. vii–viii.

15. CAB, "Who's to Write the History of the War?" *Saturday Evening Post*, 220 (4 Oct. 1947), 172.

16. The full text of CAB's letter and Benton's reply is printed in CAB, *President Roosevelt and the Coming of War, 1941* (New Haven: Yale Univ. Pr., 1948), pp 296–297.

17. CAB to F. W. Shipman, 11 Sept. 1946. Administrative Files, Franklin D Roosevelt Library; F. W. Shipman to CAB, 16 Sept. 1946.

18. CAB to George H. Smith. 5 Nov. 1946. Smith Papers.

19. CAB to Clarence B. Hewes, 7 Jan. 1947. Beard Papers in the possession of Miriam Beard Vagts; Clarence B. Hewes to Harry S. Truman, 9 Jan. 1947. Truman Papers, PPF, 1947, Truman Library.

20. Solon J. Buck to CAB, 21 Jan. 1947. Beard Papers.

21. U.S. Congress, Senate, *Hearings Before a Special Committee Investigating th National Defense Program*, 80th Cong., 1st sess., 1947, p. 24765.

22. CAB to Clarence B. Hewes, 7 Jan. 1947. Beard Papers.

23. U.S. Congress, *National Defense Hearings*, p. 24765.

24. *National Defense Hearings*, pp. 24766, 24767.

25. "Departmental Regulation," *State Department Bulletin*, 16 (25 May 1947) 1047–1049.

26. Thomas Kennedy, "Charles A. Beard and the 'Court Historians'," *Historian* 25 (Aug. 1963), 448, 449.

27. "Editorial," *Washington Post*, 10 Oct. 1947, p. 20; "Editorial," *Washington Post* 9 Nov. 1947, p. 4B; *Christian Science Monitor*, 30 Oct. 1947, n.p., clipping on Bear Microfilm.

28. William L. Langer, "Letter to the Editor," *Washington Post*, 9 Nov. 1947 p. 4B.

29. CAB to William E. Neumann, 5 Nov. 1947. Neumann Papers in the possessio of Doris Neumann.

30. G. Bernard Noble to William E. Neumann, 14 Nov. 1947. Copy in Bear Papers.

31. CAB to William Neumann, 22 Nov. 1949. Neumann Papers.

32. CAB to Merle Curti, 8 Nov. 1943. Curti Papers.

33. CAB, *The Economic Basis of Politics*, 3d ed. (New York: Knopf, 1945), p. 10

34. *Economic Basis*, p. 101.

35. *Economic Basis*, pp. 102–103, 107. See CAB's written statement against the draft in U.S. Congress, Senate, *Universal Military Training: Hearings before the Committee on Armed Services*, 80th Cong., 2d sess., 1948, pp. 1053–1057.

36. CAB, *Economic Basis*, p. 105.

37. CAB to Harry Elmer Barnes, 13 Dec. [1945]. Barnes Papers, Univ. of Wyoming Archive of Contemporary History; Edwin Borchard to CAB, 15 Oct. 1945. Borchard Papers; CAB to Edwin Borchard, 27 Oct. 1945. Borchard Papers.

38. CAB to Edwin Borchard, 18 Dec. 1945. Borchard, a professor of international law at Yale, was a close and trusted friend whom CAB had known since before World War I. Borchard had been the Law Librarian of Congress while CAB was researching his early books. During the 1930s their views of American foreign policy had coincided, and when CAB came to write his books on that foreign policy, he naturally turned to Borchard for aid and advice.

39. CAB, *American Foreign Policy in the Making, 1932–1940* (New York: Macmillan, 1946), pp. 1–6, 7–15.

40. Ibid., p. 25.

41. Ibid., quoted by Beard p. 29.

42. Ibid., pp. 34, 44–45.

43. Ibid., chap. 2, "Franklin Roosevelt Repudiates the League, 1932."

44. Ibid., p. 266.

45. CAB to George H. Smith, 19 Jul. 1945; George H. Smith to CAB, 27 Jan. 1946. Smith Papers.

46. CAB to George H. Smith, 2 Mar. 1946. Smith Papers.

47. CAB to George H. Smith, 12 Mar. 1946. Smith Papers.

48. CAB to George H. Smith. 3 Apr. 1946; Homer Ferguson to CAB, 9 Apr. 1946; George H. Smith to CAB, 19 Jun. 1946. Smith Papers.

49. George H. Smith to CAB, 8 Jul. 1946. Smith Papers.

50. CAB to George H. Smith. 10 Jul. 1946. Smith Papers.

51. CAB, *President Roosevelt and the Coming of War, 1941* (New Haven: Yale Univ. Pr., 1948), p. 362. Although he was critical of the majority's conclusions on many issues, CAB praised them for exonerating Kimmel and Short.

52. U.S. Congress, *Report of the Joint Committee on the Investigation of the Pearl Harbor Attack*, 79th Cong., 2d sess., 1946, pp. 493 passim. See also *New York Times*, 21 Jul. 1946, pp. 1, 12.

53. CAB, *President Roosevelt*, p. 364.

54. CAB to Henry Morgenstern, 7 May 1948. Morgenstern Papers, Univ. of Wyoming Archive of Contemporary History.

55. Richard Hofstadter, *The Progressive Historians* (New York: Vintage, 1970), p. 340.

56. CAB to George H. Smith, 3 Apr. 1946. Smith Papers.

57. CAB to Robert M. La Follette, Jr., 11 Jan. 1942. La Follette Family Papers, Series C, Box 19, Library of Congress.

58. CAB to Edwin Borchard, 25 Jun. 1945. Borchard Papers.

59. "John T. Flynn Charges Government Knew Jap Cabinet Intended to Break Relations," *Chicago Tribune* 2 Sept. 1945, p. 1. Beard may have seen the article in the *Congressional Record*, where it was reprinted in *Appendix to The Congressional Record*, Vol. 91, Pt. 12, 79th Cong., 1st sess., pp. A3850–A3855. In Apr. 1945, William

Neumann had published a phamplet for the Pacifist Research Bureau, *The Genesis of Pearl Harbor*, based upon *Foreign Relations of the United States, Japan: 1931–1941*, a volume of documents released by the State Department in 1943. Neumann criticized the State Department for being inflexible in negotiations with Japan over China. An excellent chapter on revisionist accounts of Pearl Harbor is found in Justus D. Doenecke, *Not to the Swift: The Old Isolationists in the Cold War Era* (Lewisburg, Pa.: Bucknell Univ. Pr., 1979), pp. 91–112.

60. CAB to Harry Elmer Barnes, 15 Sept. 1945. Barnes Papers.

61. CAB to George H. Smith, 27 Dec. 1945. Smith Papers.

62. CAB to Smith, 27 Dec. 1945.

63. CAB to Edwin Borchard, 7 Jan. 1946. Borchard Papers.

64. CAB to Borchard, 7 Jan. 1946.

65. George Morgenstern, *Pearl Harbor: The Story of the Secret War* (New York: Devin-Adair, 1947) p. 13.

66. Ibid., pp. 13–14, 168.

67. Ibid., p. 57.

68. Ibid., pp. 85, 283.

69. Ibid., p. 128.

70. Ibid., p. 271.

71. Ibid., p. 274.

72. Ibid., p. 327.

73. Ibid., p. 328.

74. CAB to Harry Elmer Barnes, 16 Jan. 1947. Barnes Papers. CAB thought Morgenstern had gone beyond the evidence, for, as he saw it, "There was only one Japanese message early in December which pointed to an attack on Pearl Harbor. . . . That was the 'one O'clock' message intercepted by our Navy about 4:50 a.m. Sunday Dec. 7—telling Nomura & Kurusa to deliver the final word to Hull at 1 p.m. that day. . . ." See CAB to Oswald G. Villard, 15 Apr. 1947, wherein Beard noted that, in his indictment of Roosevelt, Morgenstern did not distinguish between "things that were publicly known in 1941 and things that were brought out by the Congressional Committee on Pearl Harbor."

75. The characterization of Roosevelt's public behavior as "watchful indirection" is by Herbert Feis, "War Came at Pearl Harbor: Suspicions Considered," *Yale Review*, 45 (Spring 1956), 383.

76. CAB, *President Roosevelt*, pp. 210–211.

77. Ibid, p. 213.

78. Ibid., pp. 216–217.

79. Ibid., pp. 220, 432.

80. Morgenstern, *Pearl Harbor*, p. 104.

81. CAB, *President Roosevelt*, pp. 450–451.

82. Ibid., p. 486.

83. Among critics who raised this point was Samuel Eliot Morison in "History through a Beard," *By Land and by Sea: Essays and Addresses by Samuel Eliot Morison* (New York: Knopf, 1954), p. 342. An abbreviated version of this essay appeared in the *Atlantic Monthly* of Aug. 1948.

84. CAB, *President Roosevelt*, p. 506.

85. Ibid., p. 559.

86. Ibid., p. 565.

87. Ibid., p. 566. Italics added.

88. Morgenstern, *Pearl Harbor*, p. 327.

89. CAB, *President Roosevelt*, p. 566.

90. Ibid., p. 567.

91. Ibid., p. 573.

92. Arthur M. Schlesinger, Jr., Review of *American Foreign Policy in the Making, 1933–1940* by CAB, *Nation*, 163 (31 Aug. 1946), 244–245.

93. Samuel Flagg Bemis, "First Gun of a Revisionist Historiography for the Second World War," *Journal of Modern History*, 19 (Mar. 1947), 59.

94. CAB, *President Roosevelt*, pp. 575–576, 577.

95. Ibid., p. 578.

96. Ibid., p. 579.

97. Ibid., p. 580.

98. Ibid., pp. 582–583.

99. Ibid., p. 583.

100. A. A. Berle, Jr., Review of *American Foreign Policy in the Making, 1933–1940* by CAB, *Tomorrow* (Nov. 1946), 52–53.

101. CAB, *President Roosevelt*, p. 592.

102. Ibid., p. 595.

103. Ibid., p. 598.

104. Mary R. Beard to Merle Curti, 11 Nov. 1950. Curti Papers.

105. CAB to George Morgenstern, 6 Mar. 1948. Morgenstern Papers.

106. McGeorge Bundy, "Isolationists and Neutralists: A Sketch in Similarities," *Confluence*, 1 (Jun. 1952), 72.

107. S. F. Bemis, "The Shifting Strategy of American Defense and Diplomacy," *Virginia Quarterly Review*, 24 (Summer 1948), 334.

108. Gordon Craig, Review of *President Roosevelt and the Coming of War, 1941* by CAB, *Yale Review*, 37 (Jun. 1948), 763; Arthur M. Schlesinger, Jr., Review of *President Roosevelt*, *New York Times*, 11 Apr. 1948, VII, p. 4; Harry Gideonse, Review of *President Roosevelt*, *New Leader*, (12 Jun. 1948), 10.

109. Perry Miller, Review of *President Roosevelt and the Coming of War, 1941* by CAB, *Nation*, 166 (12 Jun. 1948), 665–666.

110. Blair Bolles, Review of *President Roosevelt*, *New Republic*, 119 (5 July 1948), 25–26; CAB to Harry Elmer Barnes, 9 Jul. 1948. Barnes Papers. "Bolles' escape," CAB remarked to Barnes, "is that I fail to obliterate the possibility that the United States would have fought in the war anyway, 'no matter who was President.'" However, he told Morgenstern, "Why have discussions of foreign policy if we are fated to get into war no matter who is President or what he does or says?" CAB to George Morgenstern, 9 Jul. 1948.

111. Richard Hofstadter, *Progressive Historians*, p. 340.

112. CAB to George Morgenstern, 12 Apr. 1948. See CAB to George Morgenstern, 15 and 30 Oct. 1947, in which CAB disagreed with parts of Morgenstern's *Pearl Harbor*; CAB to George Morgenstern, 3 May 1948, in which CAB praised a current editorial on fifty years of mistakes in foreign policy but recalled the *Tribune's* support of the war with Spain in 1898.

113. CAB to Oswald G. Villard, 13 Apr. 1948; CAB to George Morgenstern, 25 Apr. 1948. See the joyful letter to Bruce Barton, the advertising executive who was a neighbor of the Beards during the summers, describing the excitement of having so

many printings sold in one month. CAB to Bruce Barton, 24 Apr. 1948, Barton Papers, Wisconsin State Historical Society.

114. Richard Hofstadter, *Progressive Historians,* p. 342; CAB to George Morgenstern, 5 Jul. 1948. Morgenstern Papers.

115. Miriam Beard Vagts described her father's medical problems in an interview with the author, 16 Sept. 1976. CAB, "Neglected Aspects of Political Science," *American Political Science Review,* 42 (Apr. 1948), 224.

Selected Bibliography

Manuscripts

Alderman Library. University of Virginia. Charlottesville, Virginia.
Virginia Quarterly Review Correspondence.

Columbia University Archives. New York, New York.
Randolph S. Bourne Manuscripts
W. W. Norton Papers
Lindsay Rodgers papers
Edwin R. A. Seligman Papers
Spanish Refugee Collection
Frank Tannenbaum Papers

DePauw University Archives. Greencastle, Indiana.
Charles A. and Mary R. Beard Collection (Available on microfilm)

Doris Neumann. William Neumann Papers.

Elizabeth Schlesinger Library. Radcliffe College, Cambridge, Massachusetts.
Florence Ketchelt Collection
Elizabeth Gardiner Evans Collection

Franklin D. Roosevelt Library. Hyde Park, New York.
Administrative Files
Franklin D. Roosevelt Papers

George Arents Research Library. Syracuse University. Syracuse, New York.
Ralph Flanders Papers
William E. Mosher Papers

Harvard University Archives. Cambridge, Massachusetts.

Arthur M. Schlesinger Papers
Oswald G. Villard Papers
Miscellaneous Manuscripts Collection

Harvard University Law School Archives. Cambridge, Massachusetts.
Thomas Reed Powell Papers

Harry S. Trumen Library. Independence, Missouri.
Harry S. Truman Papers

Herbert Hoover Presidential Library. West Branch, Iowa.
Herbert Hoover Papers

Hoover Institute of War, Revolution and Peace. Stanford, California.
America First Collection
Keep America Out of War Committee, Unlisted Materials
Raymond Moley Papers

Library of Congress. Washington, D.C.
American Historical Association Papers
American Historical Review, Editorial Correspondence
James McKeen Cattell Papers
William E. Borah Papers
Albert Beveridge Papers
William E. Dodd Papers
Felix Frankfurter Papers
William J. Ghent Papers
LaFollette Family Papers
Robert P. Patterson Papers
Harlan F. Stone Papers
Carl Vrooman Papers
Henry A. Wallace Papers

Miriam Beard Vagts. Sherman, Connecticut.
Charles A. Beard Papers

Princeton University Archives. Princeton, New Jersey.
Rayond B. Fosdick Papers
David E. Lilienthal Papers

Sophia Smith Collection, Smith College. Northhampton, Massachusetts.
Mary Beard Papers

University of Chicago Archives. Chicago, Illinois.
Department of History Correspondence
Charles E. Merriam Papers

University of Minnesota Archives. Minneapolis, Minnesota.
A. H. Krey Papers

University of Wyoming Archive of Contemporary History. Laramie, Wyoming.
Harry Elmer Barnes Papers
George Morgenstern Papers
Seldon Rodman Papers

Vassar College Archives. Poughkeepsie, New York.

Lucy Salmon Papers

Wisconsin State Historical Society. Madison, Wisconsin.
  Merle Curti Papers
  Bruce Barton Papers

Yale University Archives. New Haven, Connecticut.
  Edwin Borchard Papers
  Whitney Cross Papers
  Alvin Johnson Papers
  Bernard Knollenberg Papers
  George H. Smith Papers
  Miscellaneous Collection

Newspapers and Periodicals

Baltimore Sun. February 1941.

Columbia University *Spectator*, 1917.

DePauw Palladium, 1897–1899.

The Mirage. DePauw University, 1899.

The New York Call, 1907–1908.

The New York Times, 1907–1908.

Ohio State Lantern, 29 October 1917.

Propaganda Analysis, 1937–1941.

The New Democracy, 1897.

Washington Post. October–November, 1947.

Miscellaneous

Author's interview with Miriam Beard Vagts. 16 September 1976.

Columbia University Oral History Collection.

Chronological List of the Writings of Charles A. Beard Cited

1900–1910

"Self-Education," *Young Oxford*, 1 (October 1899), 17–18.

"What Is Worth While in Education," *Young Oxford*, 1 (December 1899), 16.

"Co-operation and the New Century," *Young Oxford*, 2 (December 1900), 98.

The Industrial Revolution. London: George Allen & Unwin, 1902. First ed., 1900.

"Men Who Have Helped Us: William Cobbett," *Young Oxford*, 2 (February 1901), 171–174.

"Ruskin Hall and Temperance Reform," *Young Oxford*, 2 (March 1901), 221.

"Lessons from Science," *Young Oxford*, 2 (June 1901), 341.

"A Living Empire I," *Young Oxford*, 3 (October 1901), 24–25.

"A Living Empire II," *Young Oxford*, 3 (November 1901), 39–43.

"An Ideal Labour College," *Young Oxford*, 4 (December 1901), 79–81.

"Citizenship in the Twentieth Century," *Young Oxford*, 3 (April 1902), 243–246.

The Office of Justice of the Peace in England. New York: Columbia University Press, 1904.

Syllabus of a Course of Six Lectures on the Expansion of the United States. New York: Columbia University, Teachers College, 1904.

Review of *History of Liquor Licensing in England* by Beatrice and Sidney Webb, *Political Science Quarterly*, 19 (March 1904), 152–154.

Syllabus of a Course of Lectures on English History from the Accession of James I to the Present Time. New York: Columbia University, Teachers College, 1905.

An Introduction to the English Historians. New York: Macmillan, 1906.

"A Socialist History of France," *Political Science Quarterly*, 21 (March 1906), 111–120.

With James Harvey Robinson. *The Development of Modern Europe: An Introduction to the Study of Current History*. New York: Ginn, 1908. 2 vols.

"A Plea for Greater Stress upon the Modern Period," *Minutes of the 6th Annual Convention*, Middle States Council for the Social Studies (1908), 12–15.

"Politics," *Columbia University Lectures on Science, Philosophy, and Art, 1907–1908* (New York: Columbia University Press, 1908), 5–35.

Review of *Elements of Political Science* by Stephen Leacock, *Educational Review*, 35 (February 1908), 202.

Review of *The Spirit of American Government* by J. Allen Smith, *Political Science Quarterly*, 23 (March 1908), 136–137.

"Ballot's Burden," *Political Science Quarterly*, 22 (September 1909), 589–614.

Readings in American Government and Politics. New York: Macmillan, 1909.

American Government and Politics. New York: Macmillan, 1910 (4th ed., thoroughly revised, 1924).

"The Study and Teaching of Politics," *Columbia University Quarterly*, 12 (June 1910), 268–274.

1911–1912

Editor. *Loose Leaf Digest of Short Ballot Charters: A Documentary History of the Commission Form of Municipal Government*. New York: The Short Ballot Organization, 1911.

With C. R. Atkinson. "The Syndication of the Speakership," *Political Science Quarterly*, 26 (September 1911), 381–414.

American City Government. New York: Century, 1912.

Editor, with Birl E. Shultz. *Documents on the State Wide Initiative, Referendum and Recall.* New York: Macmillan, 1912.

The Supreme Court and the Constitution. New York: Macmillan, 1912.

"The Supreme Court: Usurper or Grantee?," *Political Science Quarterly*, 27 (March 1912), 1–35.

"Recent Activities of City Clubs," *National Municipal Review*, 1 (August 1912), 431–435.

Review of *Traité de droit constitutionnel* by Leon Duguit, *Political Science Quarterly*, 27 (September 1912), 518–519.

1913–1916

An Economic Interpretation of the Constitution of the United States. New York: Macmillan, 1913.

With Mary Ritter Beard. *American Citizenship.* New York: Macmillan, 1914.

Contemporary American History. New York: Macmillan, 1914.

"The Key to the Mexican Problem," *New Review*, 2 (June 1914), 321–324.

Review of *The New Freedom* by Woodrow Wilson, *Political Science Quarterly*, 29 (September 1914), 506–507.

"Woman Suffrage and Strategy," *New Republic*, 1 (12 December 1914), 22–23.

Economic Origins of Jeffersonian Democracy. New York: Macmillan, 1915.

"Internationalism in the United States," *New Review*, 3 (1915), 159–160.

"Section Four and Suffrage," *New Republic*, 1 (9 January 1915), 23.

"Reconstructing State Government," *New Republic*, Special Supplement, 4 (21 August 1915), 1–16.

"Historical Woman Suffrage," *New Republic*, 4 (9 October 1915), Part II, 1–3.

"The Budgetary Provisions of the New York Constitution," *Annals of the American Academy*, 62 (November 1915), 64–68.

"Jefferson and the New Freedom," *New Republic*, 1 (14 November 1915), 18–19.

"Methods of Training for Public Service," *School and Society*, 2 (25 December 1915), 904–911.

"Report of a Conference Held in Cincinnati, December 27, 1916," American Historical Association *Annual Report*, I (1916), 271–274.

"Training for Efficient Public Service," *Annals of the American Academy*, 64 (March 1916), 215–226.

"Politics and Education," *Teacher's College Record*, 17 (May 1916), 215–226.

Review of *The Need and Purpose of the Measurement of Social Phenomena* by A. L. Bowley, *National Municipal Review*, 5 (July 1916), 518.

1917–1919

"What a Budget Should Be," *New Republic*, 10 (17 February 1917), 66–67.

Review of *Political Parties* by Robert Michels, *Political Science Quarterly*, 32 (March 1917), 153–155.

"Statement," U.S. Congress. Senate. *Hearings on Production and Conservation of Food Supplies before the Committee on Agriculture and Forestry.* 65th Congress, 1st Sess., 507 (10 May 1917).

"The Perils of Diplomacy: A Communication," *New Republic*, 11 (2 June 1917), 136–138.

"Classical History," *New Republic*, 11 (7 July 1917), 282–283.

"Professor Beard's Letter of Resignation from Columbia University," *School and Society*, 6 (13 October 1917), 446–447.

"Political Science in the Crucible," *New Republic*, 13 (17 November 1917), 3–4.

"A Statement," *New Republic*, 13 (29 December 1917), 249–251.

With William C. Bagley. *The History of the American People*, Special Edition for Army Educational Commission, AEF. New York: Macmillan, 1918.

"Human Nature and Administration," *Nation*, 106 (25 April 1918), 502–504.

"The End of the War," *New Republic*, 15 (6 July 1918), 297, 299.

"A Call Upon Every Citizen," *Harper's Magazine*, 137 (October 1918), 655–656.

"English Liberty," *New Republic*, 16 (19 October 1918), 350–351.

The Advancement of Municipal Science. New York: Bureau of Municipal Research, 1919.

"The Evolution of Democracy," in F. A. Cleveland and Joseph Schafer (eds.), *Democracy in Reconstruction* (Boston: Houghton Mifflin, 1919), 486–491.

With Robert Moses, et. al. *Report of the Reconstruction Commission to Governor Alfred E. Smith on Retrenchment and Reorganization in the State Government, 10 October 1919.* Albany: J. B. Lyon, 1919.

"The Supreme Issue," *New Republic*, 17 (18 January 1919), 343.

"Propanganda in the Schools," *The Dial*, 66 (14 June 1919), 598–599.

[Pseud. J. W. Bradford]. "Could Daniel Webster Teach in New York's Schools?," *Nation*, 109 (2 August 1919), 147.

With David Zuckerman. "Bringing the Budget Home to Everybody," *New York Times*, 12 October 1919, IV, p. 1.

Review of *History of the United States, 1877–1896* by James Ford Rhodes, *New Republic*, 21 (17 December 1919), 82–83.

1920–1922

With William C. Bagley. *A First Book in American History.* New York: Macmillan, 1920 (Rev. ed., 1924).

Review of *The Degradation of the Democratic Dogma* by Henry Adams, *New Republic*, 22 (21 March 1920), 162–163.

"History and History," *Nation*, 111 (13 October 1920), 416–417.

Review of *Political Thought in England from Locke to Bentham* by Harold Laski, *New Republic*, 24 (17 November 1920), 303–304.

With others. "Final Report of a Committee on a University Center for Research in Washington," American Historical Association *Annual Report*, I (1921), 72–82.

With Mary Ritter Beard. *History of the United States*. New York: Macmillan, 1921.

Review of *The Frontier in American History* by Frederick Jackson Turner, *New Republic*, 25 (16 February 1921), 349–350.

Review of *American Political Ideas, 1865–1917* by Charles E. Merriam, *New Republic*, 25 (19 February 1921), 235–236.

"Letter to the Editor," *The Freeman*, 3 (20 July 1921), 450–451.

"Go Easy on the Professors," *New Republic*, 27 (17 August 1921), 328.

"On the Advantages of Censorship and Espionage," *New Republic*, 27 (24 August 1921), 350–351.

Review of *Workers Education in the United States*, *New Republic*, 28 (9 November 1921), 328.

Crosscurrents in Europe Today. Boston: Marshall Jones, 1922.

The Economic Basis of Politics. New York: Knopf, 1922 (Rev. ed. 1945).

With William C. Bagley. *Our Old World Background*. New York: Macmillan, 1922 (Rev. ed., 1925).

Review of *History of the United States, 1815–1846* by Edward Channing, *New Republic*, 29 (4 January 1922), 160–161.

"The Potency of Labor Education," *American Federationist*, 29 (July 1922), 500–502.

1923–1926

Administration and Politics of Tokyo. New York: Macmillan, 1923.

"Letter to Mayor Goto," *Japan Times & Mail*, 19 March 1923, p. 1.

"For a Greater Tokyo," *Far Eastern Review*, 19 (April 1923), 263–266, 277.

"Japan's Statesman of Research," *Review of Reviews*, 68 (September 1923), 296–298.

"Municipal Research in Japan: A Report to American Research Workers," *National Municipal Review*, 12 (September 1923), 520–523.

"Rebuilding in Japan," *Review of Reviews*, 68 (October 1923), 373–382.

"Goto and the Rebuilding of Tokyo," *Our World*, 5 (April 1924), 11–21.

"The Awakening of Japanese Cities," *Review of Reviews*, 69 (May 1924), 523–527.

"American Influence on Municipal Government in the Orient," *National Municipal Review*, 14 (January 1925), 7–11.

"A World Bureau of Municipal Research: Being Considered by the League of Nations," *National Municipal Review*, 14 (January 1925), 1–2.

"Municipal Research Abroad and at Home," *Journal of Social Forces*, 3 (March 1925), 495–497.

With Mary Ritter Beard. "War with Japan: What Shall We Get Out of It?," *Nation*, 120 (25 March 1925), 311–312.

"Memorandum Relative to the Reconstruction of Tokyo," *Far Eastern Review*, 21 (June 1925), 252–256.

Review of *Great Britain and the American Civil War* by Ephraim D. Adams, *New Republic*, 44 (30 September 1925), Part II, 6.

"History and an Antidote," *New Republic*, 44 (11 November 1925), 310–311.

Government Research Past, Present and Future. New York: Municipal Administration Service, 1926.

With Mary Ritter Beard. "The Issues of Pacific Policy," *Survey*, 56 (1 May 1926), 189.

Review of *The American Revolution Considered as a Social Movement* by J. Franklin Jameson, *New Republic*, 47 (11 August 1926), 344.

1927

With Mary Ritter Beard. *The Rise of American Civilization.* New York: Macmillan, 1927. 2 vols.

With James Harvey Robinson. *History of Europe: Our Own Times.* Boston: Ginn, 1921 (Rev. ed., 1927).

"Time, Technology, and the Creative Spirit in Political Science," *American Political Science Review*, 21 (February 1927), 1–11.

With Mary Ritter Beard. "Ten Years Back: The American People and the War," *Survey*, 58 (1 April 1927), 59–61.

Review of *Main Currents of American Thought* by Vernon L. Parrington, *Nation*, 124 (18 May 1927), 560–562.

"Agriculture and the Nation's Economy," *Nation*, 125 (17 August 1927), 150–151.

"Conflicts in City Planning," *Yale Review*, 17 (October 1927), 65–77.

"Recent Gains in Government," *World Tomorrow*, 10 (November 1927), 438–442.

"The Fiction of Majority Rule," *Atlantic Monthly*, 140 (December 1927), 831–836.

1928–1929

The American Party Battle. New York: Workers Education Bureau, 1928.

Editor. *Whither Mankind.* New York: Longmans, Green, 1928.

With William C. Bagley. *The History of the American People.* New York: Macmillan, 1920 (Rev. ed., 1923; 2nd rev. ed., 1928).

"Is Babbitt's Case Hopeless?," *Menorah Journal*, 14 (January 1928), 21–28.

"The Last Years of Stephen Raditch," *Current History*, 29 (October 1928), 82–84.

"Democracy Holds Its Ground: A European Survey," *Harper's Magazine*, 157 (November 1928), 680–691.

Review of *Origins of the Great War* by Sidney Fay, *Books of The New York Herald Tribune*, 11 November 1928, p. 1.

"The City's Place in Civilization," *National Municipal Review*, 17 (December 1928), 726–731.

"Political Science," in Wilson Gee (ed.), *Research in the Social Sciences* (New York: Macmillan, 1929), 269–291.

With George Radin. *The Balkan Pivot*. New York: Macmillan, 1929.

"Prospects for Peace," *Harper's Magazine*, 158 (January 1929), 133–143.

"The American Invasion of Europe," *Harper's Magazine*, 158 (March 1929), 470–479.

"The President and Congress," *Outlook*, 152 (29 May 1929), 179.

"The Contrast Between Rural and Urban Economy," *University of Georgia Bulletin of the Institute of Public affairs*, 30 (November 1929), 79–88.

1930–1931

Editor. *Toward Civilization*. New York: Longmans, Green, 1930.

"Individualism and Capitalism," in E. R. A. Seligman and Alvin Johnson (eds.), *Encyclopaedia of the Social Sciences*, (New York: Macmillan, 1930) I, 145–163.

With William Beard. *The American Leviathan*. New York: Macmillan, 1930.

"Conditions Favorable to Creative Work in Political Science," *American Political Science Review*, 24, Supplement (February 1930), 25–32.

"The Dear Old Constitution," *Harper's Magazine*, 160 (February 1930), 281–291.

"Government by Technologists," *New Republic*, 63 (18 June 1930), 115–120.

"Money in Federal Politics," *New Republic*, 63 (30 July 1930), 305–307.

"Squirt-gun Politics," *Harper's Magazine*, 161 (July 1930), 148–151.

"A Historian's Quest for Light," Proceedings of the Middle States Council for the Social Studies, 29 (1931), 12–21.

"Statement," U.S. Congress. Senate. *Hearings Before a Select Committee on Senatorial Campaign Expenditures*. 72nd Congress, 1st Sess., 4, 5, and 7 May 1931, 53–61.

"A 'Five-Year Plan' for America," *Forum*, 86 (July 1931), 1–11.

"Conservativism Hits Bottom," *New Republic*, 68 (19 August 1931), 7–11.

"Captains Uncourageous," *Virginia Quarterly Review*, 7 (October 1931), 500–506.

"Rushlights in Darkness," *Scribner's*, 90 (December 1931), 571–578.

"The Myth of Rugged Individualism," *Harper's Magazine*, 164 (December 1931), 13–22.

1932–1934

A Charter for the Social Sciences in the Schools. New York: Scribner, Sons, 1932.

Editor. *America Faces the Future*. New York: Macmillan, 1932.

"Introduction," in J. B. Bury, *The Idea of Progress* (New York: Macmillan, 1932; original Ed., 1920), ix–xl.

The Navy: Defense or Portent? New York: Harper, 1932.

"A Search for the Center," *Scribner's*, 91 (January 1932), 2–7.

"Teutonic Origins of Representative Government," *American Political Science Review*, 26 (April 1932), 223–240.

"Issues of Domestic Policy," Government Series Lecture No. 8, 24 May 1932, National Broadcasting Company. Chicago: University of Chicago Press, 1932.

"Congress Under Fire," *Yale Review*, 22 (Autumn 1932), 35–51.

Editor. *A Century of Progress.* New York: Harper, 1933.

"Introduction," in Graham A. Laing, *Towards Technocracy* (Los Angeles: Angelus Press, 1933).

With Mary Ritter Beard. *The Rise of American Civilization*, revised one-volume edition with new material. New York: Macmillan, 1933.

With George H. E. Smith. *The Future Comes.* New York: Macmillan, 1933.

With others. "Twenty-Five on Technocracy," *Common Sense*, 1 (2 February 1933), 8–10.

Review of *The Heavenly City of the Eighteenth-Century Philosophers* by Carl Becker, *American Historical Review*, 38 (April 1933), 590–591.

The Nature of the Social Sciences. New York: Scribner, Sons, 1934.

With George H. E. Smith. *The Ideal of National Interest: An Analytical Study of American Foreign Policy.* New York: Macmillan, 1934.

With George H. E. Smith. *The Open Door at Home: A Trial Philosophy of National Interest.* New York: Macmillan, 1934.

"Written History as an Act of Faith," *American Historical Review*, 39 (January 1934), 219–231.

"The World as I Want It," *Forum and Century*, 91 (June 1934), 332–334.

Review of *Miners and Management* by Mary Van Kleeck, *American Political Science Review*, 28 (August 1934), 699–700.

"Behind the New Deal," *Saturday Review of Literature*, 11 (22 December 1934), 381–383.

1935–1936

"Benjamin Franklin Forgery Exposed." New York: League for Labor Palestine, 1935.

"The Social Sciences in the United States," *Zeitschrift für Sozialforschung*, IV (1935), 61–65.

"That Promise of American Life," *New Republic*, 81 (6 February 1935), 350–352.

Review of *The Chart of Plenty* by Harold Loeb, *New Republic*, 82 (20 March 1935), 164.

"Supplemental Statement on Behalf of Independent Bondholders Committee," *Congressional Record*, 79, Pt. 6 (29 April 1935), 6513–6519.

"America Must Stay Big," *Today*, 4 (14 September 1935), 3–4, 21.

"The Constitution and States Rights," *Virginia Quarterly Review*, 11 (October 1935), 481–495.

"That Noble Dream," *American Historical Review*, 41 (October 1935), 74–87.

"Forward," in Alfred D. Rosenberg, *"Mythus" I. The Worship of Race* (London: Friends of Europe, 1936), Publication No. 46.

"Statement," U.S. Congress. Senate. *Hearing on American Youth Act,* 74th Congress, 3rd Sess., 1936, Vol. 519, part 3, p. 82.

The Devil Theory of War. New York: Vanguard, 1936.

The Discussion of Human Affairs. New York: Macmillan, 1936.

"Forty-Eight Sovereigns," *Today,* 5 (11 January 1936), 3–5.

Review of *Karl Marx: The Story of His Life* by Franz Mehring, *Common Sense,* 5 (January 1936), 25.

"Industry's Attack on the New Deal," *Current History,* 43 (February 1936), 399–406.

"Statement," *Washington Daily News,* 6 February 1936, reprinted in *Congressional Record,* Vol. 80, part 2 (14 February 1936), 2021.

"Heat and Light on Neutrality," *New Republic,* 86 (12 February 1936), 8–9.

"Peace for America: The Devil Theory of History and War," *New Republic,* 86 (4 March 1936), 100–102.

"In Time of Peace Prepare for Peace," *New Republic,* 86 (18 March 1936), 158–159.

"In Defense of Civil Liberties," *Current History,* 44 (April 1936), 66–72.

"James Harvey Robinson," *Journal of Adult Education,* 8 (June 1936), 247–249.

"Ruskin and the Babble of Tongues," *New Republic,* 87 (5 August 1936), 370–372.

1937–1939

"Statement," U.S. Congress. Senate. *Federal Licensing of Corporations: Hearings before a Subcommittee of the Committee on the Judiciary on Senate Bill No. 10,* Part I, 70, 71, 74. 75th Congress, 1st Sess., 1937.

"'Going Ahead' with Roosevelt," *Events,* 1 (January 1937), 9–12.

"A New Morgan Thesis," *New Republic,* 89 (29 January 1937), 350–353.

With Alfred Vagts. "Currents of Thought in Historiography," *American Historical Review,* 42 (April 1937), 460–483.

"Will Roosevelt Keep Us out of War?," *Events,* 2 (July 1937), 1–6.

"War—If, How and When?," *Events,* 2 (August 1937), 81–86.

"Democracy and Education in the United States," *Social Research,* 4 (September 1937), 391–398.

"'Collective Security' Begins at Home," in *War—What For* (New York: Keep America Out of War Committee, 1938), 3.

"Historiography and the Constitution," in Conyers Read (ed.), *The Constitution Reconsidered* (New York: Columbia University Press, 1938), 159–166.

"Statement," U.S. Congress. House. *Hearings Before the Committee on Naval Affairs, on House Resolution 9128 to Establish the Composition of the United States Navy, to Authorize the Construction of Certain Naval Vessels and for Other Purposes.* 7th Congress, 3rd Sess., 1938, 2133–2136.

"Turner's *The Frontier in American History,*" in Malcolm Cowley and Daniel Smith (eds.), *Books That Changed Our Minds.* New York: Exposition Press, 1938.

"Letter to the Editor," *New York Times,* 23 January 1938, p. 9.

"Roosevelt's Place in History," *Events,* 3 (February 1938), 81–86.

And Earl Browder. "Collective Security: A Debate," *New Republic,* 93 (2 February 1938), 354–359.

"The Anti-Trust Racket," *New Republic,* 96 (September 1938), 182–184.

"Another Battle of the Books," *Nation,* 147 (24 September 1938), 300–302.

With others. "To Re-elect Senator Nye," *New Republic,* 96 (9 October 1938), 310.

"Monopoly in Fact and Fiction," *Events,* 4 (November 1938), 383–387.

With Mary Ritter Beard. *America in Midpassage.* New York: Macmillan, 1939. 2 vols.

Giddy Minds and Foreign Quarrels: An Estimate of American Foreign Policy. New York: Macmillan, 1939.

Review of *The Problem of Historical Knowledge* by Maurice Mandelbaum, *American Historical Review,* 44 (April 1939), 371–372.

"We're Blundering into War," *American Mercury,* 46 (April 1939), 388–399.

"The Next Step for Progressives," *The American Teacher,* 23 (May 1939), 27–28.

"Realism About Money," *New Republic,* 99 (17 May 1939), 48–49.

1940–1949

A Foreign Policy for America. New York: Knopf, 1940.

"Freedom in Political Thought," in Ruth Nanda Anshen (ed.), *Freedom: Its Meaning* (New York: Harcourt, Brace, 1940), 288–303.

With George H. E. Smith. *The Old Deal and the New.* New York: Macmillan, 1940.

"Letter to the Editor," *New York Times,* 3 April 1940, p. 22.

Review of *The American Stakes* by John Chamberlain, *Common Sense,* 9 (May 1940), 25.

"War with Japan," *Events,* 8 (November 1940), 121–123.

Public Policy and the General Welfare. New York: Farrar and Rinehart, 1941.

"Statement," U.S. Congress. Senate. *Hearings Before the Committee on Foreign Relations on S. 275, A Bill Further to Promote the Defense of the United States and For Other Purposes.* 77th Congress, 1st Sess., 4 February 1941, 307–310.

"Letter to the Editor," *Baltimore Sun,* 12 February 1941, p. 12.

Review of *John D. Rockefeller and the Heroic Age of American Enterprise* by Allan Nevins, *American Political Science Review,* 35 (October 1941), 977–980.

"Introduction," in Franklin K. Watts (ed.), *Voices of History: Great Speeches and Papers of the Year 1941* (New York: Franklin Watts, 1942), ix–xix.

With Mary Ritter Beard. *The American Spirit: A Study of the Idea of Civilization in the United States.* New York: Macmillan, 1942.

"Introduction," in Brooks Adams, *The Law of Civilization and Decay* (New York: Knopf, 1943), lix–lxi.

The Republic: Conversations on Fundamentals. New York: Viking, 1943.

"Thomas Jefferson: A Civilized Man," *Mississippi Valley Historical Review,* 30 (September 1943), 159–170.

With Mary Ritter Beard. *A Basic History of The United States.* New York: Doubleday, 1944.

The Economic Basis of Politics, 3d. ed. New York: Knopf, 1945.

"Pearl Harbor: Challenge to the Republic," *Progressive,* 9 (3 September 1945), 1–2.

American Foreign Policy in the Making, 1932–1940. New York: Macmillan, 1946.

With others. *Theory and Practice in Historical Study: A Report of the Committee on Historiography.* New York: Social Science Research Council, 1946.

"Who's to Write the History of the War?," *Saturday Evening Post,* 220 (4 October 1947), 172.

President Roosevelt and the coming of the War, 1941: A Study in Appearances and Realities. New Haven: Yale University Press, 1948.

"Statement," U.S. Congress. Senate. *Universal Military Training: Hearings before the Committee on Armed Services.* 80th Congress, 2nd Sess., 1948, 1053–1057.

"Neglected Aspects of Political Science," *American Political Science Review,* 42 (April 1948), 211–222.

"Introduction," in John P. Frank, *Mr. Justice Black* (New York: Knopf, 1949), v–xiv.

Secondary Sources

Adair, Douglass. "The Tenth Federalist Revisited," *William and Mary Quarterly,* 8 (January 1951), 48–67.

Adler, Selig. *The Isolationist Impulse: Its Twentieth Century Reaction.* New York, London: Abelard-Schuman, 1957.

Akin, William E. *Technocracy and the American Dream: The Technocrat Movement, 1900–1941.* Berkeley: University of California Press, 1977.

Allport, Gordon W. "The Functional Anatomy of Motives," in Chalmers L. Stacey and Manfred F. DeMartino (eds.), *Understanding Human Motivation,* rev. ed. (Cleveland: World, 1965), pp. 161–173.

Alsop, Joseph, and Robert Kintner. *American White Paper: The Story of American Diplomacy and the Second World War.* New York: Simon & Schuster, 1940.

Anon. Review of *An Economic Interpretation of the Constitution* by Charles A. Beard, *Educational Review,* 46 (September 1913), 207.

Aron, Raymond. *Introduction to the Philosophy of History: An Essay on the Limits of Historical Objectivity,* tr. by George J. Irwin. Boston: Beacon, 1961 (original ed., 1938).

Barnes, Harry Elmer. "James Harvey Robinson," in Howard W. Odum (ed.), *American Masters of Social Science* (New York: Holt, 1927), pp. 321–408.

Beale, Howard K. (ed.). *Charles A. Beard: An Appraisal.* Lexington: University of Kentucky, 1954.

Beard, Mary Ritter. "Letter to the Editor," *New York Times,* 5 December 1913, p. 10.

Beard. "Letter to the Editor," *New York Times,* 17 January 1915, III, p. 2.

Beard. *A Short History of the American Labor Movement.* New York: Workers Education Bureau of America, 1924.

Beard. *The Making of Charles A. Beard.* New York: Exposition, 1955.

Beard. "The Twentieth Century Woman: Looking Around and Backward," *Young Oxford,* 1 (December 1900), 100–104.

Beard. "The Nineteenth Century Woman: Looking Forward," *Young Oxford,* 2 (January 1901), 119–122.

Beard. *Woman's Work in Municipalities.* New York: Appleton, 1915.

Beard, Miriam. *Realism in Romantic Japan.* New York: Macmillan, 1930.

Beard, William. *Create the Wealth.* New York: Norton, 1936.

Becker, Carl. "Everyman His Own Historian," *American Historical Review,* 37 (January 1932), 221–236.

Becker. "Fresh Air in American History," *Nation,* 124 (18 May 1927), 561—562.

Bemis, Samuel Flagg. "First Gun of a Revisionist Historiography for the Second World War," *Journal of Modern History,* 19 (March 1947), 55–59.

Bemis. Review of *The Open Door at Home* by Charles A. Beard and George H. E. Smith, *American Historical Review,* 40 (April 1935), 541–543.

Bemis. "The Shifting Strategy of American Defense and Diplomacy," *Virginia Quarterly Review,* 24 (Summer 1948), 321–335.

Bentley, Arthur F. *The Process of Government: A Study of Social Pressures.* Chicago: University of Chicago Press, 1908.

Berdahl, Clarence, et. al. "Letter to the Editor," *New York Times,* 12 November 1939, IV, pp. 8–9.

Berle, Adolph A., Jr. Review of *American Foreign Policy in the Making, 1933–1940* by Charles A. Beard, *Tomorrow* (November 1946), 52–53.

Bernstein, Eduard. *Evolutionary Socialism: A Criticism and Affirmation.* New York: Shocken, 1961.

Bernstein, Richard J. *The Restructuring of Social and Political Theory.* Philadelphia: University of Pennsylvania Press, 1978.

Billington, Ray Allen. *The Genesis of the Frontier Thesis: A Study in Historical Creativity.* San Marino, Calif.: Huntington Library, 1971.

Blakey, George T. *Historians on the Homefront: American Propagandists for the Great War.* Lexington: University Press of Kentucky, 1970.

Blevin, Bruce. "The Hang Back Boys," *New Republic,* 110 (6 March 1944), 305–307.

Blinkoff, Maurice. *The Influence of Charles A. Beard upon American Historiography.* Buffalo: University of Buffalo Studies, Vol. XII (May 1936).

Bolles, Blair. Review of *President Roosevelt and the Coming of War, 1941* by Charles A. Beard, *New Republic,* 119 (5 July 1948), 25–26.

Borning, Bernard C. *The Political and Social Thought of Charles A. Beard.* Seattle: University of Washington Press, 1962.

Bourne, Randolph. *History of a Literary Radical.* New York: Huebsch, 1920.

Bourne. "Twilight of Idols," in Carl Resak (ed.), *War and the Intellectuals: Essays of Randolph Bourne* (New York: Harper, 1964), pp. 53–64.

Bowers, Claude A. *The Progressive Educator and the Depression.* New York: Random House, 1969.

Boyd, William K. Review of *An Economic Interpretation of the Constitution* by Charles A. Beard, *South Atlantic Quarterly,* 12 (July 1913), 269–273.

Bretz, J. P. Review of *The Rise of American Civilization,* *American Historical Review,* 33 (October 1927), 140–142.

Browder, Earl. "American Revolutionary Traditions," *Political Affairs,* 17 (December 1938), 1079–1080.

Brown, Bernard Edward. *American Conservatives: The Political Thought of Francis Lieber and John W. Burgess.* New York: Columbia University Press, 1951.

Brown, Robert E. *Charles Beard and the Constitution: A Critical Analysis of "An Economic Interpretation of the Constitution."* Princeton, N.J.: Princeton University Press, 1956.

Buell, Raymond Leslie. *Isolated America.* New York: Knopf, 1940.

Buell. Review of *The Open Door at Home* by Charles A. Beard and George H. E. Smith, *Books of The New York Herald Tribune,* 16 December 1934, p. 7.

Bundy, McGeorge. "Isolationists and Neutralists: A Sketch in Similarities," *Confluence,* 1 (June 1952), 70–78.

Burgess, John W. *Political Science and Comparative Constitutional Law.* Boston: Ginn, 1890. 2 vols.

Burgess. *Reminiscences of an American Scholar.* New York: Columbia University Press, 1923.

Busch, Noel F. *Two Minutes to Noon.* New York: Simon & Schuster, 1962.

Canby, Henry S. "History by Innuendo," *Saturday Review of Literature,* 27 (11 November 1944), 12.

Caro, Robert. *The Power Broker: Robert Moses and the Fall of New York.* New York: Harper, 1974.

Carpenter, L. P. *G. D. H. Cole: An Intellectual Biography.* Cambridge: The University Press, 1973.

Cochran, T. C. Review of *The Open Door at Home* by Charles A. Beard and George H. E. Smith, *Modern Monthly,* 8 (February 1935), 759–760.

Cohen, Warren I. *The American Revisionists: The Lessons of Intervention in World War I.* Chicago: University of Chicago Press, 1967.

Cole, Charles W. "The Relativity of History," *Political Science Quarterly*, 48 (June 1933), 161–171.

Corwin, E.S. Review of *An Economic Interpretation of the Constitution of the United States* by Charles A. Beard, *History Teacher's Magazine*, 5 (February 1914), 65–66.

Counts, George S. "Charles Beard, the Public Man," in Howard K. Beale (ed.), *Charles A. Beard* (Lexington: University of Kentucky Press, 1955), 231–254.

Cowley, Malcolm, and Daniel Smith (eds.). *Books That Changed Our Minds*. New York: Kelmscott Editions, 1938.

Craig, Gordon. Review of *President Roosevelt and the Coming of War, 1941* by Charles A. Beard, *Yale Review*, 37 (June 1948), 762—764.

Crespi, Angelo. *Contemporary Thought of Italy*. New York: Knopf, 1926.

Croce, Benedetto. *History: Its Theory and Practice*, tr. Douglas Ainslie. New York: Russell & Russell, 1960 (original Ed., 1920).

Croce. "Letter," *American Historical Review*, 39 (January 1934), 229–230.

Croce. *The Philosophy of the Practical*. New York: Longmans, Green, 1909.

Croly, Herbert. "A School of Social Research," *New Republic*, 15 (8 January 1918), 167–171.

Curti, Merle. "A Great Teacher's Teacher," *Social Education*, 31 (October 1949), 263–266, 274.

Cywar, Alan. "John Dewey: Toward Domestic Reconstruction, 1915–1920," *Journal of the History of Ideas*, 30 (July–September 1969), 385–400.

Dahlberg, Jane S. *The New York Bureau of Municipal Research*. New York: New York University Press, 1966.

Danto, Arthur C. *Analytical Philosophy of History*. Cambridge: Cambridge University Press, 1965.

Davis, Allen F. "Welfare, Reform and World War I," *American Quarterly*, 19 (Fall 1967), 516–533.

Davis, Robert Lang. *The Search for Values: The American Liberal Climate of Opinion in the 1930's and the Totalitarian Crisis of the Coming of the Second World War as Seen in the Thought of Charles Beard and Archibald MacLeish*. Ph.D. Thesis, Claremont, 1970.

De Benedetti, Charles. *Origins of the Modern American Peace Movement, 1915–1929*. Millwood, N.Y.: KOT Press, 1978.

Denninger, Whitaker T. "The Skepticism and Historical Faith of Charles A. Beard," *Journal of the History of Ideas*, 15 (October 1954), 573–588.

"Departmental Regulation," *State Department Bulletin*, 16 (25 May 1947), 1047–1049.

Destler, Chester M. "Some Observations on Contemporary Historical Theory," *American Historical Review*, 55 (April 1950), 503–509.

Dewey, Evelyn (ed.). *Letters from China and Japan by John Dewey and Alice Chipman Dewey*. New York: Dutton, 1920.

Dewey, John. "In Explanation of Our Lapse," *New Republic*, 13 (3 November 1917), 17–18.

Dewey, John. "Professorial Freedom," *New York Times*, 22 October 1915, p. 10.

Dewey, John. *Characters and Events: Popular Essays in Social and Political Philosophy*, ed. Joseph Ratner. New York: Holt, 1929. 2 vols.

Dodd, L. T., and S. A. Dale. "The Ruskin Hall Movement," *Fortnightly Review*, 73 (June 1900), 325–335.

Doenecke, Justus D. "Non-interventionism of the Left: The Keep America Out of the War Congress, 1938–1941," *Journal of Contemporary History*, 12 (1977), 221–236.

Doenecke, Justus D. *Not to the Swift: The Old Isolationists in the Cold War Era*. Lewisburg, Pa.: Bucknell University Press, 1979.

Dorfman, Joseph. Review of *The American Spirit* by Charles and Mary Beard, *American Economic Review*, 33 (September 1943), 644–647.

Ducharme, Raymond A., Jr. (ed.). *Charles A. Beard and the Social Studies*. New York: Columbia University, Teachers College, 1969.

Dye, Nancy Schrom. "Creating a Feminist Alliance: Sisterhood and Class Conflict in the New York Women's Trade Union League, 1903–1914," *Feminist Studies*, 2 (1975), 24–38.

Eddington, Arthur S. *The Nature of the Physical World*. New York: Macmillan, 1929.

Edman, Irwin. "John Dewey and Others," in Houston Peterson (ed.), *Great Teachers Portrayed by Those Who Studied Under Them* (New Brunswick, N.J.: Rutgers University Press, 1946), pp. 185–201.

Ellis, David M., et. al. *A Short History of New York State*. Ithaca: Cornell University Press, 1967.

Elton, Oliver. *Frederick York Powell*. Oxford: Oxford University Press, 1906. 2 vols.

Erskine, John. *The Memory of Certain Persons*. New York: Lippincott, 1947.

Ezekiel, Mordecai. *$2500 a Year: From Scarcity to Abundance*. New York: Harcourt, Brace, 1936.

Ezekiel. *Jobs for All Through Industrial Expansion*. New York: Knopf, 1939.

Fallows, James. "The Passionless Presidency II," *Atlantic Monthly*, 243 (June 1979), 75–81.

Feis, Herbert. "War Came at Pearl Harbor: Suspicions Considered," *Yale Review*, 45 (Spring 1956), 378–390.

Feis. Review of *The Open Door at Home* by Charles A. Beard and George H. E. Smith, *Foreign Affairs*, 13 (July 1935), 600–611.

Fischer, David H. *Historian's Fallacies: Toward a Logic of Historical Thought*. New York: Harper, 1970.

Fite, Gilbert C. *George N. Peek and the Fight for Farm Parity*. Norman: University of Oklahoma Press, 1954.

Fletcher, Robert S. Review of *A Basic History* by Charles and Mary Beard, *American Historical Review*, 50 (January 1945), 400.

Flexner, Eleanor. *Century of Struggle*. Cambridge: Harvard University Press, 1975.

Flynn, John T. "John T. Flynn Charges Government Knew Jap Cabinet Intended to Break Relations," *Chicago Tribune*, 2 September 1945, p. 1.

Flynn. "Other People's Money: Professor Beard and the Bankers—Whom Do Senators Represent?—One Sample from Many—'The People,'" *New Republic*, 82 (10 April 1935), 242.

Forcey, Charles. *The Crossroads of Liberalism*. New York: Oxford University Press, 1961.

Fox, Richard W. "The Paradox of Progressive Socialism: The Case of Morris Hillquit, 1901–1914," *American Quarterly*, 26 (May 1974), 127–140.

Frankfurter, Felix. Review of *The American Leviathan* by Charles A. Beard and William Beard, *Harvard Law Review*, 44 (February 1931), 661.

Freedlander, Etta. *Education in the Workers' Schools of New York City*. Ph.D. Thesis: New School for Social Research, New York, 1973.

Freeman, Joseph. *An American Testament: A Narrative of Rebels and Romantics*. New York: Farrar and Rinehart, 1936.

Fuller, Edmund. "Letter to the Editor," *Saturday Review of Literature*, 27 (11 November 1944), 13.

Gabriel, Ralph H. Review of *The Rise of American Civilization* by Charles and Mary Beard, *Yale Review*, 17 (January 1928), 494–496.

Garson, David. "Research on Policy Alternatives for America in the 1930's," *Political Inquiry*, 1 (1973), 50–77.

Genovese, Eugene D. "Beard's Economic Interpretation of History," in *Charles A. Beard: An Observance of the Centennial of His Birth*. Greencastle, Ind.: DePauw University, 1976.

Gerth, H. H. and C. Wright Mills. *From Max Weber: Essays in Sociology*. New York: Oxford University Press, 1958.

Gettell, Raymond G. Review of *American City Government* by Charles A. Beard. *American Political Science Review*, 7 (May 1913), 319–320.

Gideonse, Harry. Review of *President Roosevelt and the Coming of War, 1941* by Charles A. Beard, *New Leader* (12 June 1948), 10.

Gilbert, James. *Designing the Industrial State: The Intellectual Pursuit of Collectivism in America, 1880–1940*. Chicago: Quadrangle, 1972.

Goldberg, Harvey (ed.). *American Radicals: Some Problems and Personalities*. New York: Monthly Review Press, 1957.

Goldberger, Paul. "Sale of a Regal Triplex Stirs Hotel des Artistes," *New York Times*, 26 March 1974, p. 43.

Goldman, Eric F. "A Historian at Seventy," *New Republic*, 111 (27 November 1944), 496–497.

Goldman. "Charles A. Beard: An Impression," in Howard K. Beale (ed.), *Charles A. Beard* (Lexington: University of Kentucky Press, 1955), pp. 1–8.

Goodnow, Frank J. "Reform in China," *American Political Science Review*, 9 (May 1915), 209–224.

Goodnow, Frank J. *Social Reform and the Constitution*. New York: Macmillan, 1911.

Gossett, Thomas F. *Race: The History of an Idea in America.* Dallas: Southern Methodist University Press, 1963.

Graham, George A. *Education for Public Administration.* Chicago: Public Administration Service, 1941.

Graham, Otis L., Jr. *The Great Campaigns: Reform and War in America, 1900–1928.* Englewood Cliffs, N.J.: Prentice-Hall, 1971.

Graham. "The Planning Ideal and American Reality: The 1930's," in Stanley Elkins and Eric McKitrick (eds.), *The Hofstadter Aegis: A Memorial* (New York: Knopf, 1974), 257–299.

Graham. *Toward a Planned Society: From Roosevelt to Nixon.* New York: Oxford University Press, 1976.

Gregory, Alyse. "Aesthetic Astigmatism," *Dial,* 83 (October 1927), 350–351.

Grieder, Jerome B. *Hu Shih and the Chinese Renaissance: Liberalism in the Chinese Revolution, 1917–1937.* Cambridge: Harvard University Press, 1970.

Gruber, Carol S. "Academic Freedom at Columbia University, 1917–1918: The Case of James McKeen Cattell," *Bulletin of the American Association of University Professors,* 58 (Autumn 1972), 297–305.

Gruber. *Mars and Minerva: World War I and the Uses of the Higher Learning in America.* Baton Rouge: Louisiana State University Press, 1975.

Gulick, Luther. "Beard and Municipal Reform," in Howard K. Beale (ed.), *Charles A. Beard* (Lexington: University of Kentucky Press, 1954), 47–60.

Gutek, Gerald L. *The Educational Theory of George Counts.* Columbus: Ohio State University Press, 1970.

Haber, Samuel. *Efficiency and Uplift: Scientific Management in the Progressive Era, 1890–1920.* Chicago: University of Chicago Press, 1964.

Haines, Charles G., and Marshall E. Dimock (eds.). *Essays on the Law and Practice of Governmental Administration.* Baltimore: Johns Hopkins Press, 1935.

Hatcher, Sadie Bacon. *A History of Spiceland Academy.* Indianapolis: Indiana Historical Society, 1934.

Hendricks, Luther V. *James Harvey Robinson.* New York: Kings Crown, 1946.

Herring, Hubert. "Charles A. Beard: Free Lance Among the Historians," *Harper's Magazine,* 178 (May 1939), 641–652.

High, Stanley. "The Liberals' War," *Nation,* 152 (22 March 1941), 619–623.

Higham, John, Leonard Krieger, and Felix Gilbert. *History.* Englewood Cliffs, N.J.: Prentice-Hall, 1965.

Hillquit, Morris. *Loose Leaves from a Busy Life.* New York: Macmillan, 1934.

Hirschfeld, Charles. "Nationalist Progressivism and World War I," *Mid-America,* 45 (July 1963), 139–156.

History of Henry County Indiana. Chicago: Interstate Publishing Company, 1884.

Hobson, E. W. *The Domain of Natural Science.* New York: Macmillan, 1923.

Hobson, John. *John Ruskin: Social Reformer.* London: James Hisbet, 1898.

Hofstadter, Richard. Review of *The American Spirit* by Charles and Mary Beard, *New Republic*, 108 (4 January 1943), 27–28.

Hofstadter. *The Progressive Historians*. New York: Knopf, 1968.

Hofstadter, Richard, and Walter Metzger. *The Development of Academic Freedom in the United States*. New York: Columbia University Press, 1955.

Hollingsworth, J. R. "Perspectives on Industrializing Societies," in Allan G. Bogue (ed.), *Emerging Theoretical Models in Social and Political History* (Beverly Hills: Sage Publications, 1973), pp. 97–121.

Hook, Sidney. Review of *The Republic* by Charles A. Beard, *Nation*, 157 (23 October 1943), 474–476.

Howe, Frederick C. *Confessions of a Reformer*. New York: Scribner, 1925.

Howe. *Why War?* New York: Scribner, 1916.

Hoxie, Ralph G., et. al. *A History of the Faculty of Political Science: Columbia University*. New York: Columbia University Press, 1955.

Hull, Cordell. "Trade, Prosperity and Peace," radio address of 6 February 1938, reprinted in U.S. Congress. House. *Hearings before the Committee on Naval Affairs on House Resolution 9128*, 75th Congress, 3rd Sess., 2102–2106.

Iggers, Georg G. *The German Conception of History: The National Tradition of Historical Thought from Herder to the Present*. Middletown, Conn.: Wesleyan University Press, 1968.

Jacobitti, Edmund. *Revolutionary Humanism and Historicism in Modern Italy*. New Haven: Yale University Press, 1981.

Jameson, J. Franklin. *The American Revolution Considered as a Social Movement*. Princeton, N.J.: Princeton University Press, 1926.

Jay, Martin. *The Dialectical Imagination: A History of the Frankfurt School and the Institute of Social Research*. Boston: Little, Brown, 1973.

Jeans, James. *The Mysterious Universe*. New York: Macmillan, 1930.

Johnson, Alvin. *Pioneer's Progress*. New York: Viking, 1952.

Jonas, Manfred. *Isolationism in America, 1935–1941*. Ithaca: Cornell University Press, 1966.

Josephson, Matthew. *Infidel in the Temple: A Memoir of the Nineteen-Thirties*. New York: Knopf, 1967.

Josephson. "The Hat on the Roll-top Desk—II," *New Yorker*, 17 (21 February, 1942), 21–27.

Kallen, Horace M. *Education, The Machine, and The Worker*. New York: New Republic, 1925.

Kammen, Michael (ed.). *What Is the Good of History? Selected Letters of Carl Becker, 1900–1945*. Ithaca: Cornell University Press, 1973.

Katz, Michael B. *Class, Bureaucracy and Schools: The Illusion of Educational Change in America*. New York: Praeger, 1971.

Kennedy, Thomas C. *Charles A. Beard and American Foreign Policy*. Gainsville: University of Florida Press, 1975.

Kennedy. "Charles A. Beard and the 'Big Navy Boys,'" *Military Affairs*, 31 (Summer 1967), 65–73.

Kennedy. "Charles A. Beard and the 'Court Historians,'" *Historian*, 25 (August 1963), 439–450.

Keynes, John M. *The Economic Consequences of the Peace*. New York: Harcourt, Brace, 1920.

Kimball, Warren F. *The Most Unsordid Act: Lend-Lease, 1939–1941*. Baltimore: Johns Hopkins Press, 1969.

Knight, M. M. "Introduction to the American Edition," in Henri See, *The Economic Interpretation of History* (New York: Adelphi, 1939).

Koch, Adrienne, Review of *A Basic History* by Charles and Mary Beard, *New York Times Book Review*, 6 August 1944, p. 1.

Kropotkin, Peter. "Brain Work and Manual Work," in Collin Ward (ed.), *Fields, Factories and Workshops Tomorrow* (London: George Allen & Unwin, 1974), pp. 169–187.

Krutch, Joseph Wood. "A New Philosophy of History," *Nation*, 129 (16 October 1929), 423–425.

La Follette, Robert M. *La Follette's Autobiography: A Personal Narrative of Political Experiences*. Madison: The Robert M. La Follette Company, 1913.

Lamprecht, Sterling P. "Historiography of Philosophy," *Journal of Philosophy*, 36 (17 August 1939), 449–460.

Lane, Ann J. *Mary Ritter Beard: A Sourcebook*. New York: Schocken, 1977.

Langer, William L. "Letter to the Editor," *Washington Post*, 9 November 1947, p. 4B.

Langer. *Our Vichy Gamble*. New York: Knopf, 1947.

Lasch, Christopher. *American Liberals and the Russian Revolution*. New York: Columbia University Press, 1962.

Latané, John. Review of *An Economic Interpretation of the Constitution* by Charles A. Beard, *American Political Science Review*, 7 (November 1913), 697–700.

Lawson, R. Alan. *The Failure of Independent Liberalism, 1930–1941*. New York: Capricorn, 1972.

Lease, Mary E. *The Problem of Civilization Solved*. Chicago: Laird & Lee, 1895.

Lerner, Max. Review of *The Republic* by Charles A. Beard, *American Political Science Review*, 38 (August 1944), 781–784.

Lerner. "The State in Wartime," in Willard Waller (ed.), *War in the Twentieth Century* (New York: Random House, 1940), pp. 409–428.

Lerner. "The War as Revolution II: The Attitude of the Intellectuals," *Nation*, 151 (3 August 1940), 88–92.

Libby, Orin G. Review of *An Economic Interpretation of The Constitution* by Charles A. Beard, *Mississippi Valley Historical Review*, 1 (June 1914), 113–117.

Libby. Review of *Economic Origins of Jeffersonian Democracy* by Charles A. Beard, *Mississippi Valley Historical Review*, 3 (June 1916), 100.

Lilienthal, David E. *The Journals of David E. Lilienthal*. New York: Harper, 1964, Vol. I.

Lippmann, Walter. *Public Opinion*. New York: Macmillan, 1922.

Lippmann. Review of *The Economic Basis of Politics* by Charles A. Beard, *New Republic*, 31 (9 August 1922), 282–283.

Lovejoy, Arthur O., et. al. "Letter to the Editor," *Baltimore Sun*, 7 February 1941, p. 14.

Lovejoy. "Present Standpoints and Past History," *Journal of Philosophy*, 36 (31 August 1939), 477–489.

Lovejoy. "Reply to Beard," *Baltimore Sun*, 15 February 1941, p. 12.

Lurie, Edward. "Science in American Social Thought," *Journal of World History*, 8 (1964–1965), 638–665.

McNaught, Kenneth. "American Progressives and the Great Society," *Journal of American History*, 53 (December 1966), 504–520.

Macmahon, Arthur. "Charles Austin Beard as a Teacher," *Political Science Quarterly*, 65 (March 1950), 1–19.

Mailly, Bertha H. "The Rand School of Social Science," in *Workers Education in the United States* (New York: Workers Education Bureau of America, 1921).

Mandelbaum, Maurice. "Causal Analysis in History," *Journal of the History of Ideas*, 3 (January 1942), 30–50.

Mandelbaum. *The Problem of Historical Knowledge*. New York: Harper Torchbooks, 1967 (original ed., 1938).

Mannheim, Karl. *Ideology and Utopia: An Introduction to the Sociology of Knowledge*. New York: Harcourt, Brace, 1936 (original German ed., 1929).

Marcell, David W. *Progress and Pragmatism: James, Dewey, Beard, and the American Idea of Progress*. Westport and London: Greenwood Press, 1974.

Marks, Harry. "Ground Under Our Feet: Beard's Relativism," *Journal of the History of Ideas*, 14 (October 1953), 628–633.

Martin, James J. *American Liberalism and World Politics, 1931–1941: Liberalism's Press and Spokesmen on the Road Back to War between Mukden and Pearl Harbor*. New York: Devin-Adair, 1964. 2 vols.

Marx, Karl, and Friedrich, Engels. *Basic Writings on Politics and Philosophy*, ed. Lewis S. Feuer. New York: Anchor Books, 1959.

MacLeish, Archibald. "Preface to An American Manifesto," *Forum and Century*, 91 (April 1934), 195–198.

MacLeish. "The Irresponsibles," *Nation*, 150 (18 May 1940), 618–623.

McIllwain, C. H. "The Historian's Part in a Changing World," *American Historical Review*, 42 (January 1937), 207–224.

Mehring, Franz. *Karl Marx: The Story of His Life*, trans. Edward Fitzgerald. Ann Arbor: University of Michigan, 1962.

Meiland, J. W. "The Historical Relativism of Charles A. Beard," *History and Theory*, 12, No. 4 (1973), 405–413.

Melosi, Martin. "Political Tremors from a Military Disaster: 'Pearl Harbor' and the Election of 1944," *Diplomatic History*, 1 (Winter 1977), 83–95.

Melosi. *The Shadow of Pearl Harbor: Political Controversy over the Surprise Attack, 1941– 1946*. College Station and London: Texas A&M University Press, 1977.

Merton, Robert K. "The Sociology of Knowledge," *Isis*, 27 (November 1937), 493– 503.

Meyer, Agnes E. *Out of These Roots*. Boston: Little, Brown, 1953.

Meyer, Annie Nathan. "Letter to the Editor," *New York Times*, 13 October 1917, p. 10.

Miller, Arthur T. "Visualization Lost and Regained: The Genesis of the Quantum Theory in the Period, 1913–27," in Judith Wechsler (ed.), *On Aesthetics in Science* (Cambridge: Massachusetts Institute of Technology, 1978), 73–102.

Miller, Donald L. *The New American Radicalism: Alfred M. Bingham and Non-Marxian Insurgency in the New Deal Era*. Port Washington, N.Y.: Kennikat Press, 1979.

Miller, Perry. Review of *President Roosevelt and the Coming of War, 1941* by Charles A. Beard, *Nation*, 166 (12 June 1948), 665–666.

Mitchell, Lucy Sprague. *Two Lives: The Story of Wesley Clair Mitchell and Myself*. New York: Simon & Schuster, 1953.

Mock, James R., and Cedric Larson. *Words That Won the War: The Story of the Committee on Public Information, 1917–1919*. New York: Russell & Russell, 1939.

Moley, Raymond. *27 Masters of Politics*. New York: Funk & Wagnalls, 1949.

Moore, James R. *The Post-Darwinian Controversies: A Study of the Protestant Struggle to Come to Terms with Darwin in Great Britain and America, 1870–1900*. New York: Cambridge University Press, 1979.

Morgenstern, George. *Pearl Harbor: The Story of the Secret War*. New York: Devin-Adair, 1947.

Morison, Samuel Eliot. *By Land and by Sea: Essays and Addresses*. New York: Knopf, 1954.

Morison. "Did Roosevelt Start the War? History Through a Beard," *Atlantic*, 182 (August 1948), 91–97.

Mumford, Lewis. "Letter to the Editor," *Saturday Review of Literature*, 27 (2 December 1944), 27.

Mumford. *Man Must Act*. New York: Harcourt, Brace, 1939.

Mumford. Review of *A Century of Progress*, edited by Charles A. Beard, *New Republic*, 76 (6 September 1933), 106–107.

Mumford. "The Corruption of Liberalism," *New Republic*, 102 (June 1940), 568–573.

Mumford. "The New History," *New Republic*, 50 (11 May 1927), 338–339.

Munroe, William B. "Physics and Politics: An Old Analogy Revisited," *American Political Science Review*, 22 (February 1928), 1–11.

Nagel, Ernest. "Some Issues in the Logic of Historical Analysis," *The Scientific Monthly*, 74 (March 1952), 162–169.

Nash, Gerald D. "Self-education in Historiography: The Case of Charles A. Beard," Pacific Northwest Quarterly, 52 (1961), 108–115.

Nevins, Allan. "'A Challenge to Historic Truth,'" New York Times, 16 December 1945, VI, p. 8.

Nevins. Review of A Foreign Policy for America by Charles A. Beard, New York Times, 26 May 1940, VI, p. 1.

Nevins. Review of Bases Overseas by George Welles, New York Times Book Review, 16 December 1944, p. 4.

Nevins. The Gateway to History. New York: Heath, 1938.

Nichols, Roy F. A Historian's Progress. New York: Knopf, 1968.

Nicolaievsky, Boris (ed.). "Toward a History of the 'Communist League,' 1847–1852," International Review of Socialist History, 1 (1956), 249.

Niebhur, Reinhold. Review of A Foreign Policy for America by Charles A. Beard, Nation, 150 (25 May 1940), 656–658.

Noble, David. Historians Against History: The Frontier Thesis and the National Convenant in American Historical Writing since 1830. Minneapolis: University of Minnesota Press, 1965.

Nock, Albert. "The Vanished University," The Freeman, 3 (29 June 1921), 364.

North, Sterling. Review of A Basic History by Charles and Mary Beard, New York Post, 3 August 1944, p. 10.

"Oral History" [Interview with Wellington Koo], New Yorker, 53 (18 April 1977), 32–35.

Paulson, Ross E. Radicalism & Reform: The Vrooman Family and American Social Thought, 1837–1937. Lexington: University of Kentucky Press, 1968.

Pells, Richard H. Radical Visions and American Dreams: Culture and Social Thought in the Depression Years. New York: Harper, 1973.

Peters, Houston (ed.). Great Teachers. New Brunswick, N.J.: Rutgers University Press, 1946.

Phillips, Clifton J. (ed.). "Charles A. Beard's Recollections of Henry County, Indiana," Indiana Magazine of History, 55 (March 1959), 17–23.

Phillips. "The Indiana Education of Charles A. Beard," Indiana Magazine of History, 55 (March 1959), 1–15.

Phillips, Harlan B. "Charles Beard, Walter Vrooman, and the Founding of Ruskin Hall," South Atlantic Quarterly, 50 (April 1951), 186–191.

Phillips. Walter Vrooman: Restless Child of Progress, Ph.D. Thesis: Columbia University, New York, 1954.

Pinckney, Orde S. "William E. Borah: Critic of American Foreign Policy," Studies on the Left, I (1960), 48–61.

Powell, Frederick York. "Preface," in Charles A. Beard, The Industrial Revolution (London: George Allen & Unwin, 1901), pp. vii–xv.

Powell, Thomas Reed. Review of The Republic by Charles A. Beard, Harvard Law Review, 57 (April 1944), 579.

Proceedings of a Conference of Progressives to Outline a Program of Constructive Legislation Dealing with Economics and Political Conditions for Presentation to the First Session of the 72nd Congress. Washington, D.C.: n.p., 1931.

Radin, George. "Charles A. Beard's Mission to Yugoslavia (1927–1928)," in Mary Ritter Beard, *The Making of Charles A. Beard: An Interpretation* (New York: Exposition, 1955), pp. 80–81.

Radosh, Ronald. *Prophets on the Right: Profiles of Conservative Critics of American Globalism.* New York: Simon & Schuster, 1974.

Randall, John H. "On Understanding the History of Philosophy," *Journal of Philosophy,* 36 (17 August 1939), 460–474.

Rappaport, Armin. *The Navy League of the United States.* Detroit: Wayne State University Press, 1962.

Report of the Special Committee Appointed March 5, 1917, to Inquire Into the State of Teaching in the University. New York: Columbia University Press, 1917.

Rickman, H. P. *Meaning in History: Wilhelm Dilthey's Thoughts on History and Society.* London: George Allen & Unwin, 1961.

Riezler, Kurt. "Idee and Interesse in der Politischen Geschichte," *Dioskuren* (Munich), III (1924), 1–13.

Robinson, James Harvey. "History," in *Columbia University Lectures on Science, Philosophy and Art, 1907–1908* (New York: Columbia University Press, 1908), pp. 5–29.

Robinson. *The Mind in the Making: The Relation of Intelligence to Social Reform.* New York: Harper, 1921.

Robinson. *The New History: Essays Illustrating the Modern Historical Outlook.* New York: Macmillan, 1912.

Robinson. "The New School," *School and Society,* 11 (31 January 1920), 129–132.

Robinson. "The Newer Ways of Historians," *American Historical Review,* 35 (January 1930), 245–255.

Robinson. "The Threatened Eclipse of Free Speech," *Atlantic,* 120 (December 1917), 811–817.

Robinson. "War and Thinking," *New Republic,* 1 (19 December 1914), 17–18.

Rodgers, Hugh J. "Charles A. Beard, the 'New Physics,' and Historical Relativity," *Historian,* 30 (August 1968), 545–560.

Rodgers, Lindsay. Review of *The Republic* by Charles A. Beard, *Saturday Review of Literature,* 26 (9 October 1943), 5–6.

Rosenof, Theodore. *Dogma, Depression, and the New Deal: The Debate of Political Leaders over Economic Recovery.* Port Washington, N.Y.: Kennikat Press, 1975.

Russell, Bertrand. "Science," in Charles A. Beard (ed.), *Whither Mankind?* (New York: Longmans, Green, 1928), 63–82.

Russell. *The Autobiography.* New York: Bantam, 1968, Vol. I.

Schaffer, Ronald. "The New York City Woman Suffrage Party, 1909–19," *New York History,* 43 (July 1962), 269–287.

Schiesl, Martin J. *The Politics of Efficiency: Municipal Administration and Reform in America, 1800–1920.* Berkeley: University of California Press, 1977.

Schlesinger, Arthur M., Jr. Review of *American Foreign Policy in the Making 1933–1940* by Charles A. Beard, *Nation*, 163 (31 August 1946), 244–245.

Schlesinger. Review of *President Roosevelt and the Coming of War, 1941* by Charles A. Beard, *New York Times*, 11 April 1948, VII, p. 4.

Schuyler, Robert L. "Law and Accident in History," *Political Science Quarterly*, 45 (June 1930), 273–278.

Schuyler. "Some Historical Idols," *Political Science Quarterly*, 47 (March 1932), 1–18.

Schmunk, Paul L. *Charles Austin Beard: A Free Spirit.* Ph.D. Dissertation, University of New Mexico, 1957.

Schwantes, Robert S. *Japanese and Americans: A Century of Cultural Relations.* New York: Harper, 1955.

Schwarz, Jordan A. *The Interregnum of Despair.* Urbana: University of Illinois Press, 1970.

Seligman, Edwin R.A. *The Economic Interpretation of History.* New York: Columbia University Press, 1902.

Shapiro, Stanley. "The Great War and Reform: Liberals and Labor, 1917–19," *Labor History*, 11 (Summer 1971), 323–344.

Shepherd, William R. "John William Burgess," in Howard W. Odum (ed.), *American Masters of Social Science* (New York: Macmillan, 1927), pp. 23–57.

Simkovitch, Vladimir C. "Approaches to History I," *Political Science Quarterly*, 44 (December 1929), 482–484.

Simkovitch. "Approaches to History II," *Political Science Quarterly*, 45 (December 1930), 481–526.

Simkovitch. "Approaches to History III," *Political Science Quarterly*, 47 (September 1932), 419–439.

Simkovitch. "Approaches to History IV," *Political Science Quarterly*, 49 (March 1934), 44–83.

Skotheim, Robert Allen. *American Intellectual Histories and Historians.* Princeton, N.J.: Princeton University Press, 1966.

Skotheim. "Environmental Interpretations of Ideas by Beard, Parrington, and Curti," *Pacific Historical Review*, 33 (February 1964), 35–44.

Smith, Charlotte Watkins. *Carl Becker.* Ithaca: Cornell University Press, 1956.

Smith, J. Allen. *The Spirit of American Government.* New York: John Harvard Library Edition, 1965 (first published, 1907).

Smith, Preserved. "The Place of History Among the Sciences," in *Essays in Intellectual History* (New York: Harper, 1929), 209–218.

Smith, T. V. Review of *The Rise of American Civilization* by Charles and Mary Beard and *Main Currents of American Thought* by V. L. Parrington, *International Journal of Ethics*, 38 (October 1927), 112–115.

Smith, Theodore C. "The Writing of American History in America, 1884 to 1934," *American Historical Review*, 40 (April 1935), 439–449.

Solow, Herbert. "A Preliminary Notice of an Important Book," *New York Evening Post Literary Review*, 23 April 1927, p. 2.

Solow. "The Beards Catch the True Rhythm of Our Civilization's Rise," *New York Evening Post Literary Review*, 30 April 1927, p. 2.

Sonderbergh, Peter A. "Charles A. Beard, The Quaker Spirit, and North Carolina," *North Carolina Historical Review*, 46 (Winter 1969), 19–32.

Sorenson, Lloyd R. "Charles A. Beard and German Historiographical Thought," *Mississippi Valley Historical Review*, 42 (September 1955), 274–287.

Sorenson. "Historical Currents in America," *American Quarterly*, 7 (Fall 1955), 234–246.

Soule, George. "Beard and the Concept of Planning," in Howard K. Beale (ed.), *Charles A. Beard* (Lexington: University of Kentucky Press, 1954), 61–74.

Southern, David W. *The Malignant Heritage: Yankee Progressives and the Negro Question, 1901–1914*. Chicago: Loyola University Press, 1968.

Souvenir Booklet of The Spiceland Centennial. Spiceland, Ind., 1938.

Spengler, Oswald. *The Decline of the West*. New York: Modern Library, 1962.

Steele, Richard W. "Franklin D. Roosevelt and His Foreign Policy Critics," *Political Science Quarterly*, 94 (Spring 1979), 15–32.

Stenehjem, Michele Flynn. *An American First: John T. Flynn and the American First Committee*. New Rochelle, N.Y.: Arlington House, 1976.

Stephenson, Carl. "Facts in History," *The Historical Outlook*, 19 (November 1928), 313–317.

Strout, Cushing. *The Pragmatic Revolt in American History: Carl Becker and Charles Beard*. Ithaca: Cornell University Press, 1958.

Strout. "The Twentieth Century Enlightenment," *American Political Science Review*, 49 (June 1955), 321–339.

Susman, Warren I. "History and the American Intellectual: Uses of a Usable Past," *American Quarterly*, 16 (Summer 1964), 243–263.

Susman. "The Persistence of American Reform," in Daniel Walden (ed.), *American Reform: The Ambiguous Legacy* (Yellow Springs, Ohio: Ampersand Press, 1976), 94–108.

Swain, Joseph Ward. "History and the Science of Society," in *Essays in Intellectual History* (New York: Harper, 1929), 305–325.

Thelen, David P. "Social Tensions and the Origins of Progressivism," *Journal of American History*, 56 (September 1969), 323–341.

Thomas, Norman. Review of *The American Leviathan* by Charles A. Beard and William Beard, *Columbia Law Review*, 31 (19 May 1931), 906.

Thomas, Robert E. "A Reappraisal of Charles A. Beard's *An Economic Interpretation of the Constitution of the United States*," American Historical Review, 57 (January 1952), 370–375.

Tokyo and Yokohama Rebuilt. Tokyo: Jiji Shimpo, 1930.

Tokyo, Capital of Japan—Reconstruction Work. Tokyo: Municipal Office, 1930.

T.R.B., "Funny Business in the Interstate Commerce Commission," *New Republic,* 92 (20 October 1937), 293–295.

U.S. Congress. *Report of the Joint Committee on the Investigation of the Pearl Harbor Attack.* 79th Congress, 2nd sess. 1946.

U.S. Congress. Senate. *Hearings Before a Special Committee Investigating the National Defense Program.* 30th Congress, 1st Sess., 1947.

Vagts, Detlev. "A Grandson Remembers His Grandfather," in Marvin C. Swanson (ed.), *Charles A. Beard: An Observance of the Centennial of His Birth* (Greencastle, Ind.: DePauw University, 1976), pp. 17–22.

Vaihinger, Hans. *The Philosophy of 'As If,'* tr. by C. K. Ogden. New York: Harcourt, Brace, 1925.

Vaughn, Stephen L. *Holding Fast the Inner Lines: Democracy, Nationalism, and the Committee on Public Information.* Chapel Hill: University of North Carolina Press, 1980.

Veblen, Thorstein. *The Engineers and the Price System.* New York: Huebsch, 1921.

Veblen. *The Place of Science in Modern Civilization and Other Essays.* New York: Huebsch, 1919.

Vinton, Albert. "Imperialism, Old and New," *Nation,* 152 (22 March 1941), 345–348.

Wallace, Henry A. "Beard: The Planner," *New Republic,* 81 (2 January 1935), 225–227.

Warren, Frank A. "Socialism in the 1930's: Towards a New Perspective," in Daniel Walden (ed.), *American Reform: The Ambiguous Legacy* (Yellow Springs, Ohio: Ampersand Press, 1967), 51–71.

Wecter, Dixon. Review of *A Basic History* by Charles and Mary Beard, *Saturday Review of Literature,* 27 (4 November 1944), 7–8.

Weiss, Stuart. "Thomas Amlie and the New Deal," *Mid-America,* 59 (January 1977), 19–38.

Whitehead, Alfred North. *Science and the Modern World.* New York: Macmillan, 1925.

Wilkins, Burleigh T. *Carl Becker: An Intellectual Biography.* Ithaca: Cornell University Press, 1960.

Wilkins. "Charles A. Beard on the Founding of Ruskin Hall," *Indiana Magazine of History,* 52 (September 1956), 277–284.

Wilkins. "Frederick York Powell and Charles A. Beard: A Study in Anglo-American Historiography and Social Thought," *American Quarterly,* 11 (Spring 1959), 21–39.

Wilkins, Burleigh T., and Harold Kirker. "Beard, Becker and the Trotsky Inquiry," *American Quarterly,* 13 (Winter 1961), 516–525.

Williams, William A. "A Note on Beard's Search for a General Theory of Causation," *American Historical Review,* 62 (January 1956), 59–80.

Williams. "Charles Austin Beard: The Intellectual as Tory-Radical," in Williams (ed.), *History as a Way of Learning* (New York: Franklin Watts, 1974), pp. 229–242.

Willoughby, Westel. "The Political Theories of Professor John W. Burgess," *Yale Review*, 17 (Winter 1908), 59–84.

Wilson, Edmund. "What Do the Liberals Hope For?," *New Republic*, 69 (10 February 1932), 345–348.

Wise, Gene. *American Historical Explanations: A Strategy for Grounded Inquiry.* Homewood, Ill.: Dorsey, 1973.

Young, Ernest P. *The Presidency of Yuan Shih-K'ai: Liberalism and Dictatorship in Early Republican China.* Ann Arbor: University of Michigan Press, 1977.

Index

Abundance: theme of in Beards' work, 118, 146

Adams, Brooks, 268–69n.32

Adams, Henry, 113

Addams, Jane, 66, 249n.43

Administration and Politics of Tokyo (1923), 105–7

A Foreign Policy for America (1940), 180

Agricultural Adjustment Act (1933), 144

Allen, Robert G., 150

Allen, William, 41

Ambler, Charles, 58

America First, 174

American Academy of Arts and Letters, 200

American Association of University Professors, 248–49n.30

American Citizenship (1914), 47

American City Government (1912), 39–41

"American continentalism," 100, 146–47, 174

American Federation of Labor, 68, 94

American Foreign Policy in the Making, 1932–1940 (1946), 209–11, 219–21

American Government and Politics (first ed., 1910), 35, 199

American Leviathan (1930), 134–36

American Political Science Association, 128, 171, 224

American Spirit (1942), 190–93

American Yugoslav Society, 129

Anderson, Troyer S., 204

Andrews, Charles M., 10, 231n.27

An Economic Interpretation of the Constitution (1913), 55–59, 63–65, 196

An Introduction to the English Historians (1906), 33

Atlantic Conference (1941), 221

Bailey, Thomas A., 210

Balkan Pivot (1929), 130–31

Bancroft, George, 55

Bangs, William E., 78

Barnes, Harry Elmer, 90, 216, 271n.3

Bartholdy, Albrecht Mendelssohn, 129

Basic History of the United States, A (1944), 199, 200, 279n.53

Bassett, John S., 60

Beard, Charles A.: alias of, 84; assists victims of fascism, 173, 272n.6; child-

Ellen Nore, awarded a 1963/64 Woodrow Wilson Fellowship, attended Stanford University and received the Organization of American Historians Pelzer Prize in 1980. She is a member of the faculty at Southern Illinois University, Edwardsville.